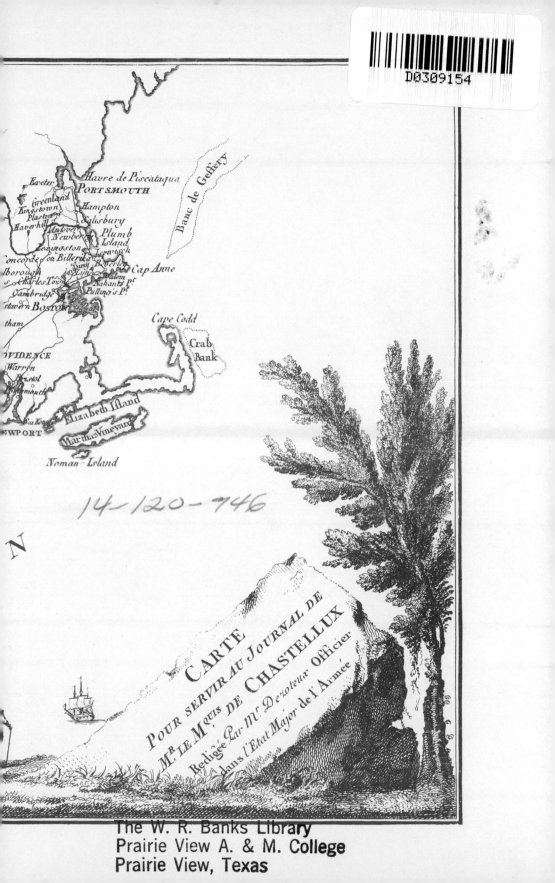

TRAVELS IN NORTH AMERICA

in the Years 1780, 1781 and 1782

The Institute of Early American History and Culture is sponsored jointly by the College of William and Mary and Colonial Williamsburg, Incorporated. Publication of this book has been assisted by a grant from the Lilly Endowment, Inc.

FRANÇOIS-JEAN, MARQUIS DE CHASTELLUX (1734-1788)
Posthumous portrait, from memory, 1789, by Mme Vigée-Lebrun
(see p. xix)

TRAVELS
IN
NORTH AMERICA

in the Years 1780, 1781 and 1782

by the

MARQUIS DE CHASTELLUX

A REVISED TRANSLATION

with Introduction and Notes

by

HOWARD C. RICE, JR.

Volume 1

Published for the
Institute of Early American History and Culture
at Williamsburg, Virginia

by THE UNIVERSITY OF NORTH CAROLINA PRESS • CHAPEL HILL

Library of Congress Catalogue Card Number: 63-18103

Manufactured in the United States of America
Van Rees Press • New York

For

France Chalufour Rice

Carolyn Hollis Chalufour, Jean-Marie Chalufour

Michel Chalufour

My Good Traveling Companions

"... *car de quelles contradictions ne se console-t'on pas*
avec un bon feu, un bon souper & une bonne compagnie?"

PREFACE

P LANS for this new edition of Chastellux's *Travels* were initiated
several years ago by Lyman H. Butterfield, then Director of
the Institute of Early American History and Culture, and have been
pursued under the present Director, Lester J. Cappon, and James
Morton Smith, Editor of Publications. The text presented here is
a drastically revised version of George Grieve's eighteenth-century
translation, through which Chastellux's book has previously been
known to English-speaking readers. Grieve's version has been carefully checked against the original text, errors have been eliminated,
awkward passages clarified, and archaisms likely to obscure the
author's meaning have been modernized. Every attempt has been
made to convey both the exact meaning and the general spirit of
Chastellux's text. Special care has been taken with proper names,
many of which were transcribed phonetically as Chastellux's ear
caught them, garbled by the original printer, and occasionally mis-
corrected by Grieve. Identifying information, such as first names,
or modern equivalents of obsolete place names, have been inter-
polated within square brackets. Occasionally the original spelling
has been retained within quotation marks, when this seemed to be
amusing or significant. English words employed in Chastellux's text
and his deliberate Anglicisms have also been retained in quotation
marks as evidence of those words and phrases which he found characteristic of American speech of the period. Here and there a French
expression from the original text has been preserved, in italics, or
added parenthetically by way of explanation. Chastellux's journals,
which were originally printed with no breaks in the text, have been
divided into chapters representing coherent geographical units, and
then into daily entries, with headings inserted. "Interludes" covering Chastellux's sojourn in America for the periods in between the
journeys described in his book have also been supplied by the
present Editor.

The notes are of three kinds. First of all come Chastellux's own notes. Then, George Grieve's notes, which, although discursive and at times irrelevant to Chastellux's text, have been retained with only an occasional abridgment, because they represent a contemporary contribution of their own and have always been, as William Short phrased it, "tacked on" to Chastellux's text in its English dress. Now, the present Editor has tacked on further notes of his contriving to this already imposing superstructure. The inconsequential notes added by the publisher of the 1827 American edition (the last reprinting of the complete book) have in a few instances been incorporated into the new editorial notes. Since this makes a rather heavy load for Chastellux's easy-flowing narrative to support, I have felt that the notes in this instance properly belonged at the back of the book. Taken together they are not, strictly speaking, footnotes, but a three-ply commentary or gloss, which will be consulted by different readers for different reasons. Means have been devised to make such consultation as convenient as possible.

In my own editorial notes I have tried to keep all interests in mind. Allusions arising from Chastellux's French background have been elucidated. His comments on historical events and on various aspects of American culture of the period have been explained, with reference to subsequent writings on the subject. Such references are intended to provide the general reader who may care to explore the subject further with the basic information and good reading as well. Inasmuch as this is a travel book, people and places perforce bulk large. Although the major American military and political figures have been identified, usually by the interpolation of a first name, no attempt has been made to repeat in the annotations the biographical information that is readily available elsewhere. The particular relationship of such persons to Chastellux has, however, been summarized. The more obscure figures have been given a note, where information was available, often in out-of-the-way sources. Chastellux's compatriots serving with the American army, or with him in the French army, have been treated at some length, on the assumption that they are less well known to the average American reader and that the sources of information about them are not so generally accessible. Each of these men has a personality of his own, though they are frequently remembered—if at all—only as lesser lights outshone by the fulgor of the incomparable Lafayette. This is a Frenchman's book, dealing with a period which laid the foundations for subsequent and fruitful cultural exchanges, so that no apology is needed for the emphasis given to Franco-American matters.

During the past few years I have visited in person virtually all the places mentioned in Chastellux's narrative, and the few exceptions, by proxy. I believe that the results of these latter-day reconnaissances, recorded in the notes, will be of interest to others, and hope that they will enable them to enjoy Chastellux's *Travels* as a field book of the American Revolution and of eighteenth-century America. The roads traveled by Chastellux have been overlaid and obscured by the elaborate network of communications woven by subsequent generations. Nevertheless, the basic routes are still there, at some points quite unchanged, at others all but obliterated. Searching them out gives a fresh awareness of the significance of hills, valleys, and watercourses, and such discovery in turn lends new meaning to the events of the Revolutionary period. Along these routes many of the houses visited by Chastellux and his suite are still standing. Some are now maintained, by local, state, or national agencies, as historic sites open to the public. Others are forgotten and unsung, hidden by later "improvements," or lost in the urban wilderness. A recapitulatory list of the surviving houses and sites that I have succeeded in identifying—a rather surprising number of them—is appended to the book as an invitation to others who, like myself, enjoy knowing *where*—exactly where. Taken as a whole, and seen in succession, these buildings present a revealing panorama of eighteenth-century American architecture and its regional variations.

Thus my own work in editing Chastellux's *Travels* has been done as much on the road as in the libraries. In both places I have encountered friendly hosts and helpful guides. To the names of my principal aides-de-camp on these travels—mentioned above in the dedication—I must add those of the auxiliaries, Alfred Bush and Robert Lewis, Jr. Carol and Willman Spawn have accompanied me in and about Philadelphia and in Rhode Island and have worked with me on the Pennsylvania chapter; William H. Gaines, Jr., has re-read and added much to the Virginia chapters; Walter Muir Whitehill has generously performed a similar service for Boston and vicinity. They should indeed be considered (with the customary disclaimers) my co-editors for these sections of the *Travels*. Help offered on specific points is recorded at appropriate places in the notes, but it nevertheless gives me pleasure to recapitulate at

least a few of the names here, for each recalls some shared predi-
lection—"those predilections or partialities," as Chastellux wrote,
"which cold and methodical minds hold up to ridicule as mere
'enthusiasm,' but which men of spirit and feeling take pride in call-
ing by this very name of 'enthusiasm.'" Ranging down the map,
from north to south, I think of them in this order: Miss Dorothy M.
Vaughan (Portsmouth, N.H.), Clifford K. Shipton (Cambridge,
Mass.), Lawrence C. Wroth, Thomas R. Adams, Jr. (Providence,
R.I.), Mrs. John Howard Benson (Newport), Mr. and Mrs. Thomas
Finley (Windsor, Conn.), Miss Kathryn Miller (Hartford, Conn.),
Mr. and Mrs. Richard Butterfield (Farmington, Conn.), Howard S.
Mott (Sheffield, Mass.), Richard G. Lucid (Westchester County,
N.Y.), Major Kenneth C. Miller (Newburgh, N.Y.), Mr. and Mrs.
William D. Wright (New York City), Mrs. Charlotte Cunning-
ham Finkel (East Fishkill, N.Y.), Mrs. Amy Ver Nooy (Pough-
keepsie, N.Y.), Martin H. Bush (Albany, N.Y.), Mr. and Mrs.
Adrian C. Leiby (northern New Jersey), the Rev. Edwin S. Ford
(Whippany, N.J.), Mrs. Mina R. Bryan (Princeton, N.J.), my
colleagues in the Princeton University Library, the Right Rever-
end Kenneth G. Hamilton (Bethlehem, Pa.), the Rev. Edward
H. Swavely (Nazareth, Pa.), David H. Wallace, Edwin Wolf II,
Whitfield J. Bell, Jr., Gertrude M. Hess (Philadelphia), Hubertis
M. Cummings (Harrisburg, Pa.), Virginius C. Hall, Jr., John Jen-
nings (Richmond, Va.), Francis L. Berkeley, Jr., Frederick D.
Nichols, and James A. Bear, Jr. (Charlottesville, Va.). Across the
seas, in Chastellux's native land, I think of the Duc de Duras (Chas-
tellux, Yonne), Yvon Bizardel (Paris), Pierre Josserand, of the
Bibliothèque Nationale, Madame Duprat, librarian of the Muséum
d'Histoire Naturelle (Buffon's great garden), and Paul Ahnne
(Strasbourg).

My indebtedness to the writings of such historians as Gilbert
Chinard and Louis Gottschalk will be evident, as it will to the
editorial labors of Julian P. Boyd and his associates. The names of
librarians, archivists, curators, custodians, and bibliographers innumerable should perhaps be added to my tally-sheet of obligations,
but, as they well know—perhaps too well—generosity is the badge
of their profession and anonymity the crown.

                                          H. C. R., Jr.

CONTENTS

Volume 1

Volume 2

PART IV: Epilogue

Maps

End Papers

ILLUSTRATIONS

Volume 1

PORTRAIT OF CHASTELLUX,
By Madame Vigée-Lebrun   frontispiece

This oil painting of Chastellux, preserved by collateral descendants
in France, was painted, presumably for his young widow, a few
months after his death. Although it has hitherto been considered
the work of an unknown artist, the Editor here attributes it to
Mme Elisabeth Vigée-Lebrun (1755-1842), because of stylistic re-
semblances to her other male portraits of the period (for example,
the Comte de Vaudreuil, 1784, Musée Jacquemart-André), and also
because she lists in the catalogue of her own work appended to her
Souvenirs (Paris, 1835-37, I, 336) a portrait of "M. de Chatelux"
done in 1789 "from memory." Other portraits executed in 1789,
on the eve of the artist's emigration, include one of the Duchesse
d'Orléans (Musée de Versailles), protectress of the Marquise de
Chastellux. Chastellux's three decorations (cross of the Order of
Saint Louis, cross of the order of Saint Lazarus of Jerusalem, and
eagle of the Cincinnati), originally shown in Mme Vigée-Lebrun's
portrait of him, were painted over at some subsequent date, probably during the French Revolution, when such emblems of aristocracy were suspect and provided a pretext for persecution.
(Courtesy of the Duc de Duras.)

CHÂTEAU DE CHASTELLUX   between pp. 8-9

The Château de Chastellux, in the Morvan hills on the confines of
Burgundy (still standing in the present Department of Yonne), was
the home of Chastellux's paternal ancestors. Although the author
of the *Travels in North America* was familiar with this family estate
and made occasional visits there, he was essentially more at home
in the *hôtels* and *salons* of Paris, where he spent the greater part of
his time when not engaged in military duties. The view reproduced
here, showing the south-eastern front of the château, is a lithograph
by Victor J.-B. Petit, published in 1840 during the Romantic Period,
when feudal castles were again the fashion. (Courtesy of the Bibliothèque Nationale, Cabinet des Estampes, and Archives Photo-
graphiques.)

CHASTELLUX WAS HERE. . . .   between pp. 8-9

These six houses, all closely associated with Chastellux's travels in America, are notable examples of eighteenth-century dwellings now maintained by public or private agencies as historic sites open to the public. Chastellux's book not only records information about the sticks and stones, but also supplies living glimpses of the former inhabitants. For other examples see the list of "Surviving Buildings Mentioned by Chastellux" at the end of Volume II.

MAWDSLEY HOUSE, corner of Spring and John Streets, Newport, Rhode Island, Chastellux's quarters during the winter and spring of 1780-81. It was here that he wrote Part I of his *Travels*. Now owned by the Society for the Preservation of New England Antiquities. This photograph was taken in 1936. (Courtesy of the Society for the Preservation of New England Antiquities.)

DEY MANSION, Preakness Valley Park, Wayne Township, New Jersey, where Chastellux was Washington's guest, November 23-26, 1780. Restored and maintained by the Passaic County Park Commission. See Pt. I, chap. 2, n. 13. (Courtesy of the Passaic County Park Commission; photograph by Carl W. Baumann.)

SCHUYLER MANSION, corner of Clinton and Catharine Streets, Albany, New York, where Chastellux enjoyed the hospitality of Philip Schuyler during his visit to Albany and vicinity, December 24, 1780—January 1, 1781. The Schuyler Mansion is one of the historic sites administered by the New York State Education Department. See Pt. I, chap. 5, n. 3. (Courtesy of the New York State Education Department, Supervisor of Historic Sites.)

HASBROUCK HOUSE, Washington's Headquarters at Newburgh, New York. Chastellux made his farewell visit to Washington here, December 6-7, 1782; his account of the house has remained the authoritative description of its interior arrangement during Washington's occupancy. It has been owned by the state of New York since 1850, and thus ranks as one of the oldest of the publicly maintained historic sites in the country. See Pt. III, chap. 3, n. 15. (Courtesy of Washington's Headquarters and Museum; photograph by Maj. Kenneth C. Miller.)

GEORGE WYTHE HOUSE, Williamsburg, Virginia. The Wythe House served as general headquarters for Rochambeau's army during the winter and spring of 1781-82, following the victory at Yorktown. Although there is no positive evidence to show that General Chastellux—the second in command—was himself quartered here, he was at least a daily visitor, and perhaps wrote Part II of his *Travels* under this roof. (Courtesy of Colonial Williamsburg, Inc.)

MONTICELLO, Charlottesville, Virginia. Chastellux's memorable account of his visit to Thomas Jefferson at Monticello, April

13-17, 1782, is one of the now classic descriptions of the man and the place. At the time of his visit Monticello had not yet been completed in the form which has become familiar to subsequent generations, as shown here. See Pt. II, chap. 2, n. 5. (Courtesy of the Thomas Jefferson Memorial Foundation.)

NEWPORT, RHODE ISLAND,
March or April 1781   between pp. 72-73

This pen and watercolor drawing serves as an extra-illustration to a manuscript copy of the *Journal* of Cromot du Bourg, an aide-de-camp of General Rochambeau. It was presumably drawn not by Cromot du Bourg himself, but by one of his brother officers. The approximate date can be deduced by the presence among the ships of the *Romulus,* captured from the English on February 19, 1781 and brought in to Newport on the 24th, and from mention in the title of Destouches, who relinquished his temporary command of the French squadron to Admiral de Barras upon the latter's arrival early in May. The drawing thus depicts Newport at the time Chastellux was writing up his first journal and having it printed by the Imprimerie Royale de l'Escadre. The view is taken from the south side of the harbor (near present Chastellux Avenue), looking north; Brenton's Point (where Fort Adams is now situated) is in the foreground at the far left. (Courtesy of the Historical Society of Pennsylvania.)

THE HUDSON, FROM WEST POINT
TO STONY POINT   between pp. 72-73

This map (south at top of page) showing the localities visited by Chastellux November 21-22, 1780, was drawn from data gathered some nine months later by Louis-Alexandre Berthier, a young officer serving with Rochambeau's army, who subsequently became famous as Marshal Berthier, Napoleon's chief of staff. It is part of a larger map drawn primarily to record the route (not shown here) to King's Ferry from the eastward taken by the French army in August 1781. It can also serve to illustrate Chastellux's earlier journey: at the lower left may be seen the road by which he approached West Point when he left the heights to go down to the river, as well as the several forts, the chain, and other features mentioned in his account. After spending the night at West Point Chastellux was taken down the river by barge to Verplanck's Point. (Courtesy of the Princeton University Library.)

REDOUBTS AND EMBRASURE
AT WEST POINT   between pp. 72-73

These drawings are also the work of Louis-Alexandre Berthier, and appear as marginal ornaments on the map described in the note to

the preceding plate. Fort Clinton was at this time the principal fort
at West Point; not to be confused with a fort of the same name
situated at the entrance to the Highlands opposite Anthony's Nose,
which was no longer maintained in 1780-81. (Courtesy of the
Princeton University Library.)

TOTOWA, OR PASSAIC, FALLS, 1761 between pp. 72-73

Totowa Falls, also known as the Great Falls of the Passaic (in what
is now the city of Paterson, New Jersey), which Chastellux visited
November 23, 1780, was by then already famous as one of the natural wonders of America. This engraving by Paul Studley after a
drawing by Governor Thomas Pownal, was but the first of a long
series of pictures portraying the "astonishing spectacle" described
by Chastellux. See Pt. I, chap. 2, n. 10. (Courtesy of the New Jersey
Historical Society.)

PHILADELPHIA AND VICINITY between pp. 136-137

This map by Louis-Alexandre Berthier showing the route of march
and encampments of Rochambeau's army early in September 1781,
when it was on the way to Yorktown, also depicts many of the
places mentioned by Chastellux in his account of his earlier visit to
the national capital in December 1780: for example, the former
English lines, the river forts, Germantown, and La Luzerne's country house below Falls of Schuylkill. Concerning the latter, see
Pt. I, chap. 3, n. 100. (Courtesy of the Princeton University Library.)

PENNSYLVANIA STATE HOUSE between pp. 136-137

This view of the State House (now Independence Hall) corresponding closely to the description of it in Chastellux's journal,
December 4, 1780, appears in the background of Charles Willson
Peale's portrait of Conrad-Alexandre Gérard, painted in the autumn
of 1779. Since the portrait was a tribute to Louis XVI's first Minister
to the United States, the artist appropriately chose to include a view
of the seat of the Continental Congress as it appeared when seen
from the French Minister's residence at the corner of Chestnut and
7th Streets. Gérard was succeeded by the Chevalier de La Luzerne,
Chastellux's host and mentor in Philadelphia. See Pt. I, chap. 3, n. 44.
(Courtesy of Independence National Historical Park Collection.)

PORTRAIT OF WASHINGTON,
By Charles Willson Peale between pp. 136-137

This is the portrait that Chastellux saw in the State House, December 4, 1780, and described as the "handsomest ornament" of the hall
where Congress met. On the basis of the evidence supplied by
Chastellux's journal, a modern copy of the original has recently

been hung in the hall. In the background of the portrait, commissioned by the state of Pennsylvania to commemorate Washington's campaigns, is Nassau Hall at Princeton, the "immense building ... remarkable only for its size," noted by Chastellux on his journey through New Jersey, November 29, 1780. See Pt. I, chap. 3, n. 45. (Courtesy of the Pennsylvania Academy of the Fine Arts.)

CHEVALIER DE LA LUZERNE,
By Charles Willson Peale   between pp. 136-137

Peale's painting, executed from life *ca.* 1782, shows the features of the second French Minister to the United States, with whom Chastellux was on a footing of warm friendship and intimacy. Before serving his King as a diplomat, Anne-César, Chevalier de La Luzerne (1741-91), had been an army officer; he remained in the United States from 1779 to 1784. Chastellux concludes his account of his own sojourn in Philadelphia (see under date of December 15, 1780) with a tribute to the talents of La Luzerne: "so well fitted for the station he occupies that one cannot imagine that any other but himself could fill it." (Courtesy of Independence National Historical Park Collection.)

THOMAS ELLISON HOUSE,
NEW WINDSOR, N.Y.   between pp. 200-201

The Thomas Ellison House on the west bank of the Hudson north of The Highlands, where Chastellux was Washington's guest on December 20-21, 1780, was demolished *ca.* 1833-34. This landscape, painted in 1832 by John Ludlow Martin (1792-1871), preserves the appearance of the "small house," while presenting the artist's imaginary reconstitution of the military activity surrounding it when it served as Washington's headquarters from December 1780 to June 1781. The painting hangs today in the "Knox Headquarters" at Vails Gate; concerning variant versions of it see Pt. I, chap. 4, n. 13. (Courtesy of New York State Education Department, and Washington's Headquarters, Newburgh.)

COHOES FALLS,
By John Trumbull   between pp. 200-201

Trumbull's India-ink and wash drawing is endorsed by him: "Cohoes Falls, 12 miles from Albany on Mohawk River, 27th Sept. 1791." Chastellux saw this "vast sheet of water" a decade earlier, on December 25, 1780, when "the picture was rendered still more awful by the snow which covered the firs, the brilliancy of which gave a black color to the water, gliding gently along, and a yellow tinge to that which was dashing over the cataract." See Pt. I, chap. 5, n. 12. (Courtesy of Addison Gallery of American Art, Phillips Academy, Andover, Massachusetts.)

"THE UNFORTUNATE MISS McCREA"   between pp. 200-201

When Chastellux was journeying along the road to Fort Edward
on December 30, 1780, he was shown the house of "the unfortunate
Miss McCrea," and heard again the story of her death in 1777. This
"sad catastrophe," he noted, "would furnish a most pathetic subject
for a drama or an elegy." Anker Smith's engraving after a painting
by Robert Smirke, one of the numerous representations of the
scene, was published as an illustration to Joel Barlow's American
epic, *The Columbiad* (Philadelphia, 1807), in which Jane McCrea
is elegized under the guise of "Lucinda." See Pt. I, chap. 5, nn. 36-37.
(Courtesy of the Princeton University Library.)

JEUNE FILLE PLEURANT SON OISEAU MORT,
By Greuze   between pp. 200-201

During his travels in America Chastellux was often reminded of
familiar paintings—landscapes by Hubert Robert, Le Prince or
Vernet, portraits and genre scenes by Greuze. At Sheffield, Massachusetts, for example, on January 2, 1781, he saw at Dewey's Inn
a girl of twelve "whom Greuze would have been only too happy
to have taken for a model when he painted his charming picture of
the young girl weeping over the loss of her canary bird." Greuze's
"Jeune Fille pleurant son oiseau mort"—one of his most popular
nymphettes—was first shown at the Salon of 1765. See Pt. I, chap. 6,
n. 2. (Courtesy of the National Gallery of Scotland, Edinburgh.)

*Descriptive notes on the illustrations included in Vol-
ume 2 will be found at the beginning of that volume.*

INTRODUCTION

O F the many books on the United States published in Europe during the years immediately following the American Revolution, Chastellux's *Travels* remains one of the most readable. It is this quality of readability that has recommended it for reprinting once again, a century and three-quarters after its first publication in 1786. The author accompanied the French Expeditionary Forces to America as one of three major generals ranking immediately below General Rochambeau. He was present at Yorktown among the other high-ranking French and American officers whose features have been preserved for us in John Trumbull's painting of the Surrender of Cornwallis. Chastellux's book is not, however, a soldier's report on the military events in which he played an honorable role, but rather an account of journeys made between campaigns, when he was freed from the active duties of his command.

Chastellux was a professional soldier, but he was also a man of letters who wielded the pen as skillfully as he did the sword. The *Travels* is not strictly speaking a diary, but a journal written up from daily jottings as a sort of round-robin letter for friends at home. In spite of the writer's protestations that the journal was for such friends alone, he no doubt suspected that it would one day reach a wider circle, and, as in so many similar cases, eventually consented without too much urging to its publication. The very personal character of Chastellux's narrative accounts for its original success, for the mild scandal that it stirred, and for its perennial appeal. It was reprinted several times in the years following its original publication, and has been quoted and extracted by historians ever since. Here is no "objective observer's" report, but the narrative of an alert traveler, revealing his personal reactions on every page. Chastellux's book will be read, as it was in the 1780's, for the light it casts on the America of that period. It can also be read as a portrait of the traveler. Indeed, as the reader will soon discover, Chastellux is rarely absent from the account, so that the man him-

self, with all his enthusiasms and foibles, is revealed in a full-length
portrait. Chastellux wrote other books, but in none of them does
he reveal so much of himself as in these informal journals. Although
he probably thought that his future reputation would rest on some
of his more formal literary exercises, it is chiefly as the author of
the *Travels in North America* that he is remembered. The book is
indeed so much a chapter of autobiography that any further biography may seem superfluous here. Nevertheless, since the reader
may be curious to know how Chastellux came to be the man that
he himself portrays in his *Travels,* some account of his earlier life
and background is given by way of introduction; and since the
book has also had an interesting life of its own, some account is given
of the circumstances of its publication and of its fortunes with
earlier generations of readers.

The Author and His Background

In the Morvan hills of France, not far from Avallon and Vézelay,
stands the Château de Chastellux, the ancestral home of the author
of the *Travels in North America.* To an American mind, at least,
its castled walls and turrets suggest the feudal age and images of
warring knights in armor. Many generations of the Chastellux
family had indeed fought for their lords and their King, risen to
high ranks in the army, and died on the battlefields of Europe before
the birth of François-Jean de Beauvoir, Chevalier de Chastellux, on
May 5, 1734.[1] He was the youngest son of Count Guillaume-
Antoine de Chastellux (1683-1742) and of Claire-Thérèse d'Aguesseau (1699-1772), daughter of Chancellor Henri-François d'Aguesseau (1668-1751), the learned and public-spirited magistrate of the
age of Louis XV. The father, a soldier like those before him, died
in 1742, when François-Jean was but eight years old. His maternal
grandfather's country estate at Fresnes and Parisian residence in the
Place Vendôme (now the Ministry of Justice)—with its rich library
and distinguished visitors—henceforth became a home for the young
Chevalier. His future career was to reflect his double heritage: following in the steps of his paternal ancestors, he entered the army
at the age of thirteen with a second-lieutenancy in the Auvergne
Regiment, but letters, learning, and the public weal were always
to be of equal concern to him.

At twenty-one Chastellux became a colonel. The same year he

performed a public service that forever endeared the name of Chastellux to philosophers and friends of man. This deed is duly recorded in the great *Encyclopédie*, where Dr. Théodore Tronchin relates: "The doctrine of *inoculation* had as yet been dealt with in France only in speculative and controversial terms; and nobody had heretofore made use of the new preventative. The first Frenchman who voluntarily risked his life with it was the Chevalier de Chastellux. . . . He got himself *inoculated* in the month of May 1755. M. Tenon, master of Surgery, and now a member of the Academy of Sciences, performed the operation. It had been preceded, and was followed by several other such experiments that the Chevalier Turgot, from zeal for the welfare of mankind, had caused to be performed by the same surgeon on some children of the people, with the consent of their parents." [2] Buffon later recalled hearing young Chastellux upon his return from the country, bearing scars which the naturalist fancied to be "the stigmata of courage," joyously proclaim, "I am saved, and my example will save many others from this scourge!" [3] During the decade following his own successful inoculation against smallpox, Chastellux struck further blows in the war against prejudice by publishing two pamphlets to refute current arguments against inoculation.[4] Twenty-five years later, when he was with the French army in America, inoculation had become an accepted practice among the troops under his command.

The Seven Years' War, which pitted France and her allies against Prussia and England, introduced Chastellux to active warfare. He participated in the campaigns in Germany from 1756 to 1763, serving as *aide-major général* of the Army of the Lower Rhine (1757), colonel of the Marche Regiment (1759), and colonel of the Guyenne Regiment (1761). After the French victory at Wolfenbüttel (1761) he had the honor of bringing to Louis XV the standards captured from the enemy. In spite of such temporary successes, the war ended in defeat for France—on the fields of Germany, as well as in North America. To later generations, who have seen in him the seeds of that Prussian militarism from which they suffered, it has always seemed a bit paradoxical that Frederick the Great, the victor in the Seven Years' War, should have continued to enjoy tremendous prestige in France, especially among the liberal intellectuals. He was to them an example of the "enlightened despot" (as was Catherine the Great of Russia), whom they might hope to convert to their humanitarian cause. A decade or so after the end of the war, when D'Alembert, one of Frederick's most notable correspondents, sent to the monarch one of Chastellux's books, he pointed out that the constant attention bestowed by the author on his profession—Chastellux was by then *brigadier* in the royal army—had not prevented him from cultivating successfully letters and philosophy, thus following the example set by Frederick himself.[5] Even earlier than this, Chastellux's name was linked, more or less accidentally, with that of the great Frederick. In 1761 Chastellux published in the *Journal Etranger*, edited in Paris by Abbé Arnaud, an analysis of the King of Prussia's *Instruction militaire pour ses Généraux;* the article was soon picked up by an alert publisher, who prefixed it to a new edition of the *Instruction* under the heading "Réflexions de M. le Chevalier de Chastelus"—with the remark that "this young and learned soldier, who carries a taste for letters amidst the tumult of the camp, was indeed worthy of being the commentator of a Prince who can mingle the harmonious song of the Muses with the fierce cries of War." [6]

A number of articles and brochures indicate the various fields that Chastellux cultivated. Memorial tributes to two of his comrades-in-arms in Germany, published in the *Mercure de France*, gave him an opportunity to evoke again the consoling and beneficent effects of "philosophy" upon warfare itself.[7] To the *Journal Etranger* he contributed, for example, a translation of a German poem deploring the miseries of War and invoking the return of Peace,[8] as well as a lengthy study of "the mechanism of Italian, English and German versification." [9] Poetry and its relationship to music was the subject of a small book published in 1765 under the title *Essai sur l'Union de la Poésie et de la Musique*,[10] in which Chastellux discoursed incidentally upon the music of the ancient Greeks, but chiefly upon that of the modern Italians: Metastasio's librettos were held up as the most successful examples of harmonious adaptation of words to music. In the current debates on musical theory and the respective merits of "French" and "Italian" opera —in which Rousseau, D'Alembert, and many others participated— Chastellux thus ranged himself on the side of the Italians. He entered the lists again with some "Observations" printed in the *Mercure de France*,[11] a translation of Francesco Algarotti's "Essay on the Opera," [12] and still later, in the 1780's, when partisans of Piccinni and of Gluck split Parisian connoisseurs into warring camps, Chastellux campaigned with the Piccinnists.[13]

Another of Chastellux's early writings brought him to the attention of the "economists" like Turgot, Trudaine de Montigny, and Abbé Morellet. This was his letter to the editors of the *Journal Encyclopédique* (May 1, 1759) on the subject of the manufacture of *toiles peintes*, or printed cottons, which was at the time prohibited in France as a means of protecting the existing monopolies.[14] Abolition of the restrictions had become a significant test case to the theoreticians of economic liberalism, and produced an abundant pamphlet literature. Abbé Morellet's "Reflections on the advantages of the free manufacture and use of printed cottons in France" (1758) spoke forth resoundingly for the liberals. Chastellux's letter, a lively defense of Morellet's work, placed him on the winning side, for a royal decree of September 1759 at length granted the desired freedom to the manufacturers of those decorative textiles since known by the generic term of *toiles de Jouy*.

After 1763 Chastellux's professional life as a military man does not appear to have been especially burdensome. In between tours of duty to boresome garrison towns he found time to devote his seemingly inexhaustible energies to a variety of good causes, and even to such diversions as amateur theatricals. He was, for example, the leading spirit in the productions at the Château de La Chevrette, the country estate of M. Savalette de Magnanville, whose niece, the Marquise de Gléon, was Chastellux's chief collaborator.[15] Both of them wrote plays: several of hers were later collected into a book edited by Chastellux himself;[16] his own were never printed. Several of the titles, at least, have survived: *Agathe, Les Amants portugais, Les Prétentions* (a title that inevitably lent itself to puns at the author's expense), and *L'Officier importun* (which must have been equally irresistible to the jesters).[17] The most ambitious of Chastellux's productions was, however, an adaptation from Shakespeare, for, like Mme de Gléon, he was something of an "Anglomaniac" in literary matters.[18] "It is *Romeo and Juliet* that I have dared to arrange for a French stage," he wrote to David Garrick, whom he had known in Paris and visited in England. "It appears to have made the greatest impression. I have made several changes in the plot, and I have cut out all the comic parts. I am very vain at having won the approbation of some Englishmen, but I should like to have yours." [19] Garrick's reply is not extant, but we have a letter written to him by another of his Parisian correspondents, Madame Riccoboni, who reported: "Here [at La Chevrette] was recently performed the Chevalier's masterpiece, which is, with all due respect to you, *Roméo et Juliette*. The whole town started off to see this pretended imitation of the poet cherished and revered by Great Britain. I followed the stream with two Englishmen, friends of mine, who were very eager to see Shakespeare disguised in French dress. But we found him neither Gaul, Briton, nor Italian: no interest, no warmth whatever; wit where thought should have been—great words and little action. As for the last act—ah, there's the rub! Instead of wasting their time taking poison or stabbing themselves, Juliet and Romeo go off gaily from the abode of the dead to get married—where is not known; to live together—how is not made plain; to be happy—as you may please to imagine. Everyone looks at everyone else, wondering where the terrible catastrophe is, so pathetic and so touching! The curtain falls, and leaves the astonished spectator to ask himself what questions he will." [20]

It is evident from these examples of Chastellux's various interests and enthusiasms that he is to be classed among the Encyclopedists and *Philosophes*, and that he belongs to that world of the Paris *salons* where sociability stimulated thought and refined sensibility. He was indeed a familiar figure there, knew everybody, and counted many of the well-known names among his acquaintances: D'Alembert, Diderot, D'Holbach, for example, and Helvétius, to whom he paid tribute in an "Eulogy" published in 1772.[21] He was a bit young to have contributed any articles to the *Encyclopédie*, the principal part of which was completed by 1765; but he was invited to write for its Supplement edited in the 1770's an article on public happiness—*Bonheur public*. His manuscript, it is said, was eliminated by the royal censor on the grounds that the word "God" was nowhere mentioned.[22]

Foreign visitors to Paris were also among his acquaintances: the English actor, David Garrick;[23] John Wilkes, the "illustrious prisoner of King's Bench";[24] David Hume, whom he met as early as 1759 and whose name, he said, was "as much respected in the republic of letters as that of Jehovah was among the Hebrews";[25] the Marquis de Caraccioli, the Neapolitan ambassador, and his chargé d'affaires, the Abbé Galiani, whom Chastellux visited in Naples in 1773;[26] and, among many others, the omnipresent Baron Grimm, correspondent of the monarchs of the North, and Count de Creutz, the much-loved ambassador from Sweden. Horace Walpole, during a visit to Paris in 1765, noted Chastellux among those present at the dinner tables of Holbach and Helvétius.[27] Benjamin Franklin's path must also have crossed Chastellux's at some point, for he, too, was welcomed by scientists and economists during visits to the French capital in 1767 and in 1769.

In this Paris world, as reflected in its inexhaustible legacy of memoirs, correspondences, newsletters, and gossip sheets, there are frequent glimpses of the Chevalier de Chastellux, not one of its greatest figures, but certainly one of the most representative and most "amiable." Some of his contemporaries, to be sure, smiled at his eagerness and candor, others found his ideas and his style a bit imprecise, but few could dislike him. Although he once fought a duel at Calais with an officer who had been dismissed from his regiment,[28] he had no real enemies. Mrs. Montagu, "Queen of the Blues," who met Chastellux at Madame Necker's dinner table, described him as "the most pleasing of the beaux esprits . . . whose manners like his birth are truly noble." [29] Marmontel's reminiscence deserves quotation, not only for what it reveals of Chastellux, but also because it well exemplifies the art of the character sketch or "portrait," which was part of the literary tradition of Chastellux's world and which he himself was to apply so happily when portraying his acquaintances of another world across the Atlantic:

Although Chastellux's mind was ever seeking further enlightenment, he possessed a great store of intelligence, and brilliant flashes would from time to time pierce the slight haziness that enveloped his ideas. He brought to this society the most winning disposition and the most likable candor. Whether he were mistrustful of the soundness of his own opinions and sought reassurance, or whether he wished to refine them by discussion, he was fond of controversy and willingly engaged in it, but with grace and fairness; and as soon as his eye caught a glimpse of truth, whether it came from you or from himself, he was happy. Never has a man made better use of his own understanding to enjoy that of others. A witticism, a clever remark, a good story opportunely told, delighted him; you might see him leap for joy upon hearing them; and as conversation became more brilliant, the eyes and countenance of Chastellux would become more animated: all success flattered him as if it had been his own.[30]

The crowning achievement of Chastellux's career as a philosopher was the two-volume work published in 1772 under the title *De la Félicité Publique, ou Considérations sur le sort des hommes dans les différentes époques de l'histoire*. As was the case with many of the other liberal writings of the period, the book was published outside of France—in this instance by Marc-Michel Rey of Amsterdam—and without the author's name, "because of circumstances unfavorable to literature," as he tactfully phrased it. There was a reprinting in 1774; a new edition, "revised, corrected and enlarged by the author," but still without his name, issued in 1776 from the presses of the Imprimerie de la Société Typographique at Bouillon in Belgium.[31] Meanwhile, the first edition was published in an English translation by John Kent as *An Essay on Public Happiness, Investigating the State of Human Nature, under each of its Particular Appearances, through the Several Periods of History, to the Present Time* (London, 1774).[32] A German translation appeared at Leipzig in 1780;[33] extracts of the work in Italian were published at Naples in 1782;[34] two more editions in English were brought out in 1790 and in 1792.[35]

"Is society capable of attaining, if not perfection, at least amelioration?" Such is the starting point of Chastellux's long investigation of the fate of mankind during the successive periods of human history. Voltaire's *Essai sur les Moeurs* (1756)—his "Essay on the Manners and Mind of Nations, and on the Principal Facts of History from Charlemagne to the Death of Louis XIII"—provided the pattern for the inquiry; indeed, as Chastellux himself stated, "it is in that immortal work that the seeds of all the truths which we are merely developing must be sought." Nor are Chastellux's conclusions very different from those already set forth by Voltaire. After demonstrating how ignorance and superstition had in previous centuries prevented governments from achieving "sound policy" and "genuine morality" and from fulfilling what should be their sole aim, "the greatest happiness for the greatest number of individuals" (*le plus grand bonheur du plus grand nombre d'individus*), Chastellux finds heartening evidence of the progress of enlightenment in his own century. Such watchwords as tolerance, liberty, agriculture, and industry have made themselves heard throughout Europe and are resounding abroad as far as America. Enlightened views— "*les lumières*"—have already bettered, and are daily bettering, the lot of man. Far from having to envy past centuries, we should re-

CHÂTEAU DE CHASTELLUX
lithograph by Victor Petit, 1840
(see p. xix)

MAWDSLEY HOUSE, NEWPORT, RHODE ISLAND (see p. xx)

DEY MANSION, PREAKNESS, NEW JERSEY (see p. xx)

SCHUYLER MANSION, ALBANY, NEW YORK (see p. xx)

HASBROUCK HOUSE, NEWBURGH, NEW YORK (see p. xx)

WYTHE HOUSE, WILLIAMSBURG, VIRGINIA (see p. xx)

MONTICELLO, CHARLOTTESVILLE, VIRGINIA (see pp. xx-xxi)

gard ourselves as far happier than the ancients. "I shall not say that all is well, but that all is better. There is progress; there is hope for the world." Lest none should mistake the author's message there appeared as a motto on the title page of the book Horace's phrase: *Nil desperandum*, nothing should be despaired of.

Between the first publication of Chastellux's book, in 1772, and the revised edition of 1776, events in faraway America gave special timeliness to his "considerations," as several allusions in the new edition show. "We shall abstain," he wrote, "from any prophecy concerning the course of events taking place overseas . . . . Nevertheless we may point out that all wars are not contrary to the welfare of mankind, just as all sicknesses are not harmful to the individual they attack. In both cases there may come a favorable crisis, which cures previous ills and produces a permanent state of robust health. What every philosopher must hope for is that the outcome of the present war may be such that America will continue to grow in population and in perfection; for reason, legislation, and the happiness that results from them, can never cover too much of this globe where all is interrelated and all is linked as by a chain, now apparent, now hidden." [II, 235]

The numerous editions of *Public Happiness* indicate that Chastellux's book enjoyed a certain reputation in its day, although several of the surviving comments lack enthusiasm. Madame d'Epinay, who was out of sympathy with its main premise and doubted that human nature was susceptible of improvement, complained that though it was well written and clearly composed, there was not a new idea in it.[36] La Harpe reported that the book, "whose object is to prove that we are in general better than we used to be," had wit and knowledge, but that it was more widely read in Europe than in Paris.[37] Grimm judged it "an estimable work, whose sole and very real fault is that it finds no readers." [38] An anonymous Parisian versifier, commenting on *Public Happiness*, ended his quatrain with the assertion that the Public was Happy, because it knew the book not: *Le public est heureux, car il n'en a rien su!*

Such indifference, as far as Chastellux was concerned, was compensated for by the approval of several of his friends, such as Turgot, Dupont de Nemours, Abbé Morellet, and Condorcet. D'Alembert transmitted to Frederick the Great a copy of the book with the flattering remark that it would prove that the author "joined to his extensive knowledge of history, philosophic views, and love of humanity, a talent for writing." [39] M. de Malesherbes said that it was worthy of the author's grandfather, Chancellor d'Aguesseau. Voltaire's enthusiasm knew no bounds. The Patriarch of Ferney had exchanged a few letters with Chastellux prior to the publication of *De la Félicité Publique*, although the two had never met. Voltaire had written thanking Chastellux for intervening in one of his perennial quarrels with the authorities over his book-smuggling activities: "Continue, Sir, to take the side of humanity. The example of your name and merit can accomplish much. My age and my maladies do not allow me to hope for many years more, but I shall die consoled leaving in the world such men as you." [40] *De la Félicité Publique* now confirmed his favorable impression of the younger man: "Sir," Voltaire wrote to Chastellux from Ferney, December 7, 1772, "the first time I read *la Félicité Publique*, I was struck by a light that brightened my eyes, and which should blind those of the fools and fanatics; but I knew not whence this light came. I have since learned what I should have easily recognized, had I but had the honor of conversing with you, for I am told that you speak as well as you write: but I have not had the private happiness of paying my court to the illustrious author of *Public Happiness*. I loaded my copy with notes, and that is something I do only when the book charms and instructs me. . . . I thank you for all you have said; I thank you for the honor you do to letters and human reason, and for the honor you do me in deigning to send me your work. I am very old and very sick, but such reading gives me a new lease on life. . . . A great revolution is indeed taking shape in the human mind. You are bringing splendid columns to this new and necessary edifice." [41]

In the spring of 1773, on his return from a journey to Italy (where he had visited Abbé Galiani at Naples), Chastellux at last made his pilgrimage to Ferney to sit at the master's feet. Henceforth Voltaire adopted Chastellux as one of his bright hopes and lost no opportunity of praising *Public Happiness*. He continually punned on the title, mentioned it in his letters, slipped in references to it in prefaces and footnotes, and predicted that it would become a catechism for the youth of France. Voltaire's extravagant, and slightly senile, infatuation with the book—which he was soon placing above Montesquieu's *Spirit of Laws*—finally brought forth from Condorcet a friendly rebuke and suggestion that he refrain from publishing an article he had written on Montesquieu and the Chevalier de

Chastellux. *Public Happiness,* Condorcet told his "dear and illustrious master," had had no success, and people had not even done it justice in Paris. "The idea that the world must continue to perfect itself is not an original one with the author: this opinion is that of the economists, who have proved it much better. People will always be offended to see these two works compared—Montesquieu will lose nothing from the comparison, and the author placed on a level with him will be made ridiculous. . . . Such a publication would have unpleasant consequences for the author of *Public Happiness,* because should anyone decide to attack his work he would be deeply grieved; it would furthermore hurt the good cause, because the scoundrels who inveigh against Montesquieu and you, would exult over the dissension that would arise in the camp of the defenders of mankind." [42]

Although it has not attained the immortality that Voltaire claimed for it, *De la Félicité Publique* has not been entirely forgotten. In 1822 Voltaire's own annotated copy of it served as the basis for a new edition.[43] It has earned for Chastellux a modest place in the history of ideas—the idea of progress, in particular—and of economic and social thought.[44] Recently, it has even been the subject of an article entitled, "A Forerunner of Marxism: François-Jean de Chastellux." [45] If nothing else, the book remains as a reflection of the preoccupations of Chastellux's "enlightened" contemporaries, a characteristic product of the age that also produced Adam Smith's *An Inquiry into the Nature and Causes of the Wealth of Nations* (1776) and Condorcet's *Esquisse d'un Tableau Historique des Progrès de l'Esprit Humain* (1795). In the present instance, it provides us with a valuable key to the frame of mind in which this soldier-philosopher was to view the American scene.

With the publication of *De la Félicité Publique,* Chastellux had emerged as a full-fledged man of letters. He might now, with such an achievement to his credit, even aspire to membership in the French Academy. This was an honor—so the gossip ran—that he sought as passionately as other military men of his rank coveted the marshal's baton or the cross of the Order of St. Louis.[46] Mademoiselle de Lespinasse, whose *salon* in the Rue Saint-Dominique was a gathering place for the literati, let slip the remark that Fontenelle was right, there are playthings for all ages.[47] Nevertheless, Chastellux's undisguised eagerness was so contagious, so irresistible, that her cynical heart melted, she took matters in hand, and it was soon a foregone conclusion that only a death among the Forty was needed to elevate Chastellux to their company. M. Dupré de Saint-Maur died opportunely in December 1774. Meanwhile, however, it had been noted by some that the venerable M. de Malesherbes, the wise magistrate and protector of the Encyclopedists, was not a member of the Academy. Chastellux (he was then only forty) was urged to withdraw his candidacy. This he graciously and tactfully did, realizing full well that such a deferential gesture would in turn operate in his own favor. He waited but a short time. The poet Chateaubrun died in February, Chastellux was elected to succeed him in March, and on the 27th of April, in Seventy-Five, he was formally received into the ranks of the Immortals at a ceremony that attracted an unusually large and fashionable public to their meeting place in the Louvre.[48] None other than the great Buffon pronounced the discourse of welcome, reviewing Chastellux's accomplishments and paying tribute to his ardent zeal for the happiness of man.[49] Chastellux's own *discours de réception*, which might be described as a supplementary chapter to his book, dealt with the subject of taste—*le Goût*—taste and the circumstances of its formation, from ancient times to the enlightened present. This dissertation might have passed into the oblivion reserved for most such Academic formalities, had not Voltaire been moved to write a poem about it: *A Monsieur le Chevalier de Chastellux, Qui Avait Envoyé à l'Auteur Son Discours de Réception à l'Académie Française, Lequel Traitait du Goût.*[50] The elderly versifier took occasion to recall that he himself, in his venturesome youth, had built a frail "Temple of Taste," but now a still finer was raised, and Taste had a new high priest to serve by the side of the master. Viewing the proceedings from his exile in Ferney, Voltaire in a personal letter further assured his young friend (once again!) that his own private happiness was now complete, and that the reception of the author of *Public Happiness* was the Academy's finest hour.[51]

"He was a contemporary of Monsieur de Voltaire and he was esteemed by him." Such were the words, Chastellux confessed, by which he most wanted posterity to remember him. This anticipatory auto-epitaph is to be found in one of his letters to Voltaire, written in May 1777, a year before the latter's death, when there seemed little hope of another meeting with him.[52] The patriarch, however, managed to astonish his friends and confound his foes by returning early in 1778 to Paris, where he spent the final months of his life. Chastellux was thus a witness to the extraordinary popular consecration of his idol. Voltaire, now a dying man, held court in the *hôtel* of the Marquis de Villette, on the Quai des Théatins, and upon several legendary occasions appeared at the Comédie Française to witness his own plays. At a meeting of the French Academy on May 7—at what was to be his last appearance there, for he died on the 30th—Voltaire produced his plan for a new dictionary, exhorting the august body to embark at once upon this patriotic task. He himself assumed responsibility for the letter "A," while work on the other letters was peremptorily parceled out among his colleagues. Having overcome the objections of the more indolent, Voltaire took leave of the gathering in the best of humor and with a final quip: "Gentlemen, I thank you in the name of the Alphabet!" To which the youngest of the group, the Chevalier de Chastellux, responded in a flash: "And we, Sir, thank *you* in the name of Letters!" [53]

During the spring of 1778 Voltaire's name was often linked with that of Benjamin Franklin, the patriarch and philosopher from the New World. "Voltaire still shares with Franklin the applause and acclaim of the public," Madame d'Epinay reported. "Whenever they appear together at the theater, in the parks, or at the academies, there is no end to the shouts and the hand-clapping. Princes may appear, but no attention is paid them. But whenever Voltaire sneezes, Franklin says 'God bless you!', and the applause starts all over again." [54] All Paris knew, too, that Voltaire gave his benediction to Franklin's grandson with the words "God and Liberty," and that Sophocles and Solon embraced *à la française* at a meeting of the Academy of Sciences. Franklin had been in Paris since December 1776; the treaty of alliance between France and the United States was signed at Versailles on February 6, 1778; a few weeks later France and England were at war. Franklin had, to be sure, visited Paris still earlier, but only briefly, in 1767 and in 1769, when he had been welcomed in the circle of the scientists and the economists as the discoverer of electricity and the author of *The Way to Wealth.* Chastellux had already paid tribute to him in his book *De la Félicité Publique:* surveying the great scientists like Descartes and Newton, whose labors were improving the lot of humanity, he spoke of the recent discovery of electricity and of Monsieur Franklin, who like a new Prometheus "stole the celestial fire and subdued it to his laws." [55] This was in 1772. Now, in 1778, Franklin had further claims to glory, for he had also, as Turgot's famous Latin epigram neatly phrased it, snatched the scepter from the tyrants.

Chastellux moved in the same circles as did Franklin and must have had frequent occasions to speak with him of trans-Atlantic affairs. The revised edition of *De la Félicité Publique*, published in 1776, indicates that he was following events in America and speculating upon their general import in the scheme of history. As a soldier who might soon be called back to the field of battle, Chastellux now had more than abstract ideas to exchange with the new Prometheus. We know, for example, that he discussed with Franklin's predecessor and associate, Silas Deane—and presumably therefore with Franklin himself—matters connected with the French volunteers who were slipping off to serve with the Americans even before France openly espoused their cause.[56] He must also have been aware of the clandestine shipments of supplies under the management of Monsieur de Beaumarchais. With the Alliance of 1778 the period of "secret aid" came to an end. Henceforth, supplies, financial aid, military campaigns, and naval expeditions were matters of avowed national policy. The first of these expeditions left many doubts in American minds about the efficacy of the Alliance: the joint action of American land forces and D'Estaing's naval forces at Rhode Island in 1778 ended in disappointment; the Admiral's attempt against Savannah the following year was likewise unsuccessful. In 1778 and 1779 Chastellux was with the French army that gathered in Normandy and Brittany for a trans-Channel invasion. With the abandonment of this enterprise against England itself, came the decision to send a substantial expeditionary force to America. On March 1, 1780, Chastellux was promoted to the rank of *maréchal de camp* and designated as one of the major generals to serve overseas under General Rochambeau. Spring therefore found him at Brest, far from the *salons* of Paris, absorbed in administrative details connected with the embarkation of the troops.

Chastellux sailed from Brest on May 1, 1780, aboard the *Duc de Bourgogne*, flagship of Admiral de Ternay's fleet, and reached Newport, Rhode Island, on July 11. His sojourn in America is related in detail in the present book, so that only the general outline need be repeated here. Chastellux made his headquarters at Newport until the following summer, when he took an active part in the Allied campaign that culminated victoriously at Yorktown in

October 1781. He remained in Virginia until the summer of 1782; marched northward with the French army to New England, where he relinquished his command; then returned to Philadelphia and Annapolis, whence he sailed for home on the frigate *Émeraude* early in January 1783. He reached Nantes on February 12. A few days later he was back again among his friends in Paris, after an absence of nearly three years.

In spite of the absorbing spectacle presented by new sights and new experiences, the Paris world was never entirely absent from Chastellux's mind during his sojourn in America. Indeed, a bit of this world was transplanted there with Rochambeau's army. This was not yet a "national" army, or a "citizens' " army, as it would have been two decades or so later, after the reforms initiated by the French Revolution had produced their effect. Officers were still, by definition, members of the nobility; few, if any, had risen from the ranks. They were all gentlemen, from established families, often blood relations, and with the same friends and same social background. The discipline of camp and field required, to be sure, a strict regard to the hierarchy of military rank, but once this necessity was relaxed, social precedence and personal relationships ruled again.[57] Chastellux was thus not only a superior officer—third in the military hierarchy—but also an amiable companion, perhaps a cousin, or the intimate friend of some subordinate officer's family. In America he found a number of old acquaintances among the French volunteers serving with the Americans—the "Gallo-Americans," as he calls them—to whom he brought the latest gossip from the Court and from the Paris *salons*. Several of the younger men in Rochambeau's army—mere lieutenants or aides-de-camp—looked up to Chastellux as a sort of philosophical mentor who carried with him all the prestige of his literary and social success. The letters and memoirs of Mathieu Dumas, Axel Fersen, and the Comte de Ségur, for example, speak of him with both admiration and affection.[58]

Chastellux was less appreciated perhaps by the drillmasters and the old campaigners. Claude Blanchard, chief quartermaster, complained in his diary that generals rarely appreciated the practical problems with which the commissariat was beset, and upon one occasion witnessed an "unbecoming scene" when, he thought, M. de Chastellux was not only unjust to a subordinate, "but did not behave as a philosopher or a man of quality." [59] An unidentified engineer remarked that Chastellux might have wit and knowledge, but he unfortunately did not know the first thing about warfare.[60] There was even a rather unkind joke (deeply resented by Chastellux) which implied that at Yorktown a certain general allowed himself to be surprised by the enemy because he was busy composing a philosophical treatise.[61] Rochambeau himself, upon at least one occasion, found it necessary to reprove Chastellux for his indiscretion.[62] Nevertheless, Rochambeau was willing to entrust Chastellux with the command of the army in his own absence, and in spite of the occasional incident and the pleasantries bandied about in the officers' mess and among the rank and file, there is every reason to conclude that Chastellux fulfilled his military duties with competence and distinction. Following the siege of Yorktown he was commended for his role in the campaign, and as a recognition of his services a royal order dated December 5, 1781, secured for him the military governorship of Longwy with its annual allowance of 10,000 *livres*.[63]

Chastellux's knowledge of English made of him an important intermediary in the French dealings with the Americans—"the diplomat of Rochambeau's army," as one writer has called him. It is obvious from his own account of his travels that the characteristics which had endeared him to his friends in France also endeared him to the Americans: to Washington, first of all, as well as to countless others in all walks of life. He was equally at ease in staff conferences, in the drawing rooms of Philadelphia or Boston, and in roadside taverns. To the literati he brought with him something of the glamour of Paris, of the French Academy, of the great Republic of Letters, which knew no boundaries. Ezra Stiles, who met him at Newport soon after his arrival, noted in his diary: "Dined at Gen. de Chatelux in a splendid manner on 35 dishes. He is a capital Literary Character, a Member of the French Academy. He is the Glory of the Army." [64] In a similar vein William Knox, who also enjoyed Chastellux's hospitality at Newport, wrote to his brother, the General: "If I recollect, the Comte Rochambeau doesn't speak a word of English, nor do the two brothers Vioménil, Marquis Laval, or Comte St. Maime. The two counts Deux-Ponts, on the other hand, speak pretty well; and the most amiable General Chastellux, *à merveille*. If you have opportunity, I am sure you must be very intimate [with] General C[hastellux], if the two characters of the man of letters and the polite gentleman are recommendations. I know nobody who can be more strongly recommended. I have reason to

speak of the civility of all the gentlemen I have named, and of many
which I have not, and who belong to that army, but more particularly of those shown me by the Chevalier de Chastellux, at whose
petits soupers I was invited two evenings out of three when at
Newport. I mention this as being a particular mark of his attention, for the being invited to dine is a common compliment from
him to recommended strangers; but the evening circle is always
selected." [65]

Chastellux returned to Paris in 1783, not only with the laurels of
a victorious general, but with academic honors, which must have
given him equal satisfaction: membership in the American Philosophical Society and the American Academy of Arts and Sciences,
and honorary doctorates of civil law from the College of William
and Mary and the University of Pennsylvania.[66] Early in 1784 he
became the Marquis de Chastellux, through the death of his eldest
surviving brother, Philippe-Louis, who had previously carried this
title. The *Almanach Royal* for 1785—the Who's Who and Social
Register of the period—could therefore list among the members of
the French Academy: "Le Marquis de Chastellux, Maréchal des
Camps et Armées du Roi, Chevalier de l'Ordre de St. Lazare, de la
Société de Cincinnati, Gouverneur de Longwi, des Académies de
Boston et de Philadelphie." His residence is given as the "Quai des
Théatins"—where he had apartments in a house adjoining the Pont
Royal, at the corner of the Quai and the Rue du Bac.[67]

Chastellux's duties as military governor of Longwy, and later as
inspector general, took perhaps more of his time than he could
have wished, but did not prevent him from resuming his multi-
farious literary activities. The publication of the *Travels*, as related
below, represented his major effort. A short essay entitled
"Thoughts on Motion," published in 1784 as an appendix to Nico-
las Bergasse's "Considerations on Animal Magnetism," reflects his
interest in Dr. Mesmer's experiments, which were then attracting
interest in Parisian circles—until they were discredited by none
other than Dr. Franklin.[68] At the French Academy Chastellux delivered speeches for the reception of his old friend Abbé Morellet
in 1785, and of the historian M. de Rulhière in 1787.[69] His preface
to a volume of plays by his former collaboratrix at La Chevrette,
the Marquise de Gléon, gave him an opportunity to discourse about
sense and sensibility on the stage.[70] America was again his theme in
a "Discourse on the Advantages or Disadvantages to Europe result-

ing from the Discovery of America," published in 1787.[71] This was
a substantial brochure which might be described as both a postscript
to *Public Happiness* and a continuation of the "Letter to Mr. Madison on the Progress of the Arts and Sciences in America" which
had been appended to the *Travels*. Chastellux explained the circumstances of its publication in a letter to his American acquaintance,
Gouverneur Morris: "To convince you, my dear Morris, that I
have not forgotten America, I send you a work, which I found
time to compose last spring. It has met with great success here, and
an incident very agreeable to me occurred, relative to it. Custom
does not permit members of the French Academy to become com-
petitors for a prize, adjudged by a provincial academy. For this
reason, I did not send my production to the Academy of Lyons,
and I even printed it under a fictitious name. But it so entirely
eclipsed all those sent to the Academy, that this body dared not
crown one of them, and sent the prize-money [back] to the Abbé
Raynal." [72]

Chastellux had indeed not forgotten America or his American
friends. After his return to France he continued to correspond with
several of them—with Gouverneur Morris and Washington, for
example—and renewed acquaintance with others in Paris, when
they in turn traveled to the Old World. Franklin was still there and
remained until the summer of 1785. Jefferson came on an official
mission in August 1784; a few days after his arrival Chastellux
helped him find a boarding school for his daughter Martha at the
Abbaye Royale de Pentemont.[73] Young William Short arrived from
Virginia a few months later to serve as Jefferson's secretary and
learn the ways of the Paris world. Several of the junior officers
whom Chastellux had known as members of Washington's military
family also crossed the seas: David S. Franks, William Stephens
Smith, and David Humphreys. With characteristic generosity Chastellux translated the latter's poem on the American army into
French, wrote a glowing introduction for it, and arranged to have
it printed by his own Paris publisher.[74] There were others, too, to
revive agreeable recollections of his wartime travels: Jeremiah
Wadsworth from Connecticut; Wadsworth's erstwhile partner in
the business of supplies for Rochambeau's army, Mr. "Carter," now
become Mr. Church again, and his wife Angelica Schuyler Church;
and Mr. and Mrs. William Bingham from Philadelphia. If we are
to credit the complaints echoed by one young traveler, Chastellux

did not devote quite as much time to these American visitors in Paris as they expected, or as he himself might have wished. "A great many people are kind to me here," Thomas Shippen wrote back home, "Mr. Jefferson invites me to dine twice a week and I amuse myself vastly well in every way. Chastellux has treated me with the same neglect that he has shewn invariably to every American of my acquaintance." [75] Tommy Shippen had first seen Chastellux in Philadelphia at a time when Monsieur Otto, one of the young secretaries of the French Legation, was playing sweet melodies on the harp to his sister Nancy, and when Monsieur de Marbois, another of the French diplomats, was paying court to Elizabeth Moore. It probably did not occur to him that such an oldster as the worldly General Chastellux might be troubled by his own *affaires de coeur*, and that there was now perhaps some excuse for his "neglect."

Chastellux had referred discreetly to such matters in a letter written to Jefferson from Marly in the spring of 1785.[76] Expressing his regret that he had had so little opportunity to enjoy the Virginian's presence in Paris, he explained that he was in a "cruel situation" at the bedside of an intimate friend (*une de mes amies les plus intimes*) who was suffering from a continuous fever: "I have been very unhappy for the past eight months, unhappy from a feeling that is better known in the country which you have left than in the one you now inhabit." Then, early in 1788—at the time Tommy Shippen was complaining of his neglect—Chastellux related the whole story to another American friend:

It is a very long time, my dear [Gouverneur] Morris, since I have written to you, and this is not for want of having thought of you; still less is it, I am sure, for want of interesting matter, to confide in your friendship, whether relating to public affairs, or to what peculiarly concerns myself. I will begin my protasis with the last-mentioned subject, as the most interesting for two friends, conversing together, at last, after so long a silence. A revolution has been wrought in my destiny, my dear Morris, diametrically opposite to that which has taken place in your country. When I saw you, I was free; I am no longer; or rather I have exchanged a painful and heavy chain for the most gentle bands. [...] In this sad situation, obliged to be absent from Paris, to attend to my business as inspector, I resolved to visit the waters of Spa, in the interval between my reviews. My soul, my dear Morris, was withered and overwhelmed. I saw nothing, in the remainder of my career, to attach me to life, when

that vast concourse of strangers who assemble at Spa, presented to
me one charming in my eyes as in those of all others; but especially
fascinating by her mind, and most lovely character. She was Irish,
of good family, and about twenty-eight years of age. The first
blessing to which I was indebted to her, was the recovery of the
pleasure of loving, which I believed I had lost forever. The second,
the happiness of inspiring in her enough esteem and friendship, to
make her consent to unite her fate with mine. I married her, my
dear Morris, and for three months, she has made me the happiest
of men. [...] [77]

This is Chastellux's own story—or at least as much of it as the
scissors of a nineteenth-century American censor have spared for
us. The charming young Irishwoman was Marie Brigitte Plunkett,
lady-in-waiting to the Duchesse d'Orléans.[78] The marriage took
place at Liège on October 14, 1787. News of it inevitably stirred
ripples of surprise and amusement in the Paris *salons,* and even
beyond. In her memoirs the Baroness d'Oberkirch recorded some
of the gossip:

The Duchesse de Bourbon has written to me about the Marquis
de Chastellux's marriage. A few years ago he published the account
of his travels in America. He attaches great importance to what he
eats, for the book consists mainly of a detailed description of the
dishes served to him each day. One must conclude that he is more
of a *gourmand* than a *gourmet,* for otherwise it would be impossible
to understand his weakness for American cooking, which enjoys no
great reputation; he speaks of the most outlandish dishes, and describes them all with a complacency that really borders on the
ridiculous. He is none the less quite vain about this book, which is
the cause of the marriage with Mademoiselle Plunkett. She was at
Spa when the Duchesse d'Orléans was there, and, as she is pretty,
she was singled out by the princess for special favors. She met the
Marquis de Chastellux several times. He appeared to her a good
match, but as she had no fortune of her own, she had to find ways
to please him, which was not easy when she had only her pretty
face to offer. Knowing of his great vanity, she contrived to be surprised by him when absorbed in the reading of his book. He was
so charmed by this mute praise that he straightway made up his
mind. The Duchesse d'Orléans, who was enchanted by such literary
devotion, has taken young Madame de Chastellux into her en-
tourage. People in high society are still chuckling about it. They
even say that she has a specially bound copy of this book which

never leaves her, and that the newlyweds read it aloud to each other, and begin all over again whenever they reach the end.[79]

The news was of course relayed to America. William Short, for example, lost no time in informing his Virginian friend, William Nelson (the Governor's son, whom Chastellux had known at Williamsburg): "I am going to give you a piece of news which will surprise you. Your old friend the Marquis de Chastellux was at Spa the last season and fell so much in love with an Irish lady as to marry her although she was entirely without fortune. The Duchess of Orleans, who was at Spa also, and was pleased with the lady, has made her *dame de compagnie,* with a lodgings and a pension of 4,000 *livres* per annum, equal to 160 guineas. The Marquis arrived at Paris a few days ago with his Lady. She seems an agreeable woman about 28 years of age, and pretty enough without being too handsome for the peace of an old husband in Paris. General Chastellux has been during thirty years the *bon ami* of an old lady, who is in despair and rage on account of his *inconstancy.* Madame de Boufflers, one of the wits of Paris, observed on this subject that the lady ought to console herself for having preserved a lover during thirty years rather than mourn the loss of him at the end of them. General Chastellux seems gay and contented himself. That is the principal, especially if it should remain, which I wish most ardently." [80] The story apparently went the rounds in America, too, for eight years later the Duc de Liancourt, then an *émigré* in Philadelphia, discovered that the Misses Dickinson, like certain ladies in Paris, still could not pardon the Chevalier de Chastellux "for having married a young woman that he loved, because he had formerly loved an old lady who still loved him a bit." [81]

The story of Chastellux's marriage would not be complete without the letter received from Mount Vernon:

My dear Marquis, [wrote General Washington,] in reading your very friendly and acceptable letter of 21st December 1787, which came to hand by the last mail, I was, as you may well suppose, not less delighted than surprised to come across that plain American word, 'My wife.'—A Wife!—well my dear Marquis, I can hardly refrain from smiling to find you are caught at last. I saw, by the eulogium you often made on the happiness of domestic life in America, that you had swallowed the bait and that you would as surely be taken (one day or another) as you was a Philosopher and a Soldier. So, your day has, at length, come. I am glad of it, with all my heart and soul. It is quite good enough for you. Now you are well served for coming to fight in favor of the American Rebels, all the way across the Atlantic Ocean, by catching that terrible contagion, domestic felicity, which time like the small pox or the plague, a man can have only once in his life: because it commonly lasts him (at least with us in America—I don't know how you manage these matters in France) for his whole life time. And yet after all the maledictions you so richly merit on the subject, the worst wish which I can find in my heart to make against Madame de Chastellux and yourself is, that you may neither of you get the better of this same domestic felicity during the entire course of your mortal existence.

If so wonderful an event should have occasioned me, my dear Marquis, to have written in a strange style, you will understand me as clearly as if I had said (what in plain English, is the simple truth) do me the justice to believe that I take a heartfelt interest in whatever concerns your happiness. And in this view, I sincerely congratulate you on your auspicious Matrimonial connection.[82]

Chastellux's domestic felicity lasted but a short time. In the autumn of 1788 he returned to Paris after an inspection of army posts in Normandy, contracted a sudden illness (*"une fièvre soporeuse"*), and died on October 24, at the age of fifty-four. He was buried in a chapel of the church of St. Germain l'Auxerrois, in the heart of the city which was more truly his nurturer than the ancestral castle at Chastellux. He never knew the son who was born four months after his death. Nor did he have the satisfaction of embracing his "dear Morris," the American friend to whom he had related the revolution in his destiny, and who at length arrived in Paris early in 1789.

"Poor Genl. de Chattellux is no more," Gouverneur Morris wrote to Washington on March 3. "I have seen his Widow, an amiable Woman who is not the less lovely for the Tears she sheds to his Memory. A fine Boy remains as the Pledge of connubial Tenderness. I think it would give her great Pleasure if you took the Trouble to mingle in a short Letter Condolence for one Event and Congratulations for the other. You would in that Case oblige me by confiding the Letter to my Care. Excuse me, I pray, for dropping this Hint."[83] The day before he penned these lines Morris called at the Palais Royal where the Duchesse d'Orléans and her ladies-in-waiting resided. There, he noted in his diary, he saw Madame de Chastellux "who presents her little Son, now ten Days old. While I hold him in my Arms: '*Ah! Monsieur Morris, cet Enfant a bien des Droits sur vous.*'—'*Oui Madame, aussi j'espère lui être de quelque Utilité.*' " [84] A few weeks later, when Morris was again at the Palais Royal, he detected a glance from the Duchesse d'Orléans which seemed to imply that "*Monsieur Morris est un peu amoureux de Madame la Marquise.*" "But Madame la Duchesse is mistaken," Morris noted. "However, this Mistake can do no Harm to any Body." [85] The Duchesse was indeed mistaken: that same evening, after taking leave of the Marquise de Chastellux, Morris went to what he described as "a snug Party" at Madame de Flahaut's apartments in the Louvre; henceforth his attentions were diverted in this other direction. He continued, however, to be a faithful caller at the Palais Royal, and often during the difficult days ahead used his good offices in behalf of the Duchesse d'Orléans and her young lady-in-waiting. The Marquise de Chastellux survived the trials of the Revolution, including imprisonment and exile, by the side of her royal patroness. She died in Paris, on December 18, 1815, a few months after Napoleon's downfall, when the Bourbons were again on the throne of France. Her son Alfred rose to an honorable position in the world—although not, it must be admitted, with any special help from the American friends of his father, whose patronage she solicited in his behalf upon several occasions. Towards the end of the Empire he obtained a civil post in the government, then, with the invasion of his country, entered the army. In 1815 he was in the service of his King, as so many other Chastelluxes had been before him. In 1822 he sponsored the publication of a new edition of *De la Félicité Publique* (with marginalia from Voltaire's copy), for which he wrote a brief memoir of the father he had never known. In the 1830's, under the Orleans Monarchy, he represented the Department of Yonne in the Chamber of Deputies. He died in 1856 at Lucy-le-Bois, the estate which his mother had acquired during the latter years of her life. Although married, Comte Alfred de Chastellux died without issue. Thus, only collateral descendants of the author of the *Travels in North America* bear the name of Chastellux today.

The date of Chastellux's death, in October 1788, when France was alive with plans for the forthcoming convocation of the Estates General, inevitably leads us to speculate on what the fate of the author of *Public Happiness* might have been had he lived a few years longer. The name of Condorcet comes to mind: another Academician, ten years Chastellux's junior, who composed his *Historical Survey of the Progress of the Human Mind* while in hiding from his Jacobin enemies—and then cheated the guillotine by taking his own life. We think, too, of those other French soldiers who appear in the pages of the *Travels in North America*. General Rochambeau, after commanding the Armies of the North in 1792, was then retired at his own request, was imprisoned during the Reign of Terror, but nevertheless died in peace at his estate in Vendôme in 1804. Baron de Vioménil, Chastellux's other superior officer in America, was mortally wounded when defending the royal family at the Tuileries on the 10th of August 1792. Baron de Montesquieu, Chastellux's aide-de-camp during his American travels, emigrated, fought on the other side, and finally settled down to a country gentleman's life in England; his other aides, Frank Dillon and the Vicomte de Vaudreuil, likewise served in the *émigré* armies, while Lynch distinguished himself on the battlefield of Valmy, made his peace with changing régimes, and resumed his military career under Napoleon. The Duc de Lauzun, who greeted the Revolution with eagerness and sat as a deputy to the Estates General, met death on the guillotine in 1793, as did Custine that same year. Gouvion died on a battlefield in Flanders. Lafayette figured prominently on the French political scene for two years or more, sought refuge with the opposing powers, spent five years in Austrian jails, and eventually, when in his late sixties, revisited the battlefields of America, a miraculous survivor of the legendary days of the Revolution. Duportail, the engineer, who took part as Chastellux did in the staff conferences preceding Yorktown, became Minister of War in 1790-91, only to find himself back in America a few years later, living as a refugee on a farm near Valley Forge. Ternant returned to America in 1791 as Minister of His Most Christian Majesty, but when the monarchy fell, he chose to linger on in America, an embittered exile, disillusioned with the Americans and the cause which he had once so eagerly supported. The Vicomte de Noailles, he who proposed the abolition of the privileges of the nobility during the memorable night session of the National Assembly on the 4th of August 1789, came back to America in 1793 with plans for a refugee colony on the Susquehanna; still later, in 1804, he died from wounds received in a naval engagement in the

West Indies. Duplessis-Mauduit, like Noailles and Lafayette one of Chastellux's gay companions on the trip to Brandywine and the river forts in December 1780, met his death in 1791 when attempting to quell a slave revolt in Santo Domingo.

No such sequel as these need be added to Chastellux's story. We can still think of him as he painted himself in the pages of his journal: conversing with Washington at Preakness over a bottle of Madeira and hickory nuts, reciting Ossian's poetry with Jefferson at Monticello, chatting with Mrs. Powel in Philadelphia or with Mrs. Tudor in Boston, scrutinizing the rocks and the waterfalls as Monsieur Buffon had taught him to do, studying the map of his next day's journey with a group of lanky New Hampshire drovers looking over his shoulder, riding happily along the roads of America with a blue jay's feather in his cap.

Chastellux's Travels: *A Biblio-biography*

The sequel, if any, to the history of Chastellux's life is to be found in the story of what has proved to be his most enduring book, the *Travels in North America*. Although its beginnings are part of the author's own biography, there came a time, as with other books, when it journeyed forward along paths of its own making.

Part I of the *Travels*, recounting Chastellux's journey from Newport to Philadelphia and Albany (Nov. 11, 1780–Jan. 9, 1781), was written up from rough notes made during the trip soon after he returned to Rhode Island, and was privately printed for him there on the press of the French fleet. This part of the book was presumably written, therefore, in the Mawdsley House on Spring Street in Newport, where Chastellux had his lodgings. It appeared as a small quarto of 192 pages, printed for private circulation among the author's friends in an edition of twenty-four copies (according to the preface of the later trade edition) under the title: *Voyage de Newport A Philadephie, Albany, &c.* The title page carries the imprint "A Newport, De l'Imprimerie Royale de l'Escadre," without date and without the author's name [§1].[86] Assuming that it took Chastellux several weeks to complete his manuscript, and that he oversaw its printing before the army moved from Newport to the Hudson early in June, we may conjecture the date of the book's completion as April or May 1781.

The *Voyage* is the most substantial of the Newport publications of the French Fleet Press, which also issued a short-lived newspaper, the *Gazette Françoise,* a *Calendrier François* for 1781, a four-page *Relation* of the naval engagement of March 16, 1781, as well as a variety of administrative blank-forms for the army and navy.[87] Although the printing equipment (including the paper) belonged to the French navy and was transported on its vessels—in this instance the *Neptune*—it was of course moved on shore during the sojourn at Newport. According to the French billeting list for the winter of 1780-81 the "Imprimerie de la Marine," designated as billet No. 641, was on the "Rue de la Pointe" and was near the other navy installations along the waterfront; the same location is given by the colophon of the *Gazette Françoise.* Newport antiquarians identify this as present Washington (formerly Water) Street, "the street which runs in a northerly direction from the westerly end of Long Wharf, along what was formerly designated as the Point." The house used as the printing shop has not been positively identified and has apparently not survived, but a bronze tablet commemorating the French press may be seen in the general vicinity, on the west foundation wall of the Nichols-Wanton-Hunter House, Washington Street.[88]

Of the twenty-four or so copies of the first edition of Part I of Chastellux's *Travels*—now one of the rarest and most prized Americana—at least eight copies have survived. One of these survivors (New York Public Library) formerly belonged to Barbé-Marbois, Secretary of the French Legation in Philadelphia, and must have circulated rather widely in polite circles there. This is presumably the copy which Thomas Jefferson once had in hand, and which led him to say that the "malice and curiosity of the world" had "fished out" certain passages and concluded that the book was "a collection of personal strictures and satyre"—whereas it was really in his opinion "the most flattering account of America that had ever been written." [89] The book evidently circulated, too, among Chastellux's brother officers in the French army, and, as he himself notes, seven or eight copies of it were sent to France soon after its completion.[90]

Part I of Chastellux's *Travels* was thus being passed around, in printed form, even before he wrote the sequels. Part II, describing a journey in Virginia in April 1782, was written the following month at Williamsburg (perhaps in the Wythe House); Part III, relating a journey in New England in November-December 1782, was written at the turn of the year, on the eve of Chastellux's embarkation for France, probably in the French Legation at Chestnut and Seventh Streets in Philadelphia, where he was La Luzerne's guest. For the moment neither Part II nor Part III was printed, but soon after Chastellux's return to Paris, early in 1783, he evidently had a few manuscript copies made to circulate among his closest friends. As might be expected, he soon yielded to the instances of one of them—Baron Grimm—who was allowed to print extracts from the manuscripts in the *Cahiers de Lecture*, published at Gotha, one of the numerous French periodicals edited outside France for the purpose of bringing the latest productions of Paris, literary and other, to the Republic of Letters and to the lesser capitals of enlightened Europe.[91] These "fragments," taken from Parts I and II, each one forming a self-contained anecdote or episode, ran serially in the monthly *Cahiers de Lecture* from January through December, 1784 [§2].

The inevitable of course happened. Publishers outside France—who were beyond the reach of the Royal Censor and who were old hands at pirated and clandestine editions—collected the extracts into book form. The first of these unauthorized editions, apparently printed at Kassel in Germany, appeared in 1785 under the title *Voyage de Mr. Le Chevalier de Chastellux en Amérique* [§3]. At least two other editions were in turn copied from this: one dated 1785 with no indication of place [§4], and another, dated 1786, with the imprint of B. Le Francq, Imprimeur-Libraire in Brussels [§5]. From the same source were derived the anonymous German translation published at Hamburg by the Nordische Typographische Litterarische Gesellschaft in 1785 as *Des Ritters von Chastellüx Reisebeobachtungen über Amerika* [§6], and another (also anonymous, but a different translation) published by Joseph Stahel, Frankfort and Leipzig, 1786 [§8].

Unwilling to see his book multiply in this truncated form, Chastellux at length consented to the publication of the entire work, duly revised by himself. Thus the complete authorized version of his *Travels*, in two volumes, was issued in the spring of 1786 by Prault, Printer to the King, at his shop "A l'Immortalité" on the Quai des Augustins in Paris [§10]. Extracts from Part I (previously printed at Newport) and from Part II had been included in the pirated editions; Part III appeared for the first time. The royal "approbation" signed by Suard and dated April 4, 1786, found its place on the last page of the work, which bore the title: *Voyages de M. le Marquis de Chastellux dans l'Amérique Septentrionale Dans les années 1780, 1781 & 1782.* The author, it will be noted, was now no longer the Chevalier de Chastellux, as he had been when he made the journeys in America, but the Marquis de Chastellux, this title having devolved upon him with the death of his elder brother in 1784. Included in Prault's handsome volumes were three engraved plates of the Natural Bridge, from drawings made by Baron Turpin in Virginia—the first published pictures of this American natural wonder. Two engraved maps, from drawings by M. Dezoteux,[92] one of the officers who had been in America with Chastellux, added to the usefulness and attractiveness of the book. The Paris edition of 1786 serves as the basis for the present new edition, as it did for the English translation published the year following its original publication.

How much did Chastellux revise his book for the complete authorized edition of 1786? His manuscripts have apparently not survived,[93] but the printed Newport edition of 1781 provides a basis for at least a partial comparison. He added a certain number of footnotes, where his subsequent experiences had contributed new information about people and events, but the text of Part I differs relatively little in the two versions. Chastellux made but twenty or so changes in all, and these in general concerned people he had met during his journey. (These changes or deletions are indicated in the Editor's footnotes to the present edition.) Thus, as Jefferson and others had suggested, Chastellux did strike out or alter some of the "personal strictures" that had been fished out by the curious and apparently given offense. In some instances he merely substituted an initial and asterisks for a name: for the Dorrance family of Voluntown with the unfortunate daughter; for Colonel Armand's ladylove, Mademoiselle Beaumesnil; for Mrs. Plater, the American protagonist of French fashions; and for Miss Vining, the Philadelphia apostle of liberty. He also softened or deleted some of his comments about public figures: Ethan Allen, General Samuel Holden Parsons, Samuel Huntington, General Robert Howe, Robert Morris, David Rittenhouse, Thomas Paine, William Stephens Smith, and General James Clinton. Finally, he edited some of his remarks about the ladies: Mrs. Knox's indescribable headgear, Martha Washington's resemblance to a German princess, Mrs. Powel's loquaciousness, Mrs. Bland's stolidity, the disposition and the indispositions of Mrs. Schuyler, and young Peggy Schuyler's toothlessness. None of these passages was seriously damaging, and Chastellux had, as he said, no real grounds for remorse. Still, he could not help realizing that certain of his little barbs, which were harmless in a journal privately printed for a few intimate friends in France, would perhaps carry more of a sting when published in a book intended for general circulation, not only in France but in the United States as well. So, he magnanimously made his small sacrifice on the altar of Franco-American friendship and smoothed over such passages as he thought likely to offend.

The two volumes of Prault's authorized edition of Chastellux's *Voyages* must have been ready by May 1786, for on the 11th of that month the French Academy received a copy of the work from the author.[94] Less than a year later, early in January 1787,[95] an English translation of the book was issued in London by G. G. J. and J. Robinson, Pater-Noster Row, under the title *Travels in North-America, in the Years 1780, 1781, and 1782* [§12]. The author is identified as "the Marquis de Chastellux, One of the Forty Members of the French Academy, and Major General in the French Army, serving under the Count de Rochambeau." The translator, however, is described only as "An English Gentleman, who resided in America at that period." The lengthy, discursive, and often provocative notes added by the translator inevitably arouse curiosity about the identity of this anonymous "English Gentleman." Since his notes have always formed an integral part of Chastellux's book for English-speaking readers, and as they are again included in the present edition, an outline of his life is appropriate here.

Something about the Translator

Although the English translation of Chastellux's *Travels* has been attributed to various persons—notably to John Kent, who did in fact translate Chastellux's *De la Félicité Publique*—the translator's real identity was established nearly a century ago by J. Hammond Trumbull in a communication published in the Massachusetts Historical Society *Proceedings* for 1869-70.[96] Trumbull's carefully-reasoned argument—admittedly based on circumstantial evidence alone—is convincing, and can now be corroborated by other sources not known to him.[97] Taking as an initial clue the statement inscribed by the German scholar and collector of Americana, Christoph Daniel Ebeling (1741-1817), in his copy of Chastellux's *Voyages* (subsequently acquired by the Harvard Library), Trumbull demonstrated, largely by a close analysis of the notes printed in the *Travels*, that the translator was George Grieve (1748-1809), the younger son of Richard Grieve, an attorney-at-law at Alnwick in Northumberland, near the Scottish border.

George Grieve has been described by his English biographer as an "hereditary agitator" and an "ardent politician." He was also, it may be added, a commercial adventurer, a journalist and hack writer of some ability, a strenuous Whig who eventually became a *sans-culotte*. When he had reached this latter stage he described himself as a "disorganizer of despotism in both hemispheres," and, when the occasion required it, did not hesitate to call himself a "citizen of the United States of America" and claim the friendship of such "liberators of mankind" as Franklin, Washington, Jefferson, Price, and Priestley!

But all this is an anticipation. As a young man in England Grieve was an advocate of parliamentary reform, an ardent admirer of John Wilkes, and a participant in fence-leveling activities in Northumberland. For a number of years he worked for the firm of Peter Thellusson, a merchant of Swiss origin established in London, and presumably traveled on the Continent in pursuing his business. With the coming of the American Revolution he was thus well prepared to launch out into that mercantile and political *demi-monde* which had its ramifications on both sides of the Atlantic. Grieve appears to have been in the West Indies early in the war. In 1777 he met Silas Deane, American agent in France, and soon made the acquaintance of Benjamin Franklin. In 1779 and 1780 he was associated in the management of the "London Courant," was involved in a libel suit, and fled England for the Continent. Letters of introduction written in Grieve's behalf early in May 1781 by Deane and Franklin describe him as "the warm and zealous friend of America" and indicate his intention of setting out for the United States on business "with respect to some lands" in Virginia. At this same time he took an oath of allegiance to the United States, dated Passy, April 29, 1781.[98] According to Grieve's statement in one of his notes he was in Holland in August 1781.[99]

Grieve's sojourn in America, which he reached late in 1781 or early in 1782, lasted only a year. From the notes that he appended to his translation of Chastellux's *Travels*, it is possible to deduce the rough lines of his itinerary.[100] Until early May 1782 he was mainly in Philadelphia, whence he made trips into other parts of Pennsylvania. By June or July he was in Virginia, journeying inland at least as far as General Gates's residence (in what is now Jefferson County, West Virginia). About the 20th of July he was at Alexandria, where he saw the encampment of the French army, and then "attended" this army "nearly the whole way" on its march northward to join forces with the Americans on the Hudson. In early October he "spent a day or two at Verplanck's Point," where the American army under Washington was encamped not far from the French. By November he had reached New England: his notes indicate that he crossed Connecticut, that he was in Providence, in Boston, and at Salem, where he just missed seeing Chastellux on November 14, 1782. It was from Salem, the following month, that he set sail for Europe, reaching Bordeaux after a seven weeks voyage some time in January 1783. A letter written by Grieve from Bordeaux (where his address is "at Messrs. French & Neveu," merchants there), January 21, 1783, to Silas Deane, then in Paris, mentions that he had "arrived a few days ago in the General Galvez, of Salem," and had the pleasure of transmitting a letter from Deane's brother (Barnabas Deane) whom he saw at Hartford in October.[101]

The statement on the title page of the English edition of the *Travels* that the translator "resided in America" at the period Chastellux was there is thus substantially correct. In the course of the year 1782 Grieve himself covered a good part—but not all—of the route described by Chastellux. It might be noted, for example, that he did not pursue his Virginia travels as far as Williamsburg, Monticello, or the Natural Bridge, nor did he travel up the Hudson as far as Albany and the Saratoga battlefields; Portsmouth, New Hampshire, too, was beyond the range of his own experience. Grieve's notes thus shed considerable light on Chastellux's narrative, but they also raise many tantalizing questions about his own activities and reasons for being in America. Grieve evidently had some bona fide business to transact for English acquaintances with family connections in America; he specifically mentions, for example, that he had business to transact with Washington "respecting the estates of an old friend to whom he was executor." [102] From his frequent references to trade, money values, and privateering, it seems fairly obvious that he was himself speculating in war supplies of some sort, or engaged in land-jobbing. His consistent "name dropping," as well as his insistently proclaimed "intimacy" with

American personalities who were then under a cloud, confirm his gift for politics and intrigue. Indeed, one cannot help wondering in what secret missions and undercover activities he may have been involved. Whatever his mission, Grieve never returned to America again, and the oath of allegiance taken at Passy notwithstanding, never became a citizen of the United States in the real sense of the term.

After his return to France early in 1783—for he apparently resided rarely, if ever, in England again—Grieve resumed his journalistic and literary activities. If the summary of these activities written under his own signature a decade later may be trusted, he translated into English, among other works, *Le Jeune Anacharsis* by the Abbé Barthélemy and *Mémoires sur les Turcs et les Tartares* by the Baron de Tott, as well as writings by Mirabeau, Volney, and Savary; and translated into French works relating to the French Revolution by Richard Price, Priestley, and others.[103] In this recapitulation, dated 1793, Grieve pointedly omits specific mention of the Marquis de Chastellux's *Travels*, for by then such aristocrats were anathema to the Revolutionary potentates whom he was trying to appease.

As might be expected from what has been said of his earlier life, George Grieve was one of that international confraternity of the "friends of mankind" who hailed the dawn of the French Revolution with enthusiasm, and yearned to play a part therein. Grieve's role, alas, was not a glorious one. Any idealism that he may have possessed forsook him, and he is remembered today only as the spiteful and vicious persecutor of Madame Du Barry, whom he literally hunted down to her death.[104] Grieve had been living in Marly; the aging favorite of Louis XV lived nearby in her château at Louveciennes. Early in 1791 the countryside was agog with the news that thieves had made off with the Countess's fabulous jewels. Not long thereafter rumors circulated that the theft was simulated, that the Countess herself had devised this means of transferring her wealth beyond the reach of possible confiscation. Grieve, who was becoming something of an oracle in the revolutionary clubs of the locality, propagated such rumors, and was suspected by some of being their originator. In 1793, when the Countess returned from the third of her fruitless attempts to recover her jewels in London, where they had turned up in the hands of thieves and brokers, she found Grieve and his coadjutors (Blache and Rotondo) installed in her château as guardians of such treasures as remained. The persecution continued relentlessly. Grieve not only published an inflammatory pamphlet describing Madame Du Barry's licentious life and odious conspiracies,[105] but tirelessly assembled the evidence to be used against her at her trial. She was arrested on September 27, 1793, incarcerated in the Prison de la Force, brought before the Revolutionary Tribunal on December 7, and guillotined next day in the Place de la Révolution, *18 Frimaire, An II de la République une et indivisible.*

The persecutor in turn found himself among the persecuted. A few months after Robespierre's fall had brought an end to the Reign of Terror, Grieve was arrested at Corbie in Picardy in November 1794 and taken back to the prison at Versailles. It was here on *4 Nivôse, An III*—December 24, 1794—that he penned in his defense the fulsome memoir in which he styles himself "Citizen of the United States of America" and recapitulates his services to liberty and to letters.[106] His arrest, it seems, was merely a result of mistaken identity, while his fortune, suspected by his denunciators, had come to him legitimately from his elder brother (deceased on December 16, 1793).[107] Indeed, it was through Henry Walter Livingston, secretary to the late American Minister, Gouverneur Morris, that this news had been conveyed to him from London. His American banker in Paris, Citizen Mark Leavenworth, among others, could vouch for his generous use of his funds; his passports and other papers were in order; and he possessed a "certificate from the Ambassador of the United States of America." Further details of this particular *affaire Grieve* have not been unearthed, but the prisoner must have been released; there are no further traces of him in France, and several years later he was residing, obscurely but comfortably, in Brussels. He died there on February 23, 1809, at the age of sixty-one. The death certificate, preserved in the municipal archives, states that "George Greive" was born "à Newcastel, en Amérique"! [108]

There is a certain irony in the fact that a man like George Grieve should have come down to posterity hand in hand with the urbane and kindly Chastellux. The coincidence appears to be largely fortuitous, for no evidence has come to light to show that Grieve's translation was specifically authorized or actively encouraged by the Marquis. The translator in his notes makes no claim to "an intimate acquaintance" with Chastellux, as he was so ready to do in the case of other prominent figures. He must, however, at least have seen him in America, or in Paris at some time after both had returned there in 1783, for we have his comment—which sounds like a firsthand one—that "the Marquis de Chastellux is a well made, handsome man, of about four and forty, with eyes full of intelligence and fire, the carriage and deportment of a man of rank, and with a disposition extremely remote from an indifference to beauty." [109] There was of course no international copyright to protect an author's work; it was the custom at the time for publishers to disregard such amenities as "permissions" and to make the most of any potentially salable foreign works that came their way. Chastellux perhaps became aware that Grieve was translating his work, but since he could not prevent it, he could do little but close his eyes and submit to the inevitable.

On the other hand, it appears likely that he himself had another translator in mind. In March 1786—that is, while the French edition of the *Voyages* was still in press—David Humphreys, then resident in Paris, who *was* well acquainted with Chastellux, wrote that he had begun to translate the *Travels* and expected to make some progress during his voyage back to America.[110] Just how much progress Humphreys made is not known, but he was able at least to show certain pages of his translation to General Washington when he visited Mount Vernon that summer.[111] It must therefore have been something of a disappointment to the aspiring young American man of letters—and to Chastellux as well—to learn that his own labors were rendered superfluous by the work of the anonymous "English gentleman" who had "resided in America." Grieve did his work quickly, spurred on no doubt by a desire to get ahead of others.

Although there is some evidence of haste in his work, Grieve's translation is on the whole an acceptable one. The translator's notes, interesting or curious as they may be in themselves, form a somewhat discordant accompaniment to Chastellux's harmonious text. Chastellux himself—whatever his real thoughts may have been—appears to have made the best of the situation. The second Paris edition of his *Voyages*, prepared not long before his death in 1788 and to which he added a few more notes of his own, indicates that he was familiar with Grieve's translation and notes. Although he in one instance (Pt. II, chap. 3, n. 24) contradicts Grieve's generalizations about American curiosity, in another (Pt. I, chap. 1, n. 23) he translates the Englishman's note as a confirmation of his own integrity, and further pays tribute to the loftiness of "Mr. G***"'s sentiments, his love of mankind, and the "facility and elegance of his style." On the other hand, William Short, who was a bit more detached and thus perhaps more perceptive than the author, spoke of Grieve as one of that numberless class of men, then swarming in Europe, who felt the *besoin d'écrire:* "He seems to have translated the Marquis's travels merely for the purpose of tacking his own to them and thus sending them into the world in good company."[112] Henceforth, as far as English-speaking readers were concerned, the travels of the omniscient and ubiquitous George Grieve were engrafted, for better or for worse, upon the *Travels* of the Marquis de Chastellux.

Within less than a year, then, Chastellux's *Travels* was ready to take its chance with readers in both its French and its English versions. "By some it is exalted to the clouds, by others levelled to the dust—both parties wrong, as literary parties always must be," William Short reported from Paris.[113] La Harpe, for example, commented favorably: the book was both agreeable and instructive, the work of a well-informed professional soldier and an amiable philosopher; the summaries of battles were interesting contributions to history, while the letter to Mr. Madison was both well conceived and well written. The editor of Grimm's newsletter, somewhat more reserved, reproached the author for having published so many details of interest only to friends, but nevertheless concluded, a bit grudgingly, that no book was better calculated to give a fair idea of the nature of the country and of the manners and government of the "new republicans" who dwelt there.[114] Of all the comments that he heard, directly or indirectly, none could have pleased Chastellux more than the letter he received from Buffon:

From the very first page the reader is by your side as your traveling companion. . . . Your reflections are all judicious and penetrating, your general views broad and discerning; and the great art of matching the colors and tones appropriate to each object—a rare merit in the travel writer, because he is so rarely a philosopher and painter—increases the charm of your narrative. . . . I must tell you, my illustrious friend, more out of simple justice than of gratitude, that no one knows better than you how to render your subject attractive; it is impossible not to love the country and people you speak of, while loving you still more. We stop with you at every inn; and I kept regretting that this was but an illusion and that it was only within the covers of your book.[115]

A second edition of the *Voyages*, revised by Chastellux not long before his death [§11], included several additional notes in which he took occasion to reply, somewhat obliquely, to certain of the criticisms that had been leveled against the book and which had evidently ruffled him. The English translation was likewise re-issued by Robinson of London [§13], and was copied in Dublin [§14]. These further printings are one indication that Chastellux's book found enough readers to be termed a "success." It is probable, too, that two pamphlets which sharply attacked it also stimulated interest in it. The first of these came from a Frenchman, the other from an Englishman.

The French attack, by Jacques-Pierre Brissot de Warville (1754-1793), was contained in his *Examen critique des Voyages dans l'Amérique Septentrionale de M. le Marquis de Chatellux*, published in Paris during the summer of 1786 [§17]. The title page indicates London as the place of publication, but this was a common subterfuge resorted to by pamphleteers who sought to circumvent the censors. The subtitle of the work sufficiently indicates its purpose and tone: "a refutation of his [Chastellux's] opinions concerning the Quakers, the Negroes, the People and Mankind"! [116] The author was the radical journalist and reformer who subsequently became leader of the ill-fated Girondist or "Brissotin" party in 1792-93. At the time he wrote his pamphlet Brissot had not yet visited America, but America—and especially the Quakers—had already become to him and to many like himself a glowing legend and ideal. Chastellux had dared touch their sacred ark, he had profaned the temple of their dreams by his irreverent and frivolous comments. The Marquis was, besides, an aristocrat, an Academician, a man of the *salons*, and thus represented all that Brissot disliked. Brissot later visited America, briefly, in 1788, and in turn produced his own *Nouveau Voyage dans les Etats-Unis de l'Amérique Septentrionale* (Paris, 1791), in which he again resumed his tilt with Chastellux. The debate was basically a clash of temperaments; America was only a pretext. At this late date it is not necessary to enter the lists. Temperament governs readers' judgments even today: those who are still touched by Rousseau's prose will respond to Brissot; those who find that Voltaire has worn better will favor Chastellux. At the time Brissot's pamphlet appeared several writers did come to Chastellux's defense. A contributor to the *Journal de Paris*, for example, went to some lengths to demonstrate that the Quakers, as Chastellux implied, had not preserved their primitive purity of the age of William Penn.[117] La Harpe, in the newsletter that he sent regularly to the Russian Court, qualified the *Examen critique* as a "furious diatribe."[118] Chastellux himself, however, evidently thought that silence was the best answer to such impertinence, for when his friend and fellow Academician, the Abbé Morellet, proposed publishing a "response" to Brissot's pamphlet, he firmly dissuaded him.[119]

No sooner was the translation of Chastellux's *Travels* published in London than there appeared in the *Gentleman's Magazine* an open letter to Chastellux from Lt. Col. John Graves Simcoe, who had also served in the American war but on the other side.[120] Soon thereafter came the anonymous pamphlet entitled *Remarks on the Travels of the Marquis de Chastellux in North America*, printed for G. and T. Wilkie, St. Paul's Church-Yard [§19]. This pamphlet was also by Simcoe, but his authorship was a carefully guarded secret at the time, and during his life.[121] Whereas Brissot de Warville's tract was the outburst of a distressed philanthropist, Simcoe's pamphlet—directed as much against the anonymous translator's notes as against Chastellux himself—sprang from other motives. The British officer was still smarting from defeat. He resented what he termed "the variety of abuse that has been thrown upon British generals and the British armies." He was especially nettled by the references to the Loyalists (he had himself commanded The Queen's Rangers, a Tory regiment), and so devoted a good part of his rather disconnected remarks to refuting and correcting the *Travels* in matters of military detail. "The American buzzard should be stripped of the eagle's plumage," was the theme of his animadversions on Washington. In an ironically polite peroration, addressed to Mr. Jefferson, he observed: "Let Great Britain and America pursue their proper advantages; they will soon lead to reconciliation: let all retrospect be avoided; let all harsh and aggravating expressions cease; and such incendiaries as the Translator of the Marquis de Chastellux's Memoirs be treated with deserved contempt. This conduct religion recommends, and history points out in the most forcible manner to Britons and their American descendants." In spite of such professions, Simcoe's anonymous pamphlet was an ill-tempered performance, and a questionable contribution to reconciliation.

The fortune of Chastellux's book in America forms still another chapter in its history. American friends were among those who had urged the author to publish it. Jefferson, it will be recalled, judged it "the most flattering account of America that had ever been written." Franklin's comment was equally cordial. "The portrait you have made of our country and people," he wrote to the author, "is what in painting is called *a handsome likeness,* for which we are much obliged to you. We shall be the better for it, if we endeavour to merit what you kindly say in our favour, and to correct what you justly censure." [122] Washington, too, responded gracefully to Chastellux's gift of the book.[123] Ezra Stiles, president of Yale College, after reading the two volumes in French during a violent snowstorm in December 1786, straightway wrote to Jefferson:

They have afforded me a most delicious and exquisite satisfaction. The Observations on our Country political, physical or natural, military, historical, literary and characteristics made by so ingenious, sagacious learned and patriotic a Foreigner, are highly informative. I am surprised that a Stranger should enter so deeply and judiciously into the genius, Manners, Laws, and political Institutions of our Country. Will you be pleased to make my most Respectful Compliments to that illustrious Nobleman and General, and beg him to accept my Thanks for the Honor he has done us by his Pen and his Arms; even tho' I might not in every Thing concur with some of his critical and learned Remarks, particularly on the wonderful Pont-naturel.[124]

Jefferson in turn transmitted Stiles's compliments to the author—which led William Short, Jefferson's secretary, to report back to America, with the irreverence of youth, that "General Chastellux insisted on my copying that part of the letter for him and he has certainly shown it to half of Paris before this time." [125]

It would seem then from such comments as these that the American literati, at least, had no serious quarrel with Chastellux's book. There are indications, however, that not all American readers were able to view it with this philosophical equanimity. Stiles himself implied as much when he wrote again to Jefferson, a year and a half after his letter of praise. "I am ashamed that any of our Countrymen should take Umbrage at some of his free and humorous

Remarks upon our American customs, especially when most of them are very judicious, and the greater part of his Travels are most excellent." [126] One reader who took umbrage was James Watmough, a Philadelphia merchant, who wrote home to his wife from London, where he had just seen a copy of Chastellux's book: "I never read so foolish a piece in my life, not one remark therein worth noticing and his information very erroneous and a bigot in his political principles which he carries to illiberality." Then, after transcribing some choice bits about Philadelphia society, the outraged merchant concluded: "I am ashamed to see a man publish a Book in such a manner mentioning names at full length. If Miss V. [Vining] should see her Character as published in France and England, she will lose her partiality for the French Nation. In the course of his Book, some hundred of Ladies are mentioned in the same manner. Mrs. Powel is his favorite, and Mrs. Meredith, the sister of Mr. Cadwallader." [127] In the same vein, others referred to the "trifling and superficial pages" of the Marquis de Chastellux.[128]

Reactions like these may perhaps help to explain why no American publisher felt inclined to reprint the *Travels.* The London and Dublin editions were apparently adequate to meet the demands of American readers. One might also be inclined to attribute some significance to the publication at Philadelphia in 1788 of an English translation of Brissot de Warville's anti-Chastelluxian tract [§18], were it not for the fact that Brissot himself evidently had a finger in this publication during his pilgrimage to the Quaker City. However this may be, it was not until 1827—when "mentioning names" could no longer give much umbrage—that an American edition of Chastellux's *Travels* was brought out in New York by White, Gallaher, & White, 7 Wall Street [§15]. This edition in a single volume, which was re-issued the following year [§16], followed the English edition of 1787; it included as a supplement nine letters from General Washington to Chastellux, copies of which had been obtained earlier from Chastellux's widow. "We have not admired the taste of the Translator, in some of his notes," the new publishers announced in their preface, "and occasionally an observation of the Author is omitted, in a case where he would not, on the same occasion have offered it to a Protestant neighbor.[129] Yet when we keep in view his character as a stranger, a Frenchman, and a Roman Catholic, we must admit that he displays no common degree of discernment, of frankness, of good sense and liberality, in his discussion of the various topics before him; many of which have proved the soundness of his abstract reasoning, while others, from local or incidental causes, have exhibited effects widely different from the Author's anticipations."

The 1827 publisher's prediction that Chastellux's *Travels* would be "an acceptable addition to the literary and historical reading of our country" has been amply confirmed. The very "trivialities" which distressed earlier readers at length became recognized as one of the book's chief attractions. It has been quarried and requarried by successive generations of American local historians. Indeed, the present Editor, when seeking to confirm some statement of Chastellux's, has found that the local historians, in a great many instances, merely quote back Chastellux as the sole authority. Frequently, too, Chastellux—or Grieve—has turned out to be the ultimate, though unrecognized, source of some "local tradition" or "personal recollection." In the mid-nineteenth century the indefatigable Benson J. Lossing carried Chastellux's *Travels* in his baggage when journeying up and down the country to collect materials for his *Pictorial Field-Book of the American Revolution*. Not only has Chastellux been consulted and quoted, but whole passages and chapters have been reprinted in a variety of sourcebooks and anthologies. Interest in the book, quite properly, has not been confined to the local antiquary. The chronicler of events, and more recently the "social historian," have likewise found grist for their mills in Chastellux's pages. The *Travels*, in short, has become one of the classic sources for the period of the American Revolution. It also has its place in that great body of European writing about America, which has formed the Old World's image of the New and thus at the same time influenced America's own destiny.[130]

A twentieth-century historian and connoisseur of Americana has written of Chastellux's *Travels*, in words that may appropriately conclude this sketch of the book's earlier vicissitudes and serve to launch it upon further adventures:

A journal of a trip of this sort could be anything—a mere record, for example, of bed, board, bait, and mileage. The fact that Chastellux's journal is the purest delight, the most interesting work on the country in the period of the Revolution, is the good fortune of the American historian and general reader. Chastellux put down something about everything and everybody he saw—buildings, people, trees, birds, flowers, and the animals of forest and farm. He wrote of all this without the customary down-the-nose glance of many European travelers. If certain customs he encountered were primitive, they were not therefore contemptible; if manners were simple, they were not always without dignity. He sought to understand, and succeeded in understanding, and in recording for his friends in France, the life and thinking of the Americans, the physical feel of the country, and the shape of events in a period of crisis.[131]

CHECK-LIST OF THE
DIFFERENT EDITIONS OF
CHASTELLUX'S *TRAVELS*

THE list provides sufficient information for ready identification of the different editions, but does not purport to give detailed bibliographical descriptions. Measurements, intended only to indicate the relative size of the different items, are of necessity approximate, since they vary from copy to copy according to the whim of the binder's knife; when the measurement is taken from an uncut copy that fact is stated. Except in the case of §1 no attempt at a complete census of all known copies has been made. Copies are located in representative American collections, with emphasis on the regions visited by Chastellux. The following location symbols are used:

CSmH	Henry E. Huntington Library, San Marino, Cal.
CtY	Yale University Library
DLC	Library of Congress
ICN	Newberry Library, Chicago
MB	Boston Public Library
MBAt	Boston Athenaeum
MH	Harvard University Library
MHi	Massachusetts Historical Society
MWA	American Antiquarian Society, Worcester, Mass.
MiU-C	William L. Clements Library, Ann Arbor, Michigan
NN	New York Public Library
NjP	Princeton University Library
PHi	Historical Society of Pennsylvania
PP	Free Library of Philadelphia
PPAP	American Philosophical Society, Philadelphia
PPL-R	Library Company of Philadelphia
PU	University of Pennsylvania
RPJCB	John Carter Brown Library, Providence, R.I.

Vi   Virginia State Library
ViHi   Virginia Historical Society
ViU   University of Virginia
ViW   College of William and Mary

§1. Voyage de Newport à Philadephie [*sic*], Albany, &c. [Ornament]. A Newport, [rule]. De l'Imprimerie Royale de l'Escadre. [1781]. [iv], 188 pp. 16.5 x 22.5 cm.

Author's name does not appear. Printed in an edition of twenty-four copies for private distribution. Only eight surviving copies have been located, as noted below. Of the five copies (including Harvard and New York Public Library) recorded in the Church Catalogue (1907), No. 1180, the Church copy itself is now the Huntington Library copy, the Halsey copy is now the Princeton copy, while the New York State Library copy was destroyed in the fire of 1911. A copy in the Newport Historical Society, noted in Alden, *Rhode Island Imprints* (1949), is excluded from our census since its existence cannot now be confirmed. For the same reason, a copy said by Monaghan to be in the Hugh Campbell Wallace, U.S. Embassy, Paris, is omitted.

Sabin, No. 12225. Monaghan, No. 403.

Bib. Nat., CSmH, MH, NN, NjP, RPJCB, two copies in private hands in France.

§2. "Fragmens du voyage de M. le chevalier de Châtellux en Amérique"; "Fragmens d'un voyage de Williamsburg à Charlotte-ville, au Natural-Bridge, Petersburg, Richmond etc. par M. le marquis de Châtellux." In *Cahiers de Lecture*, [Gotha], January-December 1784: Vol. I, 3-24, 99-114, 195-202, 291-96; Vol. II, 99-106, 195-204, 269-82; Vol. III, 3-18, 99-114, 197-206, 293-300. 12.5 x 20.5 cm.

These extracts, printed serially with the author's consent, were drawn from his first journal, previously printed as §1, and from his second journal (Virginia), as yet unpublished. They were first collected into book form in the pirated editions listed below, §'s 3-9. See note 91.

No copies of the *Cahiers de Lecture* have been located in American libraries. The above information is derived from a set in the Landesbibliothek Gotha, and an incomplete set (January-March 1784 only) in the Bibliothèque Nationale, Paris.

§3. Voyage de Mr. le Chevalier de Chastellux en Amérique. [Ornament, basket of flowers on a stone slab, reversed]. [No place]. 1785. 228 pp. 13 x 20 cm. (uncut copy).

Unauthorized edition. Compiled from the "fragments" published the previous year in the *Cahiers de Lecture* at Gotha; see §2.

Sabin, No. 12226. Monaghan, No. 404.

Bib. Nat., CSmH, CtY, DLC, ICN, MB, MBAt, MHi, MiU-C, NN, NjP, PU, RPJCB, ViHi.

§4. Voyage de Mr. le Chevalier de Chastellux en Amérique. [No ornament except two typographic rules]. [No place]. 1785. 191 pp. 9.5 x 15 cm. (uncut copy).

Unauthorized edition. Contents, deriving from §2, same as in §3. A facsimile of the title page will be found in the Church Catalogue, No. 1210, where it is assumed (on what grounds not stated) that this, rather than §3, is the first of the unauthorized editions, the one brought out by the unscrupulous printer of Kassel, referred to in the publisher's foreword to the authorized Paris edition of 1786.

Monaghan, No. 1532. Not in Sabin, but perhaps the edition described as "Leipzig, 1785" under his No. 12228-[b].

Brit. Mus., CSmH, NjP, PU, RPJCB, ViU.

§5. Voyage de M. le Chevalier de Chastellux, en Amérique. [Typographic ornament, with small crown at top]. A Paris; Et se trouve à Bruxelles, Chez B. Le Francq, Imprimeur-Libraire, rue de la Magdelaine. M. DCC. LXXXVI. 136 pp. 12 x 19 cm.

Unauthorized edition. Contents, deriving from §2, same as in §3 and §4.

Sabin, No. 12228-[a]. Monaghan, No. 1533.

Brit. Mus., CtY, MH, MiU-C, NN, NjP, PHi, PPAP, RPJCB, Vi, ViU.

§6. Des Ritters von Chastellüx Reisebeobachtungen über Amerika. [Ornament, musical instruments and knotted ribbon]. Hamburg, bey der Nordischen typographischen litterärischen Gesellschaft. 1785. viii, 182 pp. 10 x 18 cm. (uncut copy).

Unauthorized edition. Contents same as §3, §4, §5. Translated from §3 or §4. Name of translator not given. Includes occasional footnotes by the translator and a publisher's preface, pp. [iii]-viii.

Sabin, No. 12231-[a].

Brit. Mus., Stadtbibliothek Mainz, MiU-C.

§7-? Des Ritters von Chastellüx Reisebeobachtungen über Amerika. Hamburg, Chaidron, 1786.

Sabin gives this edition under his No. 12231-[b], but locates no copy. His information is apparently derived from Kayser, *Bücher-Lexicon* (1834) and Heinsius, *Bücher-Lexicon* (1812), both of which record such an edition. No copy has been located in the United States or in any of the several representative German libraries consulted.

§8. Des Herrn Ritters von Chastellux Reise durch Amerika. Aus dem Französischen. [Ornament, two horsemen and a barking dog]. Frankfurt und Leipzig, bey Joseph Stahel, 1786. 213 pp. (212-213 are misnumbered 112-113!). 10 x 16 cm.

Unauthorized edition. Contents same as §3, §4, §5, §6. Translated from §3, §4, or possibly, §5. This is an entirely different German translation from §6. Translator's name not given. No prefatory matter or notes.

Sabin, No. 12232-[a].

Bayerische Staatsbibliothek—Munich, Württembergische Landesbibliothek—Stuttgart, NjP, PPL-R, PU, RPJCB.

§9-? Des Herrn Ritters von Chastellux Reise durch Amerika. Wien, Schaumburg, 1786.

Sabin records this edition under his No. 12232-[b], but locates no copy. Kayser and Heinsius also list such an edition, but since they record neither our §6 nor §8, it is possible that there is some confusion and that both this Vienna 1786 edition and the Hamburg 1786 edition (our §7) should be relegated to the status of ghosts. No copy of this edition is to be found in the Österreichische Nationalbibliothek or Universitätsbibliothek in Vienna, or in any of the American and German libraries consulted.

§10. Voyages de M. le Marquis de Chastellux dans l'Amérique Septentrionale Dans les années 1780, 1781 & 1782. [Line in Greek from the Odyssey]. Multorumque hominum vidit urbes, & mores cognovit. Odissée, Liv. I. Tome Premier [... Second]. [Printer's device]. A Paris, Chez Prault, Imprimeur du Roi, Quai des Augustins, à l'Immortalité. 1786. 2 vols. 8, 390 pp.; [iv], 362 pp. and one additional leaf with errata on recto and "Approbation" (4 Avril 1786) on verso. 14 x 21 cm. (uncut copy). In Vol. I: folding map, engraved by Aldring, "Carte pour servir au Journal de Mr. le Mquis. de Chastellux redigée par Mr. Dezoteux. . . ." In Vol. II: folding map of Virginia, engraved by Aldring, "Carte pour servir au Journal de Mr. le Marquis de Chastellux rédigée par Mr. Dezoteux. . . ." Vol. II includes also three folding engraved plates of the Natural Bridge from drawings made by Baron de Turpin; the third of these is signed, lower left, by the engraver, "Coiny," presumably Jacques-Joseph Coiny (1761-1809).

First complete edition, authorized by Chastellux. Part I ("Voyage de Newport à Philadelphie-Albany, &c.") had been previously printed in §1. Extracts from Part I and from Part II ("Voyage dans la Haute Virginie . . .") had been printed in §'s 2-9. Part III ("Voyage dans le New-Hampshire, l'État de Massachusset & la Haute Pensylvanie") and Part IV ("Lettre de M. le Marquis de Chastellux à M. Madisson") appeared here for the first time. This edition serves as the basis for the present 1963 edition, which reproduces the original title page, the two maps (end papers) and the three plates of the Natural Bridge.

Sabin, No. 12227-[a]. Monaghan, No. 405.

Bib. Nat., Brit. Mus., CSmH, CtY, DLC, ICN, MB, MBAt, MHi, MWA, MiU-C, NN, NjP, PHi, PP, PPAP, PPL-R, PU, RPJCB, Vi, ViHi, ViU.

§11. Voyages de M. le Marquis de Chastellux dans l'Amérique Septentrionale, Dans les années 1780, 1781 & 1782. [Quotation from Odyssey]. Seconde Édition. Tome Premier [... Second]. [Printer's device]. A Paris, Chez Prault, Imprimeur du Roi, Quai des Augustins, à l'Immortalité. 1788, 1791. 8, 408;

[iv], 351 pp. (321-351 are misnumbered 221-251!). 13.5 x 21.5 cm. (uncut copy). Two maps and three plates, as in §10; struck from the same plates, but perceptibly less crisp and black than the earlier impressions.

Internal evidence shows that this edition was prepared by Chastellux before his death in October 1788. Volume I is dated that year; the printing, or at least the publication, of Volume II, which is dated 1791, was evidently delayed for some reason. There are a few verbal changes and corrections, as well as several additional notes by Chastellux.

Sabin, No. 12227-[b]. Monaghan, No. 406.

Brit. Mus., CSmH, CtY, DLC, ICN, MB, MBAt, MH, MHi, MiU-C, NN, PHi, PPAP, RPJCB, Vi, ViHi, ViU.

§12.   Travels in North-America, in the Years 1780, 1781, and 1782. By the Marquis de Chastellux, One of the Forty Members of the French Academy, and Major General in the French Army, serving under the Count de Rochambeau. Translated from the French by an English Gentleman, who resided in America at that period. With Notes by the Translator. [Line in Greek]. Odyssey. B. I. Multorumque hominum vidit urbes, & mores cognovit. Volume I [. . . II]. London: Printed for G. G. J. and J. Robinson, Pater-Noster Row. M DCC LXXXVII. xv, 462; xii, 432 pp. 12.5 x 20.5 cm. Two maps (both intended to be bound in Vol. I) and three plates of the Natural Bridge (Vol. II) copied from those in §10. The titles of the maps have been translated ("Chart for the Journal of Mr. le Mquis. de Chastellux . . ."), and a few names have been anglicized ("Philadelphia" for "Philadelphie," for example); no engraver's name on either. The first of the Natural Bridge plates is signed with engraver's name "Cook," the second has no signature, the third that of "T.Cook." All maps and plates have volume references engraved upper right.

Translated from §10. The translator is George Grieve (or Greive); see above, "Something about the Translator." Sometimes erroneously attributed to John Kent.

Sabin, No. 12229-[a]. Monaghan, No. 407.

Brit. Mus., CSmH, CtY, DLC, ICN, MB, MBAt, MH, MHi, MWA, NN, NjP, PHi, PPAP, PPL-R, PU, RPJCB, Vi, ViHi, ViU, ViW.

§13. Travels in North-America ... [etc., as in §12]. With Notes by the Translator. Second Edition [on the title-page of Vol. II only]. [Quotation from Odyssey in Greek and Latin]. Volume I [... II]. London: Printed for G. G. J. and J. Robinson, Pater-Noster Row. M DCC LXXXVII. xv, 462; xii, 432 pp. 14 x 22.5 cm. (uncut copy). Two maps and three plates of the Natural Bridge as in §12, restruck from the same plates.

Contents similar to §12, but many slight typographic variations distinguish the two editions. Although the number of pages is the same and the lines generally correspond, closer examination shows that this second edition has been reset throughout. The indication "Second Edition" appears only on the title page of Vol. II and thus serves to identify it. In Vol. I, page [vii], Table of Contents, of the first edition (§12) ends with reference to p. 37 and the catchword "Manufacture," whereas the same page of this second edition ends with reference to p. 33 and the catchword "The"; the first line of p. 36 in the first edition is "The road I had to travel becoming hence-," in the second edition it is "forth difficult and rather desert, it was deter-"; the last line of p. 462 in the first edition is "hopes at length to find some repose," in the second edition it is "length to find some repose." Such variations are especially noticeable in the footnotes. (Description based on NN copy).

Sabin, No. 12229-[b]. Monaghan, No. 408.

CSmH, CtY, MiU-C, NN, ViU, ViW.

§14. Travels in North-America ... [etc., as in §12]. Dublin: Printed for Messrs. Colles, Moncrieffe, White, H. Whitestone, Byrne, Cash, Marchbank, Heery, and Moore. M, DCC, LXXXVII. 2 vols. xv, 462; xv, 430 pp. 12 x 20 cm. Two maps and three plates copied from the London edition, §12. The two maps have the engraver's signature "J. Duff"; the first of the Natural Bridge plates (which are noticeably inferior to their prototypes) also has the signature of "J. Duff," the second and third are without signature. Maps and plates all lack engraved volume references.

Contents similar to §12.

Sabin, No. 12229-[c]. Monaghan, No. 1534.

Brit. Mus., CSmH, DLC, ICN, MB, MH, NN, NjP, PHi, PPL-R, PU, RPJCB, ViHi, ViU.

§15. Travels in North-America, in the Years 1780-81-82. By the
      Marquis de Chastellux, One of the Forty Members of the
      French Academy, and Major-General in the French Army,
      serving under the Count de Rochambeau. Translated from
      the French, by an English Gentleman, who resided in America
      at that period. With Notes by the Translator. Also, a Bio-
      graphical Sketch of the Author: Letters from Gen. Washing-
      ton to the Marquis de Chastellux: and Notes and Corrections,
      by the American Editor. New-York: White, Gallaher, &
      White, 7 Wall-Street. 1827. One volume, 416 pp. 14 x 23 cm.

Reprinted from §12, but with some omissions. "Preface to the American Edition," pp. 3-5; "Letters from General Washington," pp. 388-99;
"Additional Notes and Corrections by the American Editor," pp. 403-
16. The nine letters from Washington to Chastellux, as explained in the
preface, were "extracted from the New-York Literary Journal." Ten
such Washington letters had appeared serially in *The New-York
Literary Journal, and Belles-Lettres Repository*, published by C. S. Van
Winkle, Vols. III, IV, between May 1820 and April 1821; the editor of
the *Travels* apparently did not see fit to "extract" Washington's letter
of July 18, 1781, concerning Chastellux's gift of a cask of claret. Fifteen
Washington-Chastellux letters had also been issued as a pamphlet ded-
icated to Lafayette: *General Washington's Letters to the Marquis de
Chastellux* (Charleston, S.C., Printed by C. C. Sebring, 1825), 35 pp.
An introduction by William Willis explains that he had been shown the
originals in 1808 by Chastellux's widow, who had permitted him to
make copies for the Charleston Library Society; another set of copies
had been sent to Mrs. Washington. All these letters have subsequently
been published (from retained copies in the Washington Papers) in
Fitzpatrick's edition of the writings of George Washington.

Sabin, No. 12230. Monaghan, No. 409.

CSmH, CtY, DLC, ICN, MB, MBAt, MH, MHi, MWA, MiU-C, NN,
NjP, PHi, PU, RPJCB, Vi, ViU, ViW.

§16. Travels in North-America, in the Years 1780-81-82. By the
      Marquis de Chastellux . . . [etc., as in §15]. New-York: 1828.
      416 pp.

Reprint of §15. The publisher's name is omitted, as is the copyright
notice on verso of title-page; otherwise similar to §15.

Not in Sabin or Monaghan.

CSmH, DLC, MHi, MWA, NN, Vi, ViH.

No attempt is made to list here the selections from Chastellux's work appearing in anthologies and other historical collections. A partial reprint of the book, consisting of extracts joined by narrative summaries, was issued in 1919 in the "Great American Historical Classics Series," Bowling Green, Ohio; Chastellux's *Travels* is the second item in an unnumbered volume of the series which also includes Brissot de Warville's *New Travels* and S. A. Ferrall's *A Ramble . . . through the United States of America.*

> [*The three concluding numbers of this Checklist are contemporary pamphlets by others criticizing Chastellux's book.*]

§17. Jacques Pierre Brissot de Warville.—Examen Critique des Voyages dans l'Amérique Septentrionale, de M. le Marquis de Chatellux [*sic*]; ou Lettre à M. le Marquis de Chatellux, Dans laquelle on réfute principalement ses opinions sur les Quakers, sur les Negres, sur le Peuple, & sur l'Homme. Par J. P. Brissot de Warville. Je suis toujours pour les Persécutés. Sidney. A Londres. 1786. [iv], 143 pp. 12 x 19 cm.

Probably printed in France, in spite of the London imprint.

Sabin, No. 8019. Monaghan, No. 292.

Bib. Nat., Brit. Mus., CSmH, CtY, DLC, ICN, MB, MBAt, MH, MHi, MiU-C, NN, NjP, PHi, PPAP, PPL-R, PU, RPJCB, Vi, ViU.

§18. Jacques Pierre Brissot de Warville.—A Critical Examination of the Marquis de Chatellux's [*sic*] Travels, in North America, in a Letter addressed to the Marquis; principally intended as a refutation of his opinions concerning the Quakers, the Negroes, the People, and Mankind. Translated from the French of J. P. Brissot de Warville, with Additions and Corrections of the Author. Je suis toujours pour les persecutés. Philadelphia: Printed by Joseph James, in Chesnut-Street. M, DCC, LXXXVIII. [ii], 89 pp. 14 x 22 cm. (uncut copy).

Name of translator not given. The additions and corrections are only minor ones. This translation was probably published at the instigation of the author, who was in Philadelphia in 1788.

Sabin, No. 8017. Monaghan, No. 293.

CSmH, CtY, DLC, MiU-C, NjP, PHi, PPL-R, RPJCB, ViU.

(The American Antiquarian Society has the same pamphlet with an added title-page: "The Minor Library, being a Collection of Select Pamphlets, American and European, on Various Interesting Subjects.—The Intention of this Selection is to rescue from Oblivion, and to preserve to Posterity some of the most celebrated fugitive pieces on the interesting topics of the times.—Philadelphia: Printed 1804.")

§19. [John Graves Simcoe].—Remarks on the Travels of the Marquis de Chastellux, in North America. London, Printed for G. and T. Wilkie, in St. Paul's Church-Yard. MDCCLXXX-VII. [Price Two Shillings]. [iv], 80 pp. 12.5 x 20.5 cm.

Concerning the authorship of this anonymous publication, see n. 121. Erroneously attributed by some libraries to Jonathan Boucher or Benedict Arnold.

Sabin, Nos. 12233, 69508, 81137.

Brit. Mus., CSmH, CtY, MB, MH, MiU-C, NN, PPL-R, RPJCB, ViU.

(This pamphlet was reprinted by W. Abbatt, *Magazine of History*, 43, Extra No. 172 (1931) and also separately, 49 pp.).

VOYAGES

DE M. LE MARQUIS

DE CHASTELLUX

DANS L'AMÉRIQUE

SEPTENTRIONALE

Dans les années 1780, 1781 & 1782.

Πολλῶν δ' ἀνθρώπων ἴδεν ἄϛεα, καὶ νόον ἔγνω.
Multorumque hominum vidit urbes, & mores cognovit.
ODISSÉE, Liv. I.

TOME PREMIER.

A PARIS,

CHEZ PRAULT, IMPRIMEUR DU ROI,
Quai des Auguſtins, à l'Immortalité.

1786.

Title Page, First Trade Edition of Chastellux's Travels

PUBLISHER'S FOREWORD

*to the first trade edition of Chastellux's Travels
Paris, 1786*

IT has long been known to the public that the Marquis de Chastellux wrote journals of the different travels he made in North America, and it seems to have been the general wish that these Journals might be more widely available. The Author, who compiled them only for himself and his friends, has until now constantly refused to make them public. The first and most extensive of the journals was, in fact, printed in America, but the Author had only 24 copies printed, his sole object being to avoid the necessity of making multiple hand-written copies, indispensable in a country and at a time when one could not hope that any communication would reach its destination in Europe unless duplicates were sent. Furthermore, the small printing-press aboard the squadron at Rhode Island provided facilities of which he judged proper to avail himself. Of these twenty-four copies, barely ten or twelve reached Europe, and he addressed these all to reliable persons who were requested not to permit copies to be made. Nevertheless, that curiosity which then surrounded anything concerning America aroused much eagerness to read them. They passed successively through many hands, and there is reason to believe that all were not equally trustworthy; there can even be no doubt that manuscript copies are in existence; and as these were most likely made very hastily, it may be presumed that they are likewise very incorrect.

In the spring of the year 1782 the Marquis de Chastellux made a journey into upper Virginia; and in the autumn of the same year, another into the States of Massachusetts, New Hampshire and upper Pennsylvania. According to his custom, he wrote journals of these tours; but as he was then about to return to Europe, he kept them among his papers. These two journals were at first known only to a few friends to whom he lent them, for he had continued to refuse requests from several persons, ourselves in particular, to be allowed to publish them. However, one of his friends, who has an extensive correspondence in foreign countries, having urged him strongly to give him at least a few detached extracts from these journals, for the purpose of inserting them in a periodical publication printed at Gotha, which aims especially to collect works which have not been made public, he consented, and during an entire year there appeared in each number of this Journal a few pages selected at random from the Marquis de Chastellux's journals. These extracts did not form a connected narrative, and were selected from both the first and second journeys. The Author had taken these precautions to prevent any foreign booksellers from collecting them and deceiving the public by giving them out as a complete work. Experience has shown the insufficiency of these precautions. It so happens that an unscrupulous printer of Kassel has indeed collected these detached extracts, and without stating that they form an unconsecutive account, has published them under the title of *Voyages de M. le Chevalier de Chastellux*, a rank still held by the Author two years ago.

The publicity resulting from such a mutilated and formless work, and which the Marquis de Chastellux did not expect, far from gratifying him, could only displease him. Under these circumstances we thought fit to renew our instances, and we have obtained from the Marquis his original manuscript, to which he has graciously added the maps and plans which we have used. We hasten to offer them to the public, and we can assure our readers that we have taken great pains to present this work in a form worthy of the importance of the subject and of the name and reputation of the Author.

The two maps present with all possible accuracy not only the countries where the Author traveled, but all the places where he stopped and which he mentions in his journal. We owe these two maps to Monsieur Dezoteux, Captain of Dragoons, and Aide-Maréchal-des-Logis Adjoint, who has both drawn them and reduced them. This Officer, who was with the Army in America, has himself visited most of the places indicated on these maps.*

* See end papers of the present edition.

Journey from Newport,
to Philadelphia, Albany, &c.

VOYAGE

DE NEWPORT

A PHILADEPHIE, ALBANY, &c.

A NEWPORT,

DE L'IMPRIMERIE ROYALE DE L'ESCADRE.

Title Page of Privately Printed Edition of Part I of Chastellux's Travels,
Newport, 1781

59

AUTHOR'S FOREWORD

*to the first, privately printed, edition
of Part I of his Travels*

NEWPORT, RHODE ISLAND, 1781

INASMUCH as this journal will only pass from my hands into those of my most intimate friends, it may seem that I might rely on their indulgence and dispense with forestalling their criticism. But is not their approval the most precious and desirable of all to me? Does it not behoove me to please them, and is it not from them alone that I must seek the reward for my vigils and my labors? So I shall tell these friends that I have made a journey of nearly four hundred leagues in America and have seen several interesting sights, and it is natural that I want to preserve some recollection of them and aid my own memory in which I have never placed much confidence, and which will deserve still less as time goes on. It is well known that the accumulating years sharpen a man's judgment but diminish his memory: I fear that in my case this process is half accomplished; and I want to prevent time's ravages, even though I may not hope for its benefits.

Any traveler whose aim is not merely to move from place to place takes notes on the remarkable things he sees; but when such notes are written in haste; when they suffer from the inconveniences of inns and the fatigues of travel; when they are so badly scrawled that after three months they are illegible even to the person who wrote them down, it is indispensable to arrange them and transcribe them. This has been my task since my return; I shall not say during my leisure moments, for leisure is nonexistent in an army however small; especially when one is busy with daily duties, and when the days are taken up in whole or in part and working hours are interrupted by plans being carried out and others abandoned after having been formed, by continual correspondence with the

Americans, frequent visits from their principal Officers, and even the presence of their General. Be this as it may, I have written up a Journal of my tour. I first began it for myself alone, but what work can hold its interest when one labors for oneself alone? Indeed it seems that this word "alone" removes the very life from all our actions, and spoils solitude itself. No, never for myself alone shall I prize retirement and meditation; never for myself alone shall I cross the seas, and visit new peoples and new lands. It should be no surprise therefore that a Journal, first undertaken for my own instruction, should soon have become a homage offered to my friends. May they bear me some gratitude for it, and if they derive some profit from it, may they pardon me for having also worked for my own. I beg of them to agree to this sharing; because I have often entered into certain details which will serve solely to aid my own memory and which are of use only to myself. I would beg them to believe, however, that whenever I have been most barren and boresome, I was working for myself. I need not add that as camps, battlefields, and all that relates to war have been the principal objects of my curiosity, only military men can read me from beginning to end with some interest; but it is easy to skip these passages, which are recognizable from the first lines, or at least to skim through them rapidly. Doubtless it is not too much to expect people who live in Paris to read rapidly and carelessly. Nevertheless I must give fair warning that one should obtain several maps of this country, no matter what part of the Journal one may wish to consult. They may be found at the shops of Le Rouge, Beaurain, and all geographers. Those that are indispensable come to four: the map of New England, which includes the four eastern States; the map of New York, of the Jerseys, and of Pennsylvania. If one will add to these a map of Canada, including Lake Champlain and Lake Ontario, the chapter dealing with plans for a northern campaign and with my conversations with General Schuyler will be read with much greater interest.

FROM NEWPORT, ACROSS
CONNECTICUT, TO WEST POINT

For several months following my landing at Newport, on July 11 [1780], it was impossible for me to be away from there even for so little as two days.[1] On the 19th of that month the English fleet began to show itself before the port: the next day we counted twenty-two sail, and a few days later we learned that the enemy [in New York] were embarking troops. It was not until the middle of August that we were informed of their decision to disembark these troops at New York and on Long Island. But it was still not wholly clear that they had abandoned their undertaking [against Rhode Island]: we received every day fresh advices, which bespoke new embarkations.[2] Meanwhile we were adding to our fortifications, and our still recent establishment furnished me with daily employment of such a nature as not to admit of my absence.[3] M. de Rochambeau, who had long proposed visiting his posts at Providence, was unable to carry his project into execution before August 30. I accompanied him, and we returned the next day. On September 18, he set out, with the Chevalier de Ternay,[4] for Hartford on the mainland, where General Washington had given him a rendezvous.[5] I did not attend him on this journey, and as fortune would have it, we found ourselves, during his absence, in the most critical situation in which we had been since our arrival. The general belief at Rhode Island was that M. de Guichen,[6] who was known to have left [France] for Santo Domingo, was coming to join forces with us, and that we would then go into immediate action. On the 19th, we found that instead of M. de Guichen, Admiral Rodney had arrived at New York with ten ships of the

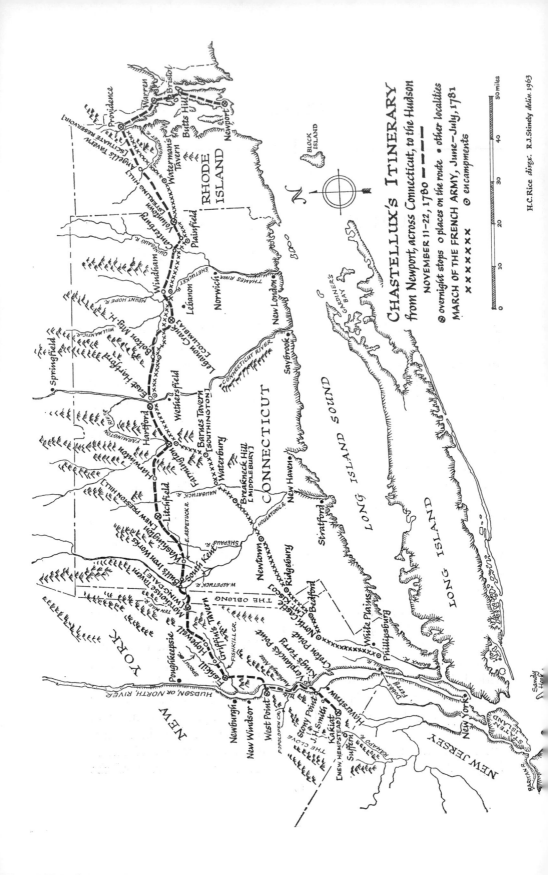

CHASTELLUX'S ITINERARY
from Newport, across Connecticut, to the Hudson
NOVEMBER 11–22, 1780
⊗ overnight stops   ○ places on the route   • other localities
MARCH OF THE FRENCH ARMY, June–July, 1781
××××××
⊙ encampments

H.C.Rice direx. R.J.Stinely delin. 1963

0   10   20   30   40   50 miles

line. Not the smallest doubt was entertained among us of an attack upon the French fleet, and even the army. Our vessels in consequence were laid across the harbor, secured fore and aft, and their anchorage was protected by new batteries, which were constructed with great skill and rapidity.[7] At the beginning of October, the season being already well advanced, and Admiral Rodney having undertaken nothing, we had reason to expect that we should remain undisturbed for the remainder of the year, and our sole occupation was henceforth to prepare winter quarters for the troops. They took possession of them on November 1. For the first time I might now without risk absent myself from the army; but not wishing to show too much impatience, and desirous of seeing discipline and the arrangements relative to the cantonments well established, I deferred until the 11th setting out on a long tour upon the continent.

November 11, 1780: Newport, R.I.—Bristol—Warren

I left Newport that day with M. Lynch and M. de Montesquieu,[8] each of whom had a servant. I myself had three, one of whom led an extra horse, and another drove a small cart which I was advised to take to convey my portmanteaus, and thus avoid hurting my riding horses. There was then a hard frost, the ground was covered with snow, and the northwesterly wind blew very sharp. In going to the Bristol "Ferry," [9] I went out of my way to view the fortifications at Butt's Hill,[10] and I reached the "Ferry" at about half past eleven. The passage was long and difficult, because the wind was contrary. We were obliged to make three tacks, and it was necessary to make two trips to pass over our horses and the cart. At two o'clock I arrived at Warren, a small town in the state of Massachusetts,[11] eighteen miles distant from Newport. I alighted at a good inn, the keeper of which, named Mr. [Shubael] Burr, is remarkable for his enormous size, as are his wife, his son, and all his family.[12] My intention was only to have my horses fed, but the cold continuing to increase, and the cart not arriving before three o'clock, I gave up all thought of going to spend the night at Providence, and I determined to stay at Warren, where I was very comfortable. After dinner I went to the bank of the little Barrington River, which runs near this town, to see a sloop from Port-au-Prince come in. This sloop belonged to Mr. Porter [Potter?], brigadier general of the militia, a nephew of Mr. Burr, and still more bulky than he. Colonel [Christopher] Greene, whom I met upon the quay, made me acquainted with Mr. Porter, and we drank tea with him, in a simple but comfortable house, the inside and the inhabitants of which presented a specimen of American manners.[13]

November 12, 1780: Warren–Providence

The 12th I set out at half past eight for Providence, where I arrived at noon. I alighted at the college,[14] that is to say, at our hospital, which I examined, and dined with M. Blanchard, *Commissaire des Guerres*.[15] At half past four I went to Colonel [Ephraim] Bowen's, where I had lodged on my first journey to Providence [August 30]; I drank tea with several ladies, one of whom, rather pretty, was called Miss Angell.[16] I was then conducted to Mrs. Varnum's, where I again found company, and from thence to Governor [Jabez] Bowen's, who gave me a bed.[17]

November 13, 1780: Providence–Scituate, R.I.–Voluntown [Sterling Hill], Conn.

The 13th I breakfasted with Colonel [George] Peck; he is an amiable and polite young man, who spent last summer with General Heath at Newport.[18] He received me in a charming small house, where he lived with his wife, who is young also, and has a pleasing, although undistinguished, countenance. This little establishment, where comfort and simplicity reign, gave an idea of that sweet and serene state of happiness, which appears to have taken refuge in the New World, while leaving mere pleasure to the Old.

The town of Providence is built on the bank of a river only six miles long, which empties into the same bay in which Rhode Island, Conanicut and Prudence Islands, etc., are situated. It has only one street, which is very long; the suburb, which is rather extensive, is on the other [western] side of the river. This town is handsome, the houses are not spacious, but well built and well appointed within. It is pent in between two chains of mountains, one to the north, and the other to the southwest, which causes unbearable heat in the summer; but it is exposed to the northwest wind, which rakes it from one end to the other, and renders it extremely cold in winter. It may contain twenty-five hundred inhabitants. Its situation is very advantageous for commerce, which accordingly was very considerable in peacetime. Merchant ships may load and unload their cargoes in the town itself, while ships of war cannot approach the harbor. Their trade is the same as that of Rhode Island and Boston; they export lumber and salt provisions, and bring back salt and a great quantity of molasses, sugar, and other products from the West Indies; they also fit out vessels for the cod and whale fisheries. The latter is carried on successfully between Cape Cod and Long Island; but they go often as far as Baffin's Straits, and the Falkland Islands. The inhabitants of Providence, like those of Newport, also carry on the Guinea trade; they buy slaves there and carry them to the West Indies, where they take bills of exchange on Old England, for which they receive woolens, stuffs, and other merchandise.[19]

On leaving Colonel Peck's, I mounted my horse for Voluntown,[20] where I proposed sleeping. I stopped at Scituate, in a rather bad inn, called Angel's Tavern,[21] which is about halfway to Voluntown; I baited my horses there and set out in an hour, without seeing my cart arrive. From this place to Voluntown the road is very bad; one is continually going up and down hill, and always over rough roads. It was six o'clock and night had closed in, when I reached D[orrance]'s Tavern,[22] which is only twenty-five miles from Providence. I dismounted with the more pleasure as the weather was extremely bad. I was well accommodated and very well received at Mr. D***'s. He is an old gentleman of seventy-three years of age, tall, and still vigorous; he is a native of Ireland, first settled in Massachusetts, and afterwards in Connecticut. His wife, who is younger than he, is active, kind, and obliging, to be sure; but his family is truly charming. It consists of two young men, one twenty-eight, and the other twenty-one years old; a boy of twelve, and two girls from eighteen to twenty, as pretty as pictures. The elder of these young women was sick, kept her chamber, and did not show herself. I have since learned that she was with child and near her confinement: she was deceived by a young man, who after promising to marry her, absented himself and has not returned.[23] Chagrin and the consequences of her situation had thrown her into a state of languor; she never came down to the ground floor on which her parents lived; but great care was taken of her, and she had always somebody to keep her company. While a good supper was preparing for me, I went into the room where the family assembled; I observed a shelf with forty or fifty volumes on it; on opening them I found that they were all classical authors, Greek,

Latin, or English. They belonged to Mr. D***'s eldest son [John]. This young man had received a good education and was "tutor" at Providence college, until the war interrupted his studies. I conversed with him on various points of literature, and particularly on the manner in which the dead languages should be pronounced. I found him well informed and possessed of much simplicity and modesty.[24]

We were waited on at supper by a most beautiful girl, called Miss Pearce. She was a neighbor of Mrs. D***, and had come on a visit to assist her in the absence of her younger daughter. This young person had, like all American women, a very becoming, even serious bearing; she had no objection to being looked at, having her beauty commended, or even receiving a few caresses, provided it was without any appearance of familiarity or wantonness. Licentious manners, in fact, are so foreign in America that conversation with young women leads no further, and that freedom itself there bears a character of modesty unknown to our affected bashfulness and false reserve. But neither my excellent supper, nor the books of Mr. D***, nor even the fair face of Miss Pearce, made my cart arrive, and I was obliged to go to rest without hearing any news of it. As I desired a chamber with a fire in it, Miss Pearce prepared me one, informing me at the same time, that it communicated with that of the sick lady with whom she slept, and inquired of me very politely, whether it would incommode me if she should pass through my chamber after I was in bed. I assured her, that if she disturbed my sleep, it would not be as a frightful dream. And, in fact, she came a quarter of an hour after I was in bed. I pretended to sleep, in order to examine her countenance; she passed very gently, turning her head the other way, and hiding the light for fear of awakening me. I do not know whether I shall pronounce my own praise or condemnation, by saying that I soon afterwards fell into a profound sleep.

November 14, 1780: Voluntown [Sterling Hill]

On rising I found Miss Pearce, but not my cart, which it seemed more than probable was broken into a thousand pieces. I was determined to give up that mode of conveying my small baggage, but to do so I still had to have it. I therefore decided to wait for the baggage; and also decided—which was still easier—to take my breakfast. At length, about eleven o'clock, my observation posts announced the cart's appearance. It was a matter of great joy to the whole crew to see it arrive, although crippled, and towed by a hired horse, which they had been obliged to hitch in front of mine. It is proper to observe that my servants, proud of possessing ample means of transporting my effects, had loaded it with many useless articles; that I myself, being apprised that wine was not always to be met with in the inns,[25] had thought proper to furnish myself with canteens which held twelve bottles, and having taken the further precaution to ask for two or three loaves of white bread from the commissary (*Munitionnaire des vivres*) at Providence, he had packed up twenty, which alone weighed upwards of eighty pounds, so that my poor cart was laden to the point of sinking. Its greatest misfortune, however, arose from striking on the rocks, which had broken one wheel and greatly damaged the other. I soon determined to leave it with Mr. D***, who undertook to get it repaired, and it was resolved that my wine should be divided into three parts, one of which should be drunk the same day, the other left with the landlord, with a request to keep it till my return, and that the third should be given to him, with a request to drink it, which met with no difficulty. The rest of the day, however, being needed to make new arrangements, I decided to remain at Voluntown. I made a general inspection of my baggage: everything unnecessary was packed up and left with Mr. D***, the rest put into portmanteaus, and by a promotion *à la Prussienne* on the field of battle, my cart horse was elevated to the rank of a saddle horse. The reading of some English poets, and conversation with Messrs. Lynch and Montesquieu, as well as with my hosts, made the day pass very agreeably for me. Towards evening, two travelers came into the room I was in, seated themselves by the fire, and began to yawn and whistle, without paying the least attention to me. Gradually, however, conversation began, and was very interesting and agreeable. One of them was a colonel of the militia, who had served in Canada, and had been in several engagements, in which he was wounded. I shall observe once for all, that among the men I have met with, above twenty years of age, of whatsoever condition, I have not found two who have not borne arms, heard the whistling of bullets, and even received some wounds; so that it may be asserted that North America is entirely military and inured to war, and that new levies may continually be made without making new soldiers.[26]

November 15, 1780: Voluntown [Sterling Hill]—Plainfield—Canterbury—Windham—[Columbia]

The 15th, I set out from Voluntown at eight in the morning. I traveled five miles farther in the mountains, after which I saw the horizon expand, and my eye very soon had it in full view. On descending the hills, and before reaching the valley, is the town, or rather, hamlet of Plainfield; for what is called in America a "town" or "township" is only a certain number of houses dispersed over a great space, but which belong to the same corporation and send deputies to the General Assembly of the state. The center or headquarters of these towns is the "meeting-house" or church. This church sometimes stands alone, and is sometimes surrounded by four or five houses only; whence it happens, that when a traveler asks the question, "How far is it to the town?" he is answered, "You are already there"; but if he happens to specify the place he wishes to be at, either the "meeting-house," or such and such a tavern, he is not unfrequently told, "It is seven or eight miles away." As for Plainfield, it is a small town, but a large place, for there are full thirty houses within reach of the "meeting-house." [27] Its situation is agreeable; but it offers, besides, a good military position: this was the first such position that I had noticed. An army might encamp there on little heights, behind which the mountains rise in an amphitheater, thus presenting successive positions as far as the great woods, which might serve as the last retreat. The foot of the heights of Plainfield is fortified by marshland, which can be crossed only by a single causeway, which would oblige the enemy to file off to attack you. The right and left are supported by escarpments. On the right also is a pond, which renders it more difficult of access. This camp is fit for six, eight, or even ten thousand men; it might serve to cover Providence and the state of Massachusetts against troops which had crossed the Connecticut River.[28] Two miles beyond Plainfield the road turns towards the north, and two or three miles farther along, is the Quinebaug River, along the edge of which we traveled about a mile before crossing it at Canterbury, over a fairly long and tolerably well-built wooden bridge. This river is neither navigable nor fordable, but flows amid stones, which renders its bed very uneven. The inhabitants of the neighborhood form dams here in the shape of a projecting angle to catch eels: the point of the angle is in the middle of the river; there they place nets in the shape of a purse, where the fish which follow the current seldom escape getting caught. The bridge at Canterbury is built in a rather deep and narrow valley. The meetinghouse of the town is on the right [western] bank, as are most of the houses, but there are some also on the heights towards the east, which appeared to me well built and agreeably situated. These heights being of the same elevation as those to the west, Canterbury offers two positions, equally advantageous for two armies, which might contest the passage of the Quinebaug.[29] Immediately after leaving Canterbury, you enter the woods and a chain of hills, crossed by very rugged and difficult roads. Six or seven miles farther along, the country begins to open up, and you descend agreeably to Windham. This is a very pretty little town, or rather the seedling of a pretty town. There are forty or fifty houses fairly near each other, and so situated as to present the appearance of a large public square, and three large streets. The "Seunganick" or Windham [Shetucket] River flows near this town, but is of no great use to its trade, for it is no more navigable than the Quinebaug, with which it joins its waters to form the Thames River. It may be observed from reading this journal, and still more from the examination of maps, that the rivers in general, and many towns, have retained their Indian names: this nomenclature has a certain raciness, because it records the still recent origin of these multiple settlements, and continually presents to the mind a very striking contrast between the former and present state of this vast country.

Windham is fifteen miles from Voluntown [Sterling Hill]. I there found Lauzun's Hussars who were stationed here for a week, until their quarters were prepared at Lebanon.[30] I dined with the Duc de Lauzun, and being unable to get away before half past three, darkness, which soon came on, obliged me to stop six miles beyond Windham, at a solitary little tavern, kept by Mrs. Hill.[31] As the house had an indifferent appearance, I asked if we could have beds, which was all we needed, for the Duc de Lauzun's dinner had left us with no worry about supper. Mrs. Hill told me, after the manner of the country, that she could only "spare" one bed, as she had a sick traveler in the house whom she did not want to disturb. This traveler was a poor soldier of the Continental Army, who was going home on a furlough for the benefit of his health. He had his furlough in his pocket in regular form, as well as the exact account of what was due him, but he had not a farthing either in paper or in "hard money." Mrs. Hill, notwithstanding, had given him a good bed, and as he was too ill to continue his journey, she had kept him and taken care of him for four days. We arranged matters in the best way we could: the soldier kept his bed; I gave him some money to help him on his journey, and Mrs. Hill appeared to me much more affected by this charity than by the good "hard money" I gave her to pay our "bill."

November 16, 1780: [Columbia]—Bolton—East Hartford—Hartford

The 16th, at eight in the morning, I took leave of my kind land-lady, and followed the road to Hartford, beginning my journey on foot, on account of the extreme coldness of the morning. After descending a gentle slope for about two miles, I found myself in a rather narrow, but agreeable and well-cultivated valley: it is watered by a rivulet which flows into the "Seunganick" [i.e., into the Willimantic, which flows into the Shetucket], and which is adorned with the name of "Hope" [Hop] River; you follow this valley to Bolton, town or "township," which has nothing remarkable about it. There you traverse a chain of fairly high mountains, which extend from north to south like all the mountains in Connecticut. On leaving the mountains, you come to the first houses of East Hartford. Though we were but five miles from Hartford Courthouse, we wished to rest our horses, which had traveled twenty-three miles in a stretch. The inn we stopped at was kept by Mr. "Mash" [Marsh]; [32] he is, according to the English phrase, a good "farmer," that is, a good cultivator. He told me that he had just begun a settlement in the state of Vermont, where he had purchased two hundred acres of land for forty dollars, which is about two hundred *livres* of our money.[33] The state of Vermont is a vast country, situated to the eastward [34] of New Hampshire and Massachusetts, and to the north of Connecticut, between the river of that name and the Hudson River. As it has been only recently settled, and has always been an object of contention between the states of New York and New Hampshire, there is, properly speaking, no established government. A certain [Ethan] Allen, celebrated for the expedition he undertook in 1775 against Ticonderoga, of his own accord, and without any other aid than that of the volunteers who followed him, has made himself the leader of that country. He has formed there an assembly of representatives; this assembly grants lands, and the country is governed by its own laws, without having

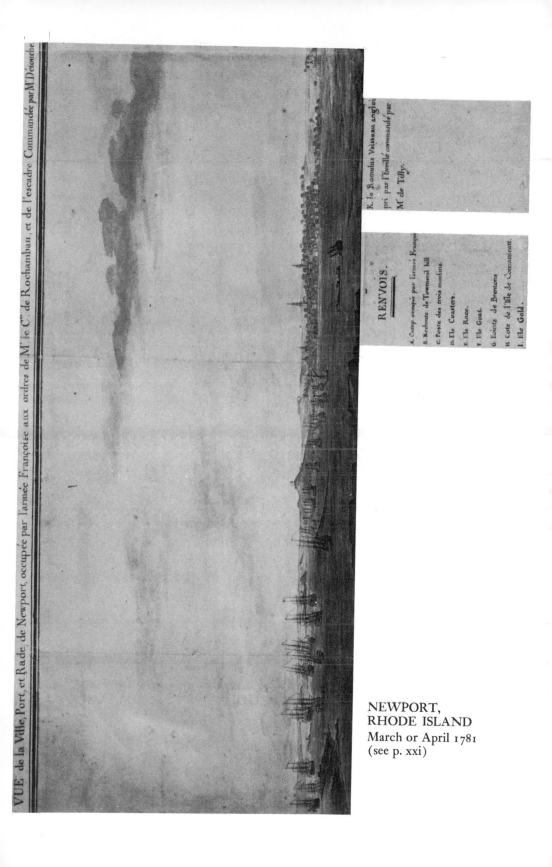

VUE de la Ville, Port, et Rade, de Newport, occupée par l'armée Françoise aux ordres de Mr. le Cte. de Rochambau, et de l'escadre Commandée par Mr. Destouche.

RENVOIS.

A. Camp occupé par l'armée Françoi[se]
B. Redoute de Townsend hill
C. Poste des trois moulins.
D. Ile Coasters.
E. Ile Race.
F. Ile Goat.
G. Pointe de Brentons
H. Cote de l'Isle de Connanicutt.
I. Ile Gold.

K. le Romulus Vaisseau angloi[s]
    pri par l'Ibreille commandé par
    Mr de Tilly.

NEWPORT,
RHODE ISLAND
March or April 1781
(see p. xxi)

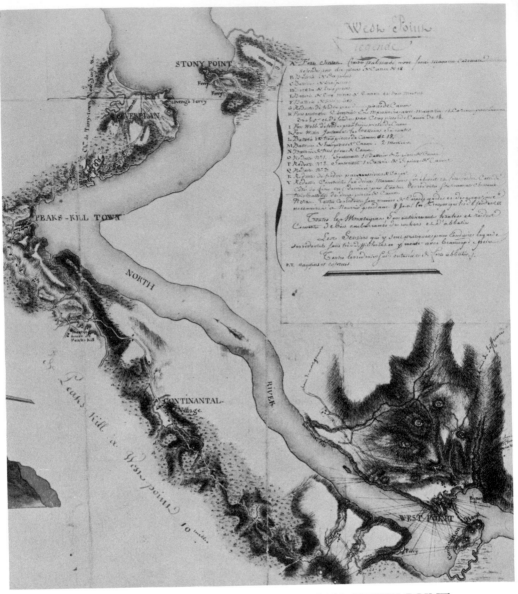

THE HUDSON, FROM WEST POINT TO STONY POINT
Map by L.-A. Berthier, August 1781
Chastellux: November 21-22, 1780 (see p. xxi)

A. Profile of the wooden redoubts built at West Point
B. Profile of an embrasure at Fort Clinton; the fraise can be raised to close
the embrasure

(see pp. xxi-xxii)

A View of the Falls on the Pafsaick, or second River in the Province of New Jersey.

Vue de l'extremité du Pasaick, ou second Riviere, dans la Province du Nouveau Jersey.

TOTOWA, OR PASSAIC, FALLS, 1761
Chastellux: November 23, 1780 (see p. xxii)

any connection with Congress. The inhabitants however are none-theless enemies of the English; but under the pretext that they are on the frontier of Canada, and are obliged to protect themselves, they furnish no contingent to the expenses of the war. They long had no other name than that of "Green Mountain's Boys," but thinking this not noble enough for their new destiny, they trans-lated it into French, which made *Verd Mont,* and by corruption, Vermont; it remains to be seen whether it is by corruption also that this country has claimed for itself the title of state of Vermont.[35]

About four in the afternoon, I arrived at Hartford ferry, after traveling over a very inconvenient road, a great part of which forms a narrow causeway through a marshy wood. We crossed this ferry, like all the others in America,[36] in a flat boat with oars. I found the inns at Hartford so full that it was impossible to procure a lodging. The four eastern states, that is, Massachusetts, New Hampshire, Rhode Island, and Connecticut, were then holding their assemblies in this town. These four states have long maintained a particular connection with each other, and they thus meet together through deputies, sometimes in one state, sometimes in another. Each state "legislature" then sends deputies.[37] Under these circumstances, so uncommon in America, where there was insufficient space for a gathering of men, Colonel [Jeremiah] Wadsworth's house offered me a most agreeable asylum;[38] I lodged with him, as did the Duc de Lauzun, who had passed me on the road. M. Dumas,[39] who be-longed to the general staff of the army and who was then attached to the Duc de Lauzun, M. Lynch, and M. de Montesquieu were very well lodged in the neighborhood.

Colonel Wadsworth is about thirty-two, very tall and well built, and has a countenance as noble as it is agreeable. He formerly lived on Long Island; and from his infancy was engaged in commerce and navigation: he had already made several voyages to the coast of Guinea and the West Indies, when according to the American ex-pression, the present "contest" began. He then served in the army, and was in several actions; but General Washington discovering that his talents might be still more usefully employed, made him commissary of purchases. This is a military post in America, and those who fill it enjoy as much consideration as the principal officers of the line. The Commissary General is charged with all the pur-chases, and the Quartermaster General with all the conveyances: it is the latter who designates the locations, establishes the magazines,

provides carriages, and distributes the rations; it is also on his receipts and orders that the "Paymasters" or *Trésoriers* make their
payments; he is, in short, properly speaking, an *Intendant Militaire*,
while the Commissary General may be compared to one of our
Munitionnaires, combining responsibility for forage and provisions.
I think this arrangement as good as ours, though these departments
have not been exempt from abuses, and even blame, in the course
of the present war; but it must be observed that wherever the government lacks political strength and the treasury is without money,
the administration of affairs is always ruinous and often culpable.
This reflection alone will afford sufficient praise for Col. Wadsworth, when it is known that throughout all America there is not
one voice raised against him, and that his name is never pronounced
without added homage to his talents and his probity. The particular
confidence of General Washington is sufficient to place the seal of
authority on the consideration he justly enjoys.[40] Not without good
reason, then, did the Marquis de La Fayette advise M. de Corny [41]
to employ him for the supplies that the expected arrival of the
French troops made necessary. As soon as they were disembarked
at Rhode Island, he again proposed him as the best man to assist
them in all their wants; but the army administration did not at that
time think proper to employ him. They even conceived some suspicions of him from false reports, and hastily substituted for this
agent (*commissionnaire*) of understanding and reputation, purvey-
ors (*entrepreneurs*), without fortune and without character, who
promised everything, performed nothing, and soon threw our affairs into confusion: first by augmenting the price of provisions by
purchases hastily made, and frequently in competition with one
another, and finally by throwing into circulation and offering at a
great discount the bills of exchange they had agreed to receive for
two-thirds of all payments. These bargains and contracts eventually succeeded so badly, that we were obliged, but too late, to have
recourse to Mr. Wadsworth, who resumed the business as nobly
as he had quitted it; always as superior to injuries by his character,
as he is by his talents to the innumerable obstacles that surround
him.[42]

Another interesting personage was then at Hartford, and I went
to pay him a visit: this was Governor [Jonathan] Trumbull, Governor *par excellence*, for he has been so these fifteen years, having
always been rechosen at the end of every two years, and enjoying

equal public confidence under both the English government, and
under that of the Congress.[43] He is seventy years old; his whole life
has been devoted to public affairs, which he passionately loves,
whether important or not; or rather, as far as he is concerned, there
are no unimportant affairs. He has all the simplicity in his dress, all
the importance, and even the pedantry becoming the great magistrate of a little republic. He brought to my mind the burgomasters
of Holland in the time of the Heinsiuses and the Barnevelts. I had
been informed that he was working on a history of the present
revolution, and I was very curious to read this work; I told him that
I hoped to see him on my return at Lebanon (his place of abode),
and that I should then request permission to look over his manuscript; but he assured me that he had only written the introduction,
which he had addressed to the Chevalier de La Luzerne, our ambassador. I procured it during my stay at Philadelphia, but it is only
an historical recapitulation, rather superficial, and by no means free
from partiality in the manner of representing the events of the war.
The only interesting fact I found in it, was that one may read in
the journal of Governor Winthrop, for the year 1670 [1640], that
the members of the Council of Massachusetts, being advised by
their friends in London to address themselves to Parliament, to
whom the King then left a great deal of authority, as the best means
of obtaining the redress of certain grievances, the Council, after
mature deliberation, thought proper to decline the proposal, reflecting that if they once put themselves under the protection of
Parliament, they should be obliged to submit to the laws that this
assembly might impose, whether on the nation in general, or on
the colonies in particular. Now, nothing can more strongly prove
that these colonies, even in the very beginning, never acknowledged
the authority of Parliament, nor imagined they could be bound by
laws of its making.[44]

November 17, 1780: Hartford–Farmington

The 17th, in the morning, I parted with regret from my host and
from the Duc de Lauzun; but this was not till after breakfast, for
it is a thing unheard of in America to set off without breakfast.[45]
By this indispensable delay I had an opportunity of making the
acquaintance of General [Samuel Holden] Parsons. He appeared
to me a sensible man, and he is so regarded in his country; but he
has had little opportunity of displaying great military talents; he is,

in fact, what one must never be, in war or in anything else, unlucky. His début was on Long Island, where he was captured, and he has since been in all the bad affairs, so that he is better known for his capacity in business than for the share he has had in the events of the war.[46]

The roads I had to travel becoming henceforth difficult and rather wild, it was determined that I should not exceed ten miles that day, that I might meet with good quarters, and get my horses in shape for the next day's journey. The place I was to stop at was Farmington. Mr. Wadsworth, fearing I should not find a good inn there, gave me a letter of recommendation to one of his relatives of the name of [Phinehas] Lewis, where he assured me I should be well received, without inconveniencing anyone, and without inconveniencing myself, for I would pay my reckoning as at an inn. In fact, when the taverns are bad, or when they are so situated as not to suit the convenience of the traveler, it is the custom in America to ask for hospitality from some well-to-do individual, who can spare room in his house for you, and give stabling for your horses: the traveler and his host then converse together as equals, but he is paid as an ordinary innkeeper.

The town of Hartford is not worth lingering over, either when traveling through it or when speaking of it. It consists of a long, very long, street, parallel to the river, which is fairly considerable and continuous, that is, the houses are not far distant from each other. It has, furthermore, many appendages; everything is Hartford for six leagues round; but East Hartford, West Hartford, and New Hartford are distinct towns, although composed of houses scattered through the country. I have already mentioned what constitutes a town; that is, having one or two "meetings," its own assemblies, and the right of sending deputies to the general assembly. These "townships" may be compared to the *curiae* of the Romans. From a very high plateau on the road to Farmington, one discovers not only all the possible Hartfords, but all that part of the continent watered by the river of that name [i.e., the Connecticut], situated between the eastern and western chains of mountains. This place is called Rocky Hill. The houses of West Hartford, frequently dispersed, and sometimes grouped together, and everywhere adorned with trees and meadows, make of the road to Farmington a *jardin anglais*, which art would have difficulty in equaling. The inhabitants engage in some industry in addition to their prosperous agriculture;

some cloths and other woollen stuffs are manufactured here, rather rough, but durable and suitable for clothing people who live in the country, that is in any town other than Boston, New York, or Philadelphia. I went into a house where they were preparing and dyeing the cloth. This cloth is woven by the country people, and is then sent to these little factories, where it is dressed, pressed, and dyed for two shillings "lawful money" per yard, which makes about thirty-five French *sols*, the Connecticut pound being equal to something more than three dollars. I reached Farmington at three in the afternoon. It is a pretty little town, with a handsome "meeting," [47] and fifty houses grouped together, all neat and well built. It is situated on the slope of the mountains: the river which bears the same name runs at the foot of them and turns towards the north, without showing itself, but the view of the valley is notwithstanding very agreeable. After dismounting, I took advantage of the good weather to take a walk in the streets, or rather in the roads. I saw through the windows of a house that they were working at a loom; I entered, and found them making a sort of camlet, as well as another woollen stuff with blue and white stripes for women's dress: these stuffs are sold at three shillings and six pence the yard "lawful money," [48] which makes about forty-five *sols*. The sons and grandsons of the family were working at the loom: one workman can easily make five yards a day. The cost of the raw materials being only one shilling, the day's work may bring him ten or twelve shillings. On my return from this walk I found an excellent dinner prepared for me, without my having said a word to my hosts.[49] After dinner, about the close of the day, Mr. [Phinehas] Lewis, who had been abroad on his affairs during a part of the day, came into the "parlour" where I was (in England and America the room where company is received is called the "parlour"), seated himself by the fire, lighted his pipe, and entered into conversation with me. I found him an active and intelligent man, well acquainted with public affairs and with his own: he trades in cattle, like all the "farmers" of Connecticut; he was then employed in furnishing provisions for the army, and was principally taken up in slaughtering and salting the cattle that the state of Connecticut was to send to Fishkill. For each state is obliged to furnish not only money, but other articles for the army: those to the eastward supply it with cattle, rum, and salt; and those to the westward with flour and forage. Mr. Lewis has also borne arms for his country: he was at the affairs of Long

Island and Saratoga, of which he gave me a very accurate account; in the last he served as a volunteer. At tea time Mrs. Lewis and her sister-in-law joined the company. Mrs. Lewis had just recovered from lying-in and had her child in her arms: she is near thirty, with a very agreeable face, and of such an amiable and polite a bearing as to present a picture of decency itself in any country in the world. The conversation was maintained with interest during the whole evening. My hosts retired at nine o'clock; I did not see them next morning, and paid my "bill" to the servants: it was neither dear nor cheap, but the fair price of everything, settled without interest and without compliments.

November 18, 1780: Farmington–Harwinton–Litchfield

I got on my horse at eight o'clock on the 18th, and at the distance of a mile fell in with the Farmington River, along which I rode for some time. There was nothing interesting in this part of my journey, except that having fired my pistol at a jay, to my great astonishment the bird fell. This species of bird had been for several days an object of curiosity to me, and it is really a most beautiful creature. It is all blue, but it unites all the various shades of that color so as to surpass the invention of art, and be very difficult of imitation. I must remark, by the way, that the Americans call it only by the name of "blue bird." It is nevertheless a real jay; but the Americans have not notably enriched their native language. Anything that had no English name has here been given only a simple designation: the jay is the blue bird, the cardinal the red bird; every water bird is simply a duck, from the teal to the wood duck, and to the large black duck which we do not have in Europe. They call them "red ducks," "black ducks," "wood ducks." It is the same with respect to their trees: the pine, the cypresses, the firs, are all included under the general name of "pine trees"; and if the people characterize any particular tree, it is from the use to which it is applied, as the "wall-nut," from its being used for the walls of houses.[50] I could cite many other examples, but it is sufficient to observe that this poverty of language proves how much men's attention has been employed in objects of utility, and how much at the same time it has been circumscribed and straitened by the only prevailing interest, the desire of augmenting wealth, rather by dint of labor, than by industry. But to return to my jay; I resolved to make a trophy of it, in the manner of the Indians, by removing its skin and feathers as a scalp, and content with my victory, I pursued my way, which soon brought me amid the steepest and most difficult mountains I had yet seen. They are covered with woods as old as creation, but which do not, for all that, differ from ours. These hills, heaped confusedly one upon another, oblige you to be continually mounting and descending, without your being able to distinguish in the midst of this wild republic the summit rising above the rest, which tells you that there will eventually be an end to your labors. This disorder of Nature reminded me of the lessons of him whom she has chosen for her confidant and interpreter. A vision of M. de Buffon appeared to me here in this primeval wilderness. He seemed to be in his proper element, and to point out to me, under a slight crust formed by the decay of vegetation, the uneven surfaces of a globe of glass, which has slowly cooled after a long fusion. The waters, said he, have done nothing here; look around you, you will not find a single calcareous stone; everything is quartz, granite, or flint. I looked, I made experiments on the stones with aqua fortis, and I reached the conclusion, not sufficiently credited in Europe, that not only does M. de Buffon express himself well, but that he is always right.[51]

While I was meditating on the great process of Nature, which takes fifty thousand years to make the earth habitable, a new spectacle, well calculated as a contrast to those which I had been contemplating, fixed my attention, and excited my curiosity; this was the work of a single man, who in the space of one year had cut several acres of woodland and had built himself a house in the middle of a fairly extensive tract, which he had already cleared. I saw, for the first time, what I have since observed a hundred times. For, whatever mountains I have climbed, whatever forests I have traversed, whatever bypaths I have followed, I have never traveled three miles without meeting with a new settlement, either beginning to take form, or already under cultivation. The following is the manner of proceeding in these "improvements," or "new settlements," as they are called. Any man who is able to procure a capital of five or six hundred *livres* of our money,[52] and who has strength and inclination to work, may go into the woods and purchase a tract of land, usually a hundred and fifty or two hundred acres, which seldom costs him more than a dollar or one hundred *sous* an acre,[53] and only a small part of which he pays in cash. There he takes a cow, some pigs, or a full sow, and two indifferent horses which do not cost him more than four *louis* each. To these precautions he adds that of having a provision of flour and cider. Provided with this first capital, he begins by felling all the small trees, and some of the big branches of the large ones: these he uses to make "fences" for the first field he wishes to clear; he next boldly attacks these immense oaks, or pines, which one might take for the ancient lords of the territory he is usurping; he strips them of their bark, or rings them round with his axe. These trees, mortally wounded, find themselves robbed of their honors the following spring; they put forth no more leaves, their branches fall, and their trunks soon become only hideous skeletons. These trunks still seem to brave the efforts of the new settler; but whenever they show the smallest chinks or crevices, they are surrounded by fire, and the flames consume what the iron was unable to destroy. But it is enough for the small trees to be felled, and the great ones to lose their sap. This object completed, the ground is "cleared"; the air and the sun begin to operate upon that earth which is wholly formed of decayed vegetation, that fertile earth which asks but to produce. The grass grows rapidly; there is pasturage for the cattle the very first year; after which they are left to increase, or fresh ones are bought, and they are employed in tilling a piece of ground which, when planted, yields the enormous increase of twenty or thirty fold. The next year, more trees are cut, more "fences" built, more progress made; then, at the end of two years, the settler has the wherewithal to subsist, and even to send some articles to market; and after four or five years he completes the payment of his land and finds himself a comfortable "farmer." Then his dwelling, which at first was no better than a large hut formed by a square of tree trunks, placed one upon another, with the intervals filled by mud, changes into a handsome wooden house, where he contrives more convenient, and certainly much cleaner apartments than those in most of our small towns [in France]. This is the work of three weeks or a month; his first habitation, that of twice twenty-four hours. I shall be asked, perhaps, how one man or one family can be so quickly lodged? I reply that in America a man is never alone, never an isolated being. The neighbors, for they are everywhere to be found, make it a point of hospitality to aid the newcomer. A cask of cider drunk in common, and with gaiety, or a gallon of rum, are the only recompense for these services. Such are the means by which North America, which one hundred years ago was nothing but a vast forest, has been peopled with three million inhabitants; and such is the immense and certain profit from agriculture, that notwithstanding the war, it not only maintains itself wherever it has been established, but it extends to places which seem the least favorable to its introduction. Four years ago one might have traveled ten miles in the woods I traversed without seeing a single habitation.

Harwinton is the first "township" I met with on my road. This place is sixteen miles from Farmington, and eight from Litchfield. Four miles before you come to this last town you cross a wooden bridge over the Waterbury [Naugatuck] River [at East Litchfield]; this river is fairly wide, but not navigable. Litchfield, or the "meeting-house" of Litchfield, is situated on a large plateau more elevated than the surrounding heights; about fifty houses quite near each other, with a large square, or rather a space in the middle, seem to foretell the progress of this town, which is already the county seat; [54] for America is divided into districts, called counties in some states, as in England. It is in the capital of these counties or districts that the court of "sessions" is held, at which the "sheriff" presides, and it is here that the chief judges come every four months to decide civil and criminal cases. Half a mile this side of Litchfield, I noticed on the right a shed surrounded by palisades which looked to me like a guardhouse; I approached it, and saw in this small enclosure ten handsome pieces of brass cannon, a mortar, and a swivel. This I learned was a part of Burgoyne's artillery, which fell to the share of the state of Connecticut, and was kept in this place as the most conveniently situated for the army, and at the same time the least exposed to the incursions of the English.

It was four o'clock, and the weather very bad, when I approached the house of a Mr. Seymour, to whom Mr. Lewis had given me a letter, assuring me that I should find better "accommodation" there than at the local taverns; but M. Lynch, who had gone on a little before to make inquiries, informed me that Mr. Seymour was not at home, and that from all appearances his wife would be much embarrassed to receive us. Indeed, American women are very little accustomed to give themselves trouble, either of mind or body; the care of their children, that of making tea, and seeing the house kept clean, constitute the whole of their domestic province. I determined therefore to go straight to the tavern, where I was still unlucky enough not to find Mr. Philips the landlord: [55] so that I was received, to say the least, with indifference, which often happens in the inns in America, when they are not in much frequented situations. Travelers are there considered as bringing more trouble than money. The reason for this is that the innkeepers are all of them well-to-do farmers who do not stand in need of this slight profit: most of those who follow this profession are even compelled to it by the laws of the country, which have wisely provided that on any road there shall be a "public house," as these taverns are commonly and appropriately called, every six miles.

A still greater difficulty I had at Mrs. Philips's was to find room for the nine horses I had with me. The quartermaster at length had some of them put in the stable of a private person, and everything was arranged to my satisfaction and to that of my hostess. It is worth pointing out that nothing can be more useful than such an officer, both for state business and for anyone traveling in an official capacity. I have already spoken of the functions of the Quartermaster General, but I did not mention that he names a "Deputy Quartermaster General" in each state, and that the latter in turn names an "assistant" in each district to act as his representative. My horses and baggage were scarcely under cover when a dreadful storm came on, which however was in my favor, as it brought home Mr. Philips: everything now assumed a new face in the house, the pantry flew open, the Negroes redoubled their activity, and we soon saw a supper preparing under the most favorable auspices. Mr. Philips is an Irishman, transplanted to America, where he has already made a fortune; he appears to be a sharp and clever man; he is cautious in talking to strangers for fear of compromising himself; in other respects he is more gay than the Americans, and even given to banter (*même un peu persifleur*), a turn of mind but little known in this hemisphere, and for which they have no specific term, any more than they do for the different species of trees and birds. Mrs. Philips, now seconded by her husband, and no longer above her task, now resumed her natural serenity. She is of American birth, and a true "Yankee," [56] as her husband told us; her face is gentle and agreeable, and her manners are entirely in keeping with her features.

*November 19, 1780: Litchfield—Washington [New Preston Hill]
—South Kent—Bull's Iron Works [Bull's Bridge], Conn.—
Morehouse's Tavern [Wingdale], N.Y.*

The 19th I left Litchfield between nine and ten in the morning, and pursued my journey through the mountains, partly on foot and partly on horseback; for having got into the habit of traveling from morning till night without stopping, I from time to time took pity on my horses, and spared them especially those descents which seemed formed for the roebuck rather than for carriages and laden horses. The name of the first town I came to proclaims it to be of recent origin; it is called Washington. A new county being formed in the woods of Connecticut, the state has bestowed on it this respectable name, the memory of which will doubtless last still longer than the city intended to perpetuate it. There is another county of Washington in Virginia, belonging to the protector of America; but its great distance from this new town prevents all possible inconvenience arising from the identity of name. This capital of a rising county has a "meeting-house," and seven or eight houses grouped together; it is in a beautiful situation, and the cultivation appears rich and well managed; [57] a stream [East Aspetuck River] which flows at the bottom of the valley renders the meadows more fruitful than they generally are in mountainous countries.[58] From Litchfield to here they reckon seventeen miles: I still had ten miles to go to reach Morehouse's Tavern, where I intended sleeping, but not taking the shortest road, I traveled at least twelve, and always among the mountains. The road I took brought me to a fairly considerable hamlet, called "New-Milford-Bordering-Skirt," that is, the confines of Milford County,[59] and from thence into so deep and wild a valley that I thought myself completely lost until a small clearing in the wood revealed, first a meadow surrounded by fences, then a house, and soon after another, and at length a charming valley, with several considerable farms, covered with cattle [South Kent]. I soon crossed this valley, which belongs to the county [town] of Kent, as well as the brook [Womenshenuk] which flows through the middle of it, and after traveling three miles farther in the mountains, I reached the banks of the Housatonic, or Stratford, River. It is unnecessary to remark that the first is the genuine name, that is, the name given it by the Indians, the former inhabitants of the country. This river is not navigable, and is easily forded near

Bull's iron works.[60] You then turn to the left and pass along its banks; but if one is sensible to the beauties of Nature, if the paintings of [Claude-Joseph] Vernet and [Hubert] Robert have taught one to admire them, it is impossible not to be lost in admiration at the view of the charming landscape formed by the combination of the forges, of the waterfall which serves to work them, and of the variegated prospect of trees and rocks, with which this picturesque scene is embellished. At a distance of a mile we again cross the same river but this time over a wooden bridge; you soon meet with another which flows into one called Tenmile River, and which you follow for two or three miles, and then come in sight of several handsome houses, forming a part of the district called the "Oblong." This is a long narrow strip of land, ceded by Connecticut to the state of New York, in exchange for some other territory.[61] The inn I was going to is in the Oblong, but two miles farther on.[62] It is kept by Colonel [Andrew] Morehouse; for nothing is more common in America than to see an innkeeper a colonel: they are in general militia colonels, chosen by the militia themselves, who seldom fail to entrust the command to the most worthy and most esteemed citizens.[63]

I pressed forward my horses and hurried on to get ahead of a traveler on horseback, who had joined me on the road and who would have had the same right as myself to the lodgings, had we arrived together. I had the satisfaction, however, to see him pursue his journey; but soon afterwards I was pained to learn that the little inn where I intended to pass the night was occupied by thirteen farmers and two hundred and fifty cattle coming from New Hampshire. The cattle were the least inconvenient part of the company, as they were left to graze in a meadow hard by, without even a dog to guard them; but the farmers, their horses, and dogs, were in possession of the inn. I inquired the reason they were on the road, and learned that they were conveying to the army a part of the contingent of provisions furnished by New Hampshire. This contingent is a sort of tax divided among all the inhabitants, on some of whom the imposition amounts to one hundred and fifty, on others to one hundred, or eighty pounds of meat, according to their means; so that they agree amongst themselves to furnish a larger or smaller sized animal, no matter which, as each is weighed. Conveying them to the army is then entrusted to several farmers and drovers. The farmers are allowed about a dollar a day, and their expenses, as well as those of the cattle, are paid them on their return, according to the receipts they are obliged to produce from the innkeepers where they have halted. The usual price is from six to ten French *sols* [64] per night for each head of cattle, and in proportion for the noon feeding.

I informed myself of these particulars while my people were endeavoring to find me lodgings; but all the rooms and all the beds were occupied by the drovers, and I was in the greatest distress, when a tall, fat man, the principal person amongst them, being informed who I was, came to me and assured me that neither he nor his companions would ever suffer a French general officer to want a bed, and that they would rather sleep on the floor than permit this to happen; adding that they were accustomed to it and that it would be attended with no inconvenience. In reply I told them that I was a military man, and as much accustomed as they were to make the earth my bed. There was a long debate on this point of *politesse;* theirs was rustic, but more cordial and affecting than the best-turned compliments. The result was that I had a room and two beds for myself and my aides-de-camp. But our acquaintance did not terminate there: after parting from each other, I to clean up and take some repose, they to continue drinking their "grog" (a drink made with rum and water) and cider, they came into my room. I was then busy tracing my route on the map of the country; this map excited their curiosity. They saw there with surprise and satisfaction the places they had passed through. They asked me if they were known in Europe, and if it was there I had bought my maps. On my assuring them that we knew America as well as the countries closer to us, they seemed much pleased; but their joy knew no bounds when they recognized New Hampshire, their country, on my map. They immediately called their companions who were in the next room; and mine was soon filled with the strongest and most robust men I had yet seen in America. On my appearing struck with their size and stature, they told me that the inhabitants of New Hampshire were strong and vigorous, for which there were many reasons; that the air was excellent, their sole occupation was agriculture, and above all that their blood was unmixed, this country being inhabited by families of former emigrants from England. We parted very good friends, touching, or rather "shaking" hands in the English fashion, and they assured me that they were very happy to have an opportunity "to shake hands with a French General." [65]

November 20, 1780: Morehouse's Tavern [Wingdale], N.Y.— Hopewell—Fishkill

The horse which carried my portmanteaus, not traveling so fast as I, did not join me till the next morning, so that it was ten o'clock on November 20 before I could set out. Three miles from More-house's Tavern is a very high mountain; you then descend, but not quite so much as you ascended; after this you travel along over elevated ground, leaving large mountains on the left. The country is well cultivated, affording the prospect of several pretty farms, with some mills; and notwithstanding the war, building is going on, especially at "Hopel" [Hopewell] township,[66] which is inhabited chiefly by Dutch people, as is the greatest part of the state of New York, for it formerly belonged to the Republic of Holland, which subsequently exchanged it for Surinam. My intention was to sleep five miles on this side of Fishkill, at Colonel Griffin's Tavern.[67] I found him cutting and preparing wood for fences: he assured me his house was full, which was easy to believe, for it was very small. So I continued my journey and reached Fishkill about four o'clock. This town, in which there are not more than fifty houses in the space of two miles, has long been the principal depot of the American army: it is there they have placed their magazines, their hospitals, their workshops, etc., but all these form a town in themselves, composed of handsome large barracks, built in the wood at the foot of the mountains; for the Americans, like the Romans in many respects, have for winter quarters only wooden towns, or camps, composed of barracks, which may be compared to the *hiemalia* of the Romans.

As for the position of Fishkill, the events of the campaign of 1777 had proved how important it was to occupy it. It was clear that the plan of the English had been, and was still, to render themselves masters of the whole course of the North [Hudson] River, and thus to separate the eastern states from those to the west and the south. It was necessary therefore to secure a post on this river; West Point was chosen as the most important point to fortify, and Fishkill as the place the best adapted to the establishment of the principal depot of provisions, ammunition, etc.; these two positions are connected with each other. I shall soon speak of West Point, but I shall note here that Fishkill has all the qualifications necessary for a place of depot, for it is situated on the high road from Connecticut and near the North River, and is protected at the same time by a chain of inaccessible mountains, which occupy a space of more than twenty miles between the Croton and the Fishkill Rivers.

The approach of winter quarters and the movement of the troops occasioned by this circumstance made lodgings very scarce: it was with difficulty that I found any, but I got at last into a middling inn, kept by an old Mrs. Egremont.[68] The house was not as clean as they usually are in America; but the most disagreeable circumstance was the lack of several panes of glass. In fact, of all repairs, that of windows is the most difficult in a country where, from the scattered situations and distance of the houses from each other, it is sometimes necessary to send twenty miles for a glazier. We made use of everything that came to hand to stuff the windows as best we could, and we made an excellent fire. Soon after, the "Doctor" of the hospital, who had seen me pass by and recognized me as being a French general officer, came with great politeness to inquire if I wanted anything, and to offer me every service in his power. I use the English word "Doctor," because the distinction between surgeon and physician is as little known in the army of Washington as in that of Agamemnon.[69] We read in Homer that the physician Macaon himself dressed wounds; but our physicians, who are no Greeks, will not follow that example. The Americans conform to the ancient custom and are none the worse for so doing; they are well pleased with their doctors, whom they hold in the highest consideration. Doctor [James] Craik, whom I knew at Newport, is the intimate friend of General Washington; and recently the Marquis de La Fayette had as aide-de-camp Colonel [James] McHenry, who last year performed the functions of doctor in the same army.[70]

November 21, 1780: Fishkill—West Point

The 21st, at nine in the morning, the quartermaster of Fishkill, who had come the night before with the utmost politeness to offer me his services, and to place two sentinels at my door, an honor I refused in spite of everything he could say, called upon me; and after drinking tea according to custom, he conducted me to the barracks, where I saw the magazines and workshops of the different

workmen employed in the service of the army.[71] These barracks
are regular wooden houses, well built and well covered, having gar-
rets and even cellars, so that we should form a very false idea were
we to judge of them by what we see in our armies when our troops
are "in barracks." The Americans sometimes make them like ours,
but this is merely to shelter the soldiers when they are more within
reach of the enemy. They call the latter "huts," and they are very
expert in constructing both. They require only three days to build
the barracks, reckoning from the moment they begin to cut down
the trees; the huts are finished in twenty-four hours. They consist
of little walls made of heaped-up stones, the intervals of which are
filled with earth kneaded with water or simply with mud; a few
planks form the roof; but what renders them very warm is that the
chimney occupies the outer side, and that you can only enter by a
small door, at the side of the chimney. The army has passed whole
winters in such huts, without suffering and without sickness. As for
the barracks, or rather the little military town of Fishkill, such
ample provision is made for everything which the service and discipline of the army may require that a provostry and a prison, surrounded by palisades, have been built there. One gate only affords
access to the enclosure of the provostry and in front of this is placed
a guardhouse. Through the window bars of the prison I distinguished some prisoners in English uniform; these were about thirty
soldiers, or "Tories" enrolled in English regiments. These wretches
had accompanied the Indians on the raids they had just made by
way of Lake Ontario and the Mohawk River. They had burned
upwards of two hundred houses, killed horses and cows, and destroyed above one hundred thousand bushels of wheat. The gallows
should have been the reward for these exploits, but the enemy having also made some prisoners, reprisals were dreaded, and so these
brigands were only confined in rigorous and close imprisonment.

　　After passing some time in visiting these different establishments,
I got on horseback, and under the conduct of a state guide whom
the quartermaster had given me, I entered the woods and followed
the road to West Point, where I wanted to arrive for dinner. Four
or five miles from Fishkill I saw some felled trees and a clearing in
the wood, which on coming nearer I discovered to be a camp, or
rather huts inhabited by several hundred invalid soldiers. These
invalids were all in very good health; but it is necessary to observe
that in the American armies every soldier who is unfit for service is

called an invalid: now these had been sent here behind the lines because their clothes were truly invalid. These honest fellows, for I will not say these unfortunates (they know too well how to suffer, and are suffering in too noble a cause) were not covered, even with rags; but their assured bearing and their arms in good order seemed to cover their nakedness, and to show only their courage and their patience. Near this camp I met with Major [Daniel] Lyman, aide-de-camp to General [William] Heath, with whom I was particularly intimate at Newport, and M. de Villefranche, a French officer, serving as an engineer at West Point.[72] General Heath had been informed of my arrival by an express, sent without my knowledge by the quartermaster of Fishkill, and he had dispatched these two officers to meet me. I continued my journey in the woods, in a road hemmed in on both sides by very steep hills, which seemed admirably adapted for the dwelling of bears, and where in fact they often make their appearance in winter. You at length take advantage of a spot where the mountains are a bit less high to turn to the westward and approach the river, but you still cannot see it. Descending slowly, at a turn of the road, my eyes were suddenly struck with the most magnificent picture I have ever beheld.[73] It was a view of the North River [Hudson], running in a deep channel formed by the mountains, through which in former ages it had forced its passage. The fort of West Point and the formidable batteries which defend it, fix the attention on the western bank, but on lifting your eyes you behold on every side lofty summits, all bristling with redoubts and batteries. I leaped off my horse and stood there for a long time looking through my spyglass, the only method of acquiring a knowledge of the whole of the fortifications with which this important post is surrounded. Two lofty heights, on each of which a large redoubt is constructed, protect the eastern bank. These two works have no other name than the Northern and the Southern Redoubt; but from the fort of West Point proper, which is on the edge of the river, to the very top of the mountain at the foot of which it stands, are six different forts, all in the form of an amphitheater, and protecting each other. I was urged to leave this place, where I should willingly have spent the whole day, but I had not traveled a mile before I saw why I had been hurried along. I perceived a corps of infantry of about two thousand five hundred men, ranged in battle formation on the bank of the river. They had just crossed it in order to proceed towards King's Bridge and cover a large foraging party which it was proposed to send towards White Plains and to the gates of New York.[74] General [John] Stark, who beat the English at Bennington, had the command of these troops, and General Heath was at their head; he was desirous of letting me see them before they marched. I passed before the ranks, being saluted with the spontoon by all the officers, and the drums beating a march, an honor paid in America to major generals, who are the first in rank, though it only corresponds to our *Maréchal de camp*. The troops were ill clothed, but made a good appearance; as for the officers they left nothing to be desired either in their bearing or in their manner of marching and giving commands. After I had passed in front of the line it broke, filed off before me, and continued its route. General Heath then conducted me to the river, where his barge was waiting to take me across to the other side. As we were going down towards the river bank a new scene opened to my view, not less sublime than the former. We were facing towards the north: in that direction is an island covered with rocks, which seems to close the channel of the river, but you soon perceive, through a sort of embrasure which the river bed has formed by separating immense mountains, that it comes obliquely from the westward, and that it has made a sudden turn round West Point to open itself a passage and rush on to reach the sea, without hereafter making the smallest bend. The eye looking towards the north beyond Constitution Island (the island I have been speaking of) again perceives the river, discerns New Windsor on the western bank, and is then attracted by different amphitheaters formed by the Appalachian Mountains, whose nearest summits, terminating the scene, are more than ten leagues away. We embarked in the barge and crossed the river, which is nearly a mile wide. As we approached the opposite shore the fort of West Point which, seen from the eastern bank, had seemed humbly situated at the foot of the mountains, rose before our eyes and itself appeared like the summit of a steep rock; this rock however was only the bank of the river. Had I not remarked that the chinks on it, in several places, were embrasures for cannon and formidable batteries, I should soon have been apprised of this fact by thirteen 24-pounders, which were fired successively. This was a military salute, with which General Heath was pleased to honor me in the name of the thirteen states.[75] Never was honor more imposing nor more majestic; every shot was, after a long interval, echoed back from the opposite bank with a noise nearly equal to that of the discharge itself. When we recollect that two years ago West Point was an almost inaccessible wilderness, which has since then been covered with fortresses and artillery, by a people, who six years before had scarcely ever seen cannon; when we reflect that the fate of the thirteen states has depended in great measure on this important post, and that a horse trader, transformed into a general, or rather become a hero, always intrepid, always victorious, but always purchasing victory at the price of his blood; that this extraordinary man, at once the honor and the opprobrium of his country, sold and expected to deliver this *Palladium* of American liberty to the English; [76] when, indeed, so many wonders, of both the physical and moral order, are brought together, it may easily be imagined that I had sufficient food for thought, and that my mind was not idle on the road.

On landing, or rather on climbing up over the rocks on the banks of the river, we were received by Colonel [John] Lamb and Major [Sebastian] Bauman, both artillery officers; by Major [Nicholas] Fish, a handsome young man, witty and well informed; and Major [David S.] Franks,[77] formerly aide-de-camp to General Arnold. Major Franks had just been tried and honorably acquitted by a council of war, requested by himself after the escape and treason of his general. He speaks good French, as does Colonel Lamb, which they both learned in Canada, where they were settled. The latter received a musket shot in his jaw at the attack on Quebec, fighting by the side of Arnold, after having nearly penetrated into the upper town. Pressed by dinner time, we went immediately to General Heath's barrack. The fort, which was begun on much too extensive a plan, has since been compressed by M. Duportail,[78] so that this barrack is no longer within its walls. Around it are some magazines, and farther to the northwest, barracks for three or four battalions; they are built of wood and similar to those at Fishkill. While dinner was preparing, General Heath took me into a little closet which serves as his bedchamber, and showed me the instructions he had given General Stark for the foraging party he commanded. This expedition required a movement of troops in an area of more than fifty miles; and I can affirm that the instructions were as well conceived as any of that kind I have ever seen, either in print or manuscript. He also showed me a letter in which General Washington merely ordered him to send this detachment, and pointed out its object, without informing him, however, of another operation con-

nected with it, which was to take place on the right [western] bank
of the North River.[79] From various intelligence, received indirectly,
General Heath was persuaded that in case the enemy collected his
force to interrupt the foraging party, M. de La Fayette would then
attack Staten Island, and he was not mistaken; but Mr. Washington
contented himself with announcing in general terms some movements on his side, merely adding that he awaited a more safe method
of communicating the nature of them to General Heath. Indeed
secrecy is strictly observed in the American army; very few persons
are in the confidence of the Commander in Chief, and in general
there is less talk about operations of war, of what we call "news,"
than in the French armies.

General [William] Heath is so well known in our little army,
that I should dispense with entering into particulars respecting him,
if this journal, in which I endeavor to recollect what little I have
seen in this country, were not destined at the same time to satisfy
the curiosity of a few persons who have not crossed the sea, and to
whose amusement I am desirous of contributing. So I must explain
that this general was one of the first who took up arms, at the
time of the blockade of Boston, and having first joined the army in
the capacity of colonel, he was immediately raised to the rank of
major general. He was at that time a substantial farmer or rich gentleman; for we must not lose sight of the distinction, that in America "farmer" means cultivator, as opposed to "merchant," the name
given to any man employed in commerce. Here, as in England, by
"gentleman" is understood a person possessing a considerable "freehold," or land of his own. General Heath, then, was a "farmer" or
"gentleman," and raised on his estate a great number of cattle,
which he sold for ships provisions. But his natural taste led him to
the study of war, to which he has principally applied himself since
the period in which his duty has concurred with his inclination; he
has read our best authors on military tactics, and especially the
Tactics of M. Guibert, which he holds in particular esteem.[80] His
fortune enabling him to continue in the service, notwithstanding
the want of pay, which has compelled the less rich to quit it, he
has served during the whole war; but chance has prevented him
from being present on the most important occasions. His countenance is noble and open; and his bald head, as well as his corpu-
lence, give him a striking resemblance to Lord Granby.[81] He writes
well and with ease, has great sensibility of mind, and a frank and

amiable character; in short, if he has not been in the way of displaying his talents in action, it may at least be asserted that he is
well adapted to what we call "the business of the cabinet." His
estate is near Boston, and he commanded there when Burgoyne's
army was brought prisoner thither. It was he who put the English
General Philips under arrest, for want of respect to the Congress; [82]
his conduct on this occasion was firm and noble. On our arrival at
Rhode Island, he was sent there; and soon after, when Clinton was
preparing to attack us, he assembled and commanded the militia
who came to our assistance.[83] During his stay at Newport he lived
honorably and in great friendship with all the French officers. In
the month of September, General Washington, on discovering the
treason of Arnold, sent for him and gave him the command of West
Point; a mark of confidence the more honorable, as none but the
most honest of men was proper to succeed, in this command, the
basest of all traitors.

After giving this advantageous but just idea of General Heath,
I cannot but congratulate myself on the friendship and thorough
good understanding which subsisted between us during his stay at
Newport, where my knowledge of the English language rendered
me the intermediary in all affairs we had to transact with him. It
was with real satisfaction that he received me at West Point; [84] he
gave me a plain but very good dinner: it is true there was not a
drop of wine, but I find that with excellent cider and "toddy" [85]
one may very well dispense with it. As soon as we rose from table,
we hurried to avail ourselves of the remaining daylight to examine
the fortifications. The first fort we met with above West Point, on
the declivity of the mountain, has been named for General Putnam.
It is placed on a rock very steep on every side; the ramparts were
at first constructed with trunks of trees; they are being rebuilt of
stone and are not yet entirely finished. There is a bombproof powder magazine, a large cistern, and a souterrain for the garrison.
Above this fort, and on reaching the highest peak, you can still see,
on three other summits, three strong redoubts lined with cannon,
each of which would require a formal siege. The day being nearly
spent, I contented myself with judging by the eye of the very intelligent manner in which they are calculated for mutual protection. Fort "Wallis" [Wyllis], whither General Heath conducted
me, was nearer and more accessible. Though it is placed lower than
Fort Putnam, it still commands the river to the south. It is a large

pentagonal redoubt, built of huge tree trunks; it is picketed (*fraisé*) and lined with artillery. Under the fire of this redoubt, and lower down, is a battery of cannon to range more obliquely the course of the river. This battery is not closed at the gorge, so that the enemy may take it, but never keep it; which leads me to remark that this is the best method to follow in all field fortifications. Batteries placed in works have two inconveniences: the first is that if these works be ever so little elevated, they do not graze sufficiently; and the second, that the enemy may at the same time attack the redoubt and the battery: whereas if the battery is exterior and protected by the redoubt, it must be attacked first; in which case it is supported by troops who have nothing to fear for themselves, and whose fire is consequently better directed and more deadly. A battery still lower down and nearer to the river completes the security of the southern part.[86]

While returning to West Point we saw a redoubt that has been allowed to go to ruin, as being useless, which in fact it is. It was dark when we got home, but what I still had to observe did not require daylight. This was a vast souterrain, formed within the fort of West Point [Fort Clinton], where not only the powder and ammunition necessary for this post are kept in reserve, but also the depot for the whole army. These magazines neatly filled, the numerous artillery one sees in these different fortresses, the prodigious labor necessary to transport and pile up on steep rocks, huge trunks of trees and enormous hewn stones, impress the mind with an idea of the Americans very different from that which the English ministry have labored to give to Parliament. A Frenchman would be surprised that a nation, just rising into notice, should have expended in two years upwards of twelve millions *livres* [87] in this wilderness. He would be still more so on learning that these fortifications cost nothing to the state, having been built by soldiers, who received not the smallest gratification and who did not even receive their stated pay; [88] but he would doubtless feel some satisfaction upon hearing that these beautiful and well-contrived works were planned and executed by two French engineers, M. Duportail and M. de Gouvion, who received no more pay than their workmen.[89]

But in this wild and warlike abode, where one seems transported to the heart of Thrace and the retreat of the god Mars, we found, on our return in the evening, pretty women and an excellent cup of tea. Mrs. Bauman, wife of the major of that name, and a younger sister who had accompanied her to West Point, were waiting for us. They both lodged in a very neatly arranged little barrack. The room they received us in was hung with pretty paper, furnished with mahogany tables, and even ornamented with several prints. After staying a little while, it was necessary to return to General Heath's quarters and to make our arrangements for passing the night there, which was not an easy affair, for the company had much increased in the course of the evening. The Vicomte de Noailles, the Comte de Damas, and the Chevalier Duplessis-Mauduit had reached West Point, which post they had intended to examine minutely; [90] but the movements of the American army determined them to set out with me, in order to join M. de La Fayette the next evening or early the following morning. Although General Heath had a great deal of company to provide for, his *maréchal général des logis* had not much to do: there were only three rooms in the barracks—the General's chamber, that of his aide-de-camp, who resigned it to me, and the dining-room, in which some blankets were spread before a large fire, where the other gentlemen passed as "comfortable" [91] a night as could be expected.

November 22, 1780: West Point—Verplanck's Point—Stony Point —Haverstraw—Kakiat [New Hempstead]

The morning gun soon summoned them from their beds; the blankets were removed, and the dining room, resuming its rights, was quickly furnished with a large table covered with "beef-stakes," which we ate with a very good appetite, while drinking from time to time a cup of tea with milk. Europeans would not find this food and drink, taken together, to their taste; but I can assure you that it made a very "comfortable" breakfast. Most un-comfortable, however, was a very heavy rain, which had begun in the night and still continued, with a dreadful wind; it rendered the passage of the ferry very dangerous for our horses, and prevented us from making use of the sail on the barge General Heath had given us to carry us to King's Ferry. In spite of all these obstacles we embarked to the sound of thirteen guns, notwithstanding my representations to the contrary. Another circumstance, however, gave additional value to these honors, for I learned that the cannon I heard discharged had belonged to Burgoyne's army. Thus did the artillery that the

King of England sent from Woolwich to Canada in 1777 now serve to defend America and to do homage to her allies, while waiting to be employed in the siege of New York.[92]

General Heath, who was detained by business at West Point, sent Major Lyman to accompany me to Verplanck's Point, where we did not arrive till half past twelve, after a continuous journey amidst the immense mountains which cover this country and through which the bed of the river is the only passage. The highest of them is called Anthony's Nose; it projects into the river and compels it to change its course a bit. Before reaching this point, you see the ruins of Fort Clinton: this fort, which was named after the Governor of the state of New York [George Clinton], was attacked and taken in 1777 by the English General [Sir Henry] Clinton, as he was coming up the river towards Albany to join hands with Burgoyne.[93] It was then the principal fort on the river, and had been built on a rock at the foot of a mountain, thought to be inaccessible, and was also defended by a little "creek" [Popolopen] which flows into the main river. Sir "Harry" Clinton scaled the top of the mountain, himself carrying the British colors, which he kept holding aloft, while his troops descended the steep rock, crossed the "creek," and carried the post. The garrison, consisting of 700 men, was almost all taken. Since the defeat of Burgoyne and the alliance with France have changed the face of affairs in America, General Washington has not thought proper to repair Fort Clinton; he has preferred to place his communication and to concentrate his forces at West Point, because the Hudson there makes a bend which prevents vessels from coming upstream with the wind abaft, or with the tide; and because Constitution Island, which is precisely at the turn of the river, in a north-and-south direction, is perfectly situated to protect the chain [94] which closes the passage to ships of war.

The English, however, had preserved a very important post at King's Ferry, where they were sufficiently well fortified; so that with the aid of their ships, they were masters of the course of the river for the space of more than fifty miles, and were thus able to push to the northward the very important [American] communication between the Jerseys and Connecticut. Such was the state of things when, in the month of June 1779, General [Anthony] Wayne, who commanded in the Clove [95] a corps of 1500 men, formed the project of surprising Stony Point. This fort consisted of a retrenchment surrounded with an abatis, which crowned a steep rock, and the *réduit* of which formed a well-picketed (*bien fraisé*) redoubt. General Wayne marched during the night in three columns, the principal of which was commanded by Monsieur de Fleury,[96] who, without firing a musket, forced the abatis and retrenchments, and entered the redoubt with the fugitives. The attack was so brisk on the part of the Americans, and such the terror of the English, that M. de Fleury, who was the first to enter, found himself in an instant loaded with eleven swords which were delivered to him by those who asked for quarter. It must be added to the honor of our allies, that from that moment not a drop of blood was spilled.[97] Once the Americans were masters of one of the banks of the river, they lost no time in getting possession of the other. M. de Gouvion constructed a redoubt at Verplanck's Point [nearly opposite, on the eastern bank], where we now landed, and where, by a lucky accident, we found our horses, which arrived at the same time we did. This redoubt is of a peculiar form, hardly ever used in America: the ditch is within the parapet, which is made steep on both sides, and picketed (*fraisé*) at the level of the cordon; lodgings for the soldiers are formed below. The middle of the work is a *réduit* constructed of wood, and in the form of a square tower. It has battlements everywhere and commands the rampart. An abatis formed of interwoven tops of trees surrounds the whole and is a substitute for a covered way. We may easily perceive that such a work cannot be surprised, nor taken without cannon. Now as this is backed by the mountains, of which the Americans are still masters, it is almost impossible that the English should besiege it. A "creek" which flows into the Hudson River, and runs to the southward of this redoubt, renders its position still more advantageous. Colonel [James] Livingston, who commands at King's Ferry, has established himself there in preference to Stony Point, to be nearer White Plains, where the English frequently make incursions. He is a very amiable and well-informed young man. Previous to the war he married in Canada, where he acquired a knowledge of the French language; in 1775 he was one of the first who took up arms; he fought under the orders of Montgomery, and took Fort Chambly, while the former was besieging St. John's. He received us in his little citadel with great grace and politeness; but to leave it with the honors of war, the American laws required that we should breakfast. It was the second we had taken that day, and consisted of "beef-stakes," and tea with milk, accompanied by a few bowls of grog, for the commander's cellar was no better supplied than the soldiers' wardrobe. The latter had been sent into this garrison as being the worst clothed of the whole American army, so that one may form some idea of their dress.

About two o'clock we crossed the river, and stopped to examine the fortifications of Stony Point. The Americans finding them too extensive, have reduced them to a redoubt, nearly similar to that of Verplanck's, but not quite so good. There I took leave of Mr. Livingston, who gave me a guide to conduct me to the army, and I set off, preceded by Messrs. de Noailles, de Damas, and de Mauduit, who wished to join M. de La Fayette that night, though they had thirty miles to go over very bad roads. This impatience was well suited to their age; but the intelligence I collected proving to me that the army could not move before the next day, I determined to stop on the road, content to profit by the little daylight that remained to travel ten or twelve miles. On leaving the river, I frequently turned round to enjoy the magnificent spectacle it presents in this place, where its bed becomes so large, that in viewing it to the southward, it has the appearance of an immense lake, whilst the northern aspect is that of a majestic river. I was shown a sort of promontory,[98] from whence Colonel Livingston had intended to take with a single cannon the *Vulture*, the sloop of war which had brought André and was waiting for Arnold. This vessel having come too near the shore, grounded at low water; the Colonel informed Arnold, and asked him for two pieces of heavy cannon, assuring him that he would place them so as to sink her. Arnold eluded the proposal on frivolous pretences, so that the Colonel could only bring one four-pounder, which was at Verplanck's, to bear on her. This piece raked the vessel fore and aft, and did her so much damage, that if she had not got off with the flood tide, she would have had to surrender. The next day, Colonel Livingston, on the shore, saw Arnold pass in his barge, as he was going down the river to get on board the frigate. He declares that he had such a suspicion of him, that had his guard boats been near, he would have gone after him instantly, and asked him where he was going. This question probably would have embarrassed the traitor, and Colonel Livingston's suspicions being thus confirmed, he would have arrested him.[99]

My thoughts were occupied with Arnold and his treason, when my road brought me to Smith's famous house where he had his interview with André and formed his horrid plot.[100] It was in this house that they passed the night together and that André changed his clothes. It was here that the liberty of America was bargained for and sold; and it was here that chance, which is always the arbiter of great events, upset this horrible project, and that, satisfied with sacrificing the imprudent André, she prevented the crime only by saving the criminal. Indeed, André would have been quietly re-crossing the river, to gain New York by White Plains, had not the cannon fired at the frigate made him fear meeting up with the American troops. He imagined that, favored by his disguise, he should be safer on the right [west] bank: a few miles from thence he was stopped, and a few miles farther he found the gibbet.[101]

Smith, who was more than suspected, but not convicted of being a party in the plot, is still in prison, where the law protects him against justice.[102] But his house seems to have experienced the only chastisement of which it was susceptible; it is punished by solitude, and is in fact so deserted that there is not a single person to take care of it, although it is the mansion of a large farm. I pursued my route, but without being able to give so much attention as to recollect it; I only remember that it was as gloomy as my reflections; it brought me into a deep vale, covered with cypresses; a torrent rolled over the rocks; I crossed it, and soon afterwards night came on. I had still some miles to an inn, where I was tolerably well lodged. This inn is situated in Haverstraw, and is kept by another Smith, but who in no way resembles the former; he assured me he was a good Whig, and as he gave me a good supper, I readily believed him.[103]

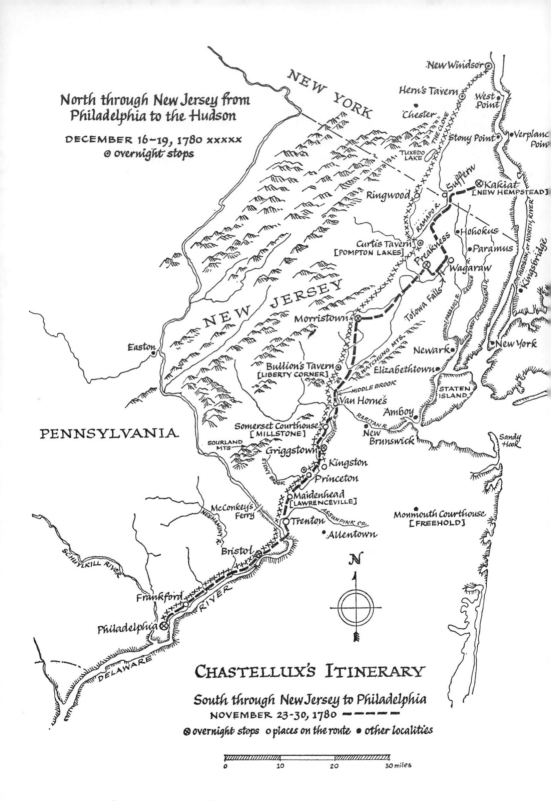

North through New Jersey from Philadelphia to the Hudson

DECEMBER 16–19, 1780 ×××××
⊙ overnight stops

NEW YORK

New Windsor
Hern's Tavern
West Point
Chester
THE CLOVE
Stony Point
Verplanck Point
TUXEDO LAKE
Suffern
Ringwood
Kakiat [NEW HEMPSTEAD]
RAMAPO R.
Hohokus
Curtis Tavern [POMPTON LAKES]
Preakness
Paramus
Wagaraw
Totowa Falls
NEW JERSEY
Morristown
Easton
WATCHUNG MTS
Newark
New York
Bullion's Tavern [LIBERTY CORNER]
Elizabethtown
STATEN ISLAND
MIDDLE BROOK
Van Horne's
Amboy
PENNSYLVANIA
Somerset Courthouse [MILLSTONE]
RARITAN R.
SOURLAND MTS
New Brunswick
Sandy Hook
Griggstown
STONY BROOK
Kingston
Princeton
Maidenhead [LAWRENCEVILLE]
McConkey's Ferry
NESHAMINY R.
Trenton
ASSUNPINK CR.
Monmouth Courthouse [FREEHOLD]
Allentown
Bristol
SCHUYLKILL RIVER
N
Frankford
DELAWARE RIVER
Philadelphia

CHASTELLUX'S ITINERARY

South through New Jersey to Philadelphia
NOVEMBER 23–30, 1780 – – – – –
⊗ overnight stops ○ places on the route • other localities

0   10   20   30 miles

H.C.Rice direx. R.J.Stinely delin. 1963

Chapter

=========== 2 ===========

SOUTH THROUGH NEW JERSEY

November 23, 1780: Kakiat [New Hempstead], N.Y.—Totowa
Falls [Paterson], N.J.—Preakness

THE 23rd I set out at eight o'clock, with the intention of arriving
in good time at the Marquis de La Fayette's camp; for I had
learned from some travelers that the army was not to move that
day, and I wanted him to present me to General Washington.[1]
The shortest road was by way of Paramus; but the guide I had been
given insisted on my taking a more circuitous route, assuring me
that the other road was not safe, that it was infested with Tories,
and that he himself always avoided it when he had letters to carry.[2]
So I took the road to the right, and followed for some time the
Ramapo River; I then turned to the left, and soon got into the
"township" of Pompton and on to the Totowa road; but being informed that this would take me straight to the main body of the
army, without passing by the vanguard commanded by M. de La
Fayette, I inquired for some crossroad which would take me to his
quarters, and one was pointed out to me, by which, passing near a
sort of lake which forms a very agreeable point of view, and then
crossing some very beautiful woods, I arrived at a stream [Goffle
Brook] which flows into Second River [Passaic] exactly at the
spot where M. de La Fayette was encamped.[3] His outposts were
strung along the brook; they were well distributed and in very good
order.

At length I arrived at the camp itself, but M. de La Fayette was
not there: apprised of my coming by the Vicomte de Noailles, he
had gone to wait for me seven miles away, at general headquarters,
to which he thought I was proceeding. He had however sent Major

Gimat and one of his aides-de-camp to meet me, but they had taken the two roads leading to Paramus; so that as a result of both his precautions and those of my guide, I was, as they say in English, completely "disappointed," for it was two o'clock and I had already traveled thirty miles without stopping. I was most impatient to embrace M. de La Fayette, and to see General Washington, but I could not make my horses share my impatience; they would have been frozen to the spot had they heard the suggestion made to me of proceeding directly to headquarters, because, it was said, I might *perhaps* still arrive there in time for dinner. However, I realized the impossibility of this, and being among friends, I asked for some oats for my horses. While they were making this slight repast, I went to see the camp of "the Marquis"; it is thus they call M. de La Fayette, the English language being fond of abridgments, and titles uncommon in America.[4] I found this camp placed in an excellent position; it occupied two heights separated by a small hollow, but with very easy communication between them. The river Totowa or Second River [Passaic] protects the right of the camp, and it is here that it makes a rather sharp bend, and turning towards the south, flows at length into the Bay of Newark. Most of the front and the entire left flank of the camp, to a great distance, are covered by the stream [Saddle River] which comes from Paramus and flows into the main river [Passaic]. This position is not more than twenty miles from the island of New York, and was accordingly occupied by the vanguard, consisting of light infantry, that is to say, by the picked corps of the American army, for the regiments composing this army have no grenadiers, but only a company of light infantry, corresponding to our *chasseurs*, from which battalions are formed at the beginning of each campaign. These troops made a very good appearance, were better clothed than the rest of the army; the uniforms both of the officers and soldiers were smart and military, and each soldier wore a helmet of hard leather, with a crest of horsehair. The officers are armed with spontoons, or rather with half-pikes, and the subalterns with fusils; but both were provided with short and light sabers, brought from France and presented to them by M. de La Fayette.[5] The tents, following the American custom, formed only two ranks; they were very well aligned, as were those of the officers; and as the season was advanced, they all had good fireplaces, but placed differently from ours, for they are built on the outside and conceal the entrance of the tents, which has the double effect of keeping off the wind, and of preserving heat night and day. I saw no stacks of arms, and was informed that the Americans made no use of them. When the weather is fair, each company places its fusils on a wooden horse; but when it rains, they must be brought inside the tents, which is undoubtedly a great disadvantage; this will be remedied when the means of doing it are more abundant, but I greatly fear that this will still not be the case next year.[6]

As I was walking along the front of the camp, I was joined by an officer, who spoke to me in very good French; which was not astonishing, as he turned out to be as much a Frenchman as myself. This was Major Galvan. This officer came to America for commercial business; in this connection he even had some sort of a lawsuit with Congress; but he had the backing of several persons, particularly of the Chevalier de La Luzerne [the French Minister], so that when he asked to enter the service, he obtained the rank of major and the command of a battalion of light infantry. He is a man of abilities, and they are well satisfied with him in the American army.[7] He took me to his tent, where I found a table very neatly spread: he proposed that I dine with him, but I did not accept, imagining I should lose nothing by waiting for the dinner which General Washington would give me. After all that has been said in Europe about the distressed state of the American army, it will perhaps seem extraordinary that such a thing as a dinner was to be found in the tent of a mere major. Doubtless it is impossible to live without money, when everything one eats has to be paid for, and in this respect American officers enjoy no special privileges. But it must be understood that they receive rations of meat, rum, and flour, that they have in each regiment bakers to bake their bread and soldiers to serve them, so that an officer who takes the field with a tent and a sufficiency of clothing may get along very well until winter without having to spend anything. Unfortunately provisions sometimes fail or do not arrive in time; in which case they really suffer, although these are emergencies which do not often occur and which may be avoided in the future, if the states perform their engagements and the Quartermaster General and commissaries do their duty.[8]

I let Mr. Galvan begin his dinner, and went to hasten my horses through theirs, so that I could get to headquarters before dark. Colonel [James] McHenry, whom I have mentioned above, offered to take me there. We kept along the river, which was on our left.

After riding two miles we came in sight of the left of the army. It was also [like the vanguard] encamped on two heights and in one line, in an extended but very good position, having a wood in the rear, and the river in front. This river [Passaic] is difficult to cross except at Totowa Bridge, but the locality would be wholly in favor of an army defending the left [west] bank, as the heights on that side everywhere dominate those on the right [east] bank.[9] Two miles beyond the bridge is a meetinghouse of hexagonal form, the shape given to their churches by the Dutch Presbyterians [Dutch Reformed] who are very numerous in the Jerseys.

I was pursuing my journey, conversing with Mr. McHenry, when I was apprised by a considerable noise that I could not be far from the great cataract known by the name of Totowa Falls.[10] I was torn between my impatience to view this curiosity and my eagerness to be with General Washington; but Mr. McHenry informing me that it would not take me two hundred paces out of my way to see the cataract, I determined to avail myself of the remainder of a fine day, and I had not in fact gone a hundred paces before I had the astonishing spectacle of a great river which hurls itself down a height of seventy feet and is then engulfed in the hollow of a cliff, which seems to swallow it up, but from whence it escapes by turning sharply to the right, as if it were slipping through a secret doorway. It seems to me impossible to give an idea of this waterfall, except by a drawing. Let us however attempt the picture, leaving the finishing to the imagination, which is the rival of Nature, and sometimes also her friend and interpreter. Let the reader imagine, then, a river flowing between mountains covered with spruces, the dark green of which contrasts with the color of its waters and renders its course more majestic; let him then represent to himself an immense rock, which would totally close up the passage, had it not, by some earthquake or other subterranean revolution, been rent in several pieces, from its summit to its base, thus forming long and perfectly vertical crevices. One of these crevices, the depth of which is unknown, may be twenty-five or thirty feet wide. It is into this sort of caldron that the river, after clearing a part of the rock, noisily hurls itself; but as this rock crosses its whole bed, it can only escape by that end which offers it an outlet. There a fresh obstacle appears; another rock opposes its flight, and it is obliged to form a right angle and turn sharp to the left. What is most extraordinary, after this tremendous fall, the river neither froths, nor boils, nor forms whirlpools, but quietly slips off through the channel open to it, and in silence reaches a deep valley, where it pursues its course to the sea. This perfect calm, after such rapid movement, can only proceed from the enormous depth of the cavern into which it plunged and from the great churning in such a restricted space. I did not test the rock with aqua fortis; but as no calcareous stone is found in this country, I take it to be hard rock, and of the nature of quartz; but it presents a peculiarity worthy of attention, which is, that its whole surface is *guilloché*, that is, hollowed into little squares, like old-fashioned *boîtes de Maubois*.[11] Was it in a state of fusion when it was raised from the bowels of the earth and blocked the passage of the river? These vertical crevices, these cracks on the surface, are they a result of its cooling? These are questions I leave to the discussion of the learned: I shall only observe that there is no volcanic appearance here and that throughout this whole region no trace of a volcano is to be seen, at least of such as are posterior to the last epochs of Nature.[12]

Although Mr. McHenry began by being a "doctor" before he was an officer, and is well educated, I did not find him much versed in natural history, and I preferred questioning him on the subject of the army along the front of which I rode, continually meeting with posts who presented arms, drum beating, and officers saluting with the spontoon. All these posts were not for the safety of the army; many of them were stationed to guard houses and barns which served as magazines. At length, after riding two miles beyond the right flank of the army, and after passing through thick woods on the right, I found myself in a little plain, where I saw a rather handsome farm: a small camp which seemed to cover it, a large tent pitched in the yard, and several wagons round it convinced me that this was the headquarters of "his Excellency," for it is thus that Mr. Washington is called in the army and throughout America.[13] M. de La Fayette was conversing in the yard with a tall man, five feet nine inches high,[14] of a noble and mild countenance. It was the General himself. I soon dismounted and approached him. The greetings were brief; the feelings which animated me and his kindly disposition towards me were not feigned. He conducted me into his house, where I found the company still at table, although the dinner had long been over. He presented me to Generals [Henry] Knox, [Anthony] Wayne, [Robert] Howe, etc., and to his "family," then composed of Colonels [Alexander] Hamilton and [Tench]

Tilghman, his secretaries and his aides-de-camp, and of Major [Caleb] Gibbs, commander of his guards; for in England and America, the aides-de-camp, adjutants, and other officers attached to the General form what is called his "family." A fresh dinner was prepared for me and for mine; and the one that had ended was prolonged to keep me company. A few glasses of claret and Madeira accelerated the acquaintances I had to make, and I soon felt myself at my ease near the greatest and the best of men. The goodness and benevolence which characterize him are evident in all that surrounds him; but the confidence he calls forth is never familiar, for the sentiment he inspires has the same origin in every individual, a profound esteem for his virtues and a high opinion of his talents.[15] About nine o'clock the general officers withdrew to their quarters, which were all at a considerable distance; but as the General wished me to make mine in his own house, I remained with him for some time longer, after which he conducted me to the chamber that he had had prepared for my aides-de-camp and me. This chamber represented the fourth part of the lodgings he occupied; he apologized to me for the little space he had at his disposal, but always with a noble politeness, which was neither embarrassing nor excessive.

November 24, 1780: Headquarters at Preakness

At nine the next morning they informed me that his Excellency had come down into the "parlour." This room served both as audience chamber and dining room. I joined him there, and found breakfast prepared. Lord [William Alexander] Stirling came to breakfast with us. He is one of the oldest major generals in the army; his birth, his title and rather extensive estates have given him more importance in America than his talents could ever have acquired for him. The title of "Lord," which was refused him in England, is not here contested: he claims to have inherited this title and went to Europe to support his pretensions, but lost his case. A part of his estate has been dissipated by the war and by his taste for spending; he is accused of liking the table and the bottle, full as much as becomes a Lord, but more than becomes a General. He is brave, but without capacity, and has not been fortunate in the different commands with which he has been entrusted. He was made prisoner at the affair of Long Island [August 1776]; in June 1777 he got into difficulties at Elizabethtown, losing two or three hundred men and three pieces of cannon, while General Washington was facing 20,000 English on the heights of Middle Brook; at Brandywine [September 1777] he commanded the right of the army, or rather the body of troops defeated by Cornwallis; but on all these occasions he displayed great personal courage and firmness. I conversed a long time with him, and found him to be a sensible man, not ill informed of the affairs of his country. He is old and rather dull; but in spite of this he will continue to serve, because military service, though not lucrative, makes up a bit for the disorder in his affairs, and not having quitted the army since the beginning of the war, he has, at least, his zeal and seniority in his favor; thus he will retain the command of the first line, to which his rank entitles him; but care will be taken not to employ him on special expeditions.[16]

While we were at breakfast, horses were brought, and General Washington gave orders for the army to get under arms and form in parade at the head of the camp. The weather was very bad and it had already begun raining; we waited half an hour, but the General seeing that it was more likely to increase than to diminish, determined to get on horseback. The two horses which were brought had been presented to him by the state of Virginia; he mounted one himself and gave me the other. M. Lynch and M. de Montesquieu each had also a very handsome blood horse, such as we could not find at Newport for any price. We repaired to the artillery camp, where General Knox received us: the artillery was numerous, and the gunners, in very fine order, were formed in parade, in the foreign manner, that is, each gunner at his battery and ready to fire. The General was so good as to apologize to me for the cannon not firing to salute me; he told me that having put all the troops on the other side of the [Hudson] river in motion and having informed them that he might himself march along the right [west] bank, he was afraid of giving the alarm and of misleading the detachments that were out. We next reached the right of the army, where we saw the Pennsylvania line; it was composed of two brigades, each forming three battalions, without reckoning the light infantry which was detached with M. de La Fayette. General Wayne, who commanded it, was on horseback, as were the brigadier generals and colonels. They were all well mounted. Their adjutants also had a very martial appearance. They were well ranged and saluted very gracefully. Each brigade had a band of music; the piece they were then playing was the march from *The Huron*.[17] I knew that this

line, though still in want of many things, was the best clothed in
the army; so that his Excellency asking me whether I wanted to
continue seeing the whole army, or go by the shortest road to the
camp of "the Marquis," I accepted this latter proposal. The troops
must have thanked me for this, for the rain was falling with redoubled force; they were dismissed, therefore, and we arrived well
drenched at M. de La Fayette's quarters, where I warmed myself
with great pleasure, partaking, from time to time, of a large bowl
of grog, which is a fixture on his table, and is presented to every
officer who enters. The rain appearing to cease, or inclined to cease
for a moment, we availed ourselves of this opportunity to follow
"his Excellency" to the camp of "the Marquis": we found all his
troops in order of battle on the height at the left, and himself at
their head, expressing by his bearing and countenance that he was
happier in receiving me here than at his estate in Auvergne. The
confidence and attachment of the troops are to him invaluable possessions, well-acquired riches, which nobody can take from him;
but what, in my opinion, is still more flattering for a young man of
his age, is the influence, the consideration he has acquired in the
political, as well as in the military order. I do not fear contradiction
when I say that private letters from him have frequently produced
more effect on some states than the strongest exhortations from
Congress. On seeing him, one is at a loss which most to admire, that
so young a man as he should already have given so many proofs of
ability, or that a man so well tried should still give hopes of so
long a career. Fortunate his country if she knows how to avail herself of them; more fortunate still should she stand in no need of him!

I distinguished with pleasure among the colonels, who were extremely well mounted, and who saluted with great grace, M. de
Gimat, a French officer, over whom I claim the rights of a sort of
military paternity, having brought him up in my regiment from his
earliest youth.[18] This whole vanguard consisted of six battalions,
forming two brigades; but there was only one picket of dragoons
or light cavalry, the remainder having marched to the southward
with Colonel [Henry, "Light-Horse Harry"] Lee. These dragoons
are perfectly mounted, and do not fear meeting the English dragoons, over whom they have gained several advantages;[19] but they
have never been numerous enough to form a solid and permanent
corps. The picket that has been with the main army was then serving as an escort to the provost marshal, and performed the func-

tions of the *maréchaussée*, or military police, until the establishment of a regular one, as was planned.[20]

The rain spared us no more here at the camp of "the Marquis"
than it had at the encampment of the main army; so that our
review being finished, I saw with pleasure General Washington set
off at a gallop to return to his quarters. We reached them as soon
as the badness of the roads would permit us. Upon our return we
found a good dinner ready and about twenty guests, among whom
were Generals Howe and Saint Clair. The meal was in the English
fashion, consisting of eight or ten large dishes of meat and poultry,
with vegetables of several sorts, followed by a second course of
pastry, comprised under the two denominations of "pies" and "pud-
dings." [21] After this the cloth was taken off, and apples and a great
quantity of nuts were served, which General Washington usually
continues eating for two hours, "toasting" and conversing all the
time. These nuts [22] are small and dry, and have so hard a shell that
they can only be cracked with a hammer; they are served half open,
and the company are never done picking and eating them. The conversation was calm and agreeable; his Excellency 'was pleased to
enter with me into the particulars of some of the principal operations of the war, but always with a modesty and conciseness, which
proved that it was from pure politeness that he consented to speak
of himself. About half past seven we rose from table, and immediately the servants came to take it down and shorten it into a smaller
one a quarter the size; for at dinner it was placed diagonally to give
more room. I was surprised at this maneuver, and asked the reason
for it; I was told they were going to lay the cloth for supper. In
half an hour I retired to my chamber, fearing lest the General might
have business, and that he remained in company only on my account; but at the end of another half hour, I was informed that his
Excellency expected me at supper. I returned to the dining room,
protesting strenuously against this supper; but the General told me
he was accustomed to take something in the evening; that if I would
be seated I should only eat some fruit and take part in the conversation. I desired nothing better, for there were then no strangers,
and nobody remained but the General's "family." The supper was
composed of three or four light dishes, some fruit, and above all, a
great abundance of nuts, which were as well received in the evening as at dinner. The cloth being soon removed, a few bottles of
good Bordeaux and Madeira were placed on the table.[23] Every sen-

sible man will be of my opinion, that being a French officer, under the orders of General Washington, and a good Whig to boot, I could not refuse a glass of wine when he offered me one; but I must confess that I had little merit in this complaisance, and that, less accustomed to drink than another, I accommodated myself very well to the English "toast": you have very small glasses, you pour yourself out the quantity of wine you choose, without being pressed to take more, and the "toast" is only a sort of refrain punctuating the conversation, as a reminder that each individual is part of the company and that the whole forms but one society. I observed that there was more solemnity in the toasts at dinner: there were several ceremonious ones; the others were suggested by the General and given out by his aides-de-camp, who performed the honors of the table at dinner, for one of them is seated each day at the head of the table, near the General, to serve all the dishes and distribute the bottles. The toasts in the evening, however, were proposed by Colonel Hamilton, as they occurred to him, without order or formality. After supper the guests are generally asked to propose a "sentiment," that is to say, a lady to whom they are attached by some sentiment, either of love or friendship, or perhaps from preference only.[24] This supper, or conversation, commonly lasted from nine to eleven, always free and always agreeable.

November 25, 1780: Headquarters at Preakness

The weather grew so bad on the 25th, that it was impossible for me to stir out, even to wait on the generals, to whom M. de La Fayette was to conduct me. I easily consoled myself for this, finding it a great luxury to pass a whole day with General Washington, as if he were at home in the country, and had nothing to do. Generals [John] Glover, [Jedidiah] Huntington, and still others, dined with us, as did Colonels [Walter] Stewart and [William] Butler, two officers distinguished in the army. The intelligence received this day caused the proposed attack on Staten Island to be given up.[25] The foraging party under General [John] Stark had indeed met with the most complete success; but, as the enemy did not think proper to disturb him, they had thus not stripped the posts in the quarter where it was intended to attack them. Besides, this expedition could only have been a *coup de main,* and the bad state of the roads as a result of the rains would have made it very difficult. It was therefore decided that the army should march the day after next to its winter quarters, and that I should continue my route to Philadelphia.

November 26, 1780: Headquarters at Preakness

The weather being fair, on the 26th, I got on horseback, after breakfasting with the General. He thoughtfully gave me the horse he had been riding on two days earlier and which I had greatly commended. I found the horse as good as he was handsome, but above all, perfectly well broken and well trained, having a good mouth, easy in hand, and stopping short in gallop without bearing the bit. I mention these minute particulars, because it is the General himself who breaks in all his own horses, and because he is a very excellent and bold horseman, leaping the highest fences, and going extremely quick, without standing upon his stirrups, bearing on the bridle, or letting his horse run wild, as do our young Frenchmen who look upon these things as so essential a part of English horsemanship that they would rather break a leg or an arm than renounce them.

My first visit was to General [Anthony] Wayne, where M. de La Fayette was waiting to conduct me to the other general officers of the line. We were received by General [Jedidiah] Huntington, who appeared rather young for the rank of brigadier general, which he has held two years; his bearing is cold and reserved, but one is not long in perceiving him to be a man of sense and knowledge. We were likewise received by General [John] Glover, about five and forty, a little man, but active and a good soldier; and by General [Robert] Howe, who is one of the oldest major generals, and who enjoys the consideration due to his rank, although, from unfavorable circumstances, he has not been fortunate in war, particularly in Georgia, where he commanded with a very small force, at the time General [Augustine] Prevost took possession of it. He is fond of music, the arts, and pleasure, and has a cultivated mind.[26] I remained a considerable time with him, and saw there a very curious, albeit most hideous, freak of nature. This was a young man of a Dutch family, whose head has become so enormous, that it has taken the whole nourishment from his body and made his hands and arms so weak that he is unable to make use of them. He lies constantly in bed, with his monstrous head supported by a pillow, and as he has long been accustomed to lie on his right side, his right arm is completely withered. He is not a complete imbecile, but has never been able to learn anything, and has no more reason than a child of five or six, though he is twenty-seven years old. This extraordinary derangement of the animal economy proceeds from a dropsy with which he was attacked in his infancy, and which displaced the bones that form the cranium. We know that these bones are joined together by sutures, which are soft in the first period of life, and harden and ossify during adolescence. Such an exuberance, so great an afflux of humour in that which of all the viscera seems to require the most exact proportion, as well in what relates to the life as to the understanding of man, affords stronger proof of the necessity of an equilibrium between the solids and fluids, than of the existence of final causes.[27]

General Knox, whom we had met, and who had thenceforth accompanied us, took us back to headquarters, by way of a short cut through the woods which joined a road leading to his house, where we wished to pay our compliments to Mrs. Knox. We found her settled in a little farm, where she had passed part of the campaign; for she never leaves her husband.[28] A child of six months and a little girl of three formed, in this instance, a real "family" for the General. As for himself, he is a man of thirty-five, very fat, but very active, and of a gay and amiable character. Previous to the war he was a bookseller at Boston, and used to amuse himself by reading the military books in his shop. Such was the origin of the first knowledge he acquired of the art of war, and of the taste he has had ever since for the profession of arms. From the very first campaign, he was entrusted with the command of the artillery, and it has turned out that it could not have been placed in better hands.[29] It was he whom M. du Coudray endeavored to supplant, and he who skillfully brushed him aside. It was perhaps fortunate for M. du Coudray that he was drowned in the Schuylkill rather than in the intrigues he was engaged in, which might have produced great harm.[30]

On our return to headquarters, we found a great many general officers and colonels, with whom we dined. I had an opportunity of conversing more particularly with General [Anthony] Wayne; he has served more than any other officer of the American army, and with the most distinction,[31] though he is still rather young. He is sensible, and his conversation is agreeable and animated. The affair at Stony Point has brought him much honor in the army; however he is still only a brigadier general. This arises from the fact that nominations to the superior ranks are vested in the states to whom the troops belong, and that the state of Pennsylvania has not thought proper to grant any promotions, apparently for reasons of economy. The remainder of the day I devoted to enjoying the company of General Washington, whom I was to leave the next day. He was so good as to map out my journey himself, to send on ahead to have lodgings prepared for me, and to give me a colonel to accompany me as far as Trenton. The next morning all the General's baggage was packed up, which did not hinder us from breakfasting, before we parted, he for his winter quarters [at New Windsor on the Hudson], and I for my journey to Philadelphia.

Here would be the proper place to give the portrait of General Washington, but what can my testimony add to the idea already formed of him? The continent of North America, from Boston to Charleston, is a great book, every page of which presents his praise. I know that since I have had the opportunity of seeing him and observing him at close range, some more particular details may be expected from me; but the strongest characteristic of this respectable man is the perfect harmony which reigns between the physical and moral qualities which compose his personality. One trait alone enables you to judge of all the rest. If you are shown medals of Caesar, of Trajan, or of Alexander, you will still, upon examining their faces, ask what was their stature and the form of their bodies; but if you discover, in a heap of ruins, the head or the limb of an antique Apollo, be not curious about the other parts, but rest assured that they all belong to a God. Let not this comparison be attributed to enthusiasm! It is not my intention to exaggerate. I wish only to express the impression General Washington has left on my mind, the idea of a perfect whole, that cannot be the product of enthusiasm, which rather would reject it, since the effect of proportion is to diminish the idea of greatness. Brave without temerity, laborious without ambition, generous without prodigality, noble without pride, virtuous without severity, he seems always to have confined himself within those limits, where the virtues, by clothing themselves in more lively, but more changeable and doubtful colors, may be mistaken for faults. This is the seventh year that he has commanded the army, and that he has obeyed Congress; more need not be said, especially in America, where they know how to appreciate all the merit contained in this simple fact. Let it be repeated that Condé was intrepid, Turenne prudent, Eugene adroit, Catinat disinterested. It is not thus that Washington will be characterized. It will be said of him, *At the end of a long civil war, he had nothing with which he could reproach himself*. If anything can be more marvellous than such a character, it is the unanimity of the public suffrages in his favor. Soldier, Magistrate, People, all love and admire him; all speak of him only in terms of affection and veneration. Can we then conclude that some virtue capable of restraining man's injustice really does exist; or are glory and happiness too recently established in America, for Envy to have deigned to cross the seas?

In speaking of this perfect whole of which General Washington furnishes the idea, I have not excluded exterior form. His stature is noble and lofty, he is well built, and exactly proportioned; his physiognomy mild and agreeable, but such as to render it impossible to speak particularly of any one of his features, so that on leaving him, you have only the recollection of a fine face. He has neither a grave nor a familiar air, his brow is sometimes marked with thought, but never with worry; in inspiring respect, he inspires confidence, and his smile is always the smile of benevolence.[32]

But it is interesting, above all, to see him in the midst of the general officers of his army. General in a republic, he has not the imposing pomp of a *Maréchal de France* who gives *the order;* a hero in a republic, he excites another sort of respect, which seems to spring from the sole idea that the safety of each individual is attached to his person. Furthermore, I must observe on this occasion, that the general officers of the American army have a very military and a very becoming bearing; and even that all the officers, whose functions bring them into public view, unite much politeness to a great deal of ability; that the headquarters of this army, in short, presents neither the picture of inexperience, nor of want. When one sees the battalion of the General's guards encamped within the precincts of his house; nine wagons, destined to carry his baggage, ranged in his yard; a great number of grooms holding very fine horses belonging to the general officers and their aides-de-camp; when one observes the perfect order that reigns within these precincts where the guards are exactly stationed, and where the drummers beat a reveille and a special retreat, one is tempted to apply to the Americans what Pyrrhus said of the Romans: *Truly these people have nothing barbarous in their discipline!* [33]

November 27, 1780: Preakness—Morristown

The reader will perceive that it is difficult for me to leave General Washington: let us make up our minds briskly then, and suppose ourselves on the road. Behold me traveling with Colonel [Stephen] Moylan, whom his Excellency had given me, in spite of my protests, as a companion, and whom I should have been glad to have seen at a distance, for one cannot be too much at one's ease when traveling. However, I had to make the best of the situation: I began to question him, he to answer me, and the conversation gradually becoming more interesting, I found I had to do with the most gallant possible man, an educated man who had lived long in Europe, and who has traveled through most of America. I found him perfectly polite; for his politeness was not bothersome, and I soon conceived a great friendship for him. Mr. Moylan is an Irish Catholic; he even has a brother [Francis] who is Bishop of Cork; he has four others, two of whom are merchants, one at Cadiz, the other at Lorient; the third is in Ireland with his family; and the fourth is intended for the priesthood.[34] As for himself, he came to settle in America some years ago, where he was at first engaged in commerce; he then served in the army as aide-de-camp to the General, and has merited the command of the light cavalry. During the war he married the daughter of a rich merchant in the Jerseys, who formerly lived in New York, and who now resides on an estate not far from the road we were to take the next day. He proposed that I should go and sleep there, or at least to take dinner; I begged to be excused, from the fear of being obliged to pay compliments or of inconveniencing others, or of being myself inconvenienced; and he did not insist. I pursued my journey, sometimes through fine woods, at others through well-cultivated lands and hamlets inhabited by Dutch families. One of these villages, which forms a little "township," bears the beautiful name of Troy. Here the country is more open and continues so to Morristown. This town, celebrated for the winter quarters of 1779,[35] is about three and twenty miles from Preakness, the name of the headquarters I had just left. It is situated on a height, at the foot of which runs the stream called the Whippany River; the houses are handsome and well built; there are about sixty or eighty round the meetinghouse. I intended stopping at Morristown only to bait my horses, for it was but half past two, but on entering the inn of Mr. [Jacob] Arnold, I saw a dining room adorned with looking glasses and handsome mahogany furniture, and a table spread for twelve persons.[36] I learned that all this preparation was for me; and what affected me even more was to see a dinner, worthy of these appearances, ready to be served. I was indebted for this to the kindness of General Washington, and the precautions of Colonel Moylan, who had sent ahead to acquaint them with my arrival. It would have been very ungracious to have left this dinner, with Mr. Arnold standing the expense, for he is an honest man and a good Whig, who has nothing in common with Benedict Arnold; it would have been still more awkward to have paid for the banquet without eating it. I quickly took counsel, therefore, and determined to dine and sleep in this comfortable inn. I may perhaps be asked why the twelve covers? Because the Vicomte de Noailles, the Comte de Damas, etc., were expected to make up the dozen; but these young travelers, who had reckoned on witnessing some skirmishes during their stay with the army, were desirous of indemnifying themselves by riding along the bank of the [Hudson] river, to take a look at the island of New York and see if they could not tempt the enemy to favor them with a few shots. M. de La Fayette himself had taken them there, with an escort of twenty dragoons. They therefore deferred for a day their journey to Philadelphia, and I had no other guests but a secretary and an aide-de-camp of M. de La Fayette, who arrived as I was at table, most willing to substitute for those absent.

After dinner I had a visit from General [Arthur] St. Clair, whom I had already seen at the army, which he had left the preceding day to sleep at Morristown. It was he who commanded on Lake Champlain, at the time of the evacuation of Ticonderoga [July 1777]. A terrible clamor was raised against him on that occasion, and he was tried by a council of war, but *honorably acquitted*,[37] not only because his retreat was attended with the happiest consequences, Burgoyne having been forced to capitulate, but also because it was proved that he had been left in want of everything necessary for the defense of the post entrusted to him. He was born in Scotland, where he still has a family and property; he is considered a good officer, and, if the war continues, will certainly play a principal part in the army.[38]

November 28, 1780: Morristown—Middle Brook—Somerset Court-house [Millstone]—Griggstown

I set out from Morristown the 28th, at eight in the morning, with very lowering weather, which did not hinder me, however, from observing, to the right of the road, the huts occupied by the troops in the winter of 1779-80. Some miles from there, we met a man on horseback, who was coming to meet Colonel Moylan with a letter from his wife. After reading it, he said to me, with truly European politeness, that we must always defer to the women; that his wife "admitted no excuse" and was expecting me to dinner; but he assured me that he would take me by a road which would not be a mile out of my way, while my people pursued their journey and went to wait for me at Somerset Courthouse [Millstone]. I was now too well acquainted with my Colonel, and too much pleased with him, to refuse this invitation. I followed him, therefore, and after crossing a wood, found myself on a height, the position of which struck me at first sight. I remarked to Colonel Moylan that I was much mistaken if this spot was not well suited for an advantageous camp. He replied that it was indeed the site of the Middle Brook camp, where General Washington had stopped the English in June 1777, when Sir William Howe was endeavoring to traverse the Jerseys in order to cross the Delaware and take Philadelphia.[39] Continuing my journey, and looking about me as far as my view would reach, the shape alone of the ground made me imagine that the right could not be very good; I also learned with pleasure that General Washington had built two strong redoubts there. The reader will permit me the following short reflection, that the best method for military men, in following on the ground the campaigns of great generals, is not to have the different positions pointed out and explained to them: it is much better, before they are made acquainted with these details, to visit the places, to look well about on every side, and to propose to themselves little problems on the nature of the ground and on the advantages to be derived from it; then to compare their ideas with the facts, by which means they will be enabled to rectify the former, and to appreciate the latter.

On descending from the heights, we turned a little to the left and found ourselves on the banks of a stream, which led us into a deep vale.[40] The various cascades formed by this stream as it flows along, or rather as it plunges over the rocks; the ancient fir trees with which it is surrounded, a part of which have fallen from age and lie across its course; the furnaces belonging to some copper mines but half destroyed by the English; these ruins of nature and these ravages of war, composed the most poetic, or according to the English expression, the most romantic picture; for it is precisely what is called in England "a Romantick prospect." It is here that Colonel Moylan's father-in-law has fitted up a little rural retreat, where his family go to avoid the heats of the summer, and where they sometimes pass the night to listen to the song of the "mocking bird," for no nightingales sing in America. We know that great musicians are oftener to be found at the courts of despots than in republics. Here the songster of the night is neither the graceful Millico, nor the pathetic Tenducci; he is rather the jester, Caribaldi.[41] He has no song of his own, and consequently no sentiment peculiar to himself; he counterfeits in the evening all that he has heard during the day. If he has listened to the lark or the thrush, it is the lark or the thrush that you hear. If workmen have been employed in the woods, or he has been near their house, he will sing precisely as they do. If they are Scotch, he will repeat you the air of some gentle and plaintive "romance"; if they are Germans, you will recognize the clumsy gaiety of a Swabian, or of an Alsatian. Sometimes he cries like a child, at others he laughs like a young girl. Nothing, in short, is more entertaining than this comedian of a bird, but he performs only in summer, and so I have not yet had the good fortune to hear him.[42]

After traveling two miles in this sort of gorge, the woods begin to open, and you soon find yourself out of the mountains. On the brow of these mountains, to the south, the huts occupied by a part of the army in 1778 after the battle of Monmouth, were pointed out to me.[43] We soon arrived at Colonel Moylan's, or rather at Colonel Van Horne's, his father-in-law. This manor, for the house resembles closely what is called "a manor" in England, is in a beautiful situation; it is surrounded by some trees, the approach is adorned with a grassplot, and if this lawn were better taken care of, one would think oneself in the neighborhood of London rather than in that of New York.[44] Mr. Van Horne came to meet me: he is a tall, stout man, near sixty years of age, but vigorous, hearty, and good humored; he is called Colonel because he held this rank in the militia under the English government. He resigned some time before the war: he was then a merchant and farmer, spending the winter in New York and the summer in the country; but since the war he has left the city and retired to his manor, remaining faithful to his country, without rendering himself odious to the English, with whom he has left two of his sons who are in business at Jamaica, but who, if the war continues, are to sell their property there and come to rejoin their father. Nothing can prove more strongly the integrity of his conduct than the esteem in which he is held by both sides.[45] Situated ten miles from Staten Island, near the Raritan River, Amboy, and Brunswick, he has frequently found himself in the midst of the theater of war; so that he has sometimes had the Americans with him, sometimes the English. It even happened to him once in the same day, to give breakfast to Lord Cornwallis and dinner to General [Benjamin] Lincoln. Lord Cornwallis, informed that the latter had slept at Mr. Van Horne's, came to take him by surprise; but Lincoln, warned in time, retired into the woods. Lord Cornwallis, astonished not to find him, asked if the American General was not concealed in the house. "No," replied Mr. Van Horne, bluntly. "On your honor?" said Cornwallis. "On my honor, and if you doubt it, here are the keys, you may search everywhere." "I shall take your word for it," said Lord Cornwallis, and asked for some breakfast; an hour afterwards he returned to the army. Lincoln, who was concealed at no great distance, immediately returned, and dined quietly with his hosts.[46]

My meeting with Mr. Van Horne having been prompt and cordial, he at once conducted me to the parlor where I found his wife, his three daughters, a young lady of the neighborhood, and two young officers. Mrs. Van Horne is an old lady, who, from her countenance, her dress, and her deportment, perfectly resembles a painting by Vandyck. She punctiliously does the honors of her house, presides over her table without saying a word, and the rest of the time she is merely there, like a family portrait. Her three daughters are not unattractive: Mrs. Moylan, the eldest, is six months advanced in her pregnancy; the youngest is only twelve years old, but the second is marriageable. She appeared to be on terms of great familiarity with one of the young officers, who was in a very elegant undress, and reminded me very much of an agreeable "country squire"; at table he cracked nuts for her, and often held her hands. I imagined that he was an intended husband, but the other officer, with whom I later had the opportunity of conversing, as he accompanied us in the evening, told me he did not believe there was any idea of marriage between them. I mention these trifles only to show the extreme liberty that prevails in this country between the two sexes, as long as they are not married. It is no crime for a girl to kiss a young man; it would indeed be one for a married woman even to show a desire of pleasing.[47] Mrs. Carter,[48] a young and pretty woman, whose husband is concerned in furnishing our army with provisions, and lives at present at Newport, once told me that, going down one morning into her husband's office, not much dressed up, but in a rather elegant informal French dress, a farmer from Massachusetts, who was there on business, seemed surprised at seeing her, and asked who this young lady might be. He was told that it was Mrs. Carter. "Well!" he replied, loud enough for her to hear him, "If she's a wife and a mother, she shouldn't be so well dressed."

At three o'clock I got back on horseback, with Colonel Moylan and Captain "Hern" [John Heard], one of the young officers I had dined with. He is in the light cavalry, and consequently in Colonel Moylan's regiment [4th Continental Dragoons]. His size and figure, which I had already remarked, appeared to still more advantage when he was on horseback. I observed that he was seated in a very noble and easy manner, and in perfect conformity to our principles of horsemanship. I asked him where he had learned to ride. He told me that it was in his own regiment, that his desire to teach his soldiers induced him to learn for himself, and that he made it his business to render them as expert in the exercise as he was. Though but twenty-one, he had already acquired experience, and had distinguished himself the preceding year, in an affair where a small body of American light-horse beat a much more considerable one of English dragoons. I had a long conversation with him, and he always spoke to me with a modesty and a grace which would be favorably received by all the military in Europe, and which, to all appearances, would be as successful in Paris as in the camps.

We had scarcely proceeded three miles before we found ourselves in the Princeton road, and on the banks of the Raritan, which may be easily crossed by fording, or over a wooden bridge. Two miles farther along we crossed the Millstone, the left [west] bank of which we followed to Somerset Courthouse [Millstone]. Of all the parts of America through which I have passed, this is the most open; you find pretty little plains here, where from fifteen to twenty thousand men might be encamped. General Howe had not less when he crossed the Raritan in 1777. His right was supported by a wood, beyond which runs the Millstone; his left also extended towards other woods. General Washington at that time occupied the camp at Middle Brook, and General [John] Sullivan, at the head of only 1500 men, was six miles from the army and three miles from the enemy's left. In this position he was near enough to harass them, without committing himself, as he had in his rear the Sourland Mountains. Those who had occasion to pass through Sauerland during the last war will easily believe that the country to which the German emigrants have given this name is not very easy of access.[49] I found my suite at Somerset Courthouse [Millstone], where they were waiting for me in a fairly good inn, but as there was still some daylight, and I had calculated my next day's journey, which required that I should gain time today, I determined to proceed further. The night, which soon came on, prevented me from making any more observations of the country. After once more crossing the Millstone, and having successfully gotten through a horrible slough, we halted at "Greeg-Town" [Griggstown], where we slept at Skillman's Tavern, an indifferent inn, but kept by very obliging people. Captain Heard left us here and continued his route.

*November 29, 1780: Griggstown–Princeton–Trenton, N.J.–
     Bristol, Pa.*

Our next day's ride presented us with very interesting objects: we were to see two places which will forever be dear to the Americans, since it was there that the first rays of hope gleamed before their eyes, or, to express it more properly, that the salvation of the country was effected. These celebrated places are Princeton and Trenton. I shall not say that I was going especially to see them, for they lay exactly in my path. Let the reader judge then how much I was out of humor, on seeing so thick a fog rising, as to prevent me from distinguishing objects at fifty paces from me; but I was in the country where hope springs eternal. The fortune of the day was like that of America: the fog suddenly dispersed, and I found myself traveling on the right [east] bank of the Millstone, in a rather narrow valley. Two miles from Griggstown you go up out of this valley on to the height of Rocky Hill, where a few houses are grouped. Kingston is a mile farther along, beside the Millstone; the road from Maidenhead [Lawrenceville] comes in here, and this junction is facilitated by a bridge built over the rivulet.

It was here that General Washington halted after the affair of Princeton. After marching from midnight until two o'clock in the afternoon, fighting nearly the whole time, he wanted to reassemble his troops and give them some rest; he knew, however, that Lord Cornwallis was following him along the Maidenhead road; but he merely removed a few planks from the bridge and as soon as he saw the vanguard of the English appear, he calmly continued his march [northward along the Millstone valley] towards Middle Brook. Beyond Kingston the country becomes more open and continues so as far as Princeton. This town is situated on a sort of plateau, not very high, but which dominates the country on all sides. It has only one street formed by the high road; there are about sixty or eighty houses, all rather well built, but you scarcely notice them, for your attention is immediately attracted by an immense building which is visible from a considerable distance. This is a college built by the state of Jersey some years before the war.[50] As this building is remarkable only for its size, it is unnecessary to describe it; the reader will need only to recall, when I come to speak of the battle, that it is on the left of the road when going towards Philadelphia, that it is situated towards the middle of the town, on an isolated spot of ground, and that the entrance to it is through a large square yard surrounded by high fences.

The object of my curiosity, though far removed from letters, having brought me to the very gate of the college, I dismounted to visit for a moment this vast edifice. I was almost immediately joined by Mr. Witherspoon, president of the university.[51] He is a man of at least sixty, is a member of Congress, and much respected in this country. In accosting me he spoke French, but I easily perceived that he had acquired his knowledge of the language from reading rather than conversation; which did not prevent me, however, from answering him and continuing to converse with him in French, for I saw that he was well pleased to display what he knew of it. This is a courtesy which costs little, and is too frequently neglected by travelers in a foreign country. To reply in English to a person who speaks French to you, is to tell him "you do not know my language so well as I do yours": in which, however, you can often be mistaken. As for myself, I always prefer to have the advantage on my side, and to fight on my own ground. I conversed in French, therefore, with the president, and from him I learned that this college is a complete university; that it can contain two hundred students, and more, if the outboarders are included; that the distribution of studies is made in such a way that there is only one class for the "humanities," which corresponds to our first four classes; that two others are devoted to perfecting the young men in the study of Latin and Greek; a fourth to natural philosophy,[52] mathematics, astronomy, etc.; and a fifth to moral philosophy. Parents may support their children at this college at the annual expense of forty guineas. Half of this sum is appropriated to lodgings and masters; the rest is sufficient for meals, either in the college itself, or at board in private houses in the town. This useful establishment has fallen into decline since the war; there were only forty students when I saw it. A fairly extensive collection of books had been gathered; most of these have been scattered.[53] The English even carried off from the chapel the portrait of the King of England, a loss for which the Americans easily consoled themselves, declaring they would have no King among them, not even a painted one.[54] There still remains a very beautiful astronomical machine; but as it was then out of order, and differs in no respect from the one I saw afterwards in Philadelphia, I shall dispense with describing it here.[55]

I confess also that I was rather impatient to seek out the traces of General Washington, in a country where every object recalled his successes. I passed rapidly therefore from Parnassus to the field of Mars, and from the hands of President Witherspoon into those of Colonel Moylan. They were both upon their own ground; so that while one was pulling me by the right arm, telling me, "Here is the philosophy classroom," the other was plucking me by the left, telling me, "This is where one hundred and eighty English laid down their arms."

Anybody who, since the commencement of the war, has merely taken the trouble to read the gazettes will recall that General Washington surprised the town of Trenton the 25th of December, 1776; that, immediately after this expedition, he retired to the other side of the Delaware, but that having received a small addition to his forces, he recrossed the river again, and encamped at Trenton. Lord Cornwallis had then collected his troops, previously dispersed, in winter quarters. He marched against Washington, who was obliged to place the Assunpink, or Trenton River, between the enemy and himself. By this means the town was divided between the two armies; the Americans occupying the left [eastern] bank of the creek, and the English the right. Lord Cornwallis's army was daily receiving reinforcements; two brigades from [New] Brunswick were expected to join him, and he only waited their arrival to make the attack.[56] General Washington, on the other hand, was destitute of provisions, and cut off from all communications with the fertile country of the Jerseys, and the four eastern states. Such was his position, when, on January 2 [1777], at one o'clock in the morning, he ordered the fires to be kept up and some soldiers left to take care of them, while the remainder of the army would march by the right, to fall back afterwards on the left, pass the rear of the English army, and enter the Jerseys.[57] It was necessary to throw themselves considerably to the right, in order to reach Allentown and the sources of the Assunpink, and then to fall on Princeton. About a mile [south] from this latter town, General Washington's vanguard, on entering the main highway, met up with Colonel Mawhood, who was marching quietly at the head of his [British] regiment on his way to Maidenhead [Lawrenceville], and thence to Trenton. General [Hugh] Mercer immediately attacked him, but was repulsed by the enemy's fire; he then attempted to charge with the bayonet, but unfortunately, in leaping a ditch, was surrounded and put to the sword by the English. The troops, who were in general only militia, discouraged by the loss of their commander, retreated into the woods, to wait for the remainder of the army, which arrived soon after: but Colonel Mawhood had continued his route towards Maidenhead, so that General Washington had only to cope with the 48th Regiment, part of which had appeared upon the main road at the sound of the first attack. He pushed these troops vigorously, dispersed them, and made fifty or sixty prisoners.

Meanwhile, General [John] Sullivan was advancing rapidly, leaving on his left the Princeton road, with the design of turning that town, and of cutting off the line of retreat to [New] Brunswick still open to the English troops occupying Princeton. Two hundred English had thrown themselves into a wood through which he had to pass, but they did not remain there long, and returned in disorder to Nassau Hall, the name of the college I have spoken of. They could have taken possession of it, and made there a vigorous defense. To all appearances their officers lost their heads, for instead of entering the building, or even the yard, they remained in a sort of wide street, where they were surrounded and obliged to lay down their arms, to the number of one hundred and eighty men, not including fourteen officers. As for General Washington, after taking or dispersing everything before him, he collected his troops, marched on to Kingston, where he halted, as I have already mentioned, and then continued his route towards Middle Brook; he had thus marched near thirty miles in one day, but still regretted that his troops were too much fatigued to proceed to [New] Brunswick, which he could have then taken without any difficulty. Lord Cornwallis had now nothing better to do than to return thither with his whole army. From this moment on, Pennsylvania was in safety, the Jerseys were evacuated, and the English confined to the towns of [New] Brunswick and Amboy, where they were always on the defensive, not being able to stir, nor even to forage, without being driven back and roughly handled by the militia of the country. Thus we see that the great events of war are not always great battles, and humanity may receive some consolation from this sole reflection, that the art of war is not necessarily a sanguinary art, that the talents of the commanders spare the lives of the soldiers, and that ignorance alone is prodigal of blood.

The affair at Trenton, to which the one at Princeton was the sequel, cost no dearer, and was perhaps more glorious, without being more useful. Addison said, when visiting the different monuments of Italy, that he imagined himself treading on "classic" ground; as for myself I was treading on martial ground, and was in the same morning to see two fields of battle. I arrived early at Trenton, having remarked nothing interesting on the road, unless it be the beauty of the country, which everywhere corresponds to the reputation of the Jerseys, called the garden of America. On approaching Trenton, the road descends a little, and permits one to see at the east end of this town the orchard where the Hessians hastily collected, and gave themselves up as prisoners. This is almost all that can be said of this affair, which has been amplified by the gazettes on one side and the other. We know that General Washington, at the head of only three thousand men, crossed the Delaware in dreadful weather, on the night of the 24th and 25th of December; that he divided his troops into two columns, one of which made a circuit to gain a road upon the left, leading into the main road to Maidenhead [Lawrenceville], while the other column marched along the [Delaware] river straight to Trenton; that the main guard of the Hessians was surprised; and that the brigade had scarcely time to get under arms. The artillery was parked near a church; they were attempting to harness the horses, when the American vanguard, which had forced the picket, fired on, and killed almost all of them. General Washington arrived with the right column; the Hessians were surrounded, and fired a few random shots, without order. General Washington suffered them to do so, but he availed himself of the first moment of the slackening of their fire, to send an officer who spoke to them in French, for our language it is that supplements all others. The Hessians hearkened very willingly to his proposal. The General promised that the effects they had left in their houses should not be pillaged, and they straightway laid down their arms, which they had scarcely had time to take up. Their position was certainly not a good one; nor can I conceive it possible that this could be an appropriate field of battle in case of an alarm. They would indeed have had a sure retreat by crossing the bridge over the [Assunpink] creek at the south end of the town, but the vanguard of the American right column had got possession of it. Such, in a few words, was this event, which is neither honorable nor dishonorable to the Hessians; but which merely proves that no troops existing can be relied on when they have let themselves be surprised.

After viewing so many battles, it was but right to think of dinner. I found my headquarters well established in a fine inn kept by Mr. [Rensselaer] Williams.[58] The sign of this inn is a philosophical, or, if you will, a political emblem. It represents a beaver at work, with his little teeth bringing down a large tree, and underneath is written, *perseverando*.[59] I had scarcely alighted from my horse before I received a visit from Mr. [William] Livingston, Governor of the two Jerseys.[60] He is a much respected old man, and considered a very sensible one. He was pleased to accompany me on a little walk I took before dinner, to reconnoiter the environs of the town and see the camp occupied by the Americans before the affair of Princeton. I returned to dinner with Colonel Moylan, M. de Gimat, and two aides-de-camp of M. de La Fayette, who had arrived some time before me. We were all acquainted, very happy to be together and to dine at our ease, when a justice of the peace, who was at Trenton on business, and an American artillery captain came and sat down at the table with us, without any ceremony; it being the custom of the country for travelers when they meet at the hour of dinner, to dine together. The dinner, of which I did the honors, was excellent, but they did not seem to realize that it was I who had ordered it. There was wine on the table, a very rare and dear article in America; they drank moderately of it, and rose from the table before we did. I had given orders that the dinner should be charged to me; they learned this on going out, but set off without saying a word to me on the subject. I have often had occasion to observe that there are more ceremonies than compliments in America. All their politeness is mere form, such as drinking healths to the company, observing ranks, giving up the right of way, etc. But all this comes only from what they have been taught, none of it arises from feeling; in a word, politeness here is like religion in Italy, all in practice and nothing from principle.

At four o'clock I set out again, after separating, but not without regret, from the good Colonel Moylan. I took the road to Bristol, crossing the river three miles below Trenton.[61] Six miles from there you pass through a wood and then come closer to the Delaware, which you do not leave for the rest of the way to Bristol. It was night when I got to this town. The inn where I stopped is kept by a Mr. Benezet [Bessonett], of French extraction, and of a very respectable Quaker family; but he is a deserter from their communion, being an Anglican, and has retained none of the acknowledged principles of his brethren, except that of making you pay dearer than other people. In other respects his inn is handsome, the windows look out upon the Delaware, and the view from them is superb; for this river is nearly a mile broad, and flows through a very delightful country.[62]

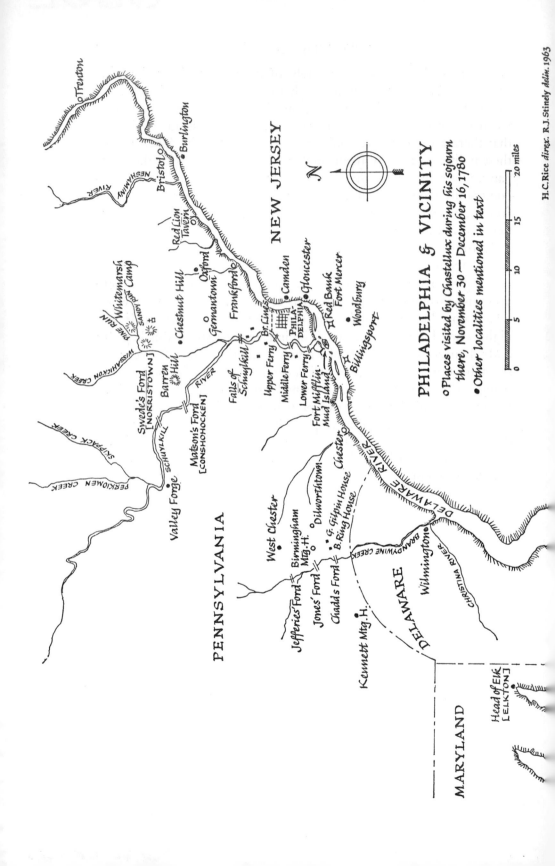

Trenton

Burlington

Bristol

NESHAMINY RIVER

Red Lion Tavern

Chestnut Hill

Oxford

Germantown

Frankford

Camden

Gloucester

Red Bank

Fort Mercer

Woodbury

Billingsport

Whitemarsh Camp

SANDY RUN

PINE RUN

WISSAHICKON CREEK

Barren Hill

Swede's Ford [NORRISTOWN]

Matson's Ford [CONSHOHOCKEN]

Falls of Schuylkill

SCHUYLKILL RIVER

Upper Ferry
Br. Lines
Middle Ferry
PHILADELPHIA
Lower Ferry
Fort Mifflin
Mud Island

NEW JERSEY

PERKIOMEN CREEK

SKIPPACK CREEK

Valley Forge

PENNSYLVANIA

West Chester

Birmingham Mtg. H.
Dilworthtown
G. Gilpin House
Chester
B. Ring House

Jefferies Ford
Jones' Ford
Chadd's Ford

Kennett Mtg. H.

DELAWARE

Wilmington

BRANDYWINE CREEK

DELAWARE RIVER

CHRISTINA RIVER

MARYLAND

Head of Elk [ELKTON]

PHILADELPHIA & VICINITY

o Places visited by Chastellux during his sojourn
  there, November 30 — December 16, 1780
• Other localities mentioned in text

N

0   5   10   15   20 miles

H.C.Rice direx. R.J.Stinely delin. 1963

Chapter

3

PHILADELPHIA AND VICINITY

November 30, 1780: Bristol, Pa.—Philadelphia

I LEFT Bristol the 30th of November, between nine and ten in the morning, and arrived at Philadelphia at two. The road leading to this city is very wide and handsome; one passes through several small towns and villages, nor can one go five hundred paces without seeing beautiful country houses. As you advance you find a richer and better cultivated country, with a great number of orchards and pastures; everything, in short, indicates the neighborhood of a large town, and this road is not unlike those leading into London. Four miles from Bristol you cross over Neshaminy Creek on a ferry. It is fairly wide, and runs in such a direction as to form a sort of peninsula of the country lying between it and the Delaware. It seemed to me from viewing the country and from inspecting the map, that at the time of General Clinton's retreat [in June 1778] General Washington might have crossed the sources of this river and then marched along it towards the Delaware. It would have covered his right flank, and, in this way he would have been free to approach the Delaware and could have crossed it as soon as Clinton. M. de Gimat, to whom I made this observation, answered me that General Washington never being sure of the moment when the English would evacuate Philadelphia, was afraid of moving far from Lancaster, where he had all his stores.

The town of Frankford, which is about fifteen miles from Bristol, and five from Philadelphia, is fairly sizable. A creek runs in the front of this town, over which are two stone bridges; for it divides itself into two branches, one of which appeared to me to be artificial and designed to turn a great number of mills that supply Philadelphia with flour. These mills, so necessary for the subsistence of the two armies, made the town of Frankford for a long time an object of contention, which gave rise to several skirmishes; but the position is such as to have been advantageous to neither party, for the river runs in a bottom, and the ground is of equal height on both sides.

The nearer you approach to Philadelphia, the more you discover the traces of the war. The ruins of houses destroyed, or burned, are the monuments the English have left behind them, but these ruins present only a picture of temporary misfortune, and not that of long adversity. By the side of these ruined edifices, those still standing indicate prosperity and plenty. You imagine you are in the country after a storm: some trees have been blown down, but the others are still clothed with flowers and verdure. Before entering Philadelphia, you cross the lines thrown up by the English in the winter of 1777-78; they are still discernible in many places.[1] The part of the lines I now saw was that of the right, the flank of which is supported by a large redoubt, or square battery, which also commands the river. Some parts of the parapet were constructed with much refinement, which however increases labor more than it strengthens fortifications: these works are in the form of a saw, that is to say, composed of a series of small redans, or teeth, each of which is capable of containing only three men. As soon as I had crossed these lines my eye was struck by several large buildings; the two principal ones were a range of barracks constructed by the English, and a large hospital previously built at the expense of the Quakers.[2] Imperceptibly I found myself in the town, and after following three or four very wide and perfectly straight streets, I arrived at the door of M. le Chevalier de La Luzerne.[3]

It was just twenty days since I had left Newport, during which time I had traveled continuously except for the day spent at Voluntown, and the three days with the American army [at Preakness]. I was not sorry therefore to get into rest quarters, and could not wish for any more agreeable than the house of the Chevalier de La Luzerne. I had ample time to converse with him before dinner, for at Philadelphia, as in London, it is the custom to dine at five, and frequently at six. I should have liked it as well had the company not been so numerous, so that I might have made acquaintance with a part of the town; but our Minister maintains a considerable state, and frequently gives large dinners, so that it is difficult not to fall into this sort of ambuscade. The guests whose names I recollect were:

Mr. Gouverneur Morris,[4] a young man full of wit and vivacity, but unfortunately maimed, having lost a leg by accident. His friends have congratulated him on this event, saying that he would now devote himself wholly to public business.

Mr. [Samuel] Powel, a man of considerable fortune, but without any part in the government, his attachment to the common cause having hitherto appeared rather equivocal.

Mr. [Henry] Pendleton, a judge from South Carolina, a remarkably tall man, with a very distinguished countenance; he had the courage to hang three Tories at Charleston, a few days before the surrender of the town [in May 1780], and was accordingly in great danger of losing his life, had he not escaped out of the hands of the English, though included in the capitulation.[5]

Colonel [John] Laurens, son of Mr. [Henry] Laurens, formerly President of Congress and now a prisoner in the Tower of London; he speaks very good French, which is not surprising, as he was educated at Geneva; but it is more surprising that being married in London, he should have left England to serve America; he has distinguished himself on several occasions, particularly at Germantown where he was wounded.[6]

Mr. [William] White, chaplain to Congress, a handsome man, and of a mild and tolerant character.[7]

General [Thomas] Mifflin, whose talents have shone alike in war and politics; he has been Quartermaster General of the army, but quitted that place on account of some preference shown to General [Nathanael] Greene.[8]

Don Francisco [Rendón], chargé d'affaires of Spain, and I believe that is all that can be said of him.

M. de Ternant, a French officer in the service of America; he had been employed in some business enterprises in America, and after executing them, he took employment in the army; he is a young man of great wit and talents; he draws well, and speaks English like his own language; he was made prisoner at Charleston.[9]

The last whose name I recollect is Colonel Armand, that is, M. de La Rouërie, nephew of M. de La Belinaye. He was as celebrated in France for his passion for Mademoiselle B * * * [Beaumesnil], as he is in America for his courage and capacity. His family having compelled him to abandon an attachment the consequences of which they dreaded, he was about to bury himself in a celebrated and deep monastic solitude, but he soon left it to go to America, where he has subjected himself to a more glorious abstinence, and to more meritorious mortifications. His character is gay, his wit agreeable, and nobody would wish to see him take the vow of silence.[10]

Such were the guests with whom I got acquainted; for I do not speak of M. de Dannemours, consul of France at Baltimore, of M. de Marbois, secretary of the embassy, nor of the "family" of M. de La Luzerne, which is rather numerous. The dinner was served in the American, or if you will, in the English fashion; consisting of two courses, one including the entrées, roast, and warm side dishes; the other, the sweet pastries and preserves. When the second course is removed, the cloth is taken off, and apples, walnuts, and chestnuts are served; it is then that healths are drunk; the coffee which comes afterwards serves as a signal to rise from table. These healths, or "toasts," as I have already observed, have no inconvenience, and only serve to prolong the conversation, which is always more lively at the end of the repast; they oblige you to commit no excess, wherein they greatly differ from the German healths, and from those we still drink in our garrisons and in our provinces. But absurd and truly barbarous is the custom, the first time you drink, and at the beginning of dinner, of calling out successively to each individual, to let him know you are drinking his health. The actor in this ridiculous comedy is sometimes ready to die of thirst, while he is obliged to inquire the names, or catch the eyes of twenty-five or thirty persons, and the unhappy persons to whom he addresses himself are dying of impatience, for it is certainly not possible for them to bestow much attention on what they are eating and on what is said to them, being incessantly appealed to from right and left, or nudged by cruelly charitable neighbors, who are so kind as to acquaint them with the courtesies they are receiving. The most civil of the Americans are not content with this general appeal; every time they drink they make partial ones, for example, to four or five persons at a time. Another custom completes the despair of poor foreigners, if they be ever so little absent-minded, or have good appetites: these general and partial attacks terminate in downright duels. They call to you from one end of the table to the other: "Sir, will you permit me to drink a glass of wine with you?" This proposal is always accepted, and does not even admit of Simkin's excuse that he didn't "care much for drinking, without knowing my company." [11] The bottle is then passed to you, and you must look your enemy in the face, for I can give no other name to the man who exercises such an empire over my will; you wait till he likewise has poured out his wine, and taken his glass; you then drink mournfully with him, as a recruit imitates his corporal in his drill. But to do justice to the Americans, they themselves feel the ridiculousness of these customs borrowed from Old England, and since laid aside by her. They have proposed to the Chevalier de La Luzerne to dispense with them, knowing that his example would have great weight; but he has thought proper to conform, and very rightly so. The more the French are in a position to give their customs to other nations, the more they should avoid the appearance of changing those of the Americans. Happy our nation if her ambassadors, and her travelers, always had such good sense, and if they never lost sight of the fact that of all men those who lead the dance should be the most nonchalant.

After this dinner, which I have perhaps spun out too long, according to the custom of this country, the Chevalier de La Luzerne took me to make visits with him.[12] The first was to Mr. [Joseph] Reed, President of the state [of Pennsylvania]. This post corresponds to that of governor in the other provinces, but without the same authority; for the government of Pennsylvania is wholly democratic, consisting only of a General Assembly, or, if you will, a House of Commons, which name an Executive Council, composed of twelve members who possess very limited powers, and who are accountable to the Assembly, in which they have no vote. Mr. Reed has been a general officer in the American army, and has given proofs of courage, having had a horse killed under him in the skirmish near Whitemarsh. It is he whom Governor [George] Johnstone attempted to corrupt in 1778, when England sent commissioners to treat with Congress; but this attempt was confined to a few insinuations, entrusted to a Mrs. [Elizabeth Graeme] Ferguson. Mr. Reed, who is a sensible man, of a rather intriguing character, and above all eager for popular favor, made a great clamor, published, and exaggerated the offers that were made him. Since he was a close friend of General Washington, he could easily justify the importance he claimed for himself. The complaints of Mrs. Ferguson, who found herself compromised in this affair, a public declaration by Governor Johnstone, whose object was to deny the facts, but which served only to confirm them, various charges, and refutations, printed and made public, produced no other effect than to second the views of Mr. Reed, and to make him attain his end, of playing a leading role in his country.[13] Unfortunately his pretensions, or his interests, led him to declare himself the enemy of Dr. Franklin.[14] When I was at Philadelphia, there was some question of recalling this respectable man, nothing less; but the French party, or that of General Washington, or to express it still better, the really patriotic party prevailed, and they were satisfied with sending an officer to France to represent the wretched state of the army, and to ask for clothes, tents, and money, of which it stood in great need.[15] The choice fell upon Colonel [John] Laurens.[16]

Mr. Reed has a handsome house, arranged and furnished in the English style.[17] I found there Mrs. Washington, who had just arrived from Virginia, and was on her way to join her husband, as she does at the end of every campaign. She is about forty or forty-five, rather plump, but fresh and with an agreeable face.[18] After passing a quarter of an hour at Mr. Reed's, we waited on Mr. [Samuel] Huntington, President of Congress. We found him in his cabinet, lighted by a single candle. Such simplicity reminded me of that of a Fabricius or a Philopoemen.[19] Mr. Huntington is an upright man, who espouses no party, and may be relied on. He is a native of Connecticut, and was delegate from that state, when chosen President.

My day having been sufficiently taken up, the Chevalier de La Luzerne conducted me to the house where he had ordered lodgings to be prepared for me. It was at the Spanish Minister's, where there were several vacant apartments; [20] for M. [Juan] Miralles who had occupied it, died a year ago [April 28, 1780] at Morristown. His secretary [Francisco Rendón] has remained chargé d'affaires, master of the house, and well contented to enjoy the *incarico*, which includes, besides the correspondence, a table maintained at the expense of the King of Spain. The Chevalier de La Luzerne, though very well and agreeably lodged, had no rooms to spare; the next day, however, he had one arranged for me, which contributed greatly to my happiness during my stay at Philadelphia, for I was situated between M. de Marbois and himself, and able to converse with them at all times of day.

December 1, 1780: Philadelphia

The 1st of December commenced, like every other day in America, by a large breakfast. As the dinners are very late at the Minister's, a few loins of veal, some legs of mutton, and other trifles of

that kind always slip in among the teacups and coffee cups at breakfast and are sure of meeting a hearty welcome. After this slight
repast, which lasted only an hour and a half, we went to visit the
ladies, according to the Philadelphia custom, where the morning is
the most proper hour for paying calls. We began with Mrs. Bache;
she deserved this special mark of our attention, for she is the daughter of Mr. Franklin.[21] Simple in her manners, like her respectable
father, she also possesses his benevolence. She conducted us into a
room filled with needlework, recently finished by the ladies of
Philadelphia. This work consisted neither of embroidered tambour
waistcoats, nor network edging, nor of gold and silver brocade—
but of shirts for the soldiers of Pennsylvania. The ladies had bought
the linen from their own private purses, and had gladly cut out and
stitched the shirts themselves. On each shirt was the name of the
married or unmarried lady who made it, and there were 2200 shirts
in all. Here is the place, no doubt, for a very moral and very trite
remark about the difference between our manners and those of
America; but as for myself, I am of the opinion that, on a similar
occasion, our French women would do as much, and I even venture
to believe that such needlework would inspire verses as agreeable
as those laboriously and awkwardly embroidered ones which accompany the annual presents of cradles, coaches, houses, castles,
etc. It must be admitted that although this custom is an abundant
source of most ingenious ideas, its heyday is past, and the ideas are
beginning to run thin. But should any stern philosopher be disposed
to censor French manners, I would not advise him to do so in the
presence of Mrs. P * * * [Plater], whom I waited upon after leaving
Mrs. Bache.[22] She is typical of Philadelphia's charming women; her
taste is as delicate as her health: an enthusiast to excess for all French
fashions, she is only waiting for the end of this little revolution, to
effect a still greater one in the manners of her country.

After paying due homage to this excellent female patriot, I hurried to make acquaintance with Mr. [Robert] Morris. He is a very
rich merchant, and consequently a man of every country, for commerce bears everywhere the same character. Under monarchies it
is free; it is an egotist in republics; a stranger, or if you will, a citizen
of the universe, it excludes alike the virtues and the prejudices that
stand in the way of its interest. It will scarcely be believed that amid
the disasters of America, Mr. Morris, the inhabitant of a town barely
freed from the hands of the English, should possess a fortune of

eight million *livres*.[23] It is, however, in the most critical times that great fortunes are acquired and increased. The fortunate return of several ships, the still more successful cruises of his privateers, have increased his riches beyond his expectations, if not beyond his wishes. He is, in fact, so accustomed to the success of his privateers, that when he is observed on a Sunday to be more serious than usual, the conclusion is, that no prize has arrived during the preceding week.[24] This flourishing state of trade, at Philadelphia, as well as in Massachusetts Bay, is entirely owing to the arrival of the French squadron.[25] The English have abandoned all their cruises in order to block up the French at Newport, and in that they have succeeded ill, for they have not taken a single sloop coming to Rhode Island or Providence. Mr. Morris is a large man, very simple in his manners; but his mind is subtle and acute, his head perfectly well organized, and he is as well versed in public business as in his own.[26] He was a member of Congress in 1776, and must be reckoned among those personages who have had the greatest influence in the Revolution of America. He is the friend of Dr. Franklin, and the decided enemy of Mr. [Joseph] Reed. His house is handsome, closely resembling the houses in London; [27] he lives there without ostentation, but not without expense, for he spares nothing which can contribute to his happiness, and that of Mrs. Morris, to whom he is much attached. A zealous republican and an Epicurean philosopher, he has always played a distinguished part at table and in business.[28]

I have already mentioned Mr. [Samuel] Powel, now I must speak of his wife; and indeed it would be difficult to separate two persons who have for twenty years lived together in happiest union, I shall not say as man and wife, which would not in America convey the idea of perfect equality, but as two friends, unusually well matched in understanding, taste, and knowledge.[29] Mr. Powel, as I have previously noted, has traveled in Europe and has brought back from there a taste for the fine arts: his house is adorned with valuable prints and good copies of several Italian paintings. Mrs. Powel has not traveled, but she has read a good deal, and profitably: it would be unjust perhaps to say, that she differs in this respect from most other American ladies; but what chiefly distinguishes her is her taste for conversation and the truly European manner in which she uses her wit and knowledge.[30]

I fear that my readers, if ever I have any, will make the obvious comment that social calls are very tiresome everywhere, and as one

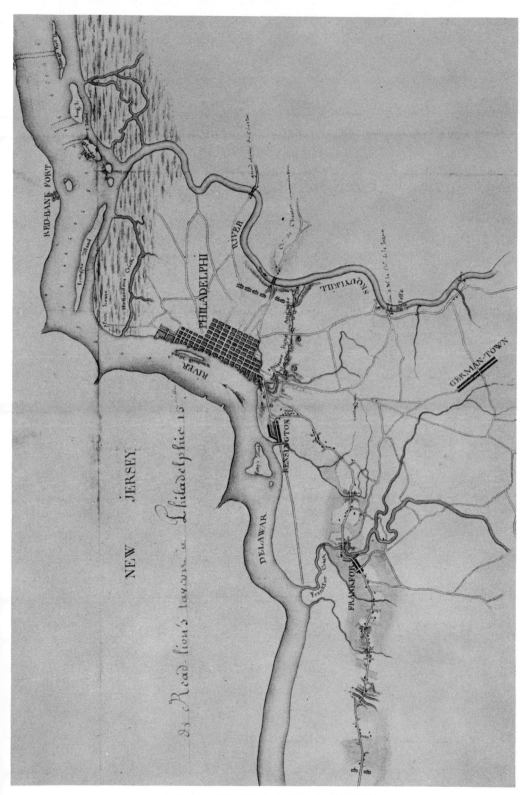

PHILADELPHIA AND VICINITY
by L.-A. Berthier, 1781 (see p. xxii)

PENNSYLVANIA STATE HOUSE (INDEPENDENCE HALL)
Detail from Charles Willson Peale's portrait of C.-A. Gérard, 1779
Chastellux: December 4, 1780 (see p. xxii)

WASHINGTON, BY CHARLES WILLSON PEALE, 1779
Chastellux: December 4, 1780 (see pp. xxii-xxiii)

THE CHEVALIER DE LA LUZERNE
French Minister to the United States
by Charles Willson Peale, *ca.* 1782 (see p. xxiii)

must be very quick to escape such remarks from the French, I shall here forestall them by hastening on. I apprise them however, that I am sparing them a long dinner, which the Chevalier de La Luzerne gave that day to the southern delegates. I shall have occasion to speak elsewhere of some of these delegates, and as for those who will not give me that opportunity, they deserve to be passed over in silence.

December 2, 1780: Philadelphia—Visit to Germantown

For fear lest the pleasures of Capua might make me forget the campaigns of Hannibal and of Fabius, I determined, on December 2, to get on horseback and visit the battlefield of Germantown.[31] It will be recalled that after the defeat of Brandywine, in 1777, the American army, not thinking proper to defend Philadelphia, retired to the upper Schuylkill, while the English took possession, without resistance, of the capital of Pennsylvania. Elated with their success, and full of that confidence which has invariably deceived them, the English divided and dispersed their forces: the greatest part of their troops was encamped upon the Schuylkill, four miles from Philadelphia; another division occupied Germantown, eight miles to the northward of that place; and they had also sent a considerable detachment to Billingsport, to support the passage of their fleet, which was making fruitless endeavors to get up the Delaware. At this juncture, General Washington thought it was time to remind the English that an American army still existed. One is at a loss whether most to extol the wise intrepidity of the Chief, or the resolution displayed by his army in making an attack on the same troops whose shock they had been unable to sustain a month before. Germantown is a long town, or village, consisting of a single street, not unlike La Villette or Vaugirard [near Paris]. From the first house, at the south, to the last, at the north end of the town, is a distance of nearly two miles and a half. The English [advanced] corps which occupied this town, or rather covered it, was encamped near the last houses to the northward, and so situated that the street, or main road, cut through the middle of the camp.[32] These troops might have amounted to three or four thousand men. General Washington, who occupied a position at ten miles distance, near Skippack Creek, left his camp towards midnight [Oct. 3, 1777], marching in two columns, one of which was to turn Germantown on the eastward, the other on the west: two brigades of the right column were ordered to form the *corps de réserve*, to separate themselves from the column at the instant of the attack, and follow the main street of Germantown. A very thick fog came on, which favored the army's march, but which rendered the attack more difficult, as it was impossible to concert the movements and deployments of the troops. The militia marched on the right and on the left, flanking the two columns just mentioned; they were not directly involved and kept along the woods, one in the direction of Frankford and the other on the Schuylkill side. General Washington halted shortly before daylight at a crossroad only half a mile distant from the picket, or advanced post of the enemy. There he learned from an English dragoon who was intoxicated and had lost his way that the Billingsport detachment had just returned. This unexpected intelligence did not change the General's plan; he continued his march at the head of the right column, and fell upon the English picket, who were surprised, put to rout, and driven back to the camp, where they brought the first news of the arrival of the Americans. They flew to arms and precipitately fell back, leaving their tents standing and abandoning all their baggage. This was a moment not to be lost, and French troops would certainly have availed themselves of it, nay, it would have been difficult to prevent them either from pursuing the enemy too far or from dispersing to plunder the camp. We can at this point form some opinion of the American character; and indeed, this army, notwithstanding the slowness of its maneuvers and its inexperience in warfare, may perhaps merit the praise of Europeans. General Sullivan, who commanded the right column, calmly and slowly formed the three brigades at its head, and after ranging them in order of battle, moved through the English camp, without a single soldier stopping for plunder. He advanced in this manner, leaving the houses on the left, and driving before him all resistance from the gardens and enclosures; he then penetrated into the town itself, and was for some time engaged with the English troops who were defending a small square near the market.

While everything thus succeeded on the right, General Washington, at the head of the reserve, was expecting to see his left column arrive, and pursued his march through the main street. But a fire of musketry, which proceeded from a large house within pistol shot of the street, suddenly checked the van of his troops.[33] It was resolved to attack this house; but cannon were necessary, for it was

known to be of stone, and could not therefore be set on fire. Unfortunately they had only six-pounders: the Chevalier Duplessis-
Mauduit brought two pieces near another house, two hundred paces
from the one just mentioned. This cannonade produced no effect;
it penetrated the walls, but did not demolish them. The Chevalier
de Mauduit, full of that ardor which led him at the age of sixteen
to undertake a journey into Greece to view the fields of Plataea and
Thermopylae, and at twenty to go in search of laurels in America,
then resolved to attack by main force this house, which he was unable to reduce by cannon. He proposed to Colonel Laurens to take
with him some determined men, and get from a nearby barn some
straw and hay which they would pile up against the front door and
set afire. One can readily imagine that such an idea should have
occurred to two spirited young men; but it is hard to believe that
of these two noble adventurous youths, one should now be on his
way to France and the other in good health at Newport.[34] M. de
Mauduit having no doubt that they were following him with all the
straw in the barn, went straight to a window on the ground floor,
broke it open and climbed up onto it. He was received, in truth,
much like the lover mounting a ladder to see his mistress, who found
the husband waiting for him on the balcony; I do not know
whether, like him too, on being asked what he was doing there, he
answered, "I am only taking a walk!" But this I do know, that while
one gallant man, pistol in hand, was asking him to surrender, another, less polite, entered briskly into the room, and fired a musket
shot which killed, not M. de Mauduit, but the officer who was trying to capture him. After this comedy of errors and this slight dispute, his difficulty was to find a way to retire. Either he would expose himself to deadly firing from the first and second floors; or,
since a part of the American army were spectators, he would look
ridiculous if he returned running. M. de Mauduit, like a true Frenchman, chose to expose himself to death rather than to ridicule; but
the bullets respected our prejudices; he returned safe and sound, and
Mr. Laurens, who was in no greater haste than he, escaped with a
slight wound in his shoulder. I must not here omit a circumstance
which proves the precarious tenure of a military existence. General
Washington thought that if the commander of this post were summoned, he would readily surrender: M. de Mauduit was therefore
requested to take a drum with him, and make this proposal; but on
his observing that he spoke bad English, and might not, perhaps, be

understood, an American officer was sent, who being preceded by a drum, and displaying a white handkerchief, it was imagined, would not incur the smallest risk; but the English replied to this officer only with musket fire, and killed him on the spot.

By this time the enemy began to rally: the English army had marched from their camp near the Schuylkill to succor German-town, and Cornwallis was coming with all haste from Philadelphia, with the grenadiers and chasseurs, while the *corps de réserve* of the American army were losing their time at the stone house, and the left column was scarcely ready for the attack. The contest had become too unequal; it became necessary to think of a retreat, which was executed in good order, and General Washington retired to an excellent position four miles from Germantown; so that on the evening of the battle he was six miles nearer the enemy than he had been before. The capacity he had just displayed on this occasion, the confidence he had inspired into an army they thought disheart-ened, and which, like the Hydra of the fable, reappeared with a more threatening head, astonished the English and kept them in awe, until the defeat of Burgoyne changed the aspect of affairs. This is the most favorable light in which we can view this day, un-fortunately too bloody for any advantage derived from it. Military men who view the ground, or have before them an accurate plan, will, I imagine, be of the opinion that the extensiveness of the object occasioned the failure of this enterprise. The project of first beating the advanced corps, then the army, and afterwards of becoming masters of Philadelphia, was absolutely chimerical: for the village of Germantown being upwards of two miles in length, presented too many obstacles for the assailants and too many rallying points for the English; besides, it is not in intersected country, and without cavalry, that those great battles which destroy or disperse armies are won. Had General Washington contented himself with pro-ceeding to Whitemarsh, and covering his march with a large body of troops which might have advanced to Germantown, he would have surprised the English vanguard, and forced them to retire with loss; and if, content with giving this sort of lesson to a victorious army, he had fallen back on the new position he wished to occupy, he would have completely fulfilled his object, and the whole honor of the day been his. But, supposing the plan of attack to be such as was adopted, it appears to me that two mistakes, both indeed quite pardonable, were committed: one, losing time in ranging in line of battle General Sullivan's column, instead of marching directly to the camp of the enemy; the other, wasting time in attacking the stone house. The first mistake will appear very pardonable to those who have seen the American troops such as they then were; they had no instruction and were so ill disciplined that they could neither preserve good order in marching in a column, nor deploy when circumstances required it; for experience, which is always at odds with M. de Mesnil-Durand, teaches us that formation in depth is the combat order most subject to disorder and confusion, and the one which consequently demands the most composure and discipline.[35] The second mistake may be justified by the hope they always had of getting possession of the stone house, the importance of which was measured by the obstinacy of the enemy in defending it. It is certain that two better measures might have been adopted: the first, to pursue the march without worrying about the musketry fire, which could always have been sufficiently slackened by detaching a few men to fire at the windows; and the second, that of leaving the village on the left, to enter it again three hundred paces further on, where it would then have been sufficient to take possession of another house opposite the one occupied by the enemy: even though this house were not quite so high as the other, the fire from it would have been sufficient to contain the English and ensure a retreat in case of necessity.[36]

In allowing myself this sort of censure, I feel how much I ought to mistrust my own judgment, especially as I was not present at the action; but I made these same observations to Mr. Laurens, M. de Mauduit, and M. de Gimat, and they seemed unable to refute them. We have seen the share the two former had in the engagement; the third has several times viewed the field of battle with General Washington, who has explained to him the movements of the two armies, and nobody is better fitted than M. de Gimat to hear well and to give a good account of what he has heard.[37]

After sufficiently examining the position of Germantown, I returned to Philadelphia by the shortest road, and faster than I came, for the cold was very piercing, and I had only time to dress myself to accompany the Chevalier de La Luzerne to dine with the northern delegates. It must be understood that the delegates, or if you will, the members of Congress, have a tavern to themselves, where they give frequent entertainments;[38] but so that the company may not be too numerous at a time, they divide themselves into two sets, and as we see, very geographically, the line of demarcation being from east to west.[39] The dinner was plain and good, and our reception polite and cordial, but not ceremonious. Two delegates placed at each end did the honors of the table. Mr. [James] Duane, deputy from the state of New York, occupied the side I was on.[40] He is of a gay and open character, has no objection to talk, and drinks without repugnance. I conversed some time, but less than I could have wished, with Mr. Charles Thomson, Secretary of Congress.[41] He passes, with reason, for one of the best informed men in the country, and though he is a man of the cabinet and mixes little with society, his manners are polite and amiable. Mr. Samuel Adams, deputy for Massachusetts Bay, was not at this dinner, but on rising from table I went to see him.[42] When I entered his room, I found him tête-à-tête with a young girl of fifteen who was preparing his tea; but we shall not be scandalized at this, considering that he is at least sixty. Everybody in Europe knows that he was one of the prime movers of the present revolution. I experienced in his company the satisfaction one rarely has in society, or even at the theater, of finding the person of the actor corresponding to the role he plays. In him, I saw a man wrapped up in his object, who never spoke but to give me a good opinion of his cause and a high idea of his country. His simple and frugal exterior seemed intended as a contrast to the energy and scope of his thoughts, which were wholly focused upon the republic, and lost nothing of their warmth by being expressed with method and precision, just as an army, marching towards the enemy, appears no less daring for observing the laws of tactics. Among several facts that he cited in honor of his country, I shall relate one which deserves to be transmitted to posterity. Two young soldiers had deserted from the army and returned to their father's house. Their father, incensed at this action, loaded them with irons and conducted them himself to their general, Lord Stirling. The latter did what any other officer would have done in his place—he pardoned them. The father, as patriotic but less austere than a Roman, was happy to keep his children; nevertheless he seemed astonished, and approaching the General: "My Lord," he said, with tears in his eyes, "Tis more than I hoped."

I left Mr. Adams with regret, promising myself to see him again, and my evening terminated by a visit to Colonel [Theodorick] Bland, a delegate from Carolina [Virginia]. He is a tall handsome man, who has been in the West Indies, where he acquired French.

He is said to be a good soldier, but at present serves his country, and serves it well, in Congress.[43] The southern delegates, in fact, are very influential; they are incessantly laboring to draw the attention of the government towards them, and to avert any idea of purchasing peace at their expense.

December 3, 1780: Philadelphia, "at home"

On the 3rd the weather was so bad that it was impossible to stir out. I had no reason to complain, however, of the employment of this day, which I passed either in conversation with M. de La Luzerne and M. de Marbois, or in reading such interesting papers as they were pleased to communicate to me.

December 4, 1780: Philadelphia

Mr. [Samuel] Huntington having informed me that the next day he would show me the hall in which the Congress meets, I went there at ten o'clock, and found him waiting for me accompanied by several delegates.[44] This hall is spacious without being lavishly decorated; its handsomest ornament is the portrait of General Washington, larger than life. He is represented at full length, in that noble and easy attitude which is natural to him; cannon, flags, and all the attributes of war form the accessories of the picture.[45] I was then conducted into the room used by the secretaries, which has nothing remarkable about it but the manner in which it is furnished; the colors captured from the enemy serve as wall hangings. From there you pass into the library, which is fairly large, but far from being filled; the few books comprising it seemed to me to be well chosen. It is in the former town hall [State House] that Congress has established its seat: this building is rather handsome; the staircase in particular is wide and noble. As for the outside ornaments, they consist only in the decoration of the doorway, and in several tablets of marble placed below the windows.[46] I noticed a refinement in the roof which appeared novel to me: the chimneys have been consigned to the extremities of the building, which is an oblong, and have been so constructed as to be linked together in the form of an arcade, thus resembling a sort of portico.

After taking leave of the President and delegates, I returned to the Chevalier de La Luzerne's, and as the streets were covered with ice, I stayed at home, where I received a visit from Mr. [James] Wilson,[47] a celebrated lawyer and author of several pamphlets on

current affairs. He has in his library all our best authors on public
law and jurisprudence; the works of President Montesquieu and of
Chancellor d'Aguesseau hold the first rank among them, and he
makes them his daily study.[48] After dinner, which was private and
à la française, I went to see Mrs. [William] Bingham, a young and
handsome woman, only seventeen; her husband, who was there
according to the American custom, is only twenty-five.[49] He was
agent of Congress at Martinique, whence he has returned with a
tolerable knowledge of French, and with much attachment to the
Marquis de Bouillé. I spent the rest of the evening at Mrs. Powel's,
where I hoped to find agreeable conversation; in this I was not disappointed, and I lingered there longer than I realized.[50]

December 5, 1780: Philadelphia

I went again to the town hall [State House] on the 5th, but this
time it was to attend a session of the Assembly of the state of Pennsylvania; for the hall where this sort of parliament meets is in the
same building as the one used by Congress.[51] I was with M. de La
Fayette, the Vicomte de Noailles, the Comte de Damas, M. de
Gimat, and all the French or the Gallo-Americans who were in
Philadelphia.[52] We seated ourselves on a bench facing the chair of
the Speaker [Frederick Augustus Muhlenberg]: on his right was
the President of the state [Joseph Reed]; the clerks [Samuel Ster-
rett *et al.*] were placed along a table which is in front of the
Speaker. The debates turned on some misconduct imputed to the
Board of the Treasury.[53] The Executive Council was sent for and
heard. Almost the only one who spoke was General [Thomas]
Mifflin; he delivered himself with grace and wit, but with a marked
intention of contradicting the President of the state, who is not one
of his friends. His manner of expressing himself, his gestures, his
bearing, the air of ease and superiority that he invariably maintained, perfectly reminded me of those members of the House of
Commons who are accustomed to set the tone for the others, and
to make everything bend to their opinion. It not being possible to
finish the business that morning, the Speaker left the chair; the
house went into committee, and adjourned.

The morning was not yet far advanced, and there was still plenty
to keep me busy. I was expected in three places: by a connoisseur
of natural history, by an anatomist, and at the college, or rather the
university of Philadelphia. I began with the cabinet of natural

history. This collection, rather small and rather paltry, is very re-
nowned in America, because it has no rival there; it was formed by
a painter from Geneva, called *"Cimetiere"* [Du Simitière], whose
cemeterial name is better suited to a doctor than to a painter.[54] This
worthy man came to Philadelphia twenty years ago to make portraits, and has remained there ever since; he is still a bachelor and
still a foreigner, a very uncommon thing in America where the titles
of husband and of citizen are generally acquired without delay. The
most curious thing I saw in his cabinet was a large quantity of the
vice, or screw, a rather common kind of shell, within which a very
hard stone, like jade, is exactly molded. It appears clear to me that
these petrifactions were formed by the successive accumulation of
lapidific molecules conveyed by the waters and aggregated with
the help of fixed air.[55] After fatiguing my legs and satisfying my
eyes, as always happens in natural history cabinets, I thought proper
to quit the earth for the heavens; that is, in common speech, I went
to the library of the university to see a very ingenious machine
which represents all the movements of the heavenly bodies.[56] I lose
no time in declaring that I shall not give a description of it, for nothing is so tiresome as the description of any machine; it is enough for
me to state that one part of it displays perfectly, on a vertical plane,
all the motion of the planets in their orbits; and that the other, which
is intended only to represent the motion of the moon, shows in the
clearest manner, its phases, nodes, and different latitudes. The President of the college [57] and Mr. [David] Rittenhouse, who invented
and executed this machine, took the trouble to explain all its details
to me: they seemed very happy that I knew enough English and
astronomy to understand them; on which I must observe, that the
latter fact is more to the shame of the Americans than to my credit,
the almanac being almost the only book of astronomy studied at
Philadelphia. Mr. "de Rittenhausen" is of German descent, as his
name sufficiently indicates, but he was born in Philadelphia, and is a
clockmaker by profession. He is a man of great simplicity and modesty, and though not a mathematician of the class of the Eulers and
the D'Alemberts, knows enough of that science to be perfectly
acquainted with the motions of the heavenly bodies.[58] As for his
mechanical talents, it is unnecessary to seek a reason for them; we
know that of all others, such talents are less the results of study,
than they are a gift of nature. It is even worth noting that, notwithstanding the slight connection discernible between such a mechani-

cal bent and the delicacy of our senses or the perfection of our organs, men are more frequently born mechanics, than they are painters or musicians. Education, even the very rigor of education, has frequently made famous artists in the two latter branches, but there is no example of its having made a mechanical genius.

This morning seemed to be devoted to the sciences, and my walks were a sort of encyclopedia, for I left the university library only to call upon a celebrated anatomist, called Dr. [Abraham] Chovet.[59] Here, in brief, is his history. He was born in England upwards of seventy years ago. After studying medicine and surgery there, he went to France to improve himself under M. Winslow. In 1734 he went to the West Indies, where he has since practiced medicine, now at Barbados, now at Jamaica, but invariably with application and hard work. During the war of 1744, there was by chance brought into Barbados a prize with a great deal of wax on board. Mr. Chovet took advantage of this fortunate opportunity to experiment with anatomical models in wax, and he succeeded so well that he has carried this art to the highest degree of perfection. On seeing him, it is difficult to conceive how he has been able to combine so much patience and perseverance with his natural vivacity; for it seems as if the sun of the tropics had preserved in him all the heat of youth; he speaks with fire, and expresses himself as easily in French as if he were still in our schools of surgery. Moreover, he is a real eccentric: his chief characteristic is contrary-mindedness; when the English were at Philadelphia he was a Whig, and since they left he has become a Tory; he is always sighing after Europe, without ever making up his mind to return there, and declaims incessantly against the Americans, while remaining among them. His reason for coming to the continent was to recover his health, so that he would be able to cross the seas; this was at about the time that the war broke out, and, since that time, he imagines he is not at liberty to leave, though nobody prevents him from going. He was to me a greater curiosity than his anatomical models, which in truth I thought superior to those at the Institute at Bologna, but inferior to those of Mademoiselle Biheron,[60] as the wax invariably had a certain unnatural glossiness.

At the end of this morning's walk I was like a bee, so laden with honey that he can hardly regain his hive. I returned to the Chevalier de La Luzerne's with my memory well stored, and after taking other food than that of the mind, I devoted my evening to society.

I was invited to drink tea at Colonel Bland's, that is to say, to attend a sort of assembly much like the *conversazzioni* of Italy; for tea here is the substitute for the *rinfresco*. Mr. [Richard] Howly, Governor of Georgia, Mr. [Ralph] Izard, Mr. Arthur Lee (the two last lately arrived from Europe), M. de La Fayette, M. de Noailles, M. de Damas, etc., were of the party. The scene was graced by several married and unmarried ladies, among whom, Miss [Nancy] Shippen, daughter of Dr. [William] Shippen and cousin of Mrs. [Benedict] Arnold, claimed particular distinction. Thus we see that in America the crimes of individuals do not reflect upon their family; not only had Dr. Shippen's brother [Edward Shippen] given his daughter [Peggy Shippen] to the traitor Arnold, a short time before his desertion, but it is generally believed, that being himself a Tory, he had inspired his daughter with the same sentiments, and that the charms of this handsome woman contributed not a little to hasten to criminality a mind corrupted by avarice, before it felt the power of love.[61]

On our return to the Chevalier de La Luzerne's we assembled all the French and Gallo-American military, and laid our plan for a very agreeable trip that began the next day.[62]

December 6, 1780: Philadelphia—Chester—Brandywine

The 6th in the morning, M. de La Fayette, the Vicomte de Noailles, the Comte de Damas, the Chevalier du Plessis-Mauduit, Messieurs de Gimat and de Neville, aides-de-camp of M. de La Fayette, M. de Montesquieu, M. Lynch, and myself, set out to visit the Brandywine battlefield, thirty miles from Philadelphia. M. de La Fayette had not seen it since at the age of twenty—after parting from his wife, his friends, the pleasures of the world, and those of youth, and a thousand leagues from his native land—he there shed the first drop of blood he offered to Glory, or rather to that so noble cause that he has continued to support with the same zeal, but with better luck. We crossed the Schuylkill south of Philadelphia, at the same ferry where M. du Coudray was drowned in 1777.[63] We there discovered the traces of some entrenchments thrown up by the English after they became masters of Philadelphia; then bearing to the left, we rode on fourteen miles to the little town of Chester. It is built at the spot where the creek of that name flows into the Delaware, and is a sort of port where vessels coming up the river sometimes anchor. The houses, to the number of forty or fifty, are pretty and built of stone or brick.[64] On leaving Chester, and following the road to Brandywine, you cross over the stone bridge where M. de La Fayette, wounded as he was, stopped the fugitives, and took the first measures for rallying the army behind the creek. The country beyond it presents no special features, but resembles the rest of Pennsylvania, that is to say, is interspersed with woods and cultivated lands. It was already late when we came within reach of the field of battle, and as we could see nothing until next morning and were too numerous to remain together, we had to separate into two divisions. Messrs. de Gimat, de Mauduit, and my two aides-de-camp, stayed with me at an inn three miles this side of Brandywine; and M. de La Fayette, attended by the other travelers, went further on to ask for hospitality from a Quaker named Benjamin Ring, at whose house he had lodged with General Washington the night before the battle.[65]

December 7, 1780: Brandywine Battlefield—Chester

I joined him early the next morning, and found him in great friendship with his host who, Quaker though he was, seemed delighted to entertain "the Marquis." We got on horseback at nine, provided with a map executed under the direction of General Howe and engraved in England; [66] but we got still more information from an American major, with whom M. de La Fayette had made an appointment. This officer had been present at the engagement, and as his house was on the battlefield itself, he was better acquainted with it than anybody else.

We must recall that in 1777 the English, having in vain attempted to cross the Jerseys [from New York] to get to Philadelphia by land, had been obliged to set to sea again and sail around the capes in order to enter Chesapeake Bay and proceed up the bay to the mouth of the Elk River. They arrived there the 25th of August, after a difficult passage at sea, but a fortunate one in the bay, up which they sailed with much less difficulty than they expected. While the sea, the winds, and three hundred vessels were assisting the maneuvers of the enemy's army, Mr. Washington had remained some days at Middle Brook [in New Jersey], in one of the most embarrassing positions in which the general of an army can find himself. To the north, the troops of Burgoyne, after having taken Ticonderoga, were advancing towards Albany; to the south, an English army of 15,000 men had embarked and might either proceed to Chesapeake Bay—as they did—or penetrate by the Delaware, or turn back up the Hudson as far as West Point to form a junction with Burgoyne and cut off the American army, which would thenceforth have been forever separated from the eastern and northern states. Of all these possibilities, this latter was certainly the most to be dreaded: accordingly General Washington did not abandon his position at Middle Brook until he received certain intelligence that the English fleet had doubled Cape May. Let us try to imagine the situation in which a general must find himself when, obliged to include in his plan of defense an immense country and a vast extent of coast, he does not know, even within one hundred and fifty miles, where the enemy is likely to appear; and having no longer any intelligence of them, either by patrols, or detachments, or even by couriers, he finds himself reduced to observing the compass and consulting the winds, before he can make a decision. As soon as the movement of the enemy was determined, General Washington lost no time in marching his army; I should say his soldiers, for a number of soldiers, however considerable, does not always form an army. His was composed of 12,000 men at most. It was at the head of these troops, the greater part of them new levies, that he traversed in silence the city of Philadelphia, while Congress was giving orders to fight, and yet was removing archives and public papers farther inland—a sinister omen of the success which must follow their council.

The army crossed the Schuylkill and marched to a first camp near Wilmington on the banks of the Delaware. This position had a double object, for the ships of war, after convoying General Howe to the Elk River, had sailed back down Chesapeake Bay, then gone up the Delaware and, seconded by some landing troops, appeared inclined to force the passage of that river. General Washington, however, soon perceived that the position he had taken became every day more dangerous. The English, having finished their debarkation, were ready to advance into the country; his right flank was exposed, and he was leaving both Philadelphia and the whole of Lancaster County uncovered. It was determined therefore that the army should cross back over Brandywine Creek and encamp on the left [eastern] bank of this river. The position chosen was certainly the best that could be taken to dispute the passage. The left of the position was very good and was supported by thick woods extending as far as the junction of the creek with the Delaware. As it approaches its mouth, this creek becomes more and more embanked and difficult to ford: the heights are equal on the two banks; but for this very reason the advantage was in favor of whoever was defending the passage. A battery of cannon with a good parapet was pointed towards Chadd's Ford, and everything appeared secure on that side; but to the right the ground was so covered that it was impossible to judge of the movements of the enemy, and to keep abreast of them, in case they should attempt—as they did—to detach a corps by their left, in order to cross the river higher up. The only precaution that could be taken was therefore to place five or six brigades [67] in echelon, to watch that sector. General [John] Sullivan had the command of these brigades; he received orders to keep abreast of the enemy, should they march by their left; and on the supposition that they would unite their forces near Chadd's Ford, he was himself to cross the river and make a powerful diversion on their flank.

When a general has foreseen everything, when he has made the best possible dispositions, and when his activity, judgment, and courage in the action are equal to the wisdom of his measures, has he not already triumphed in the eyes of every impartial judge? And if by some unforeseen misfortunes, the laurels he has merited drop from his hands, is it not for History to gather them up carefully and replace them on his brow? Let us hope that History will acquit herself of this duty better than we can, and let us now observe how such wise dispositions were upset by the mistakes of a few officers and by the inexperience of the troops.

On the 11th of September [1777], General Howe occupied the heights on the right [west] of the creek; he there formed part of his troops in line of battle and had batteries placed opposite Chadd's Ford, while his light troops were attacking and driving before them a corps of "riflemen," who had crossed over to the right bank to observe his motions more closely. General Washington seeing that the cannonade was continuing without any disposition on the part of the enemy to cross the river, concluded that they had another object. He was informed that a great part of their army had marched higher up the creek and was threatening his right; he realized how important it was to keep an attentive eye on all the movements of this corps; but the country was so covered with thickets, that the patrols could discover nothing. It must be observed that General Washington had only a very small number of horsemen, and that he had sent these to the right towards Dilworth to scout that sector. He ordered an officer, whom he judged an intelligent one, to cross the river and inform himself accurately of the route Lord Cornwallis was taking, for it was Cornwallis who commanded this separate corps. The officer returned and assured him that Cornwallis was marching by his right to join Knyphausen, in the direction of Chadd's Ford. According to this report the attack seemed to be determined on the left. Another officer was then sent, who reported that Cornwallis had changed his direction, and that he was rapidly advancing by the road leading to Jefferies's Ford, two miles above Birmingham Church. General Sullivan was immediately ordered to march thither with all the troops of the right. Unfortunately the roads were badly reconnoitered, and not at all open: with great difficulty General Sullivan got through the woods, and when he came out of them to gain a small eminence near Birmingham Church, he found the English columns were coming up this same height on the opposite side. It was no easy matter to range into order of battle such troops as his; he had neither the time to choose his position nor to form his line. The English reached the eminence, drove the Americans back on the woods, and pursued them to the edge of these woods, where they finally dispersed them.[68]

During the short time that this rout lasted, Lord Stirling and General Conway had time to form their brigade on rather advantageous ground: this was a sort of hillock, partly covered by the woods which backed it up. Their left was protected by these same woods, and on the right of this hillock, but a little in the rear, was the Virginia line, which had been ranged in battle formation, on slightly rising ground and on the edge of a sort of grove. The left column of the enemy, which had not been engaged with Sullivan, deployed rapidly and marched against these troops with as much order as vivacity and courage. The Americans made a very smart fire, which did not check the English, and it was not till the latter were within twenty yards of them, that they gave way and plunged into the woods. Lord Stirling, M. de La Fayette, and General Sullivan himself, after the defeat of his division, fought with this body of troops, whose post was the most important, and who resisted the longest. It was here that M. de La Fayette was wounded in his left leg, while rallying the troops who were beginning to waver. On the right, the Virginia line made some resistance; but the English had gained a height, from which their artillery took them obliquely: this fire must have been very severe, for most of the trees bear the mark of bullets or cannon shot. The Virginians in their turn gave way, and the American right was then entirely uncovered.

Though this was nearly three miles distant from Chadd's Ford, General Knyphausen heard the firing of the artillery and musketry, and judging that the fight was really joined, concluded from his confidence in the English and Hessian troops, that they were victorious. Towards five in the evening, he descended from the heights in two columns,[69] one at Jones's Ford, which turned the battery of the Americans, and the other lower down at Chadd's Ford. The latter marched straight to the battery and captured it; whereupon General Wayne, whose brigade was in line of battle, the left on a height and the right inclined towards the battery, withdrew his right and strengthened the heights, thus operating a sort of change of front. In a country where there are neither open columns, nor successive positions to take in case of misfortune, it is difficult to make any provision for retreat. The different corps which had been beaten all rushed headlong into the Chester road, where they formed but a single column with artillery, baggage, and troops mixed together in confusion. At nightfall General Wayne [70] also took this road, but in better order, and the English, content with their victory, did not disturb his retreat.

Such is the idea I have formed of the battle of Brandywine, from what I have heard from General Washington himself, from Messrs. de La Fayette, Gimat, and Mauduit, and from Generals Wayne and Sullivan. I must observe, however, that there is disagreement in some particulars: several persons claim for example that Knyphausen, after crossing the river, continued his march in one column to the battery, and it is thus marked on the English map, which however gives a wrong direction to that column; and furthermore General Washington and General Wayne assured me there were two, and that the left column turned the battery, which otherwise would not have been carried.[71] It is equally difficult to trace out on the plan all the ground on which Cornwallis fought. The narratives of both sides throw scarcely more light on this point; I was therefore obliged to draw my own conclusions from the different accounts, and to follow no one of them in particular.

While we were examining the field of battle in the greatest detail, our servants had gone on to Chester to have dinner and lodgings prepared for us; we soon followed after them, and got there at four o'clock. The road did not appear long to me; for chance having separated M. de La Fayette, the Vicomte de Noailles, and myself a bit from the rest of the company, we entered into a very agreeable conversation, which continued until we got to Chester. I pointed out to them that after talking of nothing but war for three hours, we had suddenly changed the subject and were speaking only of Paris and of all sorts of details concerning our private circle of friends. This transition was truly French, but it does not prove that we are less fond of war than other nations, but only that we care more for our friends. We had scarcely arrived at Chester when we saw coming down the river some state barges or boats, which the President [Joseph Reed] had sent to take us back to Philadelphia, it being our plan to proceed up the Delaware next day, in order to examine the fort at Red Bank and Fort Mifflin, as well as all the other posts which had served for the defense of the river. An officer of the American navy who had come with these barges and who had been assigned to accompany us, informed us that two vessels had arrived that very morning at Philadelphia after a thirty-five day crossing from Lorient. The hope of having some letters or news from Europe, almost tempted us to change our plans and set out immediately for Philadelphia; but as the weather was very fine and as we would have the tide in our favor next morning, which would make our voyage much easier, we determined to remain at Chester, and M. de La Fayette sent off a rider to Philadelphia, to bring back news and letters, in case there were any. This courier returned before nine; he brought only a single note from the Chevalier de La Luzerne, by which we learned that these ships had brought no letters, but that the captains stated that Monsieur de Castries was Minister of the Marine.[72]

While the courier was going and coming, we had reached the inn where dinner and lodgings were prepared for us.[73] The outside of this house was not imposing, and several of the company were already preparing to look elsewhere, when after a more thorough examination we found that there was room enough for a dozen masters, nearly as many servants, and nineteen horses. Our company had been increased by the major whom we had met on the Brandywine battlefield, and by the officer who had brought us the barges. We had an excellent dinner, and very good wine.[74] The tea, which followed on the heels of dinner, was equally good; so that all my young traveling companions were in the best humor, and so gay as never to cease laughing, singing, and dancing during the whole evening. The people of the house, who saw in this company only two generals, one French and the other American, accompanied by their "families," and not a society of friends joyously reunited in another hemisphere, could not conceive how it was possible to be so gay without being drunk, and looked upon us as people come down from the moon. This evening, which was lengthened to eleven o'clock, terminated happily, for we had excellent beds, such as one might expect in a well-furnished country house.

December 8, 1780: Chester–Billingsport–Mud Island–Red Bank, N.J.–Philadelphia

We rose at six in the morning and assembled in the dining room, where a very good breakfast had been prepared for us by candlelight. At seven we embarked, and crossing the Delaware obliquely a little higher up, we landed at Billingsport.[75] This is a fort which was constructed in 1779 [1777] to support the left of the first barrier of the chevaux-de-frise, intended to block the passage of the river. This post was of no use, for the fortifications having been commenced on too extensive a plan for the number of troops which could be spared, it was thought proper to abandon it. The fortifications have since been reduced, which is for the better, as they are now out of range of certain points which commanded the fort. As the present situation of affairs does not attract attention to this locality, the fortifications are somewhat neglected. The entire battery consisted only of one rather good brass mortar and five eighteen-pounders [*Gr.*–English twenty-fours], which Major [John] Armstrong, who commands on the river, and who had come to receive us, fired on my arrival. When America has more money and leisure she will do well not to neglect this post, as well as all those which can serve for the defense of the river. For once this war is terminated, she will see no more European armies on this continent, and all she can have to fear from England, in case of a rupture with her, will be limited to a few maritime expeditions, the sole object of which will be to destroy shipping, to ravage the country, and even to burn the towns within reach of the sea. Unfortunately Billingsport belongs to the state of Jersey, which can reap no advantage from it; and Pennsylvania, whose safety it would defend, has no other means to employ towards fortifying it than its own request and the recommendations of Congress, which are not always attended to. However this may be, Philadelphia has taken other precautions for her defense, which depend only on the state of Pennsylvania, and to this advantage is united that of an excellent position, which will soon be made into an impregnable fort. I am referring to Fort Mifflin, where we went on leaving Billingsport, still ascending the river.[76] The island on which this fort was built, and the one called Mud Island, support the right of a second barrier of chevaux-de-frise, the left of which is defended by the fort at Red Bank on the Jersey side; but it must be observed that this barrier blocked only the main channel of the river, the only passage by which it was thought that vessels could pass.[77] Near the right [west] bank is Hog Island, about two miles long, the surface of which, like that of most of the islands in the Delaware, is so low that at high tide nothing is to be seen but the tops of the reeds with which it is covered. Between this island and the mainland, a small passage remains open, but the Americans always believed that there was not water enough for any ship with guns to pass through it. At the end of this channel, proceeding upstream, there is on the left a marshy ground, so surrounded by creeks and inlets as to form a real island, called Province Island.[78] This post was in the possession of the enemy; they established batteries there, which hindered those of Fort Mifflin, but not sufficiently to force the Americans to abandon it.

The English army was at that time [autumn 1777] in a singular situation: they had purchased and maintained possession of Philadelphia at the price of two bloody battles; but they were still shut up between the Schuylkill and the Delaware, having in front of them Washington's army, which kept them in awe, and behind them several forts occupied by the Americans, which thus closed the passage of the Delaware. A large city, however, and a whole army had to be fed; it became necessary therefore to open the communication by sea and to secure the navigation of the river. Whenever one recollects the innumerable obstacles the English had to surmount in the present war, it is difficult to assign the cause of their successes; but if we reflect upon all the unforeseen events which have deceived the expectations of the Americans, and frustrated their best concerted measures, we remain convinced that they were doomed to destruction, and that the alliance with France could alone effect their salvation. During this excursion, especially, I saw proofs of it every instant. When the place was pointed out to me where the *Augusta*, a vessel of sixty-four guns, took fire and blew up in attempting to force the chevaux-de-frise, and further on, when I saw the remains of the *Merlin*, of twenty-two, which ran ashore in this same action and was burned by the English themselves, while the Hessians were vainly sacrificing five or six hundred men before the fort at Red Bank, I could fancy the English army starved in Philadelphia, retreating with disgrace and difficulty through the Jerseys, and my imagination already delighted in the triumph of the Americans. But suddenly the scene changed, and I saw nothing but the fatality which gathered towards the channel of Hog Island the waters long confined by the chevaux-de-frise, and recollected with pain, that on November 15 [1777], three weeks after the fruitless attempts I have just mentioned, the English succeeded in passing over the bar of this channel the *Vigilant* and another small ship of war [*Fury*]; that they thus got up the river and turned Fort Mifflin, the batteries of which they took from behind, and left the Americans no other resource but to abandon the defense of the chevaux-de-frise on all sides and make a precipitate retreat by the left [eastern] shore of the Delaware.

Taught by sad experience, the Americans have provided in the future against the misfortunes which cost them so dear. I saw with pleasure that they were extending the fortifications of Mifflin's Island, so as to enclose the fort on every side, which will also be surrounded on all sides by the Delaware for a ditch; and as the garrison will have a safe shelter in bombproof souterrains, this fort may henceforth be considered impregnable. The plan of these works has been drawn up by M. Duportail; Major Armstrong showed it to me upon the spot, and I found that it was fully equal to the deserved reputation of the author.[79]

We still had the Red Bank fort to visit; to reach it we had again to cross the Delaware, which in this place is nearly a mile wide.[80] The gentleman who was to do the honors there was impatient to arrive. We had amused ourselves by telling him that as the morning was far spent and the tide about to turn, we should be obliged to omit Red Bank and return directly to Philadelphia. This guide, whom we diverted ourselves in tormenting, was M. du Plessis-Mauduit, who in the double capacity of engineer and artillery officer, had been in charge of arranging and defending this post, under the orders of Colonel [Christopher] Greene. On landing from our boat, he proposed taking us to a Quaker's, whose house is half a musket-shot from the fort, or rather the ruins of the fort, for it is now destroyed, and there remains only a faint outline in relief. "This man," M. de Mauduit told us, "is a little bit of a Tory; I was obliged to knock down his barn and fell his fruit trees, but he will be glad to see M. de La Fayette, and will receive us well." We took him at his word, but never was expectation more completely deceived. We found our Quaker [James Whitall] seated in the chimney corner, busy cleaning herbs: he recognized M. de Mauduit, who introduced M. de La Fayette and me to him; but he did not deign to lift his eyes nor to reply to any of our introducer's remarks, which were at first complimentary, and at length jocose. Except for the silence of Dido, I can think of none more forbidding.[81] We easily resigned ourselves to this cool reception, and made our way to the fort. We had not gone a hundred yards before we came to a small elevation, on which a stone was vertically placed, with this short epitaph: "Here lies buried Colonel Donop." M. de Mauduit could not refrain from expressing his regret for this brave man, who died in his arms two days after the action; he assured us we could not take a step without treading on the remains of some Hessian; for near three hundred were buried in the front of the ditch.

The fort at Red Bank was designed, as I have said above, to support the left [east] of the chevaux-de-frise.[82] The bank of the Delaware at this place is steep; but this very steepness allowed the enemy to approach the fort under cover and without being exposed to the fire of the batteries. To remedy this disadvantage, several galleys armed with cannon and assigned to defend the chevaux-de-frise were stationed alongside the escarpment and could thus watch it on the river side. The Americans, little practiced in the art of fortification, and always disposed to undertake works beyond their strength, had made those of Red Bank too extensive. When M. de Mauduit obtained permission to be sent thither with Colonel Greene, he immediately set about reducing the fortifications, by making an intersection from east to west, which transformed them into a sort of large redoubt of approximately pentagonal shape. A good earthen rampart with pointed stakes projecting from below the parapet (fraisé à hauteur de cordon), a ditch, and an abatis in front of the ditch, constituted the whole strength of this post, in which were placed three hundred men,[83] and fourteen pieces of cannon.

On October 22 [1777], in the morning, news was received that a detachment of twenty-five hundred Hessians were advancing; soon afterwards they appeared on the edge of a wood to the north of Red Bank, nearly within cannon shot. Preparations were making for the defense, when a Hessian officer advanced, preceded by a drum; he was suffered to approach, but his harangue was so insolent that it only served to irritate the garrison and inspire them with more resolution. "The King of England," he said, "orders his rebellious subjects to lay down their arms, and they are warned that if they stand battle, no quarter whatever will be given." The answer was that they accepted the challenge, and that there should be no quarter on either side. At four o'clock in the afternoon, the Hessians opened very brisk fire from a battery of cannon that they had set up, and soon after they advanced and marched to the first entrenchment; finding it abandoned but not destroyed, they thought they had driven the Americans from it. They then shouted "victoria," waved their hats in the air, and advanced towards the redoubt. The same drummer, who a few hours before had come to summon the garrison, and had appeared as insolent as his officer, was at their head beating the charge; both he and that officer were mowed down by the first shot fired. The Hessians, however, still kept advancing within the first entrenchment, leaving the river on their right; they had already reached the abatis, and were endeavoring to pull up or cut away the branches, when they were overwhelmed with a shower of musket shot, which took them in front and in flank; for as chance would have it, a part of the courtine of the old entrenchment, which had not been destroyed, formed a projection at this very part of the intersection. M. de Mauduit had contrived to make of it a sort of *caponnière*, and he now threw into it some men who took the enemy's left in flank and fired on them at close range. The officers were seen continually rallying their men, marching back to the abatis, and falling amidst the branches they were endeavoring to cut. Colonel Donop could be distinguished by the marks of the order he wore, by his handsome figure, and by his courage; he was seen to fall like the others. The Hessians, repulsed by the fire of the redoubt, attempted to secure themselves from it by attacking on the side of the escarpment, but the fire from the galleys sent them back with a great loss of men. At length they relinquished the attack and regained the wood in disorder.

While this was taking place on the north side, another column attacked on the south, and, more fortunate than the other, passed through the abatis, crossed the ditch, and went up the berm; but they were stopped by the pointed stakes, and M. de Mauduit, running to this spot as soon as he saw the first attack beginning to give way, saw this second attacking column obliged to do likewise. However, they still did not dare stir out of the fort, fearing a surprise; but M. de Mauduit wanted to replace some of the stakes which had been torn out; he sallied forth with a few men, and was surprised to find about twenty Hessians standing on the berm and glued against the face of the parapet. These soldiers, who had been bold enough to advance thus far, realized that there was still more danger in turning back, and decided not to risk it; they were captured and brought to the fort. M. de Mauduit, after replacing the stakes, set to having the abatis repaired; he again sallied out with a detachment, and it was then that he beheld, insofar as the darkness of the night allowed, the deplorable spectacle of the dead and dying heaped one upon another. A voice rose from the midst of these corpses, and said in English: "Whoever you are, take me out of here." It was the voice of Colonel Donop: M. de Mauduit had the soldiers lift him up and carry him into the fort, where he was soon recognized. He had a broken hip; but whether they did not consider his wound as mortal, or that they were overheated by the battle and still angered by the threats thrown out against them a few hours before, the Americans could not help crying out: "Well now, is it agreed that no quarter will be given?" "I am in your hands," replied the Colonel. "You may take your revenge." M. de Mauduit had no difficulty in imposing silence, and turned all his attention to the care of the wounded officer. The latter, perceiving that he spoke English badly, said to him: "Sir, you appear to me a foreigner, who are you?" "A French officer," rejoined the other. "*Je suis content*," Donop replied, making use of our language, "*je meurs entre les mains de l'honneur même*" (I am content, I die in the hands of honor itself).

The next day he was removed to the Quaker's house, where he lived three days, during which he conversed frequently with M. de Mauduit. He told him that he had long been a friend of M. de Saint-Germain [French Minister of War], that he wished in dying to recommend to him his conqueror and his benefactor. He asked for paper and wrote a letter, which he delivered to M. de Mauduit, requiring of him, as a final favor, that he would warn him when he was about to die. M. de Mauduit was soon under the necessity of acquitting himself of this sad duty. *"C'est finir de bonne heure une belle carrière,"* said the Colonel, *"mais je meurs victime de mon ambition et de l'avarice de mon souverain"* (This is finishing a noble career early, but I die the victim of my ambition and of the avarice of my sovereign). Fifteen wounded officers were found, like him, upon the field of battle; M. de Mauduit had the satisfaction of taking them himself to Philadelphia, where he was very well received by General Howe. By a curious coincidence it happened that the English had that very day learned indirectly of the capitulation of Burgoyne, of which M. de Mauduit knew more than they. They pretended to give no credit to the news: "You, who are a Frenchman," they said, "speak freely, do you think it is possible?" "I know for a fact that it is true," he said, "you may explain it as you will."

Perhaps I have dwelt too long on this event; but I shall not have to apologize to those who will share the sweet satisfaction I experience in fixing my eyes upon the triumphs of America and in discovering my own countrymen among those who have reaped her laurels.

Now I must hasten my return to Philadelphia, where, on my arrival, I had only time to dress before going out with the Chevalier de La Luzerne and with my traveling companions to dine with Mr. Huntington, the President of Congress. Mrs. Huntington, a stout, rather good-looking woman, but no longer young, did the honors of the table, that is to say, she helped everybody without saying a word. I did not remain long after dinner, as I had contrived a snug little rendezvous, which I was not inclined to miss. The reader is doubtless thinking that it is high time for me to add a bit of variety to this journal; but I am obliged to confess that this rendezvous was with Mr. Samuel Adams. We had promised each other at our last interview to set aside an evening for a tranquil tête-à-tête, and this was the day appointed. Our conversation began with a topic of which he might have spared himself the discussion, that is, the justice of the cause he is engaged in. I am firmly convinced that the Parliament of England had no right to tax America without her consent, but I am even more convinced that when a whole people says "I want to be free," it is difficult to prove to it that it is wrong. Be that as it may, Mr. Adams very satisfactorily proved to me that New England, which includes the states of Massachusetts, New Hampshire, Connecticut, and Rhode Island, had not been settled with any view to trade and conquest, but wholly by individuals who were fleeing from persecution and seeking an asylum in a remote land, where they might be free to live according to their opinions; that it was of their own accord that these colonies had placed themselves under the protection of England; that the mutual relationship springing from this connection had been expressed in their charters, and that the right of imposing or exacting a revenue of any kind had not been included in them.

From this subject we passed to a more interesting one, the form of government which should be given to each state; for it is only for the benefit of the future that it is necessary to concern oneself with the past. The revolution has been accomplished, and now the Republic is beginning; it is like a newborn child, which must be nourished and reared. I expressed to Mr. Adams some anxiety concerning the foundations on which the new constitutions had been formed, particularly that of Massachusetts. Every citizen, said I, every man who pays taxes, has a right to vote in the election of the representatives who form the legislative body which may be called "the Sovereign." All this is very well for the present moment, because every citizen is about equally well-off, or can become so in a short time; but the success of trade, and even of agriculture, will introduce riches among you, and riches will produce inequality of fortunes and of property. Now, wherever this inequality exists, the real force will invariably be on the side of property; so that if the influence in government be not proportioned to that of property, there will always be a contradiction, a struggle between the form of government and its natural tendency; the right will be on one side, and the power on the other; hence the balance can only exist between the two equally dangerous extremes of aristocracy and anarchy. Besides, the ideal worth of men must ever be comparative: an individual without property is a discontented citizen when the state is poor; place a rich man near him, he becomes a *manant*, a yokel. What then will one day become the right of election in this class of citizens? A source of civil unrest, or corruption, perhaps both at the same time.

Mr. Adams's answer to my remarks was about as follows. I am very sensible of the force of your objections; we are not what we should be; we should thus labor for the future rather than for the present moment. Suppose I build a country house and that I have young children; I ought doubtless to construct their apartments with an eye to the time in which they shall be grown up and married; but we have not neglected this precaution. In the first place, I must inform you that this new constitution was proposed and accepted in the most legal manner of which there is any example since the days of Lycurgus. A committee chosen from the members of the legislative body, then existing, and which might be considered as a provisional government, was named to prepare a new code of laws. As soon as it was prepared, each county or district was requested to name a committee to examine this plan and was asked to send it back at the expiration of a certain time, with their observations. These observations having been discussed by the legislative committee, and the necessary alterations made, the plan was sent back to each of the district committees. When they had all approved it, they received orders to submit it to the people "at large," and to ask for their suffrages. If two-thirds of the voters approved it, it was to have the force of law, and be regarded as the work of the people themselves; of twenty-two thousand votes, a much greater proportion than two-thirds was in favor of the new constitution. Now these are the principles on which it was established: a state is never free except when each citizen is bound by no law whatever that he has not approved of, either directly, or through his representatives; but to represent another man, it is necessary to have been elected by him; every citizen must therefore have a part in the elections. On the other hand, it would be in vain for the people to possess the right of electing representatives, were they restricted in the choice of them to a particular class; it was necessary therefore not to require too much property as a qualification for being a *representative of the people*. Accordingly, the House of Representatives, which forms the legislative body and is the true *Sovereign*, is the people themselves represented by their delegates.

Thus far the government is purely democratic; but it is the permanent and enlightened will of the people which must constitute law, and not the passions and whims to which they are too subject. It is necessary to moderate their first emotions and force them to consider and reflect. This is the important business entrusted to the Governor and Senate, who represent with us the negative power—vested in England in the upper house and in the Crown itself—with this difference only, that in our new constitution the Senate has a right to reject a law, and the Governor to suspend the promulgation, and then return it for a consideration; but these forms complied with, if, after this fresh examination, the people persist in their resolution, and there is then, not as before, a mere majority, but two-thirds of the suffrages in favor of the law, the Governor and Senate are compelled to give it their sanction.[84] Thus this power moderates, without destroying, the authority of the people, and such is the organization of our republic, that it prevents the springs from breaking by too rapid a movement, without ever stopping them entirely. Now, it is here that we have given to property all its privileges. A man must have a pretty considerable property to vote for a member of the Senate; he must have a more considerable one to be himself eligible. Thus democracy is pure and entire in the assembly which represents the *Sovereign;* and aristocracy, or, if you will, "optimacy," is to be found only in the moderating power, where it is the more necessary, as men never watch more carefully over the state than when they have great interests linked to its destiny. As to the power of commanding armies, it ought neither to be vested in a great, nor even in a small number of men: the Governor alone can employ the land and sea forces according to the need; but the land forces will consist only of the militia, which, as it is composed of the people themselves, can never act against the people.

Such was the idea Mr. Adams gave me of his own work,[85] for it is he who had the greatest share in the formation of the new laws. It is said, however, that before his credit was employed to get them accepted, it was necessary to combat his private opinion, and to make him abandon systems in which he loved to stray, for less sublime, but more practical projects. This citizen, otherwise so respectable, has been frequently reproached with consulting his library rather than present circumstances, and of always proceeding by way of the Greeks and Romans in order to reach the Whigs and Tories. If this be true, I shall only say that study has its drawbacks, but that these must be slight indeed, since Mr. Samuel Adams, heretofore the enemy of regular troops, and the most extravagant partisan of democracy, is at present employing all his influence to maintain a regular army and to establish a mixed government. Be this as it may, I left him well content with this conversation, which was interrupted only by a glass of Madeira, a dish of tea, and a former American general [Artemas Ward], who is now a member of Congress and who lodges with Mr. Adams.

I knew that there was a ball at the Chevalier de La Luzerne's, which made me less in a hurry to return there; it was, however, a very agreeable assembly, for the ball was given for a select society, on the occasion of a marriage. There were about twenty women, a dozen or fifteen of whom were dancers; each of the latter had her "partner," as is the custom in America. Dancing is said to be the emblem both of gaiety and of love; here it seems to be the emblem of legislation and of marriage; of legislation, inasmuch as places are marked out, the *contredanses* prescribed, and every proceeding provided for, calculated, and submitted to regulation; of marriage, since each lady is supplied with a "partner," with whom she must dance the whole evening, without being allowed to take another. It is true that every strict law requires some mitigation, and so it often happens that a young lady after dancing the first two or three dances with her "partner," may take a fresh choice or accept the invitation she receives; but the comparison still holds good, for the dancer has in this case merely made a marriage *à l'Européenne*. Strangers generally have the privilege of being "complimented with the handsomest ladies." The Comte de Damas thus had Mrs. [William] Bingham for his partner, and the Vicomte de Noailles, Miss [Nancy] Shippen. Both of them, like true philosophers, testified a great respect for the custom of the country, by not leaving their handsome partners during the whole evening; they furthermore compelled the admiration of the whole assembly by the grace and nobility with which they danced; I shall even assert, for the honor of my country, that for the space of this evening they outshone a high judge from Carolina (Mr. Pendleton) and two members of Congress, one of whom (Mr. Duane) passed however for being by 10 per cent more lively than all the other dancers. The ball was interrupted towards midnight by a supper, served *café*-style, at several different tables. On passing into the dining room, the Chevalier de La Luzerne offered his hand to Mrs. [Robert] Morris, and gave her the precedence, an honor rather generally bestowed on her, as she is the richest woman in the city, and all ranks here being equal, men follow their natural bent by giving the preference to wealth. The ball continued till two in the morning, as I learned only the next morning on rising, for I had seen too many attacks and battles the day before not to have learned to make a timely retreat.

December 9, 1780: Philadelphia

Our young folks needing some rest after their travels and their late hours, did not appear at breakfast. In their stead, we had an old Quaker by the name of [Anthony] Benezet, whose small stature and humble and unimposing looks formed a perfect contrast to Mr. Pendleton. This Mr. Benezet may rather be regarded as the model, than as a specimen of the sect of Quakers: wholly occupied with the welfare of mankind, his charity and generosity brought him great consideration in happier times, when the virtues alone sufficed to render a citizen illustrious. At present, the loud clash of arms deafens ears to the small voice of charity, and love of country has prevailed over the love of mankind. Benezet, however, still continues to exercise his benevolence: he had come to ask me for some information respecting the new methods invented in France for restoring drowned persons to life.[86] I promised not only to send him this information from Newport, but to transmit to him one of the boxes such as our government has distributed in the seaport towns. Confidence being established between us, we fell on the topic of the miseries of war.

"Friend," he said to me, "I know thou art a man of letters, and a member of the French Academy. The men of letters have written a great many good things of late; they have attacked errors and prejudices and, above all, intolerance; will they not endeavor, too, to disgust men with the horrors of war, and to make them live together like friends and brethren?" "Thou art not deceived, Friend," I replied, "when thou buildest some hope on the progress of enlightened philosophy. Many active hands are laboring at the great edifice of public happiness; but vainly will they employ themselves in finishing some parts of it, as long as there is a deficiency at the base, and that base, thou hast said it, is universal peace. As for intolerance and persecution, it is true that these two enemies of the human race are not yet bound by strong enough chains; but I will whisper a word in thy ear, of which thou wilt not perhaps feel all the force, though thou art well acquainted with French: *elles ne sont plus à la mode,* they are no longer fashionable; I should even believe them to be on the point of annihilation, but for certain little circumstances thou art not informed of; which are, that they who attack them are sometimes imprisoned, and that livings of a hundred thousand *livres* a year are bestowed upon those who favor them."

"A hundred thousand *livres* a year!" cried Benezet. "But that is enough to build hospitals and establish manufactures; this doubtless is the use they make of their riches." "No, Friend," I replied, "persecution needs bribes; though it must be confessed that it is but indifferently paid and that the most splendid of these persecutors content themselves with giving a pension of ten or twelve hundred *livres* to a few satirical poets, or journalists, enemies of letters, whose works are widely read but little sold." "Friend," the Quaker said to me, "this persecution is a strange thing: I can hardly believe what has happened to myself. My father was a Frenchman, and I was born in thy country. It is now sixty years since he was obliged to seek an asylum in England, taking with him his children, the only treasure he could save in his misfortunes. Justice, or what is so called in thy country, ordered him to be hung in effigy, because he explained the Gospel differently from thy priests. My father was not much better pleased with those of England; wishing to get out of the way of all hierarchy, he came and settled in this country, where I had a happy life until this war broke out.[87] I have long forgotten all the persecutions my family underwent. I love thy nation, because it is mild and sensible, and as for thee, Friend, I know that thou servest humanity as much as in thy power. When thou shalt be again in Europe, engage thy brethren to second thee and, in the meantime, permit me to place under thy protection our brethren of Rhode Island." He then recommended to me specifically the Quakers living in that state, and who are pretty numerous; after which he took leave, asking my permission to send me some pamphlets of his making, which were principally apologies for his sect. I assured him I would read them with great pleasure, and he did not fail to send them to me the next morning.[88]

To whatever sect he belongs, a man burning with zeal and love of humanity is, let there be no doubt of it, a being worthy of respect; but I must confess that it is difficult to bestow upon this sect in general that esteem which cannot be refused to some individuals.[89] The law observed by many of them, of saying neither *you* nor *sir*, is far from giving them a tone of simplicity and candor. I know not whether it be to compensate for this sort of rusticity that they often assume a smooth and wheedling tone which is altogether Jesuitical. Nor does their conduct belie this resemblance: concealing their indifference for the public welfare under the cloak of religion, they are indeed sparing of blood, especially of their own; [90]

but they trick both parties out of their money, and that without either shame or decency. It is a commonplace maxim in trade, to beware of them, and this opinion, which is well founded, will become still more so. In fact, nothing can be worse than religious enthusiasm in its decline; for what can be its substitute, but hypocrisy? This monster, so well known in Europe, finds but too easy an access to all religions. It found none, however, into a company of young ladies, who were invited, as well as myself, to drink tea with Mrs. Cunningham [Conyngham?]. They were well dressed, seemed desirous of pleasing, and it must be assumed that their private sentiments did not belie their appearance. The mistress of the house is amiable, and her conversation graceful and interesting. This assembly recalled to my mind in every respect those of Holland and of Geneva, where one meets with gaiety without indecency, and the wish to please without coquetry.

December 10, 1780: Philadelphia

On Sunday the 10th I had resolved to make a circuit through the churches and different places of worship. Unfortunately the different sects, who agree on no other point, have chosen the same hour to assemble the faithful, so that in the morning I was only able to visit the Quakers' meeting, and in the afternoon the Anglicans. The hall where the Quakers meet is square; there are, on all sides and parallel to the walls, benches and desks, so that people are placed facing each other, without either altar or pulpit to attract the attention.[91] As soon as they are assembled, one of the more elderly makes an impromptu prayer, just as it comes to his mind; silence is then observed until some man or woman feels inspired and rises to speak. Travelers must be taken at their word, however extraordinary their tales may be. Like Ariosto, I shall be recounting wonders, *dirò maraviglia:* but the fact is that I arrived just as a woman had stopped talking. She was followed by a man who talked a great deal of nonsense about inner grace, the illumination of the spirit, and the other dogmas of his sect, which he kept repeating but avoided explaining; at length his discourse ended to the great satisfaction of the brethren and the sisters, who all looked inattentive and bored. After seven or eight minutes of silence, an old man went on his knees, dealt us out a very commonplace prayer, and dismissed the audience.[92]

After this dreary and rustic assembly, the service of the Anglicans appeared to me a sort of opera, both because of the music and the scenery: a handsome pulpit placed before a handsome organ; a handsome minister in that pulpit, reading, speaking, and singing with truly theatrical grace; a number of young women responding melodiously from the pit and the boxes (for the two side galleries are much like boxes); soft and agreeable singing, alternating with excellent sonatas played on the organ; all this, compared to the Quakers, the Anabaptists, the Presbyterians, etc., appeared to me more like a little paradise in itself than as the road to it.[93] If however we consider these many different sects, some of them strict and others lax, but all of them imperious and all of them self-opinionated, we seem to see men reading in the great book of Nature, like illiterate Montauciel at his lesson. The letters as written actually spell *"vous êtes un blanc bec"* (you are a simpleton), but he persists in misreading them as fanciful nonsense of his own imagining. There is not one chance in a million that he can guess correctly a line of writing without knowing his letters; should he, however, come to implore your help, beware of giving it; better far to leave him in error than to cut throats with him! [94]

I shall mention my dinner this day at Mrs. Powel's, only to say that it was excellent and agreeable in every respect. The conversation carried us so far into the evening, that it was near eleven when I returned home.

December 11, 1780: Philadelphia—Visit to Whitemarsh

M. de La Fayette had made up a party with the Vicomte de Noailles and the Comte de Damas to go on the morning of the 11th, first to Germantown (which the two latter had not yet seen), and then to the old camp at Whitemarsh.[95] Though I had already reconnoitered Germantown, I had no objection to going over it a second time, and besides I was curious to see the Whitemarsh camp. This is the camp that General Washington occupied after the unsuccessful attempt against Germantown [October 3-4, 1777]. As this position was a bold one and as the English never dared attack it, it enjoys much celebrity in the American army, where they like to say that only two redoubts constituted the whole entrenchment. As a matter of fact the position is excellent and does great honor to General Washington, who managed to discover it, as if by instinct, through the woods with which the country was then covered; but it is no less true that General Howe had every reason for not attacking it. Here are its main features. Descending from the heights of Germantown, you find very thick woods; on coming out of these woods, to the west, you see a fairly high hill, at the foot of which flows a brook [Wissahickon Creek], with steep banks, which turns towards the north and protects the right [west] of the camp. Six pieces of cannon were placed on this height, with four hundred men who formed an advanced post. A little church [St. Thomas's] which is on the summit of the hill has given it the name of Chestnut Church ["Church Hill"]: behind this height and behind the woods which stretch from east to west, the ground rises considerably, and forms two hills ["Fort Hill" and "Camp Hill"] with gentle slopes which command Chestnut Church ["Church Hill"]; here the army was encamped. These hills are separated only by a small hollow; the summit of each was fortified with a redoubt and the slope defended by an abatis. The hill on the left [east, i.e., "Camp Hill"] was still further protected by a brook [Sandy Run], which could be increased at pleasure, as it ran behind the camp and it was easy to make the dams necessary for raising the waters. To be sure, the front of this position is covered with woods, but these woods terminate at three hundred paces from the front lines; an enemy therefore would have had to come out of them uncovered, and how, furthermore, could they come through a wood where there is no road and which had been filled with militia and "riflemen"? I took special pains to point out to M. de La Fayette all the advantages of this position, and even amused myself by exaggerating them for his benefit, in order to convince him that he was a braggart along with the rest of them (*Gascon comme les autres*). He admitted to me that the camp was indeed a good one, and that if the English deserved the jokes made at their expense, it was only because they had said in their account of the affair that the rebels were so well *entrenched* that it was impossible to attack them. We were even more easily in agreement when I concluded that the more respectable this position was, the more honor it did to General Washington, who had divined rather than reconnoitered it. His was verily an eagle's eye, for it seems as if he must have soared above the treetops in order to see the ground beneath them.

Having completed our reconnaissance, we returned briskly to the Chevalier de La Luzerne's, where dinner came very *à propos*, after being eight hours on horseback and riding thirty-six miles. After dinner we took tea at Mrs. Shippen's.[96] This was the first time since my arrival in America that I had seen music slip into society and mingle with its amusements. Miss Rutledge played on the harpsichord, and played very well. Miss Shippen sang with timidity, but with a pretty voice. Mr. Otto, secretary to the Chevalier de La Luzerne, sent for his harp; he accompanied Miss Shippen, and also played several pieces. Music naturally leads to dancing: the Vicomte de Noailles took down a violin, which they fitted up with harp strings, and he made the young ladies dance, while their mothers and the other grave personages chatted in another room. If music and the fine arts prosper in Philadelphia; if society there becomes easy and gay, and they learn to accept pleasure when it presents itself, without a formal invitation, then they will be able to enjoy all the advantages peculiar to their manners and government, without having to envy Europe for anything.[97]

December 12, 1780: Philadelphia—Visit to Barren Hill

The 12th, in the morning, another cavalcade, and another reconnoitering party. This time it was M. de La Fayette's turn to do the honors. The interest that he rightly inspires has rendered even more famous an event, which is in itself singular enough. In June [May] 1778, the alliance with France by then being public knowledge, it seemed likely that the English would not long delay the evacuation of Philadelphia. Under these circumstances, though it was General Washington's business to risk nothing, it was important nevertheless to watch the movements of the enemy. M. de La Fayette thus received orders to march [May 18, 1778] from Valley Forge, with two thousand infantry, fifty dragoons, and as many Indians, cross the Schuylkill [at Swede's Ford], and take post on a height called Barren Hill, about twelve miles distant from Philadelphia.[98] The position was critical: he might be attacked or turned by any one of three different roads; but M. de La Fayette guarded the most direct of the three [Ridge Road]; a brigadier general of militia, named [James] Potter, had orders to watch the second, and patrols kept an eye upon the third, which was the most circuitous. Though these precautions seemed sufficient at first glance, they must not have been deemed so by General Howe, for he thought he had really caught "the Marquis" this time. He even carried his gasconade so far as to invite ladies to meet the Marquis at supper the next day, and while most of the officers were still at the play,[99] he put in motion the main body of his forces, which he marched in three columns. The first, commanded by General Howe in person, took the direct road to Barren Hill, passing through Falls of Schuylkill and keeping along the river; the second, led by General Grey, took the Germantown high road and was to head for M. de La Fayette's left flank; the third, under the orders of General Grant, made a long detour, marching first out the Frankford road, then turned [westward] at Oxford, to reach the only ford by which the Americans could retreat.

This combined march was executed the more easily as the English had positive intelligence that the militia had not occupied the post assigned them. Fortunately for M. de La Fayette, two officers had set out early from the camp to go into the Jerseys on business; these officers having successively met up with two columns of the enemy, decided to return to the camp through the woods and as quickly as possible. As for General Howe's column, it was not long in reaching the advanced posts of M. de La Fayette, which gave rise to a laughable enough adventure. The fifty Indians who had been assigned to La Fayette were placed in the woods, in ambush, after their manner, that is to say, lying as close as rabbits. Fifty English dragoons, at the head of the column, rode into the woods. They had never seen any Indians and the Indians had never seen any dragoons. So, up jumped the savages with a horrible cry, threw down their arms, and escaped to safety by swimming across the Schuylkill, while the dragoons, as frightened as they were, turned tail and fled in such a panic that they could not be stopped until they reached Philadelphia. M. de La Fayette now realized that he had been outflanked. He surmised, with good military judgment, that the column marching against him would not be the first to make the attack and that it would wait until the other was in readiness. He therefore immediately changed his front and took a good position facing the second column, having the Barren Hill Church in front of him and behind him the opening which served as a retreat. But he had no sooner occupied this position than he learned that General Grant was marching in the direction of the ford across the Schuylkill and was already nearer to it than he was. Nothing remained but to retreat: but the only road he could take brought him close to General Grant's column and exposed him to be attacked by it in front, while Grey and Howe fell upon his rear. As a matter of fact, this road, soon turning to the left, became separated by a small valley from the one that General Grant would take, but this valley itself was crossed by several roads and it must, in short, be traversed to reach the ford. In this situation, greatness of mind alone suggested to the young soldier the proper conduct, as effectively as the most consummate experience could have done. He knew that more honor is lost, than time gained, in converting a *retreat* into a *flight*. He continued his march, therefore, in such quiet and regular order, that he deceived General Grant into believing that he was supported by Washington's whole army, which was waiting for him at the end of the defile. On the other hand, Howe himself, on arriving on the heights of Barren Hill, was deceived by the first maneuver of M. de La Fayette; for seeing the Americans in line of battle, on the very spot where his second column was to appear, he thought it was General Grey who had got possession of this position, and thus lost some minutes in looking through his spy-glass and in sending scouts to reconnoiter. General Grey also lost time in waiting for the right and left columns. The result of all these mistakes was that M. de La Fayette effected his retreat as if by magic, and crossed the river [at Matson's Ford, i.e., Consho-hocken] with all his artillery without losing a man. Six alarm guns, which were fired at army headquarters [Valley Forge], on the first news of this attack, served, I believe, to deceive the enemy, who imagined the whole American army was on the march. The English, after discovering that the bird had flown, returned to Philadelphia, spent with fatigue, and shamefaced at having caught nothing. The ladies did not meet the Marquis, and General Howe himself arrived too late for supper.

In relating this affair, I am also giving an account of my ride, for I followed the road taken by the English left column. This road leads to Falls of Schuylkill, which is a small settlement where there are several very pretty country houses, the Chevalier de La Luzerne's among others.[100] A small creek which flows into the Schuylkill after a fall of ten or twelve feet, the mills turned by this creek, the trees which cover its banks and those of the Schuylkill, form a most pleasing landscape, which [Hubert] Robert and [Jean-Baptiste] Le Prince would find worth painting.

This ride, which was not so long as the one taken the day before, left me two hours at my disposal; and I took this opportunity to visit the left [west] of the English lines which I had not yet seen.[101] M. de Gimat was willing to leave the rest of the company, and instead of returning directly to Philadelphia, we turned off to the right, in order to follow the lines back to the Schuylkill. I found that from the center to the left of these lines their position was nothing less than advantageous, particularly near a burned house, towards which I should have directed my attack, had I been in circumstances to make one. From a ridge of ground, where the English had in fact formed a semicircular battery towards the Schuylkill, the glacis is against the lines; so that the assailant might first march under cover, and then command the batteries which defend them. At the very left, and very close to the Schuylkill, the ground rises considerably: the English had not failed to avail themselves of this by constructing here a large redoubt and a battery; but this summit is itself commanded and surveyed from behind by the heights on the other side of the river. Be this as it may, these works were sufficient to secure an army of 15,000 men against one of 7,000 or 8,000 at most. At every step one takes in America, one is astonished at the striking contrast between the contempt in which the English affect to hold their enemies, and the extreme precautions they take on every occasion.

Nothing can equal the beauty of the view afforded by the banks of the Schuylkill as you proceed southward to return to Philadelphia.

I found a rather numerous company assembled for dinner at the Chevalier de La Luzerne's; it was still further increased by the arrival of the Comte de Custine and the Marquis de Laval.[102] In the evening we took them first to see the President of Congress [Samuel Huntington], who was not at home, and then to Mr. [Richard] Peters, the Secretary of the Board of War, to whom it was also my first visit.[103] His house is not large, nor his office of great importance; for everything which is not in the power of the General of the army depends on each particular state, much more than on Congress; but he possesses what is preferable to all the offices in the world, an amiable wife,[104] excellent health, a fine voice, and a happy and agreeable disposition. We conversed some time together, and he spoke to me of the American army with as much frankness as good sense. He admitted that this army was formerly quite unacquainted with discipline, and he strongly emphasized the obligations it owed to Baron von Steuben, who fulfills the functions of Inspector General. Passing then to praise of Messrs. de Fleury, Duportail, and all the French officers who had served America in the late campaigns, he admitted that those who had offered their services at the beginning had not given such an advantageous idea of their country. They were almost all supplied, however, with letters of recommendation from the governors or commanders of our colonies, who, it seems to me, acted most reprehensibly in this respect. The weakness which prevents men from refusing a letter of recommendation, or the desire to get rid of an undesirable character, continually prevail over justice and good faith; not only do we deceive and compromise our allies, but what is more, we betray the interests of our own country, whose honor and character are thus shamefully prostituted.

I shall mention Mr. [James] Price, with whom we drank tea and finished the evening, only to bear witness to the generosity of this true gentleman who, born in Canada and always attached to the French, lent two hundred thousand *livres* of hard money to M. de Corny, when the [French] Court sent him [to America] with only fifty thousand *livres* to provide supplies for our army.[105]

December 13, 1780: Philadelphia

The 13th, I went with the Chevalier de La Luzerne, and the French travelers, to dine with the southern delegates. Messrs. [William] Sharpe [North Carolina], "Flowy," and [James] Madison [Virginia], were the nearest to me; I conversed a great deal with them, and was much satisfied with their conversation.[106] But I was still more so with that I had in the afternoon at Mrs. [Samuel] Meredith's, General [John] Cadwalader's daughter:[107] this was the first time I had seen this amiable family, although the Chevalier de La Luzerne was very intimate with them; but they had only just arrived from the country, where General Cadwalader was still detained by business. It is this gentleman who had a duel with Mr. C*** [Conway] and severely wounded him in the jaw with a pistol shot.[108] Mrs. Meredith has three or four sisters, or sisters-in-law. I was astonished at the freedom and gaiety which reigned in this family, and regretted not having known them sooner. I chattered more particularly with Mrs. Meredith, who appeared to me very amiable and well informed. In the course of an hour we talked of literature, poetry, novels, and above all, history; I found she knew that of France very well; the comparison between Francis I and Henry IV, between Turenne and Condé, Richelieu and Mazarin, seemed familiar to her, and she made them with much grace, wit, and understanding. While I was talking with Mrs. Meredith, M. Lynch had got possession of Miss Polly Cadwalader, who had likewise made a conquest of him, so that when we had left, the Chevalier de La Luzerne was much entertained at the enthusiasm with which this company had inspired us, and the regret we expressed at not having become sooner acquainted with them. It must be said for the honor of the ladies who compose it, that none of them is what is called pretty; this mode of expression is perhaps a little too circuitous for American women, but these would have wit enough to comprehend; and if they should also have enough to take it as a compliment, nothing further could be said in their praise.

December 14, 1780: Philadelphia

I know not how it happened that since my arrival in Philadelphia I had not yet seen Mr. [Thomas] Paine, famed in America and throughout Europe as the author of the excellent work entitled *Common Sense*, and of several other political pamphlets. M. de La Fayette and I had asked the permission of an interview for the 14th in the morning, and we waited on him accordingly with Colonel [John] Laurens. I discovered, at his apartments, all the attributes of a man of letters; a room pretty much in disorder, dusty furniture, and a large table covered with books lying open and half-finished manuscripts.[109] His dress was in keeping with the room, nor did his physiognomy belie the spirit that reigns in his works. Our conversation was agreeable and animated, and such as to form a connection between us, for he has written to me since my departure, and seems desirous of continuing a sustained correspondence with me. His existence at Philadelphia is similar to that of those political writers in England who have obtained neither credit enough in the state, nor sufficient personal consideration to have a part in the affairs of government. Their works are read with more curiosity than confidence, their projects being regarded rather as an exercise of their imagination than as plans that are well grounded and authoritative enough ever to produce any real effect: theirs is always considered as the work of an individual, and not that of a party; information may be drawn from them, but not consequences; accordingly we observe that the influence of these authors is more felt in the satirical than in the dogmatical style, as it is easier for them to decry other men's opinions than to establish their own. This is more the case with Mr. Paine than another; for having formerly held a post in the government, he has now no connection with it; and as his patriotism and his talents cannot be questioned, it is natural to conclude that the vivacity of his imagination and the independence of his character have rendered him better suited for reasoning on affairs, than for conducting them.[110] Another literary man, as much respected, though less celebrated, expected us for dinner; this was Mr. [James] Wilson, whom I have already mentioned: his house and library are in the best order; he gave us an excellent dinner, and received us with a plain and easy politeness.[111] Mrs. Wilson did the honors of the table with all possible attention; but we were particularly sensible to the mark of it she gave us, by retiring after the dessert, for then the dinner began to grow merry. Mr. [Richard] Peters, the Minister of War, gave the signal for mirth and jollity by favoring us with a song of his own composition, so broad and unrestrained that I shall dispense with giving either a translation, or a selection of it here. This was really an excellent song. He then sang another, more chaste and more musical; this was a very fine Italian *cantabile*.[112] Mr. Peters is unquestionably the minister of the two worlds who has the best voice and who sings best both the pathetic and the *bouffon*—a fact doubtless unknown in Europe and one which could not have been guessed at there. I was told that the preceding year there were still some private concerts at Philadelphia, where he sang among other comic opera pieces, a burlesque part in a trio which was in itself very pleasing, and which he seasoned with all the humorous strokes usual on such occasions. The company laughed most heartily, so that this was not the time for saying, "one cannot lose a kingdom more gaily," but only, "it is impossible to be more gay in forming a republic." After this, you may conclude from the particular to the general, judge of whole nations by one specimen, and establish your general principles!

   The assembly, or subscription ball, of which I must give an account, may be properly introduced here. In Philadelphia, as in London, Bath, Spa, etc., there are places appropriated for the young people to dance in, and where those whom that amusement does not suit play at different card games; but in Philadelphia no gambling is allowed—that is, except in trade. A "manager," or master of ceremonies presides over these methodical amusements: he presents to the gentlemen and lady dancers folded papers each containing a number; thus fate decides what "partner" you must have and keep for the rest of the evening. All the dances are previously arranged, and the dancers are called each in their turn. These dances, like the "toasts" we drink at table, have a marked connection with politics: one is called "the success of the campaign," another "Burgoyne's defeat," and a third, "Clinton's retreat." The "managers" are generally chosen from among the most distinguished officers of the army; this important place is at present held by Colonel [James] Wilkinson, who is also "clothier," that is, in charge of clothing the troops. Colonel [John] Mitchell, a little fat, squat man, fifty years old, a great judge of horses, and who was lately contractor for carriages, both for the American and French armies, was formerly the "manager"; but when I saw him, he had stepped down from the magistracy and was dancing like a private citizen. He is said to have exercised his office with great strictness, and it is told of him that when a young lady who was figuring in a square dance forgot her turn because she was conversing with a friend, he came up to her and loudly called out, "Come, come, watch what you are doing; do you think you are here for pleasure?"

The assembly I went to on leaving Mr. Wilson's was the second of the winter. I was apprised that it would be neither numerous nor brilliant, for in Philadelphia, as in Paris, the best company seldom go to the balls before Christmas. However, on entering the room, which was rather well lighted, I found twenty or twenty-five ladies dancing. It was whispered to me that having heard a great deal about the Vicomte de Noailles and the Comte de Damas, they had come with hopes of having them for partners; but they were completely "disappointed," for these gentlemen had set out that very morning. I should have been "disappointed" also, had I expected to see pretty women. There were only two passable, one of whom, called Miss Footman, was a bit contraband, that is to say, suspected of not being a very good Whig, for the Tory ladies have been publicly banned from this assembly.[113] I was here presented to a rather ridiculous personage, but who plays her part in the town, a Miss V*** [Vining], celebrated for her coquetry, her wit and sharp tongue; she is thirty, and does not seem on the point of marriage.[114] In the meantime she applies red, white, blue, and all possible colors, affects an extraordinary mode of dressing her hair and person, and, a staunch Whig in every point, she sets no bounds to her liberty.

December 15, 1780: Philadelphia

I had intended to leave Philadelphia on the 15th, but the President of the state [Joseph Reed], who is also President [Patron] of the Academy [i.e., American Philosophical Society] was so good as to invite me to a meeting of that body to be held that day.[115] It was the more difficult for me to refuse his invitation, as it had already been proposed to elect me a foreign member. The meetings are held only once a fortnight, and the elections take place but once a year: every candidate must be presented and recommended by a member of the academy; after which recommendation his name is posted during three successive meetings in the hall where the academy convenes, and the election is at length proceeded to by "ballots." I learned of mine only three days ago.[116] It was unanimous, which very rarely happens. M. de La Fayette himself, who was elected at the same time, had one "ball" against him, but this is thought to have been a mistake. I have been informed that out of twenty-one candidates, only seven of us were chosen, although the others had been strongly recommended, and there were several vacancies.

As the sittings of the academy do not begin until seven in the evening, I spent my morning in making a few calls, after which I dined at Mr. Holker's [117] with the Chevalier de La Luzerne, M. de La Fayette, and all the French officers; then I went to the academy, accompanied by M. de Marbois, who belongs to the society, as does M. de La Luzerne.[118] The latter, having other business, excused himself from attending me, but left me in very good hands. M. de Marbois combines with all possible political and social talents a great deal of literature and a perfect knowledge of the English language. The assembly consisted of only fourteen or fifteen persons; the president of the college [John Ewing] performed the office of secretary. A memoir was read on a singular native plant; the secretary then reported on the correspondence, and read a letter, the object of which was for the academy of Philadelphia to associate with, or rather adopt, several learned societies which are being formed in each state. This project tended to make of this academy a sort of literary "congress," with corresponding "legislatures" in each state, but it was not thought proper to adopt this idea; the members seeming to be afraid of the trouble inseparable from all these adoptions, and the academy not wishing to make the following lines of Racine's *Athalie* [Act III, Scene 7] applicable to it:

D'où lui viennent de tous côtés
Ces enfans qu'en son sein elle n'a pas portés?

Whence come to her from all sides
These children whom she has not given birth to?

I returned as soon as possible to the Chevalier de La Luzerne's, to enjoy once more that society which had constituted my happiness for the last fortnight: for it is unquestionably a very great satisfaction to live with a man whose amiable and mild character never varies on any occasion, whose conversation is agreeable and instructive, and whose easy and unaffected politeness is the genuine expression of his natural disposition. But however legitimate it may be to declare one's own sentiments, when dictated by justice and gratitude, there is always a sort of personal prejudice in considering public men only on the basis of their connections with ourselves: I also owe my testimony and my praise to the King's Minister in America, to a man who most ably fills a most important post. I shall say, therefore, without fear of contradiction, that the Chevalier de La Luzerne is so well fitted for the station he occupies that one cannot imagine that any other but himself could fill it: noble in his expenditures as befits the Minister of a great monarchy, but as simple in his manners as a republican, he is equally well fitted to represent the King with Congress, or the Congress with the King. He loves the Americans, and his own inclination attaches him to the duties of his mission; he has accordingly obtained their confidence, both as a private and a public man; but in both these respects he is equally inaccessible to the spirit of party which reigns only too much around him; whence it results, that he is anxiously courted by all parties, and that by espousing none, he moderates them all.

A General View of Philadelphia

The details of my daily occupations having prevented me from giving a general idea of Philadelphia, I must, on leaving it, take a backward glance and consider both its present state and the destiny which is in store for it. In observing its geographical situation, we may readily admit that Penn was not mistaken when he conceived its plan in such a way as to make it one day the capital of America. Two large rivers,[119] which take their rise in the neighborhood of

Lake Ontario, convey to it the riches of all the interior parts of the country and unite to form a magnificent port for this city. This port is at once far enough from the sea to shelter it from every insult; and so near, as to render it as easy of access as if situated on the shore of the ocean. The Schuylkill, which runs to the west of Philadelphia, and nearly parallel with the Delaware, is ornamental rather than useful to this city and its commerce. This river, though wide and beautiful near its conflux, is not navigable for boats, on account of its shallow and rocky bed. Philadelphia, placed between these two rivers, on a neck of land only three miles broad, was to have filled up this space, but trade has decided otherwise. The regular plan of William Penn has been followed, but the buildings are along the Delaware, for the convenience of being near the warehouses and shipping. Front Street, which is parallel to the river, is nearly three miles long, out of which open upwards of two hundred quays, forming as many views with vessels of different sizes in the background.[120] I could easily form an idea of the commerce of Philadelphia from seeing more than three hundred vessels in the harbor, although the English had not left a single bark in it in 1778. Two years of tranquillity, and, above all, the diversion made by our squadron at Rhode Island, have sufficed to collect this great number of vessels, the success of which in privateering, as well as in trade, have filled the warehouses with goods, to such an extent that the goods lack purchasers, and not the purchasers goods. The wisdom of the legislative council, however, has not always kept abreast with the advantages lavished by Nature. Pennsylvania is very far from being the best governed state of the Confederation. Exposed more than any other to the convulsions of credit and to the maneuvers of speculation, the instability of public wealth has made itself felt in the legislation itself. An attempt was made to fix the value of paper currency, but commodities augmented in price, in proportion as money lost its value; a resolution was then taken to fix the price also of commodities, which almost produced a famine. A more recent error of the government was the law prohibiting the exportation of grain. The object they had in view was on the one hand to supply the American army at a cheaper rate, and on the other to put a stop to the contraband trade between Pennsylvania and the city of New York [occupied by the British]; the result was the ruin of the farmers and of the state, which could no longer obtain payment of the taxes. This law has just been repealed, so that

I hope agriculture will soon resume its vigor and commerce make further gains. Wheat sent to the army will be a bit more expensive, but there will be infinitely more means to pay for it; and should there be some smuggling with New York, English money will at least circulate among their enemies.[121]

It is greatly to be wished that paper may at length obtain an established credit, no matter what value; for it signifies little whether the price of a sheep be represented by one hundred and fifty paper dollars, or two dollars in specie. This depreciation of paper money is not felt in those places where it remains the same; but Philadelphia is, so to speak, the great sink wherein all the speculation of America terminates and mingles. Since the capture of Charleston many of the inhabitants of Carolina have hastily sold their estates and crops, and having been paid only in paper, they have brought this capital with them to Philadelphia, already overstocked with it.[122] The Quakers and Tories, on the other hand, with which this province abounds, two classes of men equally dangerous, one from their timidity, and the other from their bad intentions, are incessantly laboring to secure their fortunes; they lavish the paper for a little gold or silver, to enable them to remove wherever they may think themselves in safety; for these reasons, paper money is more and more depreciated, not only because it is too common, but because gold and silver are extremely scarce and too much sought after.

In the midst of these convulsions the government is without force, nor can it be otherwise. A popular government cannot be strong whenever the people are uncertain and vacillating in their opinions; for then the leaders seek to please rather than to serve them; obliged to gain their confidence before they merit it, they are more inclined to flatter than to enlighten them, and fearing to lose popular favor as soon as they have acquired it, they end up by becoming the slaves of the multitude whom they pretended to govern. Mr. Franklin has been blamed for giving too democratic a government to his state, but they who censure him do not reflect that the first step was to make her renounce monarchical government, and that it was necessary to employ a sort of seduction in order to lead to independence a timid and avaricious people, who were besides so divided in their opinions that the party of liberty was scarcely stronger than the other. Under these circumstances he acted like Solon: he has not given the best possible laws to Pennsylvania, but the best of which the country was susceptible. Time will produce perfection: when pleading to recover an estate, the first object is to obtain possession, and then to think about further arrangements.[123]

Philadelphia contains about forty thousand inhabitants. The streets are wide and regular, and intersect each other at right angles. There are sidewalks here, as in London, for pedestrians. This city lacks none of the most useful establishments, such as hospitals, work-houses, houses of correction, etc., but it is so deficient in what might serve for the enjoyment of life, that there is not a single public walk.[124] The reason for this is that hitherto everything concerning the police and particular government of the city has been in the hands of the Quakers, and these sectarians consider every species of private or public amusement as a transgression of their law and as a "pomp of Satan." Fortunately the little zeal they have displayed in the present crisis has made them lose their credit. This revolution comes very opportunely, at a time when the public has derived every benefit from them they could expect; the walls of the house are finished—it is time to call in the cabinetmakers and upholsterers.

Chapter

================ 4 ================

NORTH THROUGH NEW JERSEY
AND UP THE HUDSON TO ALBANY

December 16, 1780: Philadelphia—Bristol, Pa.—Princeton, N.J.

I T was on the 16th of December that I left the excellent winter
quarters I had with the Chevalier de La Luzerne to make my
way northward and to seek amidst the snowdrifts the traces of
General Gates and General Burgoyne. I had sent my horses ahead
to await me at Bristol, where I was driven in a carriage which the
Chevalier de La Luzerne was so kind as to lend me. By this means
I gained time and was able to reach Princeton that night, but not
before it was dark, leaving behind me some of my servants and
horses.

December 17, 1780: Princeton—Bullion's Tavern [Liberty Corner]

I intended setting out early on the 17th, to continue my journey
to Albany, via New Windsor, where General Washington had established his winter headquarters. Indeed, I needed to push on
briskly in order to reach Morristown that night, but as my baggage
horse had not been able to cross over the Delaware at the same
time that I did, I had left one of my people there to wait and bring
him along to me later. It so happened that neither the horse and
driver, nor the other servant who was to guide him, had arrived.
One of the servants was an Irishman, the other a German, both
newly entered into my service. As I watched the morning of the
17th advance without their putting in an appearance, the neighborhood of New York began to give me some uneasiness. I feared that
they might have continued along the New York road with my

small baggage,[1] and I was already making plans to pursue them
when, to my great satisfaction, I saw the head of my baggage column appear, that is, one of the three horses which were left behind,
the remainder following soon after. Meanwhile, however, to calm
my impatience, I had entered into conversation with my landlord,
Colonel [Jacob] Hyer, who is a very good man, and with his son
the Captain, a great talker and a true *Capitan*.[2] He related to me
with many gestures, oaths, and imprecations all his feats of prowess
in the war; especially at the affair of Princeton, where he served as
a lieutenant of militia in his father's regiment; and indeed the action
he boasted of would have merited much praise, had he related it
with simplicity. It will be recalled that after beating the English at
Princeton General Washington continued his route towards Middle
Brook. An American officer, whose leg had been broken by a musket ball, was dragged into a house, where the English sooner or later
must have found him: young Hyer, and several soldiers as well disposed as himself, set out at night from Middle Brook, took a circuitous road, arrived at the house, found the officer, took him on
their shoulders, and carried him back to their quarters. During the
remainder of that winter, the Jersey militia were constantly under
arms to contain the English, who occupied Elizabethtown and
[New] Brunswick. It was a sort of continual hunting party, to
which Lieutenant Hyer one day took his little brother, a lad of
fifteen, who was lucky enough to begin his career by killing a Hessian grenadier. As all these stories were very tedious, I shall not
attempt to record them here, lest they remain equally tedious in
the retelling. I must mention however the manner in which my
Capitan entered into the service, since this will indicate the spirit
which reigned in America at the beginning of the present revolution. He was apprentice to a hatter at the time of the affair of Lex-
ington and the blockade of Boston; three of his companions and
himself set out one morning from Philadelphia with only four dollars among them in their pockets; they traveled four hundred miles
on foot to join the army, in which they served as volunteers for the
remainder of the campaign; from there they set out with [Benedict]
Arnold on his expedition to Canada, and did not return home till
the theater of war was removed into their own part of the country.

Eleven o'clock had already struck before I had managed to rally
my horses and get on my way. I therefore abandoned my plan of
spending that night at Morristown, and decided to stop at Basking

Ridge, eight miles nearer Princeton. I first left the Millstone on the right, then crossed it twice before I reached the Raritan, which I crossed at the same place as I did on my journey southward to Philadelphia. Three miles farther along I was told to take a road to the right, which leads into the woods and over the crest of the [Watchung] mountains; this route was opened for the army during the winter quarters of 1778-79; it appears to have been made with care and is still passable; but after some time, daylight failing me, I got lost and went a mile or two out of my way. Luckily for me, I found a hut inhabited by some new settlers; there I got a guide who took me to Basking Ridge, which I reached at seven o'clock. I alighted at Bullion's Tavern [Liberty Corner], where I found tolerable lodgings and the best people in the world.[3] Our supper was very good: only bread was lacking; but inquiring of us what sort we wanted, in an hour's time they served us what we had asked for. This speed will appear less extraordinary, if one knows that in America little cakes (*galettes*) which are easily kneaded and baked in half an hour often take the place of bread. Possibly one might in the long run tire of them, but I always found them to my taste whenever I met with them. Mr. Bullion [John Boylan] had two white servants, one a man about fifty, the other a woman, younger, with a tolerable good face: I had the curiosity to inquire what wages he gave them, and was told that the man earned half a crown a day, and the woman six shillings a week, or ten pence a day. If we note that these servants are lodged and fed, and have no expenses, we may see that it is easy for them very shortly to acquire a piece of land, and to start a settlement like those I have already described.

December 18, 1780: Bullion's Tavern [Liberty Corner]—Pompton [Pompton Plains]—Curtis's Tavern [Pompton Lakes]

The 18th I set out at eight in the morning, and made only one stage to Pompton; that is, thirty-six miles, without baiting my horses or stopping, except for a quarter of an hour to pay a visit to General [Anthony] Wayne, whose quarters were on the main road.[4] He was entrusted with covering the Jerseys, and had under his orders the same Pennsylvania line which revolted a fortnight after. I again saw with pleasure the environs of Morristown, because they are agreeable and well cultivated; but after crossing the Rockaway and approaching Pompton [Pompton Plains], I was astonished at the degree of perfection to which agriculture was carried and particularly admired the farms of Messrs. Mandeville.[5] They are the sons of a Dutchman, who first cleared the ground from which they now reap such rich harvests. Their domains join each other. In each of them the manor is very simple and small, the barns alone are lofty and spacious. Always faithful to their nation's traditional thriftiness, they cultivate, reap, and sell, without enlarging either their houses or their enjoyments, content with living in a corner of their farm, and with being only the spectators of their own wealth. By the side of these old farms you see new settlements forming, and have more and more reason to be convinced that if the war has retarded the progress of agriculture and population, it has not entirely suspended them. The night, which surprised me on my journey, deprived me of the beautiful prospect this country would have continued to afford. Being very dark, it was not without difficulty that I crossed over two or three rivulets on very small bridges, and reached "Courtheath's" Tavern.[6] This inn has been only recently established, and is kept by young people without fortune, consequently the best parts of the furniture are the owner and his family. Mr. "Courtheath" [Joseph Curtis] is a young man of twenty-four, who was formerly a peddler of cloth, trinkets, etc. The depreciation of paper money, or perhaps his own imprudence, so far ruined him as to oblige him to leave his house at Morristown, and set up a tavern in this out-of-the-way place, where only the proximity of the army can procure him a few customers. He has two pretty sisters, well-dressed girls, who wait on travelers with grace and coquetry. Their brother says he will marry them each to some fat lout of a Dutchman, and that as for himself, as soon as he has earned a little money, he will resume his trade and travel about again. On entering the parlor, where these young women sit, when there are no strangers, I found on a big table Milton, Addison, Richardson, and several other books of that kind. The cellar was not nearly so well supplied as the library, for there was neither wine, cider, nor rum, but only some bad cider-brandy, with which I had to make grog. The bill they presented me the next morning amounted nevertheless to sixteen dollars.[7] I observed to Mr. "Courtheath," that if he was charging me for the pleasure of being waited on by his pretty sisters, this was much too little, but if only for lodgings and supper, it was a great deal. He seemed a little ashamed at having charged too much, and offered me a rather considerable reduction, which I refused, content with having shown him that though a foreigner, I was no stranger to the price of things, and satisfied with the excuse he made me, that being himself a stranger and without property in the region he lived in, he was obliged to purchase everything. I learned on this occasion that he hired the house he kept as an inn, as well as a large barn which served for a stable, and a garden of two or three acres, all for eighty bushels of wheat a year: in fact, the depreciation of paper has compelled him to this manner of doing business, which is perhaps the best method of all, but which is in any case an effectual remedy to the present disorder.

December 19, 1780: Curtis's Tavern [Pompton Lakes]—Ringwood, N.J.—Tuxedo Lake, N.Y.—Hern's Tavern

At eight o'clock next morning I took leave of my landlord and young landladies, to plunge into the woods by a road with which nobody was too well acquainted. The country I was to pass through, called "the Clove," is extremely wild, and was scarcely known before the war: it is a sort of valley, or gorge, situated to the westward of the high mountains which extend between New Windsor and King's Ferry, and at the foot of which are West Point and Stony Point, and the principal forts which defend the river. At times when the river is not navigable, either on account of ice or of contrary winds, it is necessary to have some communication by land between the states of New York and the Jerseys, between New Windsor and Morristown. This route of communication passes through the Clove, so that when General [Nathanael] Greene was Quartermaster General he opened a road through it for convoys of supplies and the artillery. This is the road I took, leaving on my right the Ramapo road, and following up the one that comes from Ringwood. Ringwood is little more than a hamlet of seven or eight houses, formed by Mrs. Erskine's manor and the forges which she operates.[8] I had been told that I should find there all sorts of conveniences, whether in point of lodgings, if I chose to stop, or in procuring any information I might stand in need of. As it was early in the day, and I had traveled but twelve miles, I alighted at Mrs. Erskine's, only to ask her to tell me of some inn where I might sleep, or to recommend me to some hospitable quarters. I entered a very handsome house where everybody was in mourning, Mr. Erskine having died two months before. Mrs. Erskine, his widow,

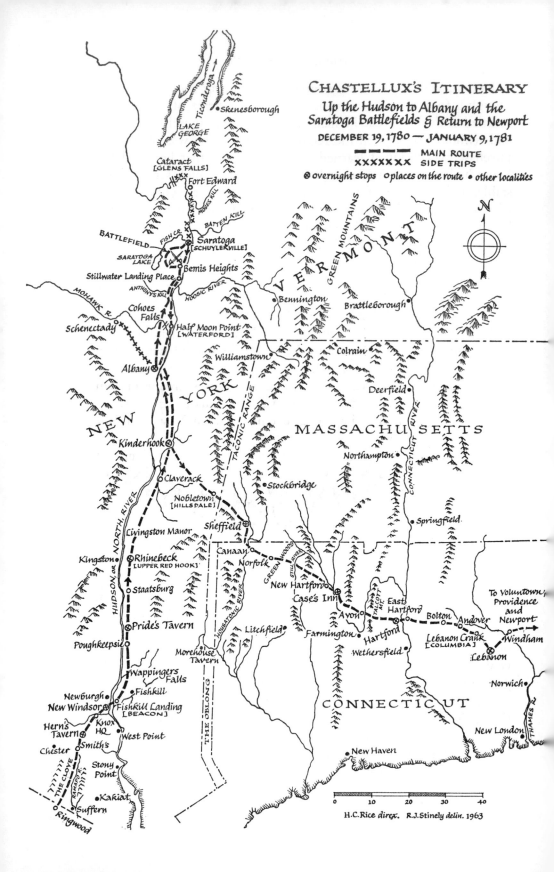

CHASTELLUX'S ITINERARY
Up the Hudson to Albany and the
Saratoga Battlefields & Return to Newport
DECEMBER 19, 1780 — JANUARY 9, 1781

━━━━━━ MAIN ROUTE
XXXXXXX SIDE TRIPS
⊗ overnight stops ○ places on the route • other localities

N

LAKE GEORGE

• Skenesborough

Cataract [GLENS FALLS]

○ Fort Edward

MOSES KILL

BATTEN KILL

BATTLEFIELD

FISH CR.

⊗ Saratoga [SCHUYLERVILLE]

SARATOGA LAKE

○ Bemis Heights

Stillwater Landing Place ○

ANTHONYS KILL

HOOSIC RIVER

MOHAWK R.

Cohoes Falls

○ Half Moon Point [WATERFORD]

Schenectady

Albany ⊗

NEW YORK

VERMONT

GREEN MOUNTAINS

• Bennington

• Brattleborough

Colrain

Williamstown

TACONIC RANGE

MASSACHUSETTS

CONNECTICUT RIVER

Deerfield

Kinderhook ⊗

○ Claverack

Northampton •

• Stockbridge

Nobletown [HILLSDALE]

Livingston Manor ○

Sheffield ⊗

• Springfield

Kingston •

⊗ Rhinebeck [UPPER RED HOOK]

HUDSON OR NORTH RIVER

Canaan ○

Norfolk ○

GREEN WOODS

STILL RIVER

FARMINGTON RIVER

○ Staatsburg

New Hartford ⊗
Case's Inn

HOUSATONIC RIVER

• Litchfield

○ Avon

TALCOTT MT.

East Hartford

Bolton ○ Andover ○

To Voluntown, Providence and Newport

⊗ Pride's Tavern

Poughkeepsie ○

Morehouse Tavern ○

• Farmington

Hartford ⊗

Wethersfield •

Lebanon Crank [COLUMBIA]

Lebanon ○

Windham ⊗

• Norwich

THE OBLONG

Wappingers Falls

Newburgh • ○ Fishkill

New Windsor ⊗ ○ Fishkill Landing [BEACON]

Hern's Tavern ⊗

Knox HQ ⊗

○ Smith's

West Point

CONNECTICUT

THAMES R.

• New London

Chester ○

Stony Point •

THE CLOVE

RAMAPO R.

• Kakiat

○ Suffern

Ringwood ○

• New Haven

0   10   20   30   40

H.C. Rice direx.   R.J. Stinely delin. 1963

is about forty, and appeared none the less sprightly or calm despite her bereavement. She had with her one of her nephews, and Mr. John Fell, a member of Congress. They gave me all the necessary information and after drinking a glass of Madeira, according to the custom of the country, which will not allow you to leave a house without drinking something, I got on horseback, and penetrated afresh into the woods, mounting and descending very high mountains, until I found myself on the borders of a lake, so solitary and concealed, that it is only visible through the trees by which it is surrounded. The declivities which form its banks are so steep, that if a deer made a false step on the top of the mountain, he would infallibly roll into the lake without being able to recover his balance. This lake, which is not marked on the maps, is called "Duck Sider"; it is about three miles long and one or two wide.[9] I was now in the wildest and most deserted country I had yet passed through; my imagination was already enjoying this solitude and my eyes were searching through the woods for some extraordinary animals, such as elk or caribou, when I perceived in a clearing a quadruped which seemed to me very large. I started with joy and cautiously approached, but on closer observation of this monster of the wilderness, I discovered to my great disappointment that it was only a forlorn horse peaceably grazing there; and the clearing was nothing less than a field belonging to a new settlement. On advancing a few steps farther I met two children, eight or ten years old, returning quietly from school, carrying under their arms a little basket and a large book. Thus I was obliged to abandon the fancies of a poet and huntsman, and to admire this new country where one cannot travel four miles without finding a dwelling, nor find one which is not within reach of all possible advantages, material as well as moral. These reflections and the fine weather we had all the afternoon made the end of my day's journey very agreeable. At nightfall, I arrived at the house of Mr. Smith, who formerly kept an inn, though at present he lodges only his friends; but as I had not the honor to be of that number, I was obliged to go a little further, to "Hern" Tavern, a rather poor inn, where I supped and slept.[10]

December 20, 1780: Hern's Tavern—New Windsor

I left it the 20th, as early as possible, having still twelve miles to New Windsor, and intending to stay there only one night, I wanted at least to spend the greater part of the day with General Washington. I met him two miles from New Windsor; he was in his carriage with Mrs. Washington, going on a visit to Mrs. Knox, whose quarters were a mile farther on, near the artillery barracks.[11] They wished to return with me, but I begged them to continue on their way. The General gave me one of his aides-de-camp (Colonel [David] Humphreys)[12] to conduct me to his house, assured me that he should not be long in joining me, and he returned accordingly in half an hour. I saw him again with the same pleasure, but with a sentiment different from that inspired by our first interview. I felt that inner satisfaction, in which self-love may perhaps have some share, but which we always experience in finding ourselves in an intimacy already formed, in real society with a man we have long admired without being able to approach him. It then seems as if this great man more particularly belongs to us than to the rest of mankind. Heretofore we desired to see him; henceforth, so to speak, we exhibit him; we know him, we are better acquainted with him than others, have the same advantage over them, that a man having read a book through, has in conversation over him who is only at the beginning.

The General again insisted on my lodging with him, though his house was much smaller than the one he had at Preakness.[13] Several officers, whom I had not seen at the army, came to dine with us. The principal of these were Colonel [William] Malcom, a native of Scotland, but settled in America, where he has served with distinction in the Continental Army; he has since retired to his estate, and is now only a militia colonel; Colonel [William Stephens] Smith,[14] an officer highly spoken of, and who commanded a battalion of light infantry under M. de La Fayette; Colonel [David] Humphreys, the General's aide-de-camp, and several others whose names I have forgotten, but who all had the best *ton* and the easiest deportment. The dinner was excellent; tea succeeded dinner, and conversation succeeded tea, and lasted till supper. War was frequently the subject: on asking the General which of our professional books he read with the most pleasure, he answered me that they were the King of Prussia's *Instruction to his Generals*, and the *Tactics* of M. de Guibert; from which I concluded that he knew as well how to select his authors as to profit by them.[15]

December 21, 1780: New Windsor—Fishkill Landing [Beacon]—
Poughkeepsie—Pride's Tavern

I should have been very happy to accept General Washington's pressing invitation to pass a few days with him, had I not made a solemn promise, at Philadelphia, to the Vicomte de Noailles and his traveling companions, to arrive twenty-four hours after them at headquarters, if they stopped there, or at Albany if they went straight on.[16] We were desirous of seeing Stillwater and Saratoga, and it would have been no easy matter for us to have acquired a just knowledge of that country had we not been together, because we were counting upon General Schuyler, who could not be expected to make two journeys to gratify our curiosity. I was thus far faithful to my engagement, for I arrived at New Windsor the same day that they left West Point; I hoped to overtake them at Albany, and General Washington, finding he could not retain me, was pleased himself to take me in his barge to the other side of the river. We went ashore at Fishkill Landing Place [Beacon], to reach the eastern road, which travelers prefer to the western. I now took leave of the General, but he insisted that Colonel Smith should accompany me as far as Poughkeepsie. The road to this town passes fairly near Fishkill, which you leave on the right; from there you travel on the heights, where there is a beautiful and extensive prospect, and traversing a "township" called Middlebush, arrive at Wapping [Wappingers] Creek and Falls. There I halted a few minutes to consider, from different points of view, the charming landscape formed by this river, with its cascade, which is roaring and picturesque, and the groups of trees and rocks, which, combined with a number of sawmills and furnaces, compose the most capricious and agreeable patterns.

It was only half past three when I got to Poughkeepsie, where I intended sleeping; but finding that the court of "Sessions" was being held there, and that all the taverns were full, I took advantage of the little remaining daylight to reach a tavern I had been told of three miles farther along. Colonel Smith, who had business at Poughkeepsie, remained there, and I was very happy to find myself in the evening with nobody but my two aides-de-camp. It was, in fact, always a fresh pleasure for us when we were left to ourselves and at perfect liberty to give mutual accounts of the impressions left on our minds by so many different objects.[17] I only regretted not having seen Governor [George] Clinton, for whom I had letters of recommendation. He is a man who governs with the utmost vigor and firmness; relentless with the Tories, whom he makes tremble, though they are very numerous, he has been able to hold in line this vast province, one extremity of which borders on Canada, the other on the city of New York. He was then at Poughkeepsie, but taken up with the business of the court of sessions; besides, Saratoga and Burgoyne's different fields of battle, being henceforth the sole object of my journey, I was intent on pushing forward for fear of being forestalled by the snow, and of the roads becoming impassable. On my arrival at Pride's Tavern,[18] I asked a number of questions of my landlord respecting the likelihood of a continuance of good weather, and perceiving that he was a good farmer, I interrogated him on the subject of agriculture, and drew the following details from him. The land is very fertile in Dutchess County, of which Poughkeepsie is the capital, as well as in the state of New York, but is commonly left fallow one year out of two or three, less from necessity than from there being more land than they can cultivate. A bushel of wheat at most is sown upon an acre, which yields twenty and twenty-five for one. Some farmers sow oats on the land that has borne wheat the preceding year, but this grain in general is reserved for newly cleared land.[19] Flax is also a considerable object of cultivation.[20] The land is plowed with horses, three or four to a plow; sometimes even a greater number when on new land, or on land that has long lain fallow. Mr. [John] Pride, while relating these details, was giving me hope of fine weather for the next day. I went to rest, highly satisfied with him and his prognostics.

December 22, 1780: Pride's Tavern—Staatsburg—Rhinebeck [Upper Red Hook]

However, in the morning, when I awakened, I saw the ground already entirely white, and snow, which continued to fall in abundance, mixed with ice and sleet. There was nothing to be done under such circumstances but to continue my journey, as if it had been fine weather, only taking a little better breakfast than I should otherwise have done. What I regretted most was that the snow or fine hail, that drove against my eyes, prevented me from seeing the country, which, as far as I could judge, was beautiful and well cultivated. After traveling about ten miles, I traversed the township of

"Strasbourg," called by the inhabitants of the country "Stratts-borough" [Staatsburg]. This township is five or six miles long, yet the houses are not far from each other. As I was noticing one which was rather handsome, the owner came to the door, doubtless from curiosity, and asked me, in French, if I would alight, and step in and dine with him. Nothing can be more seducing in bad weather than such a proposal; but on the other hand, nothing is more cruel, when one has once got under shelter, than to quit the fireside, a second time, to expose oneself to the cold and snow. I therefore refused the dinner offered me by this gallant man, but not the several questions he put to me. I asked him, in my turn, whether he had seen any French officers pass by, meaning the Vicomte de Noailles, the Comte de Damas, and the Chevalier de Mauduit, who, as they had three or four servants, and six or seven horses, might have been remarked on the road. My Dutchman, for I have since learned that his name was Le Roy,[21] that he was a Dutch merchant, born in Europe, and acquainted with France, where he lived for some time; my Dutchman, then, replied like a man who knew France and who speaks French: "Sir, it is very true that the Prince de Conti passed by here yesterday evening, with two officers, on the way to Albany." I didn't know whether it was to the Vicomte de Noailles, or to the Comte de Damas that I should attribute the principality; but as they are both my relatives, I answered, with strict truth, that as my cousin wanted to gain time, I was very glad to know at what time he had passed and when I could expect to join him; so that if Mr. Le Roy consulted his almanac, as no doubt he did, he will have concluded that I was the Duke of Orleans or the Duke of Chartres; which was the more plausible as I had nine horses with me, whereas the Prince de Conti, being further removed from the Crown, had only seven.

You scarcely get out of Strasbourg [Staatsburg], before you enter the township of Rhinebeck. It is unnecessary to observe, that all these names reveal a German origin. At Rhinebeck, nobody came out to ask me to dinner. But this snow mixed with hail was so cold, and I was so fatigued with keeping my horse from slipping, that I should have stopped here even without being invited by the handsome appearance of the inn called Thomas's Inn.[22] It was no more, however, than half past two; but as I had already come twenty-three miles, and as the house was good, the fire well lighted, my host a tall good-looking man, a hunter, a horse dealer, and disposed to chat, I determined, according to the English phrase, to "spend" the rest of my day there. The only information of interest that I learned from Mr. Thomas is the following. In time of peace, he carried on a great trade in horses, which he purchased in Canada and sent to New York, there to be shipped to the West Indies. It is incredible with what facility this trade is carried on in winter; he assured me that within a fortnight he once went to Montreal and brought back with him seventy-five horses which he had bought there. This is effected by traveling in a straight line, traversing Lake George on the ice, and on the snow, the wilderness between that lake and Montreal. The Canadian horses easily travel eighteen or twenty hours a day, and three or four men, mounted, are sufficient to drive one hundred before them. "It was I," added Mr. Thomas, "who made, or rather who repaired the fortune of that rogue of an Arnold. He had badly managed his affairs in the little trade he carried on at New Haven; [23] I persuaded him to purchase horses in Canada, and to go himself and sell them in Jamaica. This speculation alone was sufficient to pay his debts and set him once more afloat." After talking of trade, we spoke of agriculture: he told me that in the neighborhood of Rhinebeck the land was uncommonly fruitful, and that for a bushel of sown wheat, he reaped from thirty to forty. The wheat is so abundant that they do not take the trouble of cutting it with a sickle, but mow it like hay. Some dogs of a beautiful kind moving about the house awakened my passion for hunting; on asking Mr. Thomas what use he made of them, he told me that they were only for hunting the fox; that deer, stags, and bears were fairly common in the region, but they seldom killed them except in winter, either by tracing on the snow, or by tracking them in the woods. All American conversation must finish with politics. Mr. Thomas's politics appeared to me rather equivocal; he was too rich, and complained too much about the supplies of flour he sent to the army, to let me think him a good Whig. He gave himself out for such notwithstanding, but I observed that he was greatly attached to an opinion which I found widespread throughout the state of New York; that there is no expedition more useful nor easier than the conquest of Canada. It is impossible to conceive the ardor that all the inhabitants of the north still have for recommencing that enterprise. The reason is that their country is so fertile and so happily situated for trade, that they are sure to become very wealthy as soon as they have nothing more to fear from the Indians;

and indeed the Indians are formidable only when they are supported and stirred up by the English.

December 23, 1780: Rhinebeck [Upper Red Hook]—Claverack— Kinderhook

I left Thomas's Inn the 23rd, at 8 in the morning, and traveled for three hours and all this time within the district of Livingston's Manor. The road was good, and the country rich and well cultivated. You pass through several sizable hamlets, the houses of which are handsome and neat, and every object here announces prosperity. On leaving this district, you enter that of Claverack, then descend from the hills and approach the Hudson River. You soon after cross a creek, which is also called by the name of Claverack, and which flows not far from this point into the Hudson. As soon as you have crossed over this creek, an immense rock, which extends crosswise to the direction of the road, obliges you to turn sharply to the right to reach the Claverack meetinghouse, and to pursue the road to Albany.[24] This rock, or rather chain of rocks, merits all the attention of naturalists. It is about three miles in length. As I did not traverse it, I am ignorant of its width, but it is so steep on the south side, that it can be ascribed to nothing but a landslide occasioned by a violent shock. Yet one does not find, either in the space between this rock and the little river, or on the opposite bank, any correspondence indicating an accidental separation. Its flank, which is almost exposed, presents parallel layers, but rarely horizontal, which made me conjecture that it was of a calcareous nature;[25] I tried it with aqua fortis and found my conjecture correct. But I was the most struck with the strength and beauty of the trees which grow in the midst of it, the trunks of which rise out of the cracks formed by the separation of the rock. Unless you closely examine these trees, it is impossible to believe that they can grow and reach such a height without an inch of earth to nourish their roots. Several of them grow out horizontally, then rise suddenly in a vertical direction. Others have their roots quite naked, which proves that their origin is prior to the catastrophe, whatever it was, which one cannot refuse admitting. These roots are in the most whimsical directions imaginable, resembling serpents crawling amidst the ruins of an immense edifice. Most of these trees I speak of are of that sort of fir called "hemlock" by the English, but they are mixed with others, which I took to be walnut trees and soft woods; but I must observe that this conjecture cannot be relied on, as I did not see the leaves, and am not well enough acquainted with trees to distinguish them by their branches and their structure.[26]

Claverack is a rather large township and extends very far. After leaving it you must traverse some woods before reaching the first houses of Kinderhook. I found in these woods new "improvements," and several "log huts." But on approaching one of them, I perceived, with regret, that the family who inhabited it had been long settled there, without thinking of building a better house, an uncommon circumstance in America, and which is almost unexampled, except in the Dutch settlements; for the Dutch are more economical than industrious, and seek rather to amass wealth than to add to their comfort.[27] When you arrive at the first hamlet of Kinderhook, you must make a long detour to the right to reach the meetinghouse, which is the center of what may be properly called the town of Kinderhook. There you pass a pretty considerable stream, and then have the choice of three or four inns; but the best is the one kept by Mr. Van Burragh.[28] The preference given to this, however, does no honor to the others; it is a very small house, kept by two young people of a Dutch family; they are civil and attentive, and you are not badly off with them, provided you are not difficult to please. It would have ill become me now to have been so, for I had had nothing but snow, hail, and ice during the whole day, and any fireside was an agreeable asylum for me.

Chapter

5

ALBANY AND THE
SARATOGA BATTLEFIELDS

December 24, 1780: Kinderhook—Albany

IT was a big problem to know where I should the next day cross
the North River, for I was told that it was neither sufficiently
frozen over to cross on the ice, nor free enough from floes to venture it in a boat. Apprised of these obstacles, I set out early on the
24th, that I might have time to find the place where the crossing
would be the easiest. I was only twenty miles from Albany; so that
after a continuous journey through a forest of spruce, I arrived at
one o'clock on the banks of the Hudson. The valley through which
this river flows, and the town of Albany, which is built in the form
of an amphitheater on its western bank, would have afforded a very
agreeable view, had it not been a bit disfigured by the snow. A
handsome house halfway up the bank opposite the ferry seems to
attract the eye and to invite strangers to stop at General Schuyler's,
who is its owner as well as its architect. I had recommendations to
him from all quarters, but particularly from General Washington
and Mrs. Carter.[1] I had besides made an appointment with Colonel
Hamilton, who had just married another of his daughters,[2] and furthermore was preceded there by the Vicomte de Noailles and the
Comte de Damas, who I knew had arrived the night before. The
sole difficulty therefore consisted in crossing the river. While the
boat was making its way with difficulty through the floating ice,
which we were obliged to break as we advanced, M. Lynch, who
is not uninterested in a good dinner, contemplated General Schuyler's house and said to me, "I am sure the Vicomte and Damas are

now at table, where they have good cheer and good company, while we are kicking our heels here, with scarcely a hope of even getting to some wretched alehouse this evening." I shared a bit of his anxiety, but diverted myself by assuring him that they had seen us from the windows, that I had even made out the Vicomte de Noailles who was looking at us through a telescope, and that he was going to send somebody to conduct us on our landing to that excellent house, where we should find a dinner ready; I even pretended that a sleigh I had seen coming down towards the river was for us. Never was a conjecture more just. The first person we saw on shore was the Chevalier de Mauduit, who was waiting for us with the General's sleigh, into which we quickly stepped, and found ourselves in an instant in a handsome drawing room, near a good fire, with Mr. Schuyler, his wife, and daughters. While we were warming ourselves, dinner was served, to which everyone did honor, as well as to the Madeira, which was excellent, and which made us completely forget the rigor of the season and the fatigue of the journey.[3]

General Schuyler's family was composed of Mrs. Hamilton, his second daughter, who had a mild agreeable countenance; of Miss Peggy Schuyler, whose features are animated and striking; [4] of another charming girl, only eight years old, and of three boys, the eldest of whom is fifteen, and the handsomest children to be seen. The General is himself about fifty, but already gouty and infirm.[5] His fortune is very considerable, and it will become still more so, for he possesses an immense extent of land, but derives more credit from his talents and knowledge than from his wealth. He served with General Amherst in the Canadian war [Seven Years' War] as Deputy Quartermaster General, corresponding to our *Aide Maréchal-Général des logis*. From that period he made himself favorably known; he was very useful to the English, and was called to London after the peace, to settle the accounts of all the supplies furnished by the Americans. His marriage with Miss Van Rensselaer, the rich heiress of a family which has given its name to a district, or rather to a whole province, further increased his credit and his influence; so that it is not surprising that he should have been raised to the rank of major general at the beginning of the present war, and have been entrusted with the command of the troops on the Canadian frontier. It was in this capacity that he was commissioned in 1777 to oppose the progress of General Burgoyne; but having received orders from Congress, directly contrary to his opinion, without being provided with any of the means necessary for carrying them into execution, he found himself obliged to evacuate Ticonderoga, and to fall back on the Hudson. These measures, prudent in themselves, being unfavorably construed in a moment of ill humor and anxiety, he was tried by a court martial, as was General [Arthur] St. Clair, his second in command. Both of them were soon after *honorably acquitted*. St. Clair resumed his station in the army, but General Schuyler, justly offended, demanded more satisfactory reparation, and reclaimed his rank, which, since this event, was contested with him by two or three generals of the same standing. This affair not being settled, he abstained from rejoining the army, but has continued his services to his country. Elected a member of Congress the year following, he was nearly chosen President in opposition to Mr. [Henry] Laurens. Since that time he has always enjoyed the confidence of the government and of General Washington, who are at present seeking him out and pressing him to accept the office of Secretary of War.

While we were in this excellent asylum, the weather continued doubtful, between frost and thaw; there was little snow upon the ground, but it was likely that more would soon fall. The council of travelers assembled, and it appeared to them proper not to delay their departure for Saratoga. General Schuyler offered us his own house at Saratoga, which is itself part of his estate; but he could not serve as our guide, because he was indisposed and feared an attack of the gout.[6] He proposed giving us an intelligent officer to conduct us to the different fields of battle, while his son should go ahead to prepare us lodgings. We could still travel on horseback, and would be supplied with horses from the locality to replace ours which were fatigued, and some of which still remained on the other side of the river. All these arrangements being accepted, we were taken into Albany in a sleigh. On our arrival, we waited on Brigadier General [James] Clinton, to whom I delivered my letters of recommendation.[7] He is an honest man, but of no distinguished talents, and is only employed out of respect to his brother, the Governor.[8] He immediately ordered horses for our journey, and Major [William] Popham, his aide-de-camp, an amiable and intelligent officer, was chosen to accompany us. He was to take with him Major [John] Graham, who knows the ground perfectly, and who served in General Gates's army.

All our measures being well concerted, we each of us retired to our quarters; the Vicomte de Noailles and his two companions to an inn, kept by a Frenchman, called Louis, and I to that of an American of the name of "Blennissens" [?].

December 25, 1780: Albany—Visit to Cohoes Falls

At daybreak, tea was ready, and the whole caravan assembled at my quarters; but wet snow was falling, which did not promise an agreeable ride. We were in hopes that it was a real thaw, and set out upon our journey. The snow however fell thicker and thicker, and was six inches deep when we arrived at the junction of the Mohawk and the Hudson River. Here there is a choice of two roads to Saratoga: one obliges you to cross over the Hudson, to follow along the left [eastern] bank for some time and then cross back near Half-Moon [i.e., Half-Moon Point, present Waterford]; the other takes you up along the Mohawk River until you get above the Cataract, where you cross over this river and traverse the woods to Stillwater. Even had there been no difficulty in crossing over the North River which was full of floating ice, I should have preferred the other road, in order to see the cascade of Cohoes, which is one of the wonders of America. Before we left the Hudson, I remarked an island in midstream which offers a very advantageous position for erecting batteries and obstructing navigation.[9] The two majors, to whom I communicated this observation, told me that this point of defense was neglected, because there was a better one, a little higher up, at the extremity of one of the three branches into which the Mohawk River divides itself as it flows into the Hudson. They added that this position had merely been reconnoitered; the one still higher up, on which fortifications were begun, being sufficient to stop the progress of the enemy. Thus the more you examine the country, the more you are convinced that the expedition of Burgoyne was reckless, and must sooner or later have miscarried, quite apart from the engagements which decided the event.

The junction of the two rivers is six miles north of Albany, and after traveling two more in a westerly direction through the woods, we began to hear a dull sound, which kept increasing until we came in sight of Cohoes Falls. This cataract extends the whole width of the river, that is to say, nearly two hundred *toises*.[10] It is a vast sheet of water, which drops 76 English feet.[11] The river in this place is

THOMAS ELLISON HOUSE, WASHINGTON'S HEADQUARTERS
AT NEW WINDSOR, by John Ludlow Martin
Chastellux: December 20, 1780 (see p. xxiii)

COHOES FALLS, BY JOHN TRUMBULL
Chastellux: December 25, 1780 (see p. xxiii)

THE MURDER OF LUCINDA.

COLUMBIAD.

"THE UNFORTUNATE MISS McCREA"
Chastellux: December 30, 1780 (see p. xxiv)

JEUNE FILLE PLEURANT SON OISEAU MORT
by Jean-Baptiste Greuze, 1765
Chastellux: January 2, 1781 (see p. xxiv)

confined between two steep banks formed by the slope of the mountains; these precipices are covered by an earth as black as iron ore, and on which nothing grows but firs and cypresses. The course of the river is straight, both before and after the falls, and the rocks forming this cascade are nearly on a level, but their irregular shape whirls the water as it falls, and forms a variety of whimsical and picturesque appearances. This picture was rendered still more awesome by the snow which covered the firs, the brilliancy of which gave a black color to the water, gliding gently along, and a yellow tinge to that which was dashing over the cataract.[12]

After feasting our eyes with this impressive spectacle, we traveled a mile higher up to the ferry where we hoped to cross over the river; but on our arrival found the boat so entangled in the ice and snow that it was impossible to make use of it. We were assured that people had that morning crossed at a ferry two miles higher up; we immediately went there, determined to continue on our way, though the snow was greatly increased and we were benumbed with wet and cold. The boatmen of this ferry made many objections on account of the bad weather and the smallness of their boat, which could only transport three horses at a time; but this difficulty did not stop us, and we agreed to make several trips. They first attempted to take over my *valet de chambre*, with three horses: I was waiting by the fireside for my turn, when they came to inform me that the boat was coming back to shore with some difficulty, and that the current had almost carried it towards the cataract. We were obliged therefore to submit to our destiny, which was not yet disposed to let us fulfill the object of our voyage. On this occasion I displayed a magnanimity which placed me high in the esteem of the whole company: while the others were cursing and growing impatient, uncertain of the measures to be taken, I serenely gave the signal for a retreat, and henceforth thought only of supper, for which I at once took the wisest precautions. The innkeeper of the Vicomte de Noailles being a Frenchman, and consequently a better cook, or at least more active than mine, it was decided that he should provide our supper. The best-mounted cavalier of the troop was dispatched to give the necessary orders; we followed in half an hour, arrived as night was closing in, and a quarter of an hour later sat down to table. Thus passed the day of the 25th, which was not very agreeable till the hour of supper, but terminated very happily; for what are the disappointments that cannot be solaced by a good fire, a good supper, and good company?

December 26, 1780: Albany

The 26th, the rivers not yet being frozen over, nor the roads hard enough to make a long journey in a sleigh, I determined to remain at Albany. My morning was employed in writing up my notes, which occupation was only interrupted by a visit from Colonel Hamilton.[13] He told us that Mrs. Schuyler was a little indisposed, but that the General would be none the less pleased to receive us at his house during the evening. Accordingly he sent us his sleigh at nightfall. We found him in the drawing room with Mr. and Mrs. Hamilton. Conversation soon began between the General, the Vicomte de Noailles, and myself. We had already talked, two days earlier, of certain rather important facts concerning the northern campaign, about which we had asked for explanations. Mr. Schuyler appeared no less desirous of giving them. He is rather communicative, and is well entitled to be so; his conversation is easy and agreeable; he knows well what he is speaking of, and speaks well about what he knows. To give the best answer to our questions, he suggested letting us read his political and military correspondence with General Washington; we accepted the proposition with great pleasure, and leaving the rest of the company with Mr. and Mrs. Hamilton, we retired into another room. The General opening his portfolio, the Vicomte and I divided the different manuscripts, which contained upwards of sixty pages of close writing on paper à la Tellière.[14] The first dispatch I read was a letter written by him to General Washington in November 1777.[15] It contained a plan of attack on Canada, which originated in the following circumstances: two English officers, after being made prisoners with Burgoyne's army, obtained permission to return to Canada on parole, and on the road stopped at General Schuyler's at Saratoga. The conversation, as may easily be supposed, soon turned on the great event, the impression of which was still so recent. One of these officers being attached to General Burgoyne, blamed Governor Sir Guy Carleton, whom he accused of having retained too many troops in Canada; the other maintained that he had not even kept enough for the defense of the country. From assertions they came to proofs, which proofs could only be an exact account of the forces then remaining in Canada, and their distribution. General Schuyler was attentive, and took advantage of the argument. He learned in this way that Canada was in real danger; and, in consequence, proposed to General Washington to recapture Ticonderoga, in case that post was not abandoned, as it actually had been, and to proceed from thence to Montreal. This plan is extremely well conceived, and exhibits a great knowledge of the country. What struck me as most worthy of attention, is the immensity of the resources to be found in this country for a winter expedition, and the extreme facility with which an army may rapidly advance, by means of sleds carrying provisions and ammunition, and even sick and lame soldiers. It is possible, in a month's time, to collect, between the Connecticut and Hudson Rivers, fifteen hundred sleds, two thousand horses, and as many oxen; the latter may be shod for the ice, like horses, and serve to draw the sleds with provisions; and as these are consumed, or the oxen become tired, the latter may be killed as food for the army. Nor must it be imagined that these expeditions are so dreadful for the soldiers as we are accustomed to suppose them. With proper shoes and clothing, which it was easy to procure before the finances and resources of the country were exhausted, they endure extremely well the fatigue of long marches; and as they always spend the night in the woods, they easily make shelters, and light great fires, by which they sleep better than under tents. It should be noted that if the cold be severe in this country, it is always a dry cold, against which it is easier to protect oneself than against rain and dampness.

General Schuyler never received any answer to this letter, nor does he know with whom the fault lies. M. de La Fayette however came to Albany in January [February 1778] to prepare and command an expedition similar to the one that had been proposed: he showed his instructions to General Schuyler, who discovered it to be his own plan, for which he supposes some other person wished to claim the honor; but as no orders had come to him, he had made no preparations, nor had any been made in the Connecticut River country; so that M. de La Fayette, however agreeable this expedition might be to him, had enough good sense and attachment to the interest of America, to point out the difficulties and divert Congress from pursuing it.[16]

The winter following [1778-79], after the evacuation of Philadelphia and the affair of Monmouth, General Washington, always more concerned with putting an end to the misfortunes of his country than with prolonging the brilliant rôle he is playing in America, wrote to Mr. Schuyler, to consult him on an expedition to Canada, and on the means of executing it with success. In answer to this letter, Schuyler sent a memoir perfectly well conceived and no less well written, in which he proposes three different plans.[17] The first is to collect his forces near the sources of the Connecticut River, at a place called Coos; from thence there is only a fairly short portage to the rivers which flow into the St. Lawrence, below Lake Saint Pierre and near Quebec. But this plan would be difficult of execution, because resources on the Connecticut River are not very plentiful and great difficulties would be encountered in bringing there such as are available along the Hudson and Mohawk Rivers; besides which the attack would thus be carried into the heart of the English forces, and too near the sea, from which they derive their principal aid. The second project is to go up the Mohawk River, then to embark on Lake Oneida, and crossing Lake Ontario, proceed westward to besiege Niagara; then returning by the same route, to descend the [St. Lawrence] River, and attack Montreal from the north. In this plan General Schuyler finds two great disadvantages; one is the long circuit it would be necessary to make, thus giving the English time to collect their troops at the point of attack; the other is the impossibility of deceiving the enemy by threatening him from Lake Champlain and Sorel, since the preparations on the Mohawk and Hudson Rivers could not fail to disclose the whole system of the campaign. It is by Lake Champlain therefore, and in the winter, that General Schuyler would march on Montreal; but a direct march, leaving St. Johns on the right, and postponing until spring the attack on that post, which would not be secured until after the capture of the Isle of Montreal and of all the upper country: with this plan there would be no difficulty in concealing its real object, as the necessary supplies might be collected on both the Hudson and Connecticut Rivers; the shifting of them from one to the other being fairly easy. Thus the enemy would at the same time fear for Quebec, St. Johns, and Montreal. If such a supposition is correct, it seems likely that they would prefer to sacrifice Montreal. There an advantageous establishment might be formed, and measures taken to attack Quebec; but in case Montreal could not be taken, retreat would still be easy by way of the "Beaver hunting Place"[18] and Lake Champlain. Such is the object of this long dispatch, which I read with great attention and much pleasure, and of which I have attempted to give some idea, convinced as I am that this passage of my journal will not be uninteresting to military men; others may find it less boring by looking at the map and surveying the immense country embraced by these different projects.

The next memoir which fell into my hands was General Washington's reply to the preceding.[19] After expressing the greatest confidence in General Schuyler, he enters into discussion with him, and offers his comments with a modesty that is as amiable as it is estimable. He thinks that the expedition by way of Lake Ontario is perhaps too lightly rejected; that it would be easy for him to assist the attack on Niagara by means of a diversion he would effect on Lake Erie by marching the Virginia troops into the region of the Ohio and of Fort Pitt: he inquires whether it would not be possible to build boats on the Hudson River and transport them on carts to the Mohawk. It may be seen that his object is to eliminate one of the principal objections I have mentioned, that the preparations for such an expedition would too readily reveal its real object. All the other points are treated with wisdom and precision; which renders the reply of General Schuyler still more curious and interesting. This reply is worthy both of the importance of the subject and of the great man to whom it is addressed.[20] Mr. Schuyler persists in his opinion; and still attached to his project of an attack by way of Lake Champlain, he proves that it may be executed in summer as well as in winter. Everything depends, according to him, on possessing naval superiority,[21] which he thinks may be easily obtained by constructing larger vessels than those of the English, and he is persuaded that two fifty-gun ships would be sufficient to assure it. People are wrong, he adds, in dreading the navigation of the lakes, and in not daring to trust large ships on them. On all these subjects, he speaks as an enterprising man, and as one who is well informed and capable of executing what he proposes.

I shall conclude this sitting by reading the proposed plan of a campaign against the Indians, different from the one adopted by Congress in 1779, the execution of which was entrusted to General Sullivan.[22] According to Schuyler's plan, five hundred men only would have marched by way of Wyoming and Tioga, while the remainder of the army would have debouched from the headwaters of the Mohawk River, then crossed Lake Oneida, to take the Indians in the rear, and cut off their retreat to Lake Ontario; which appeared to me much more reasonable, because by this means, the double object would be fulfilled of destroying the savages, and of avoiding a long and difficult march for the main body of the army across the Great Swamp of Wyoming. To understand all this, it must be recollected that in 1779, Congress, seeing their enemies confined in New York and Rhode Island, thought they might spare a body of troops of 3,000 or 4,000 men to be sent against the Five Nations, at whose hands they had experienced a thousand cruelties. They hoped to capture or destroy them, and thus relieve the country lying between the Susquehanna and the Delaware. General Sullivan, after taking every sort of precaution to secure the subsistence and health of the soldiers, made a very long and skillful march, drove the savages before him, and burned their villages and harvests. But this was the whole fruit of his expedition, for he never had it in his power to cut them off, the corps under General [James] Clinton, which had penetrated by the Mohawk River, being found too weak to act of itself, was obliged to join the main body of the army.

I did not finish my reading before ten o'clock; and I continued in conversation with General Schuyler while we were at supper. It cannot be supposed that I was able to reason upon all the subjects he had laid before me. I contented myself therefore with remarking that any partial expedition against Canada, which did not tend to the total conquest, or rather the deliverance of that entire country, would be dangerous and ineffectual; because it would not be strengthened by any support from the inhabitants, they having already been disappointed in their expectations at the time of Montgomery's expedition [1775-76], and dreading the resentment of the English, should they again show themselves too favorable to the Americans. It gave me pleasure to find that General Schuyler was of exactly my opinion. So we separated very well pleased with one another, and I returned home to await the decision of the weather respecting the next day's journey.

December 27, 1780: Albany—Visit to Schenectady

The 27th in the morning, learning that the rivers were not yet frozen over, but seeing that the weather was fairly good but very cold, I wished to take advantage of it to go to Schenectady. This is a town situated fourteen miles from Albany, on the Mohawk

River. It excites some curiosity from being built in the very country of the Indians; from its being picketed, that is to say, surrounded
with lofty palisades like their villages, and from their still retaining
some habitations there, which form a sort of suburb, to the east of
the town. It was rather late when I thought of this ride, and it was
noon before I got a sleigh; but General Schuyler had assured me
that I should be there in two hours, on the supposition, doubtless,
that my sleigh would have better horses than it did. I found the
roads very difficult, and the horses even more difficult than the
roads; for they would not pull, and if M. de Montesquieu had not
himself taken the reins, and pressed forward with more vivacity
than their meek driver, I believe I should still be there in the snow,
with which this country is covered six months in the year. The
country which lies between Albany and Schenectady is nothing
but an immense forest of spruce trees, untouched by the axe. They
are lofty and robust, but well spaced; and as nothing grows under
their shade, a line of cavalry might traverse this wood without
breaking ranks or defiling. It was three o'clock, and I was half dead
with cold when I reached Schenectady. This town stands at the
foot of a small declivity, on your coming out of the woods; it is
regularly built, and contains five hundred houses within the palisades, without counting some dwellings which form a suburb, and
the Indian village adjoining this suburb. Two families, and eight
inhabitants, are reckoned to a house. Beyond the town, to the westward, the country is more open and the land very fertile; it produces a great deal of grain with which they carry on a great trade.
I alighted at Colonel [John] Glen's, the quartermaster general of
this district, a lively, active man. He received me in the politest
manner; an excellent fire and two or three glasses of toddy warmed
me sufficiently so that I could ask him a few questions and set out
again immediately, for night was coming on, and the Vicomte de
Noailles expected me for dinner at five o'clock. Colonel Glen lent
me horses to return to Albany, and was so good as to conduct me
himself into the Indian village. As we were preparing to set out, one
of these savages entered his house: he was a messenger dispatched
by their hunters, and came to announce that a party of one hundred
and fifty Senecas and several Tories had been seen a few miles from
Saratoga, and that they had even carried off one of their young
men. This messenger spoke very good French and very bad English; born of a Canadian, or perhaps European, father, he had mixed

with the savages, amongst whom he had lived twenty years, from preference for this unrestricted life (*libertinage*) rather than from any other motive. The news he brought was not very encouraging for the journey I was planning for the morrow or the day following, but I gave little credit to it, and I was in the right.

The Indian village Mr. Glen conducted me to is nothing but an assemblage of miserable huts in the woods, along the road to Albany. He took me into the hut of a savage from the Sault Saint Louis, who had long lived at Montreal and spoke good French. These huts are like our barracks in time of war, or like those built in vineyards or orchards, when the fruit is ripe and has to be watched at night. The framework consists only of two uprights and one crosspole; this is covered with a matted roof, but is well lined within by a quantity of bark. The inner space is rather below the level of the ground, and the entrance by a little side-door; in the middle of the hut is the fireplace, from which the smoke ascends by an opening in the roof. On each side of the fire are raised two platforms, which run the length of the hut and serve as beds; these are covered with skins and bark. In addition to the savage who spoke French, there was in this hut a *squah* (the name given to the Indian women), who had taken him as her second, and was bringing up a child by her first husband; two old men composed the remainder of this family, which had a melancholy and poor appearance. The *squah* was hideous, as they all are, and her husband almost stupid, so that the charms of this society did not make me forget that the day was advancing and that it was time to set out. All that I could learn from the Colonel, or from the Indians, was that the state gives them rations of meat and sometimes of flour; that they also possess some lands, where they sow Indian corn, and go hunting for skins, which they exchange for rum. They are sometimes employed in war, and are commended for their bravery and fidelity. Though in subjection to the Americans, they have their chiefs, to whom application is made for justice, when an Indian has committed any crimes. Mr. Glen told me that they submitted to the punishments inflicted on them; but could not comprehend that it was right to punish them with death, even for homicide. Their number at present is 350, which is constantly diminishing, as is that of the tribes called the Five Nations.[23] I do not believe that these five nations can produce four thousand men in arms. The savages of themselves therefore would not be too much dreaded, were they

not supported by the English and the American Tories. As an advanced guard they are formidable, as an army they are nothing.
But their cruelty seems to augment in proportion to their decrease
in numbers; it is such as to render it impossible for the Americans
to consent to have them longer for neighbors; and a necessary consequence of a peace, if favorable to Congress, will be their total
destruction, or at least their exclusion from all the country this side
of the lakes.[24] Those who are attached to the Americans, and live
in some manner under their laws, such as the Mohawks in the neighborhood of Schenectady and a part of the Oneidas, will ultimately
become civilized, and be intermingled with them. This is what every
feeling and reasonable man should wish, who, preferring the interests of humanity to those of his own fame, disdains the little
artifice so often and so successfully employed, of extolling ignorance and poverty, in order to win acclaim in Palaces and Academies.[25]

I had time to meditate on such matters as these, and on many
others besides, as I journeyed by the sole light of the snow, through
these majestic woods, where silence reigns by night and is seldom
disturbed by day. I did not arrive at the lodgings of the Vicomte
de Noailles until nearly eight o'clock; supper, tea, and conversation
detained me there until midnight. Nothing, however, was decided
respecting our journey, and the news we had received about the
rivers was not yet satisfactory.

December 28, 1780: Albany

The next morning I received a letter from General Schuyler, who
informed me that having sent word the evening before, he was told
that I was gone to Schenectady, and from thence to Saratoga; but
that he was glad to know I had returned to Albany, for his gout was
much better and he intended to accompany me the next day. He
requested me to come and pass the evening with him, to decide
upon our route and our departure. I answered his letter by accept-
ing all of his propositions, and spent part of the morning in walking
about Albany, not without taking many precautions, for the streets
were all covered with ice. My first visit was to the artillery park,
or rather to the trophies of the Americans; for there is no artillery
in this place other than eight handsome mortars and twenty ammunition wagons, which formed part of Burgoyne's artillery.[26] I
entered a large shed where they were making "fusils" for the army.

The barrels of these muskets, as well as the bayonets, are cast a few miles from Albany, and polished and finished here. I inquired the price of them, and found that the weapon complete costs about five dollars.[27] The armorers are hired, and receive besides their rations, wages which would be considerable if they were duly paid. From thence I went to another large barrack situated halfway towards the west of the town, which serves as a military hospital.[28] The sick are cared for by women. Each of them has a separate bed, and they appear in general to be well taken care of, and kept very clean. At dinner time all those who were to be of the Saratoga party collected at my lodgings, and we went afterwards to General Schuyler's to make arrangements for our journey.

December 29, 1780: Albany—Stillwater—Bemis Heights—Saratoga [Schuylerville]

Accordingly, we set out the next day at sunrise in five different sleighs. General Schuyler took me in his. We crossed the Mohawk River on the ice a mile above the cataract. It was almost the first attempt, and succeeded with all but Major Popham, whose two horses broke through the ice and sunk at once into the river. This event will appear disastrous to Europeans; but let them not be alarmed at the consequences. It is a very common accident, and is dealt with in two ways. One is to drag the horses onto the ice, if possible with the help of a lever or a plank to lift them up. The other is to strangle them with their halter or the reins: as soon as they have lost their breath and motion, they float on the water, and are then hauled by their forefeet onto the ice; then the binding is gradually loosened, they are bled, and in a quarter of an hour are harnessed up again. As there were a great many of us, the first method, which is the safest for the horses, was used; in five minutes' time we had pulled them out of the river. All this may be readily understood, but some people may ask what became of the sleigh, and how we dared approach the hole opened up by the horses? My answer is that these animals, being much heavier than the sleigh which is hung on four slender bases, break the ice under their feet, without ever causing the sleigh to sink, because this sleigh is itself light and its weight is supported by long pieces of wood which serve as shafts. The travelers are no less safe, the ice always being thicker than is necessary to bear them. As for the horses, they easily keep themselves on the surface of the water, by means of their four legs, and by resting their heads upon the ice.

The accident which happened to Major Popham's sleigh did not detain us above seven or eight minutes; but we went a little astray in the woods we had to pass through in order to reach the main road. We came into it between Half Moon [Waterford] and Still-water. A mile farther along I saw on the left a clearing in the wood and a fairly extensive plateau, at the bottom of which there was a creek. I said to General Schuyler that there must be a good position there; he answered that I was not mistaken, and that it had been reconnoitered for that purpose in case of need. The creek is called Anthony's Kill [at Mechanicville]; the word "kill," among the Dutch, having the same meaning as "creek" with the Americans. Three miles farther on, we went through a hamlet called "Still-water-landing-place," for it is here that boats coming down from Saratoga [29] are obliged to stop to avoid the rapids. From here there is a portage of eight or ten miles to the place where the river is again navigable. I suppose that the name of Stillwater comes from the fact that the water here is calm or still before the rapids begin. General Schuyler showed me some redoubts he had had constructed to defend the park where his boats and provisions were collected after the evacuation of Fort Ann and Fort Edward. We stopped there to refresh our horses. The General had made an appointment here with a militia officer, called Mr. "Swang" [Col. Jacob Lansing(?), Albany County militia], who lives in this neighborhood and served in the army of General Gates; he put me into his hands, and continued his route to Saratoga, to prepare our reception. I presently got into a sleigh with my guide, and, at the end of three miles, we saw two houses on the bank of the river; it was here that General Gates had his right, and his bridge of boats defended by a redoubt on each bank. We alighted to examine this interesting position, before which Burgoyne saw all his hopes vanish and his ruin take shape. I shall attempt to give some idea of it, which, though indeed incomplete, may throw some light on the accounts given by General Burgoyne, and even serve to correct them.[30]

The heights called "Beams's height" [Bemis Heights], from which this famous camp is named, are only a part of the high ground which extends along the right [western] bank of the Hudson, from the Mohawk River to the one at Saratoga [Fish Creek, at

Schuylersville].[31] At the spot chosen by General Gates for his position, they form, on the side towards the river, two different slopes (*talus*), or, one might say, two terraces. Climbing up the first slope, you see three redoubts placed parallel to each other. In front of the last, on the north side, is a little hollow; beyond this the ground rises again, and here there are three more redoubts placed nearly in the same direction as the former. In front of them is a deep ravine which comes from the west and through which flows a small creek. This ravine takes its rise in the woods, and all the ground on the right of it is very thickly wooded. If you will now retrace your steps, place yourself near the first redoubts I have mentioned, and then climb up to the second slope, while proceeding westward, you will find, on the highest plateau, a large entrenchment which extends parallel to the river, and then turns towards the northwest, where it terminates on some fairly steep summits, which were still fortified by small redoubts. To the left of these heights, and at the place where the slope becomes more gentle, begins another entrenchment which turns towards the west, and makes two or three angles, while continuing along the crest of the heights to the southwest. Towards the northwest, you come out of the lines, descend a fairly steep slope and go up another similar one; then you find a new plateau, which presents a position the more favorable as it commands the surrounding woods and stands in the way of anything which might attempt to turn the left flank of the army. It is here that Arnold was encamped with the advanced guard.

If you descend again from this height, proceeding towards the north, you are presently in the midst of the woods near Freeman's Farm, and on the ground where the actions of the 19th of September and of the 7th of October took place. I avoid the term "field of battle"; for these two engagements were fought in the woods, and on ground so intersected and covered, that it is impossible either to imagine or to discover the least resemblance between this locality and the plan of it published by General Burgoyne.[32] But what appeared very clear to me is that this General, who was encamped about four miles from the camp of Bemis Heights, wishing to approach and reconnoiter the avenues to it, marched through the woods in four columns, and that having several ravines to cross, he made General Fraser, with the advanced guard, turn them at their origin; that two other columns crossed the ravines and the woods, as best they could, without either communicating or waiting for each other; that the left column, chiefly composed of artillery, followed the bank of the river where the ground is more level, and built bridges over the ravines and brooks, which are deeper on that side, as they all terminate in the river; that the engagement first began with the "riflemen" and the American militia, who were supported as necessity required and without any prior plan; that the advanced guard and the right column were the first engaged, and that the fighting lasted until the columns on the left arrived, that is to say, until sunset; that the Americans then retired to their camp, where they had taken care to convey their wounded; and finally, that the English advanced guard and right column greatly suffered, both having been very long engaged in the woods without any support.

General Burgoyne purchased dearly the frivolous honor of sleeping on the field of battle: he now encamped at Freeman's Farm, so near the American camp that it became impossible for him to maneuver, so that he found himself in the situation of a chess player who has allowed himself to be stalemated. In this position he remained until the 7th of October, when seeing his provisions expended, having no news of Clinton, and being too near the enemy to retreat without danger, he tried a second attack, and again wanted his advanced guard to turn the enemy's left. The Americans, with whom the woods were filled, penetrated his design, themselves turned the left flank of the corps which threatened theirs, put them to rout, and pursued them so far as to find themselves, without knowing it, opposite the camp of the Germans. This camp was situated at a right angle to, and a little in the rear of the line. Arnold and Lincoln, emboldened by success, attacked and carried the entrenchments: both of them bought the victory at the price of their blood; each of them had a leg shattered by a musket shot.[33] I saw the spot where Arnold, uniting the boldness of a "jockey" [34] with that of a soldier, leaped his horse over the entrenchment of the enemy. Like all of those in this country, this was a sort of parapet, formed by trunks of trees piled one upon another. This action was very brisk, to which the fir trees, which are torn by musket and cannon shot, will long bear testimony, for the term of their existence seems as remote as does the period of their birth.

I thus continued my reconnoitering until dark; sometimes walking in the snow, into which I sank to the knees, and sometimes proceeding still less successfully in a sleigh, my driver having taken the trouble to tip me over, very gently indeed, into a beautiful pile of snow. At length, after surveying Burgoyne's lines, I came down to the main road, passing through a field where he had established his hospital. We then traveled more easily, and I got to Saratoga [Schuylerville] at seven in the evening, after a day's journey of thirty-seven miles. We found good rooms well warmed, an excellent supper, and gay and agreeable conversation; for General Schuyler, like many European husbands, is still more amiable when he is absent from his wife.[35] He gave us instructions for our next day's expedition to Fort Edward and to the great cataract of the Hudson River, eight miles above the fort and ten from Lake George.

December 30, 1780: Saratoga [Schuylerville]—Fort Edward—
[Glens Falls]—Saratoga

In consequence of these arrangements, we set out the next morning at eight o'clock, with Majors Graham and Popham, whom General Schuyler had requested to accompany us. We went up the right [west] bank of the Hudson for near three miles before we found a safe place to cross the river in our sleighs. The one we chose exposed us to no danger, the ice being as thick as we could wish; but on approaching the opposite side, the banks appeared to me so high and steep that I could not conceive how we should get up them. As it is my principle not to judge of things I do not understand, and always, whether traveling by land or by sea, to put my trust in the people who are accustomed to the route, I was sitting quietly in my sleigh, waiting the event, when my driver, a farmer of the region, *called* his horses with a ferocious cry, rather like an Indian war whoop; and in an instant, without a stroke of the whip, they set off with the sleigh, and, in three bounds, were at the top of a nearly perpendicular escarpment twenty feet high.

The road to Fort Edward goes along beside the river most of the way, but you frequently lose sight of it in the fir woods you must pass through. From time to time you see fairly handsome houses on the two banks. That of the unfortunate Miss [Jane] McCrea, who was killed by the Indians, was pointed out to me.[36] If the Whigs were superstitious, they would attribute this event to divine vengeance. The parents of Miss McCrea were Whigs, nor did she belie the sentiments which they had inspired in her, until she became acquainted in New York with an English officer [David Jones], who triumphed over both her scruples and her patriotism. From that moment she espoused the interests of England, and awaited an opportunity to marry her lover. The war, which was not long in breaking out in New York, as well as in Boston, obliged her father to retire to his country house; soon, with the approach of Burgoyne's army, he abandoned this. But Miss McCrea's lover was in this army; she wished to see him again as a conqueror, to marry him, and then share his toils and his successes. Unfortunately the Indians composed the vanguard of Burgoyne's army: these savages are not much accustomed to distinguish friends from foes; they pillaged the house of Miss McCrea and carried her off. After they had brought her to their camp, there was a dispute over who should have her; they could not agree, and to end the quarrel, some of them killed her with a tomahawk (or *casse-tête*, as the Canadians call it). The recital of this sad catastrophe, while it made me deplore the miseries of war, concentrated all my interest in the person of the English officer, who was thus torn between his passion and his duty. I know that a death so cruel and unforeseen would furnish a most pathetic subject for a drama or an elegy; [37] but the charms of eloquence and poetry can arouse sympathy for such a fate only by displaying the effect and ignoring the cause; for such is the true character of love that all noble and generous sentiments seem to be its natural attendants, and if it be true that it can sometimes ally itself with blameable vices, at least everything which tends to humiliate and degrade it either destroys or misrepresents it.

As you approach Fort Edward the houses become more rare. This fort was built sixteen miles from Saratoga, in a little valley near the river, on the only spot which is not covered with woods and where you can see for as much as a gunshot around you. Formerly it consisted of a square, fortified by two bastions on the east side, and by two demi-bastions on the river side; but this old fortification has been abandoned, because it was too easily commanded from the heights, and a large redoubt, with a simple parapet and a wretched palisade, has been built on a more elevated spot: within are small barracks which can accommodate two hundred soldiers.[38] Such is Fort Edward, so much spoken of in Europe, although it has never been in a state to resist five hundred men equipped with four pieces of cannon. I stopped here an hour to refresh my horses, and about noon set off to proceed as far as the cataract, which is eight miles beyond it. On leaving the valley and following the road to Lake George, you find a tolerable military position which was occupied during the last war; it is a sort of entrenched camp, or one which can be made so with abatis, guarding the passage from the woods and commanding the valley.

I had scarcely lost sight of Fort Edward before the spectacle of devastation presented itself to my eyes, and continued to distress them as far as my stopping place. Into these ancient forests Peace and Industry had led cultivators, happy men, until the time of this war. Only those who were in Burgoyne's path experienced the unhappy consequences of his expedition; but at the time of the most recent invasion of the savages desolation spread from Fort Schuyler (which the English call Fort Stanwix) as far as Fort Edward.[39] So I beheld around me only remains of conflagrations; a few bricks, that fire could not destroy, alone indicated the spots where houses had been built; while fences still intact, and cleared fields, proclaimed that these deplorable habitations had once been the abode of wealth and of happiness. When we got as far as the cataract, we had to get out of our sleighs and walk half a mile to the bank of the river. The snow was fifteen inches deep, which made this walk rather difficult and obliged us to proceed in single file in order to tread a path. Each of us in turn put ourselves at the head of this little column, much as wild geese relay each other at the point of the triangle they form in their flight. But even had our march been still more difficult, the sight of the cataract would have been an ample recompense.[40] It is not a sheet of water as at Cohoes or at Totowa: here the river is confined and interrupted in its course by different rocks, through the midst of which it glides and falls precipitously, as it forms several cascades. The cataract of Cohoes is more majestic, this one more terrible: the Mohawk River at Cohoes seems to fall from its own weight; here the Hudson frets and fumes, it foams and forms whirlpools, and flies like a serpent making its escape, still continuing its threats by horrible hissings.

It was nearly two o'clock when we regained our sleighs, having twenty-two miles to return to Saratoga, so that we retraced our route as fast as possible; but we still had to halt at Fort Edward to refresh our horses. We employed this time, as we had done in the morning, in warming ourselves by the fire of the officers who command the garrison. They are five in number, and have about one hundred and fifty soldiers. They are stationed in this wilderness for the whole winter, and I leave my readers to imagine whether this garrison be much more gay than those at Gravelines, or at Briançon.[41] We set off again in an hour, and night soon overtook us; but before it was dark, I had the satisfaction of seeing the first game I had met with in my journey: it was a bevy of quail, by some called partridge, though they have a much greater resemblance to quail. They were perched, to the number of seven, upon a fence. I got out of my sleigh to have a nearer view of them; they let me approach within four paces, and to make them fly off I was obliged to throw my cane at them; they all went off together, in a flight similar to that of partridge. They are bigger than quail, but their beak is like a partridge's, and they are also sedentary like partridge.[42]

Our return was quick and fortunate: the only incident was the recrossing of the river and the descent of the escarpment we had mounted. I awaited this fresh trial with as much confidence as the former; but a sleigh ahead of mine having stopped at this place and the darkness of the night preventing me from distinguishing anything, I thought that the company were going to alight and straightway did likewise. The first sleigh carried the Vicomte de Noailles and the Comte de Damas; but I was no sooner alighted than I saw this sleigh set out with its full load and slide down the bank with such speed that it could only be stopped at thirty paces from the bottom. Indeed they make no more fuss about descending these escarpments than mounting them: the horses, accustomed to this maneuver, spring forward as quickly as they launch off, so that the sleigh sliding down like the *ramasse* of Mount Cenis,[43] cannot touch their hind legs and make them fall.

At half past six, we reached General Schuyler's, where we spent our evening as agreeably as the former.

December 31, 1780: Saratoga [Schuylerville]—Bemis Heights—Half Moon [Waterford]—Albany

The 31st we got on horseback at eight o'clock, and Mr. Schuyler himself took us to the camp occupied by the English when General Burgoyne capitulated. We could not have a better guide, but he was absolutely necessary for us in every respect; for aside from the fact that he was an eyewitness of the event and thus better able than anybody else to give us an account of it, he was also the owner of the land and was himself able to conduct us safely through woods, fences, and entrenchments covered a foot deep with snow.

In looking at the map, it will be seen that Saratoga is situated on the bank of a small river which comes from a lake of that name and flows into the Hudson. On the right [south] bank of the Fish Kill [or Creek], the name of this little river, there stood formerly a handsome country house belonging to General Schuyler; a large farm belonging to it, as well as two or three sawmills, a meeting-house, and three or four middling houses, composed all the habitations of this celebrated place, the name of which will be handed down to remote posterity. After the affair of the 7th of October, General Burgoyne began his retreat; he marched in the night between the 8th and 9th, but did not manage to cross the creek until the 13th, so great was the difficulty in dragging his artillery, which he insisted upon keeping with him, although the greater part of his horses had been killed or had died from fatigue and hunger. He took four days therefore to retire eight miles, which gave the Americans time to follow him on the right [west] bank of the Hudson, and to get ahead of him on the left [east] bank, where they occupied in strength all the crossing places. General Burgoyne had no sooner reached the other side of the [Fish] Creek than he set fire to General Schuyler's house, rather from ill temper than for the safety of his army; [44] since this house, situated in a bottom, could afford no advantage to the Americans, and since, furthermore, he left the farm standing, which is at present the only asylum for the owner. It is here that Mr. Schuyler lodged us in some temporary rooms he has fitted up, until happier times allow him to build another house.[45] The creek runs between two steep banks, the summits of which are about the same height; it then descends through several rapids which turn the mills: there the ground is more open and continues so to the Hudson River, that is to say, for half a mile. As for General Burgoyne's position, it is difficult to describe it, because the ground is so very irregular, and the General finding himself surrounded, was obliged to divide his troops into three camps, forming three different fronts; one facing the [Fish] Creek, another the Hudson River, and the third the mountains to the westward.[46] General Burgoyne's plan [47] gives a fairly accurate idea of this position, which was not ill taken, and is only defective on the side of the Germans, where the ground forms an incline, the slope of which was against them. All that is necessary to observe is that the woods continually rise towards the west; so that the General might very well occupy some advantageous eminences, but never the summits. Accordingly, General Gates, who arrived at Saratoga almost as soon as the English, sent 2,000 men over the creek, with orders to entrench themselves and to construct a battery for two cannon. This battery began to fire on the 14th and considerably incommoded the English. General Schuyler criticizes this position; he pretends that this corps was so advanced as to be in danger, without being strong enough to oppose the retreat of the enemy. But when one considers that these 2,000 men were posted in very thick woods, that they were protected by abatis, had a secure retreat in the immense forest in their rear, and that their task was to harass an enemy in flight, whose courage was broken, then one will think as I do that General Schuyler's criticism is rather that of a harsh rival than of a learned and methodical tactician. Be this as it may, it remains certain that General Burgoyne had no other alternative than to let his troops be slaughtered or to capitulate. His army had only five days' provision; it was therefore impossible for him to retain his position. It was proposed that he should re-establish an old bridge of boats, which had been constructed in the very front of his camp; but a corps of 2,000 Americans was already posted on the heights on the opposite side of the river, where they had raised a battery of two pieces of cannon. Had he undertaken to march up the right [west] bank [of the Hudson], to reach the fords which are near Fort Edward, he had ravines to cross and roads to repair; besides, these defiles were already occupied by the militia, and the vanguard must have been engaged with them, while he had a whole army in his rear and on his flanks. He had scarce time to deliberate, the cannon balls were beginning to fall into the camp; one of them fell into the house where the council of war was being held, and obliged them to quit it to take refuge in the woods.

Let us now compare the situation of General Burgoyne, collecting his trophies at Ticonderoga and publishing his insolent manifesto, with that in which he now stood, when vanquished and surrounded by a band of peasants, not even a place was left him where he could discuss the manner of supplication he should make to them. I confess that when I was conducted to the spot where the English laid down their arms, and to that where they filed off before Gates's army,[48] I shared the triumph of the Americans, and at the same time admired their nobility and magnanimity; for the soldiers and officers beheld their presumptuous and sanguinary enemies pass, without offering the smallest insult, without suffering an insulting smile or gesture to escape them. This majestic silence offered a striking refutation of the vain declamations of the English general, and bore witness to all the rights of our allies to the victory. Chance alone gave rise to a remark which General Burgoyne seemed to feel deeply. It is the custom in England and in America, on approaching any person for the first time, to say, "I am very happy to see you." General Gates used this expression in accosting General Burgoyne: "I believe you are," replied the General. "The fortune of the day is entirely yours." General Gates seemed to pay no attention to this answer; he conducted Burgoyne to his quarters, where he gave him a good dinner, as well as to most of the English officers. Everybody ate and drank heartily, and seemed to forget their misfortunes, or their successes.

Before dinner, and at the moment when the Americans were choosing the English officers they wanted to entertain, somebody came to ask where her Ladyship the Baroness Riedesel, the wife of the Brunswick General, was to be conducted. Mr. Schuyler, who had followed the army as a volunteer, since he had quitted the command, ordered her to be shown to his tent; he went there soon afterwards, and found her trembling and speechless, expecting to find in every American a savage, like those who had followed the English army. She had with her two charming little girls, about six or seven years old. General Schuyler caressed them greatly; the sight of this touched Madame de Riedesel and removed her apprehension in an instant: "You are tender and sensible," said she; "you must then be generous, and I am happy to have fallen into your hands." [49]

In consequence of the capitulation, the English army was conducted to Boston. During their march the troops encamped, but lodgings had to be procured for the generals, and there being some difficulty in procuring near Albany a proper quarter for General Burgoyne and his suite, Mr. Schuyler offered him his handsome house, which I have already mentioned. He was himself detained by business at Saratoga, where he remained to visit the ruins of his other house, which General Burgoyne had just destroyed; but he wrote to his wife to prepare everything for giving him the best possible reception, and his intentions were perfectly fulfilled. Burgoyne was extremely well received by Mrs. Schuyler and her little family; he was lodged in the best apartment in the house. An excellent supper was served him in the evening, the honors of which were done with so much grace, that he was affected even to tears;

and could not help saying, with a deep sigh, "Indeed this is doing too much for the man who has ravaged their lands, and burned their retreat." [50] The next morning, however, he was reminded of his disgrace by an adventure which would have appeared gay to anyone but him. It was always innocently that he was afflicted. His bed was prepared in a large room; but as he had a numerous suite, or "family," several mattresses were spread upon the floor for some of the officers to sleep near him. Mr. Schuyler's second son, then about seven years old, a spoiled little child, as are all American children—very willful, mischievous, and likeable—was running next morning all over the house, according to custom; he opened the door of the room, burst out laughing on seeing these Englishmen collected there; and, shutting the door behind him, said to them, "You are all my prisoners." This innocent remark was cruel to them, and rendered them more melancholy than they had been the evening before.

I hope I shall be pardoned for relating these little anecdotes, which have perhaps appeared interesting to me only because I know them firsthand and because I heard them on the very spot. Besides, a plain journal deserves some indulgence, and when one is not writing history, he may at least be allowed to tell pretty stories. Henceforth I have only to take leave of General Schuyler, detained by his business at Saratoga, and to retrace my steps as fast as possible to Newport.

In passing a second time near Bemis Heights and Stillwater, I again had an opportunity of examining the right [left?] flank of General Burgoyne's camp: it seemed to me that his plan had given me a fairly accurate idea of it.[51] I was assured that I might return to Albany by the eastern road, but on arriving at Half Moon [Waterford], I learned that the ice was broken in several places, so that after resting some time in a handsome inn, kept by Mrs. "People" [Elizabeth Peebles], a Dutchman's widow, I again took the road by the Mohawk River, which I crossed without accident, and arrived at Albany about six in the evening. We immediately assembled (I speak only of the six French travelers) to concert measures for our return. Not a moment was to be lost, for the wind had changed to the south, and the thaw was beginning; and it might very well happen that we should be detained a considerable time at Albany. For, when you cannot cross the river on the ice, you are sometimes obliged to wait eight or ten days before it is navigable and you can cross over on the ferry. It was necessary therefore to set out as soon as possible; but as we were too many to travel together, it was determined that the Vicomte de Noailles and his two companions should set off the next morning at daybreak, and that they would spend the night thirty miles from Albany; and that I should set out at noon, and stay at Kinderhook. The Vicomte de Noailles had left his horses on the other side of the river, and had already sent over his sleigh; nothing therefore stood in the way of his departure, the ice being certainly thick enough for him to pass on foot. My situation was very different; I had two sleighs at Albany; they belonged to the state, and were furnished me by the deputy quartermaster general, an excellent man, called Mr. "Quakerbush" [Henry Quackenboss]. My intention was to pay for them; but he would not allow it, assuring me that I had only to deliver them to the quartermaster of Rhode Island, who would return them by the first opportunity. This is indeed a very convenient arrangement for the military on the continent, and for all such as are employed on business for the public service: each state maintains horses which can be used for traveling, the only requirement being to deliver them to the quartermaster of the place at which you leave them. In the northern states there are also sleighs for the same purpose.

As we were deliberating on our journey, Colonel [Hugh] Hughes, quartermaster of the state of New York, came to call upon us: he had just arrived from a trip towards Fishkill, and expressed great regret at not having been at Albany during our stay. I must repeat here what I have already said elsewhere, that it is impossible to imagine a more frank and noble politeness, a more courteous behavior, than I have experienced from most all of the American officers with whom I had any dealings. Mr. Hughes was so good as to undertake personally to conduct me to the other side of the river, and promised to call for me on the next day at eleven o'clock.

I had traveled far enough during the day to hope for a quiet sleep, and expected a good night; but at four in the morning I was awakened by a musket fired close to my windows: I listened but heard not the smallest noise or motion in the street, which made me imagine it was some musket which had gone off by itself without causing any accident. So I attempted to go back to sleep. A quarter of an hour later a fresh musket or pistol shot interrupted my repose: this was followed by several others; so that I no longer had any doubt that it was some rejoicing or feast, like our village christenings. The hour indeed struck me as unusual, but at length a number of voices mingled with musketry, shouting "New Year," reminded me that it was the first of January, and I concluded that it was thus that *Messieurs les Américains* celebrated the beginning of the new year. Though this manner of proclaiming it was not, I must own, especially pleasing to me, there was nothing to do but be patient; but at the end of half an hour I heard a confused noise of upwards of a hundred persons, mostly children or young people, assembled under my windows. Soon I was even better warned of their proximity, for they fired several musket shots, knocked rudely at the door, and threw stones against my windows. Cold and indolence still kept me in bed, but M. Lynch got up, and came into my chamber to tell me that these people certainly meant to do me honor and to ask me for some money. I requested him to go down and give them two louis; he found them already masters of the house and drinking my landlord's rum. In a quarter of an hour they went off to visit other streets and continued their noise until daylight.

January 1, 1781: Albany—Kinderhook

On rising I learned from my landlord that it was the custom of the country for the young folks, the servants, and even the Negroes, to go from tavern to tavern, and to many other houses, to wish a happy new year and ask for drink. So that there was no particular compliment to me in this affair, and I found that, after the example of the Roman emperors, I had made a largess to the people. In the morning, when I went out to take leave of General Clinton, I met nothing but drunken people in the streets, but what astonished me the most was to see them not only walk, but run upon the ice without falling or making a false step, while it was with the utmost difficulty that I kept on my feet.

As soon as my sleighs were ready, I took one of them to go and bid adieu to Mrs. Schuyler and her family; then I returned to meet Colonel Hughes, who was waiting for me on the edge of the town. He had learned, since he left us, that the Baron de Montesquieu was the grandson of the author of the *Spirit of Laws*. Rejoicing at this discovery, he asked me to introduce him a second time to the gentleman who bore so respectable a name; and a few minutes after, as I was expressing my sensibility for the services he was rendering me, and at the same time my regret at not having it in my power to repay them, he said to me with truly amiable feeling, "Well then! Since you wish to do something for me, try to procure for me a French copy of the *Spirit of Laws*. I do not speak your language, but I understand your books, and shall be happy to read this one in the original." I promised to get a copy for him, and I was fortunate enough to be able to make good my word upon my return to Newport.[52] After this conversation he took me to the riverside, at the place he thought the safest; but, as I was about to venture forth, the first object I beheld was a sleigh, the horses of which were sinking under the ice, at about twenty paces from me. Judge of my consternation: I must retrace my steps and remain perhaps a week at Albany until the thaw was complete and the river free from floating ice. Colonel Hughes told me to return to my inn, and remain there quietly, until he sent a man and horse along the river to find out if there were not a place where one could still cross over. Three sleighs, however, with rum for the state storehouses appeared on the other side and seemed determined to risk the crossing: he immediately sent a man on foot to stop them, after which I left him sorrowfully enough. But about one o'clock, as I was reading by my fireside, Mr. Hughes's secretary entered and told me that the sleighs they had tried to stop had persisted in crossing, and had succeeded in doing so by avoiding the hole made by the horses I had seen sinking and extricated with great difficulty. As the thaw continued, I had not a moment to lose; I had my horses harnessed and set out at once, under the auspices of Colonel Hughes, who was waiting for me at the bank of the river. As soon as I got on the other side, I parted from him; [53] but still had half a mile to go upon the ice before I could get to a landing place which led me to the main road. All perils were now past, and I reached Kinderhook with ease at about six o'clock that evening.

Chapter

FROM ALBANY BACK TO NEWPORT

January 2, 1781: Kinderhook—Nobletown [Hillsdale], N.Y.—Sheffield, Mass.

I SET out the next morning at nine, and after crossing the Kinderhook bridge, left the Claverack road on the right, and took the Nobletown road. I stopped in this township and alighted at Makingston's Tavern, a small and rather neat inn, in which two travelers may be conveniently lodged.[1] I had an opportunity of conversing with the cousin and neighbor of Mr. Makingston, of the same name. He told me he had been a major in the American army, and received a ball through his thigh in Canada. He told me that his nerves, irritated by the wound, became contracted, and he limped for upwards of a year; but that at the affair of Princeton, after traveling eighteen miles on foot, he happened to leap over a fence, and that by this effort the contracted nerves broke or rather were stretched out, so that he has never since been lame.

As soon as my horses had rested a little I continued my journey, and traveling amongst woods and mountains, it was night before I got to Sheffield. I traversed this whole town, which is about two miles long, before I got to Mr. Dewey's inn.[2] Sheffield is a very pretty place, there are a good many well-built houses, and the high road which separates them is upwards of a hundred paces wide. My inn gave me pleasure the moment I entered it; the master and mistress of the house appeared polite and well-mannered; but I admired above all a girl of twelve, who had all the beauty of her age, and whom Greuze would have been only too happy to have taken for a model when he painted his charming picture of the young girl weeping over the loss of her canary bird. When I was shown into my chamber, I amused myself by looking at some books scattered on the tables. The first I opened was the *Abridgment of Newton's Philosophy*.[3] This discovery induced me to put some questions to my landlord on physics and geometry, with which I found him well acquainted, and I saw that he was also very modest and very good company. He is a "surveyor," a very active employment in a country where there is perpetually land to measure and boundaries to fix.

January 3, 1781: Sheffield, Mass.—Canaan, Conn.—Norfolk—New Hartford—[Canton]

The 3rd in the morning, I was sorry to find that the weather, which had until then been uncertain, turned to a thaw. I had to traverse the Green Woods, a rugged, difficult, and unsettled country. The snow remaining on the ground still gave me hope of being able to continue my route in a sleigh, so I kept mine and proceeded tolerably well as far as Canaan,[4] a small town situated on the left bank of the Housatonic, seven miles from Sheffield Meetinghouse; there I turned to the left and began to climb the mountains. Unfortunately the snow failed me where it was the most necessary, and I was obliged to walk nearly all the time on foot to relieve my horses, who were at times laboring to drag the sleigh out of the mud, and at others to pull it over stones two or three feet high. This road is, in fact, so rough that it is hardly possible to make use of sleighs unless there is a foot and a half of snow upon the ground. It was with the utmost difficulty therefore that I managed to travel fifteen miles to a wretched inn in the town of Norfolk. On leaving this inn I got into the Green Woods. This forest is part of the same chain of mountains I had crossed in going to Fishkill by the Litchfield road;[5] but here the trees are particularly superb; they are spruces, so strong, so straight and lofty, that I doubt whether there are any like them in all North America. I regret that Salvator Rosa or Gaspard Poussin never saw the majestic and truly *grandioso* picture presented by this deep valley, through which flows the small river called the Naragontad [Still River?]. This valley appears even more narrow from the immense firs that shade it; some of which, rising obliquely, seem to unite their tops to intercept the rays of the sun. When you have crossed this river you ascend for four or five miles, and then descend for as many again, continually bounding over the large stones which lie across the road and make it like a stairway. Here one of my sleighs broke down, and night approaching, I was at a loss how to repair it, imagining myself in an uninhabited wilderness; I tried to get it forward broken as it was, but despaired of succeeding, when two hundred steps further on, I found a small house, and opposite it a forge, where the fire was lighted and the blacksmith was at work. A pilot discovering land in unknown seas is not more happy than I was at this sight. I politely asked the good man to leave his work and repair my sleigh, which he agreed to do, and I continued to follow on foot the one that was still intact, despairing of ever seeing the first again; nevertheless it arrived an hour at most after I did. Such are the resources travelers meet with in America, and the excellent organization [6] of this country is such that no road is destitute of what is necessary for their wants.

This day was destined to be full of vexations for me. It was seven in the evening when I arrived at New Hartford, where I expected to find a good inn, called [John] Gilbert's House.[7] Three American officers, who, being on horseback, had very easily passed me on the road, were so polite as to go further on in order to leave me the whole house; but on entering I was told, and it was evident, that it was impossible to accommodate me. The house was being repaired and masons were at work everywhere. So that my only hope now was the inn of a certain Mr. [Dudley?] Case, which was two miles further along and beyond the Farmington River; but having learned that the American officers were there, I asked if I could not be lodged elsewhere, and was recommended to an old woman, called Mrs. Wallen, who formerly kept an inn, and I was given hopes of her receiving me. I continued therefore to follow my sleigh on foot, and having with difficulty reached this house, I humbly implored Mrs. Wallen's hospitality; she consented to give me a lodging, but only to oblige me. I remained a short time in the house, which looked very poor, but on looking at the rooms intended for us, I found them so wretched, that I sent one of my people to Case's Inn, to see if he could find me some corner to lodge in. They contrived to let me have one, and I went thither on foot, leaving my horses at the other house.[8] I was lucky enough to find a good bed, and a supper, such as it was, but which appeared to me excellent, less because I had a good appetite than from being waited on by a tall woman of twenty-five, handsome, and of a noble and distinguished appearance. I inquired of my landlady if she was her daughter, but the landlady, a good-natured fat woman, very curious and talkative, and whose good grace I had already obtained by answering all her questions, told me she had never had any children, although she then had one in her arms, which she was dandling and caressing. "To whom does that one belong then?" said I. "To that tall woman you see there," she replied. "And who is her husband?" "She has none." "She is a widow then?" "No, she was never married. It is an unfortunate affair, too long to tell you: this poor girl was in want, I took her to live with me and I provide for the mother and child." Is it advancing a paradox to say that such conduct proves, more than anything else, how pure and respectable are the manners of the Americans? With them vice is so foreign and so rare, that the danger of example is almost nonexistent; so that a mistake of this nature is regarded as would be an accidental illness. The individual stricken with it must be cured without it being necessary to take measures to prevent the contagion. I must add, too, that the acquisition of a citizen in this country is so precious, that a girl, by bringing up her child, seems to expiate the weakness which brought it into existence. Thus morality, which can never differ from the real interest of society, appears sometimes to be local and modified by times and circumstances. When an infant without an asylum and without property shall become a burden to the state, a being doomed to unhappiness, owing its preservation to pity alone, and not to public utility, we shall then see the mother humiliated, perhaps even punished, and this severity will then be justified by all those austere dogmas which are now disregarded or forgotten.[9]

January 4, 1781: [Canton]−[Avon]−Hartford

I proposed making a short journey the next day to Hartford, fifteen miles only from the place I slept at, but as it seemed to me impossible to perform it except on horseback, I left the two sleighs belonging to the state of New York with Mr. Case, taking a receipt from him, which I afterwards delivered to Mr. [Jeremiah] Wadsworth. At first I was not satisfied with my decision, as I traveled sometimes on heights covered with snow, where sleighs would have been perfect, but as I came down towards the Farmington River, I found the thaw complete, and mud instead of snow. The woods I just passed through were very different from the Green Woods; they were full of small spruces, whose verdant hue pleased the eye, and the road was by accident so prettily laid out that it was impossible to imagine a better model for walks in the English style (*promenades anglaises*).

After I had crossed the Farmington River I went up a pretty long and steep hill [Talcott Mountain], on which I observed, from time to time, objects interesting to lovers of natural history.[10] You see, among other things, large masses of rocks, or rather great blocks of stone, which have no sort of relationship to the rest of the mountain, and appear to have been hurled there by some volcano. I noticed one more singular than the rest and stopped to measure it: it is a sort of *socle*, or long square, thirty feet long by twenty high, and as many wide, not unlike the pedestal of the statue of Peter the Great to be seen at St. Petersburg.[11] On the east side, it is split for the greater part of its height; the crack is about a foot and a half wide at the top, but much less at bottom. Some shrubs have sprouted in the small amount of earth collected there, and on the very summit of the rock grows a small tree, but I could not tell of what species. The stone is hard, of the nature of quartz, and is nowise volcanized.

I got to Hartford about three, and being informed that Mr. [Jeremiah] Wadsworth was absent, I was afraid of inconveniencing his wife and sister by going to lodge there, and went to a very good inn kept by Mr. [David] Bull, who is accused of being rather "on the other side of the question," which is a polite way of saying that he is thought to be a Tory.[12] I therefore made only a brief call on Mrs. Wadsworth, to invite myself to breakfast the next morning.

January 5, 1781: Hartford—Lebanon

The 5th I did not set out till eleven, although I had a thirty-mile journey to Lebanon. At the ferry-crossing I met with a detachment of the Rhode Island regiment, the same corps we had with us all last summer, but they have since been recruited and clothed.[13] The majority of the enlisted men are Negroes or mulattoes; but they are strong, robust men, and those I saw made a very good appearance. I had fine weather all day and got to Lebanon at sunset. This does not mean that I had yet reached Lebanon Meetinghouse, where the Duc de Lauzun was quartered with his Hussars; I had six miles more to go, still traveling in Lebanon. Who would not think after this, that I am speaking of an immense city? and, in fact, this is one of the most considerable towns in the country, for it consists of at least one hundred houses; but it is necessary to add that they are widely scattered and often more than four or five hundred paces from each other.

It will be easily imagined that I was not sorry to find myself again in the French army, of which Lauzun's Hussars formed the advanced guard, although their quarters are some seventy-five miles or so from Newport; but there are indeed no circumstances in which I should not be happy to be with M. de Lauzun.[14] For two months I had been talking and listening, with him I conversed: for it must be admitted that conversation still remains the natural appanage of the amiable French; a precious adjunct to our nation, which it perhaps neglects too much and may one day lose. It is told of an Englishman accustomed to be silent, that he said "talking spoils conversation." This whimsical expression contains great sense: everybody can talk, but nobody knows how to listen; so that the society of Paris, such as I left it, resembles the chorus of an opera, which a few *coryphées* alone have a right to interrupt; each theater has its own particular coryphaeus; each theater has its chorus too, which chimes in, and its pit which applauds without knowing why. Transplant the actors, or change the theater, the effect of the play is lost. Lucky indeed are the spectators if the repertory is abundant and the same production is not repeated to satiety.

January 6, 1781: Lebanon

But I have strayed far from America; I must however return there again, and this time it will be to hunt squirrels. The Duc de Lauzun entertained me with this diversion, which is much in fashion in this part of the country. These animals are larger and have more beautiful fur than those in Europe; like ours, they are very adroit in jumping from tree to tree, and in clinging so closely to the branches as to become almost invisible. You frequently wound them, without their falling; but that is a slight inconvenience, for you have only to call or send for somebody, who obligingly applies the hatchet to the tree and quickly cuts it down. As squirrels are not rare, you will conclude then, and quite correctly, that trees are very common.[15] On returning from the hunt I dined at the Duc de Lauzun's with Governor Trumbull and General [Jabez] Huntington. The former lives at Lebanon, and the latter had come from Norwich. I have already painted Governor [Jonathan] Trumbull;[16] now you have only to picture this little old man, in the antique dress of the first settlers in this colony, approaching a table surrounded by twenty Hussar officers, with perfect composure and without losing a bit of his formal stiffness, pronouncing in a loud voice a long prayer in the form of a grace. Let it not be fancied that he excites the laughter of his auditors; they are too well brought up for that: you must, on the contrary, imagine twenty *amens* issuing simultaneously from the depths of twenty pairs of mustaches, and you will have some idea of this little scene. But M. de Lauzun is the man to relate how this good, methodical Governor, didactic in all his actions, invariably says, that he must "consider," or "refer" to his council; how of little affairs he makes great ones, and how happy a mortal he is when he has any to transact. Thus, in the two hemispheres, Paris alone excepted, eccentricities must not imply inaptitude to govern: since it is through character that men govern, and through character also that men acquire eccentricities.

January 7, 1781: Lebanon—Voluntown [Sterling Hill]

I proposed leaving Lebanon the 7th at ten o'clock, but the weather was so bad that I stayed till past one, hoping it would clear up. I was finally obliged, however, to set out in a melting snow, the most continuous and the coldest I have ever experienced. The bad weather urged me on so fast that I arrived at Voluntown [Sterling Hill] about five o'clock. If the reader recollects what I have said at the beginning of my journal of Mr. D***'s [Dorrance's] house, he will not be surprised at my returning to it with pleasure.[17] Miss Pearce however was no longer there, but she was replaced by the younger Miss D***, a charming pretty girl, although not so regular a beauty as her friend. She has, like her, modesty, candor, and kindness in all her features; and has, besides, a serenity and gaiety, which render her as amiable as the other is interesting. Her elder sister had lain in since I was last in Voluntown; I found her seated in a great chair, near the same fire around which her family were seated. Her noble and imposing countenance seemed more changed by misfortune than by suffering; yet everybody about her was employed in consoling and taking care of her; her mother, seated beside her, held her baby in her arms, smiling at it and caressing it; but as for Miss D*** herself, her eyes were sorrowfully fixed upon the innocent creature, considering it with interest, but without pleasure, as if she were saying to it, *misero paragoletto il tuo destin, non sai* [unfortunate child! you know not what fate is in store for you].[18] Never will a more affecting or more moral picture inspire the brush of a Greuze, or the pen of a poet of feeling. May that man be banished from the bosom of society who is so barbarous as to leave this unlucky girl a prey to a misfortune he is capable of repairing; and may all the blessings of heaven be bestowed on the being generous and just enough to give her more legitimate titles to the names of wife and mother, and thus restore all that happiness which Nature had intended for her.[19]

January 8-9, 1781: Voluntown [Sterling Hill], Conn.—Providence, R.I.—Newport

My journey henceforward affords nothing worthy of the smallest attention. I slept next day at Providence,[20] and arrived the 9th at Newport; happy to have seen many interesting things, and to have met with no accident; but sad at the thought that the place I was arriving at, after traveling so far, was still fifteen hundred leagues from the place where I have left my friends; where I shall enjoy the little knowledge I have acquired by sharing it with them, where I shall again be happy, if there still be any happiness in store for me; the only place, in short, *dove da' lunghi errori spero di riposar.*[21]

NOTES

Notes by Chastellux are preceded by the symbol: *Ch*. Notes by the eighteenth-century translator, George Grieve, are preceded by the symbol: *Gr*. All other notes are by the present Editor, and are preceded by the symbol *Ed*. only when they form a continuation of a note by Chastellux or by Grieve.

Introduction

1. There is no full-length biography of Chastellux. Notices of him have appeared in the standard biographical dictionaries, most recently in J. Balteau, M. Barroux, and M. Prévost, eds., *Dictionnaire de Biographie Française*, VIII (Paris, 1959), 746. A brief sketch of him by his son, Alfred de Chastellux, was issued as a pamphlet of 24 pages, and is bound up with some copies of the 1822 edition of *De la Félicité Publique* (copy in Bibliothèque Nationale). A more comprehensive essay, "Le Marquis de Chastellux," by Léonce de Lavergne, is included in his *Les Economistes Français du Dix-Huitième siècle* (Paris, 1870), 279-330 (previously published in Académie des Sciences Morales et Politiques, *Séances et Travaux*, 71 [1865], 303-55; *Le Correspondant*, 63 [1864], 766-800; English translation in the *Catholic World*, 1865). H.-P.-C. de Chastellux, *Histoire Généalogique de la Maison de Chastellux* (Auxerre, 1869), includes a chapter on Chastellux as well as material on the family in general. Three doctoral dissertations have been devoted to Chastellux. Lucien Sicot, *Le Marquis de Chastellux (1734-1788)* (Paris, 1902), presented to the Faculty of Law, University of Paris, is mainly a discussion of Chastellux's economic theories as expressed in his *De la Félicité Publique*. Fanny Varnum, *Un Philosophe cosmopolite du XVIIIe siècle: Le Chevalier de Chastellux* (Paris, 1936), written for the Faculty of Letters, University of Paris, places more emphasis on Chastellux's literary activities, but is weak on American matters. George Barr Carson, Jr., The Chevalier de Chastellux, Soldier and Philosophe (unpubl. Ph.D. diss., University of Chicago, Dept. of History, 1942) is a competent and well-balanced work. Varnum and Carson, especially the latter, have provided indispensable bibliographical guidance, but I have myself returned to the sources cited by them in the preparation of the present sketch. Typed transcripts of Chastellux's letters found in different American libraries, constituting Appendix III, pp. 141-71, of Carson's thesis, are reproduced in pamphlet form as "a part of a dissertation submitted . . . in candidacy . . . etc." (Chicago, 1944).

2. Diderot, D'Alembert, *et al.*, eds., *Encyclopédie, ou Dictionnaire raisonné des sciences, des arts et des métiers*, 8 (1765), 757, in the article "Inoculation." For a modern survey of the subject see Arnold H. Rowbotham, "The 'Philosophes' and the Propaganda for Inoculation of Smallpox in Eighteenth-century France," University of California, *Publications in Modern Philology*, 18 (1935), 265-90.

3. Buffon, in his *Discours prononcé dans l'Académie Françoise à la réception de M. le chevalier de Chastellux* (Paris, 1775), 32.

4. *Réponse à une des principales objections qu'on oppose maintenant aux partisans de l'inoculation de la petite vérole* (Paris [?], 1763); *Nouveaux*

éclaircissemens sur l'inoculation de la petite vérole, pour servir de réponse à un écrit de M. Rast, médecin de Lyon (Paris [?], 1763). Copies in Bib. Nat.

5. Aug. 22, 1772, Thomas Holcroft, trans., *Posthumous Works of Frederic II, King of Prussia,* 13 vols. (London, 1789), XI, 313-18.

6. Chastellux's article in the *Journal Etranger,* July 1761, 149-94, was a digest-review of a French translation of Frederick's *Instruction* which had been published earlier that year at Frankfort and Leipzig. Chastellux's authorship of the review is indicated in this same issue of the *Journal Etranger,* p. 150, where the editor also attributes to him several earlier unsigned articles. The subsequent reprint of Frederick's *Instruction* with Chastellux's article as a preface is entitled *Instruction Militaire du Roi de Prusse pour ses Généraux, traduite de l'Allemand par Monsieur Faesch, Lieutenant-Colonel dans les Troupes Saxonnes* (no place and no publisher, 1761), "Réflexions de M. le Chevalier de Chatelus," pp. vii-xii; copy in New York Public Library. The *Instruction* was a pirated edition of Frederick's confidential manual for his generals, *General-Principia vom Kriege* (1748); see J.-D.-E. Preuss, ed., *Oeuvres de Frédéric le Grand,* 31 vols. (Berlin, 1846-57), XXVIII, 1-95, "Les Principes Généraux de la Guerre, appliqués à la tactique et à la discipline des troupes prussiennes," and the editor's bibliographical introduction, pp. xi-xvii (in which, however, the edition with Chastellux's preface is not recorded).

7. "Eloge historique et militaire de M. le vicomte de Belsunce," *Mercure de France,* Feb. 1764; "Eloge historique de M. le Baron de Closen," *ibid.,* Feb. 1765.

8. "Gedanken bey dem Beschlusse des Jahres 1759, Pensées sur la cloture de l'Année 1759," *Journal Etranger,* July 1760.

9. "Réflexions sur le Méchanisme de la Versification Italienne, Angloise & Allemande," *ibid.,* June 1760. In this connection it is worth mentioning that Thomas Jefferson's essay "Thoughts on English Prosody" was originally intended for Chastellux; see below, Pt. II, chap. 2, n. 17.

10. The author's name does not appear. It is a duodecimo of iv-94 pp. with the imprint: "A La Haye, Et se trouve à Paris, Chez Merlin, Libraire, au bas de la rue de la Harpe, M.DCC.LXV."

11. "Observations sur un ouvrage nouveau intitulé: Traité du Mélodrame ou Réflexions sur la musique dramatique," *Mercure de France,* Sept. 1771, 133-59. Chastellux's "Observations" in turn called forth an article by Diderot entitled "Lettre au sujet des Observations du Chevalier de Chastellux sur le Traité du Mélodrame," J. Assézat, ed., *Oeuvres Complètes de Diderot,* 20 vols. (Paris, 1875-77), VIII, 506-10. Diderot makes this comment on Chastellux's style: "The Chevalier de Chastellux has knowledge, wit, and sound ideas; he thinks, but his style is ambiguous, involved, diffuse. There is throughout a certain wearisome abstractness, so that little notice will be taken of his reply, although it is solid and profound."

12. *Essai sur l'opéra,* traduit de l'italien du Comte d'Algarotti (Pisa and Paris, 1773). This translation (there were others) is attributed to Chastellux by the Bibliothèque Nationale catalogue. Algarotti's work had first appeared in 1755 as *Saggio sopra l'opera in musica;* a French translation appeared in the *Mercure de France,* May 1757, 40-62.

13. Jean-François La Harpe, *Correspondance littéraire . . . ,* 5 vols. (Paris, 1801-7), II, 153; *Mémoires inédits de l'Abbé Morellet,* 2 vols. (Paris, 1821),

I, 245-49. In 1773 Chastellux had made the acquaintance of Piccinni in Naples, and, according to Abbé Galiani's report, "swooned with pleasure" upon hearing Piccinni's masterpiece, *Splende ogni astro più sereno;* Galiani to Madame d'Epinay, Naples, May 22, 1773, Lucien Perey and Gaston Maugras, eds., *L'Abbé Galiani Correspondance avec Madame d'Epinay* [et al.], 3rd ed., 2 vols. (Paris, 1890), II, 208-9.

14. "Lettre aux Auteurs de ce Journal—sur l'Examen des effets que doivent produire dans le Commerce, l'usage et la libre fabrication des Toiles peintes," *Journal Encyclopédique,* May 1, 1759, 71-93. For a discussion of the controversy and the various pamphlets, see Edgard Depitre, *La Toile Peinte en France au XVIIe et au XVIIIe siècle* (Paris, 1912), chap. 6.

15. See Auguste Rey, *Le Château de La Chevrette et Madame d'Epinay* (Paris, 1904). Madame d'Epinay leased the estate in 1764 to M. de Magnanville, "Garde du Trésor Royal."

16. Geneviève de Savalette, Marquise de Gléon, *Recueil de comédies nouvelles* (Paris, Prault, 1787), with an "avertissement" by Chastellux. Copy in Bib. Nat.

17. Maurice Tourneux, ed., *Correspondance littéraire...par Grimm* [et al.], 16 vols. (Paris, 1877-82), IX, 297; XI, 148.

18. J. J. Jusserand, *Shakespeare in France under the Ancien Régime* (N. Y. and London, 1899), 408-11, records Chastellux's adaptation as a landmark of sorts in the history of the gradual naturalization of Shakespeare in France.

19. June 15, 1771, James Boaden, ed., *Private Correspondence of David Garrick...,* 2 vols. (London, 1831-32), II, 583-84. Original in French.

20. Nov. 27, 1770, *ibid.,* 574-76. Original in French.

21. *Eloge de M. Helvétius* [Paris, 1772]. The pamphlet appeared without name of author. Concerning Chastellux's authorship see Albert Keim, *Helvétius, Sa Vie et Son Oeuvre* (Paris, 1907), 606-7. It is not to be confused with a somewhat similar biographical sketch, "Essai sur la Vie et les Oeuvres d'Helvétius," by Saint Lambert, which first appeared anonymously as a preface to Helvétius' posthumously published poem *Le Bonheur,* and which was reproduced in successive editions of his works. Chastellux's remark in his *Eloge de M. Helvétius* that "his customary sense of justice prevented him from hating men for faults which he attributed only to their ignorance or their prejudices," might well be applied to Chastellux himself.

22. Voltaire to Chastellux, Dec. 4, 1776, and note to this letter, in Louis Moland, ed., *Oeuvres Complètes de Voltaire,* 52 vols. (Paris, 1877-85), L, 439-40, letter no. 9903.

23. Frank A. Hedgcock, *A Cosmopolitan Actor, David Garrick and His French Friends* (New York, [ca. 1912]), 314-16.

24. G. Bonno, "Lettres inédites de Chastellux à Wilkes" [four letters, 1762-68], *Revue de littérature comparée,* 12 (1932), 619-23.

25. J. Y. T. Greig, "Some Unpublished Letters to David Hume" [including five from Chastellux, 1766-69], *ibid.,* 826-56.

26. Perey and Maugras, eds., *L'Abbé Galiani, Correspondance;* Fausto Nicolini, ed., *Gli Ultimi Anni della Signora d'Epinay: Lettere inedite all' Abate Galiani (1773-1782)* (Bari, 1933).

27. "Horace Walpole's Paris Journals," Oct. 6, 1765, Nov. 17, 1765, Feb. 4, 1766, in W. S. Lewis and Warren Hunting Smith, eds., *Horace Walpole's*

Correspondence with Madame du Deffand and Wiart, 6 vols. (New Haven and London, 1939), V, 267, 272, 299.

28. Chastellux to Wilkes, Calais, Apr. 9, 1768, Bonno, "Lettres inédites de Chastellux à Wilkes," *Revue de littérature comparée*, 12 (1932), 619-23; Diderot to Sophie Volland, Aug. 28, 1768, in Diderot, *Lettres à Sophie Volland*, ed. André Babelon, 3 vols. (Paris, 1930), III, 129; Abbé Galiani to Madame d'Epinay, Naples, Oct. 13, 1770, in Perey and Maugras, eds., *L'Abbé Galiani, Correspondance*, I, 281-82.

29. Mrs. Elizabeth Montagu to her sister, Paris, Aug. 11, 1776, in Reginald Blunt, ed., *Mrs. Montagu... Her Letters and Friendships from 1762 to 1800*, 2 vols. (London, 1923), I, 321-22.

30. Jean François Marmontel, *Mémoires*, Book 6. The translation of this passage as given in the several available English editions of the work is inaccurate in several particulars; a fresh version is presented here.

31. See Fernand Clément, ed., *Le Journal Encyclopédique et la Société Typographique, Exposition en hommage à Pierre Rousseau (1716-1785) et Charles-Auguste de Weissenbruch (1744-1826)* (Bouillon, 1955). Extracts from *De la Félicité Publique* were included in the *Dictionnaire des Sciences morale, économique, politique et diplomatique, ou Bibliothèque de l'Homme d'Etat et du Citoyen* (Paris, 1777-83), I, under "Agriculture," and XXVI, under "Population." A final French edition of Chastellux's book was published in 1822; see below, n. 43.

32. Published by T. Cadell. See letter from John Kent to Benjamin Franklin, Feb. 22, 1775, sending a copy of the book: "I am confident that my friend the Chevalier de Chattelux, who has joined the multitude in applauding you would be pleased that you should read his sentiments of you, in their English dress.... Do the Chevalier and me the honor to recommend it." Franklin Papers, IV, 42½, American Philosophical Society.

33. *Über die Glückseligkeit der Völker, oder Betrachtungen über das Schicksal der Menschen in den verschiedenen Epochen der Gesellschaft*, 2 vols. (Leipzig, Weygand, 1780).

34. *Considerazioni sopra la sorte dell' umanità delle diverse epoche della storia moderna* (Naples, Società Letteraria e Tipografica, 1782).

35. The 1790 edition (T. Cadell) with the title *Essays on Historic Subjects, from the Earliest Age to the Present Time;* the 1792 edition as *Agriculture and Population the Truest Proofs of the Welfare of the People; or, an Essay on Public Happiness, Investigating the State of Human Nature....* The title page of the latter, published by J. Caddel, erroneously refers to Chastellux as a "Member of the National Assembly!"

36. Madame d'Epinay to Abbé Galiani, Jan. 12, 1773, Perey and Maugras, eds., *L'Abbé Galiani, Correspondance*, II, 164-69.

37. La Harpe, *Correspondance littéraire*, I, 34 (Dec. 1, 1774).

38. Tourneux, ed., *Correspondance littéraire par Grimm*, XV, 102.

39. Aug. 22, 1772, Thomas Holcroft, trans., *Posthumous Works of Frederic II*, XI, 313-18. In his reply, Oct. 6, 1772, Frederick mentions that he is enclosing a letter for the Chevalier de Chastellux: "His equals were formerly numerous in France. Nobility destitute of knowledge is a vain title, which places an ignorant man in the glare of day, and exposes him to the irony of those who shall seek amusement."

40. Feb. 11, 1767, in Moland, ed., *Oeuvres de Voltaire*, XLV, 108, letter no. 6740. Also in Theodore Besterman, ed., *Voltaire's Correspondence* (Geneva, 1953 ———), LXIV, 198-99, letter no. 13048.

41. Dec. 7, 1772, in Moland, ed., *Oeuvres de Voltaire*, XLVIII, 239-41, letter no. 8703.

42. June 20, 1777, in A. Condorcet O'Connor and M. F. Arago, eds., *Oeuvres de Condorcet*, 12 vols. (Paris, 1847-49), I, 151-54.

43. *De la Félicité Publique ... Nouvelle édition augmentée de notes inédites de Voltaire*, 2 vols. (Paris, Renouard, 1822). A "Notice sur le Marquis de Chastellux, par M. Alfred de Chastellux, Son Fils" (pp. i-xxiv) was included in some, but apparently not all, copies of the book; it is present, for example, in one of the copies at the Bibliothèque Nationale (Z. Beuchot 1048, and as a separate, Ln^{27}.4064), but is lacking in two copies, both in contemporary bindings, examined by the Editor (N.Y. Pub. Lib., Cornell Univ.). According to a footnote to this "Notice" (p. i), Voltaire's annotated copy of Chastellux's work (see Voltaire's letter of Dec. 7, 1772, cited above, n. 41) then belonged to Count Orloff (Grégoire-Vladimirovitch Orloff, 1777-1826), who permitted the publisher Renouard to transcribe the Voltairian marginalia for his new edition. This copy, which was in 1822 in the possession of Count Orloff, then a resident of Paris, is perhaps the same which is now in the State Public Library of Leningrad among the other books from Voltaire's library acquired by Catherine II in 1779; see M. P. Alekseev and T. N. Kopreeva, eds., *Biblioteka Vol'tera, Katalog Knig; Bibliothèque de Voltaire, Catalogue des Livres* (Moscow, Leningrad, 1961), p. 247, No. 722, where a copy of the Amsterdam 1772 edition of *De la Félicité Publique* with marginal notes is recorded. The Leningrad catalogue also records, No. 723, a copy of the Bouillon 1776 edition of Chastellux's work with Voltaire's armorial bookstamp on the cover; this example of the bookstamp is reproduced in Vladimir Lublinsky, "Voltaire and His Library," *The Book Collector*, 7 (1958), 139-51, plate III, facing p. 145. Voltaire's own manuscript catalogue of his library at Ferney, reprinted as an appendix to the Leningrad catalogue, lists *De la Félicité Publique* three times (fol. 75vo, 77ro, 81vo); see also George R. Havens and Norman L. Torrey, eds., "Voltaire's Catalogue of His Library at Ferney," *Studies on Voltaire and the Eighteenth Century*, ed. Theodore Besterman, 9 (1959), 126, Nos. 612-13.

44. See, for example, works cited in n. 1 above, especially Lavergne and Sicot, and the following: Jules Delvaille, *Essai sur l'histoire de l'idée de progrès jusqu'à la fin du XVIIIe siècle* (Paris, 1910), 419-23; J. B. Bury, *The Idea of Progress, An Inquiry into its Origin and Growth* (New York, 1932), 186-91; Benedetto Croce, *Conversazioni Critiche*, 5 vols. (Bari, 1924-39), V, 321-29. Croce points out that Chastellux was one of the very few 18th-century French writers to mention G. B. Vico's *Scienza Nuova* (1725), but concludes that there was no real influence of his essential doctrine; this came only with the discovery of Vico by such 19th-century French historians as Joubert, Michelet, and Quinet.

45. Werner Stark, *Economica*, New Ser., 8 (1941), 203-7. The article, according to the author, "is only meant to show that Chastellux, to whom my attention was drawn by Professor Laski, is an interesting thinker, who has not been given the place in the history of social and economic thought which he deserves." Stark finds a parallel between Chastellux's "materialistic

conception of history" and that of Karl Marx, and also points out that "Chastellux in fact anticipated Marx's whole theory of surplus value." He further surmises that Marx probably did not know Chastellux's work: "He was an aristocrat, and, in spite of his genuine desire to promote the well-being of his fellow-men, a thorough conservative. Such men lay beyond Marx's sphere of interest."

46. La Harpe, *Correspondance littéraire*, I, 34 (Dec. 1, 1774).

47. Mlle de Lespinasse to M. de Guibert, Oct. 14, 1774, in Eugène Asse, ed., *Lettres de Mlle de Lespinasse* (Paris, 1903), 129.

48. C. Doucet and G. Boissier, ed., *Les Registres de l'Académie Françoise, 1762-1793*, 4 vols. (Paris, 1895-1906), III; Louis Petit de Bachaumont, *Mémoires secrets ...*, 36 vols. (London, 1777-89), XXX, 234-38 (Apr. 27-28, 1775).

49. *Discours prononcés dans l'Académie Françoise, Le Jeudi XXVII Avril M.DCC.LXXV. à la Réception de M. le Chevalier de Chastellux* (Paris, 1775). Buffon's speech is also printed in his *Histoire naturelle, générale et particulière, Supplément IV* (Paris, 1777), and in J.-L. de Lanessan, ed., *Oeuvres complètes de Buffon*, 14 vols. (Paris, 1884-85), XI, 575-79.

50. Moland, ed., *Oeuvres de Voltaire*, X, 594.

51. Voltaire to Chastellux, Apr. 14, 1775, *ibid.*, XLIX, 272, letter no. 9370.

52. Chastellux to Voltaire, May 23, 1777, quoted in *ibid.*, L, 226n: "Oui je voudrais n'avoir auprès d'elle [la postérité] d'autre titre que votre indulgence, et que toute ma célébrité dépendît de ces mots qu'on trouverait écrits quelque part: *Il fut contemporain de Monsieur de Voltaire et il en fut estimé.*"

53. Tourneux, ed., *Correspondance littéraire par Grimm*, XII, 94 (May 1778).

54. Madame d'Epinay to Abbé Galiani, May 3, 1778, in Perey and Maugras, eds., *L'Abbé Galiani, Correspondance*, II, 545-48.

55. *De la Félicité Publique* (Amsterdam, 1772), II, 87.

56. Silas Deane to Congress, Paris, Aug. 18, 1776, Silas Deane to Chastellux, ca. Jan. 1777, *The Deane Papers* (N.Y. Hist. Soc., *Collections*, 19-23 [1887-91]), I, 218, 468-69, hereafter cited as *Deane Papers*.

57. The general character of the army of the Ancien Régime, as contrasted with the newer one, is admirably described by Louis-Philippe, Comte de Ségur, in his *Mémoires, souvenirs et anecdotes ...*, 3 vols. (Paris, 1824-26), I, 74-77.

58. *Ibid.*, 409-11 (see below, Pt. III, chap. 3, n. 1); Mathieu Dumas, *Memoirs of His Own Time ...*, 2 vols. (Phila., 1839), I, 64 ff.; Axel Fersen, *Lettres à son père*, ed. F. U. Wrangel (Paris, 1929), 75-76, 140.

59. Thomas Balch, ed., William Duane, trans., *The Journal of Claude Blanchard, ... 1780-1783* (Albany, 1876), 144-45, 147, 149; hereafter cited as Blanchard, *Journal*.

60. Bernard Faÿ, ed., "Relation sur la guerre d'Amérique d'après une conversation avec un officier du Génie qui y étoit employé," *Franco-American Review*, 2 (1937), 114-20.

61. Bachaumont, *Mémoires secrets*, XXII, 333-35 (May 18, 1783). In an anonymous "Lettre écrite à M. Garat par un officier récemment arrivé d'Amérique," in the *Mercure de France*, Mar. 1783, 196, Chastellux himself

corrected certain statements about the siege of Yorktown made by Abbé Robin in his *Nouveau Voyage dans l'Amérique septentrionale en l'année 1781, et campagne de l'Armée de M. de Rochambeau* (Paris, 1782).

62. *Mémoires militaires, historiques et politiques de Rochambeau*, 2 vols. (Paris, 1809), I, 273-75. See below, Pt. II, Intro. and n. 8.

63. Henri Doniol, *Histoire de la Participation de la France à l'Etablissement des Etats-Unis d'Amérique, Correspondance Diplomatique et Documents*, 5 vols. (Paris, 1886-92), IV, 669n.

64. Entry of Oct. 9-10, 1780, Franklin B. Dexter, ed., *The Literary Diary of Ezra Stiles...*, 3 vols. (N. Y., 1901), II, 473-74.

65. William Knox to Henry Knox, Boston, Aug. 22, 1781, Francis S. Drake, *Life and Correspondence of Henry Knox* (Boston, 1873), 66-67.

66. For details see below: Pt. I, chap. 3, n. 56 (Univ. of Pa.) and n. 116 (Amer. Phil. Soc.); Pt. II, chap. 5, n. 17 (Wm. and Mary); Pt. III, chap. 2, n. 40 (Amer. Acad. Arts and Sciences). Chastellux was also elected an honorary member of the Charleston (South Carolina) Library Society (Apr. 2, 1783). The Société Royale des Sciences et Belles Lettres de Nancy likewise elected him an associate member in 1786.

67. Earlier editions of the *Almanach Royal* give Chastellux's residence as the Rue des Juifs (1776) and the Rue du Sentier (1777-84)—both in the "Marais," the ancient aristocratic quarter of the city which was already considered a bit old-fashioned in the 1780's. The names designating successive stretches of the Seine embankment have varied capriciously over the years. Watin's *Etat actuel de Paris* (1787, 1788, 1789), another directory, places Chastellux's residence on the "Quai d'Orsay," as does a letter from Jefferson, Dec. 24, 1784 (Julian P. Boyd et al., *The Papers of Thomas Jefferson* [Princeton, N. J., 1950——], VII, 580-81), addressed "A Monsr. le Marquis de Chastellux en son hôtel Quai d'Orsai à Paris"—but this is undoubtedly the same place as the Quai des Théatins of the *Almanach Royal*. For the moment (1963) the spot is known as the Quai Anatole France; the site of Chastellux's residence, between the Rue du Bac and the Gare d'Orsay, is occupied by the Caisse d'Amortissement et des Dépôts et Consignations. See also Félix de Rochegude and Maurice Dumolin, *Guide pratique à travers le Vieux Paris...* (Paris, 1923), 501.

68. *Considérations sur le Magnétisme Animal, ou sur la Théorie du Monde et des Êtres Organisés, d'après les Principes de M. Mesmer. Par M. [Nicolas] Bergasse. Avec des pensées sur le Mouvement, par M. le Marquis de Chatellux, de l'Académie Françoise* (The Hague, 1784). Chastellux's "Pensées" constitute pp. 143-49.

69. *Discours prononcés dans l'Académie Françoise le Jeudi XVI Juin M DCC LXXXV, à la réception de M. L'Abbé Morellet* (Paris, 1785). The "Réponse de M. le Marquis de Chastellux au Discours de M. l'Abbé Morellet" comprises pp. 34-50. The speeches are also printed in Morellet, *Mélanges de littérature et de philosophie du 18e siècle*, 4 vols. (Paris, 1818), I, 1-56. See also *Discours prononcés dans l'Académie Françoise à la réception de M. de Rulhière* (Paris, 1787).

70. See n. 16 above.

71. *Discours sur les Avantages ou les Désavantages qui résultent, pour l'Europe, de la Découverte de l'Amérique. Objet du Prix proposé par M.*

l'Abbé Raynal. Par M. P***, Vice-Consul, à E*** (Paris, Prault, 1787), 8, 68 pp. Prault was also the publisher of Chastellux's *Voyages.* Chastellux's authorship is conclusively established by his own letter to Gouverneur Morris, cited below in the text. A German version was published under the title *Abhandlung über die Vortheile und Nachtheile die für Europa aus der Entdeckung von America entstehen, Von Herrn P***, Aus dem französischen übersetzt* (Halle, 1788). For other essays published in response to the question proposed by Abbé Raynal in a contest sponsored by the Académie de Lyon, see Durand Echeverria, *Mirage in the West . . .* (Princeton, 1957), 173.

72. Chastellux to Gouverneur Morris, Jan. 18, 1788, transcript in Jared Sparks MSS., Harvard Univ. Lib.

73. Chastellux to Jefferson, [Paris], Aug. 24, 1784, in Boyd *et al.*, eds., *Jefferson Papers*, VII, 410-11. See below, Pt. II, chap. 2, n. 17.

74. See below, Pt. I, chap. 4, Dec. 20, 1780, and n. 12.

75. Thomas Lee Shippen to Dr. William Shippen, Jr., Feb. 14–Mar. 26, 1788, quoted in Boyd *et al.*, eds., *Jefferson Papers*, XII, 502-4. See below, Pt. I, chap. 3, Dec. 11, 1780, and n. 96.

76. Chastellux to Jefferson, Marly, June 2, 1785, *ibid.*, VIII, 174-75. Original in French.

77. Chastellux to Gouverneur Morris, Paris, Jan. 18, 1788, in English. A transcript of this letter, made for Jared Sparks from papers then in the possession of Morris's widow, is among the Jared Sparks MSS., Harvard University Library. Portions of the transcript have been cut away; these incisions are indicated here by square brackets. My efforts to find the original letter among the Morris Papers now in the Columbia University Library have proved fruitless.

78. Marie-Joséphine-Charlotte Brigitte de Plunkett, born in Louvain, Sept. 8, 1759, was the daughter of Baron Thomas de Plunkett, lieutenant field marshal in the Austrian service, and of Marie d'Alton. The family traced its origins to Bewly, County of Louth, in Ireland. H.-P.-C. Chastellux, *Histoire Généalogique.*

79. Comte de Montbrison, ed., *Mémoires de la Baronne d'Oberkirch*, 2 vols. (Paris, 1869), II, 325. The same story is related, with variations, in Bachaumont, *Mémoires secrets*, XXXVI, 282-83 (Dec. 14, 1787). Madame de Genlis, governess of the Orléans children, had a finger in the marriage, as related in her *Mémoires* (various editions); she evidently resented the fact that the Marquise de Chastellux eventually "supplanted" her as an intimate of the Duchesse d'Orléans.

80. William Short to William Nelson, Paris, Nov. 3. 1787, Gilpin Papers, Historical Society of Pennsylvania. (I am greatly indebted to M. Yvon Bizardel for calling my attention to this unpublished letter.) In this letter Short adds for Nelson's benefit (in a passage that curiously foreshadows his own liaison of twenty years with the Duchesse de La Rochefoucauld): "The affair of what is called *liaison de coeur* or *bonne amitié* at Paris is really a curious circumstance to a stranger. It has its rules and its morality as well established as marriage among us—an infidelity reckoned as base and inconstancy as unpardonable in that case, as amongst us between husbands and wives."

Chastellux's *bonne amie* was perhaps the Marquise de Gléon, she of the amateur theatricals at La Chevrette. If this supposition is correct, then the publication of a volume of her plays, under Chastellux's aegis in 1787, would have been a final *beau geste* at the time of the rupture. Bachaumont's *Mémoires secrets*, XXXV, 265-66 (June 21, 1787), speaks of the "*éditeur galant*" (without naming him) and adds that "the author is a woman of quality, who in her youth frequented the court of the late Prince de Conti, who was beautiful, full of talent, and who performed on the stage with taste and grace; today she is in miserable health, and has for long been a prey to mesmerism." See Chastellux to Jefferson, Marly, June 2, 1785, Boyd *et al.*, eds., *Jefferson Papers*, VIII, 174-75. Geneviève de Savalette, Marquise de Gléon, was born *ca.* 1732, which would have made her an "old lady" in the 1780's.

As Short implies, an established *liaison*, like marriage, did not in itself exclude inconstancy and infidelity. Chastellux apparently took a passing fancy to the Comtesse Golowkin, who besieged Dr. Franklin for news of her friend when he was off to the wars in America; "je suis intimement liée avec le Chevalier de Chastellux, et j'ai vu dans le Courier de l'Europe qu'il avoit été tué à une affaire que Mr. de Rochambeau a eue—rassurez moi s'il est possible . . . mon bon et cher Papa." Gilbert Chinard, "Benjamin Franklin and the Mysterious Madame G——," Amer. Phil. Soc., *Library Bulletin* (1946), 49-72. Wilhelmina von Mosheim, Comtesse Golowkin, was born *ca.* 1745, and did not settle in Paris until *ca.* 1770; she does not therefore qualify as the *bonne amie* of thirty years' standing.

81. Duc de Liancourt (La Rochefoucauld-Liancourt), *Journal de voyage en Amérique et d'un Séjour à Philadelphie, 1 Octobre 1794-18 Avril 1795 . . .*, ed. Jean Marchand (Baltimore, 1940), 90-91 (Jan. 26, 1795).

82. Washington to Chastellux, Mount Vernon, Apr. 25—May 1, 1788, John C. Fitzpatrick, ed., *The Writings of George Washington . . .*, 39 vols. (Washington, 1931-44), XXIX, 483-86; also printed in 1827 edition of Chastellux's *Travels*, 397-99. In his postscript Washington acknowledges the receipt of a duplicate copy of Chastellux's letter in the handwriting of his wife and adds a gracious word of thanks to the "fair transcriber" and "amiable amanuensis," which will be appreciated by any who have attempted to decipher the Marquis's handwriting.

83. Gouverneur Morris to Washington, Paris, Mar. 3, 1789, in Gouverneur Morris, *A Diary of the French Revolution*, ed. Beatrix Cary Davenport, 2 vols. (Boston, 1939), I, xxxviii-xxxix.

84. *Ibid.*, 2-3 (Mar. 2, 1789).

85. *Ibid.*, 24-25 (Mar. 31, 1789).

86. The bracketed numbers in this section refer to the items in the "Check-List of the Different Editions of Chastellux's *Travels*," 43-52.

87. A.-Jacques Parès, *Imprimeries d'Escadre* (Paris, 1928) (reprint from *Bulletin de la Section de Géographie, Comité des travaux historiques et scientifiques*, 1927); John Eliot Alden, ed., *Rhode Island Imprints, 1727-1800* (N. Y., 1949), Nos. 811, 853, 865; *Gazette Françoise, A Facsimile Reprint of a Newspaper printed at Newport on the Printing Press of the French Fleet*, introduction by Howard M. Chapin (N. Y., 1926); Lawrence C. Wroth, "The French Fleet Press in the American Revolution," in souvenir program, *Washington-Rochambeau Celebration* (Newport, 1955), 24-31.

88. The restored house is maintained by the Preservation Society of Newport County. The tablet, presented on July 10, 1955, by *France-Amérique*, French newspaper published in the United States, to commemorate the 175th anniversary of the arrival of Rochambeau's army in Newport, recalls that the *Gazette Françoise* was the first foreign-language newspaper published in the United States, as well as the first service newspaper published abroad by an expeditionary force, and as such, the ancestor of *Stars and Stripes*, published by the American expeditionary forces in France during the two World Wars.

89. Jefferson to Chastellux, Paris, Dec. 24, 1784, Boyd *et al.*, eds., *Jefferson Papers*, VII, 580-83; see below, Pt. I, chap. 3, n. 30.

90. See below, Pt. I, chap. 1, Chastellux's n. 23. The publisher's foreword to the 1786 edition (q.v.) says that "of these twenty-four copies, barely ten or twelve reached Europe."

91. The publisher's foreword to the authorized Paris 1786 edition of the *Travels* (q.v.) describes this only as "un receuil périodique qu'on imprime à Gotha, & où l'on s'attache sur-tout à rassembler des ouvrages qui n'ont pas été rendus publics." Subsequent bibliographers and writers on Chastellux have merely repeated or paraphrased this statement without further identifying the periodical. A footnote added by Maurice Tourneux to his edition of *Correspondance littéraire par Grimm*, XIV, 380, supplies the information that "Le véritable titre de ce journal, fondé par Otto Reichard, est *Cahiers de lecture*. Ces cahiers parurent de 1784 à 1794, et forment 36 vol. in-8° et in-12." The three issues of this apparently very scarce periodical comprising the incomplete set in the Bibliothèque Nationale, Paris–those for Jan., Feb., and Mar. 1784–contain "Fragmens du voyage de M. le Chevalier de Châtellux en Amérique." A more extensive set in the Landesbibliothek Gotha shows that the fragments continued to appear monthly until the end of 1784. I am indebted to M. Pierre Josserand of the Bibliothèque Nationale and to Dr. Küttler of the Landesbibliothek Gotha for their help in finally solving this elusive bibliographical riddle.

92. Pierre-Marie-Félicité Dezoteux (1751-1812), trained as an engineer, served in America as aide-de-camp to Baron de Vioménil; in 1791 he was involved in the attempted escape of the King, emigrated, and subsequently participated in the counter-revolutionary guerrilla in Vendée (the "Chouannerie") under the name of Baron de Cormatin. E. T. Hamy, "Les Cartes du Voyage de Chastellux," Société des Américanistes de Paris, *Journal*, 1 (1895-96), 73-79. Ludovic de Contenson, *La Société des Cincinnati de France et la Guerre d'Amérique, 1778-1783* (Paris, 1934), 163-65, portrait 45. Mathieu Dumas met Dezoteux at Nancy in 1791 shortly before his emigration with his then general, the Marquis de Bouillé; Dumas *Memoirs*, I, 121.

93. The Duc de Duras, present owner of such of Chastellux's papers as have survived at the Château de Chastellux (Yonne), has informed me that no manuscripts of the *Voyages* are to his knowledge extant in his branch of the family. The Newberry Library, Chicago, Ill., has a manuscript entitled "Voyage de Williamsburg en Virginie Amérique Septentrionale, à Charlottesville, au Natural Bridge, Petersburg, Richmond etc," North American MS. 154, Ayer Collection. A MS. note in an unidentified 19th-century hand describes it thus: "Cet ouvrage est le manuscrit original du Chevalier de Chastellux, c'est la relation de son second voyage dans l'intérieur des

Etats-Unis. Il fait suite à celui publié à Newport et imprimé à bord de l'Escadre royale en 1781. Brest 1860." The text follows very closely the printed version of Part II of the *Voyages;* it is not in Chastellux's handwriting, but in that of an 18th-century copyist. In my opinion this cannot properly be described as "*the* original manuscript," but is probably one of the fair copies which circulated before publication.

94. Doucet and Boissier, eds., *Les Registres de l'Académie Françoise*, III, 574.

95. The *Gentleman's Magazine*, 57 (Jan. 1787), published an open letter from Lt. Col. J. G. Simcoe to Chastellux, incited by the appearance of the English translation. See also the Mar. 1787 letter of James Watmough (James H. Watmough, ed., "Letters of James H. Watmough to His Wife, 1785," *Pennsylvania Magazine of History and Biography*, 29 [1905], 308-9), who had a copy in hand in late Feb. or early Mar.; William Short to William Nelson, Feb. 7, 1787, Gilpin Papers, Hist. Soc. of Pa.

96. Pp. 5-9. The communication is in the form of a letter to Robert Winthrop, President of the Society, from J. Hammond Trumbull, a Corresponding Member, dated Hartford, Conn., Mar. 29, 1869.

97. William Short, in a letter to William Nelson, Paris, Feb. 7, 1787, Gilpin Papers, Hist. Soc. of Pa., specifically states: "It [General Chastellux's work on America] has been already translated into English and published by an Englishman by the Name of Greive—who travelled a great deal in America during the war and is at present here." Other sources for Greive's story are to be found in the writings of John G. Alger: "English Actors in the French Revolution," *Edinburgh Review*, 166 (1887), 445-64; article on George Grieve in *DNB*; *Englishmen in the French Revolution* (London, 1889), 187-92. Alger was not familiar with Trumbull's article, and his references to Greive's sojourn in America are erroneous. Grieve was the family name, although the man himself spelled it Greive (presumably a Gallicized form) in at least two signed documents that I have seen (see below nn. 98, 106). To avoid confusion I have arbitrarily retained the former spelling in my text, except for purposes of direct quotation.

98. Deane to Washington, Paris, May 2, 1781; Deane to Jefferson, Paris, May 2, 1781; Deane to Barnabas Deane, Paris, May 2, 1781; *Deane Papers*, V, 305-7; Franklin to Jefferson, Passy, May 6, 1781, Boyd *et al.*, eds., *Jefferson Papers*, V, 610. Greive's oath of allegiance is in the Franklin Papers, LXXIV, 17, Amer. Philos. Soc.; his signature here reads "George Greive."

99. See below, Pt. I, chap. 3, Greive's n. 16.

100. All the dated or datable references to incidents of American travel in Greive's notes fall within the year 1782, with one exception. In Pt. I, chap. 1, n. 100, he mentions having been at Joshua Hett Smith's house in Haverstraw in 1780, but this is evidently a typographical error and he was probably there in the fall of 1782 at the time he visited the American army at Verplanck's Point.

101. The letter from Grieve to Silas Deane is quoted by J. Hammond Trumbull, Mass. Hist. Soc., *Proceedings*, 11 (1871), 7.

102. See below, Pt. I, chap. 2, n. 15.

103. Although no extensive investigation has been undertaken, the following works—all anonymous translations and all published by G. G. J. and J.

Robinson of London (publishers of Grieve's translation of Chastellux)—lend credibility to his claim: *Memoirs of Baron de Tott, containing the State of the Turkish Empire and the Crimea* ..., 2 vols. (1785); *Letters on Egypt* ... *by Mr. [Claude Etienne] Savary*, 2 vols. (1786); Comte de Volney, *Travels through Egypt and Syria, in the years 1783, 1784, and 1785* ..., 2 vols. (London, 1787-88).

104. The story is told briefly by J. G. Alger in the works cited above, n. 97. More details are given by G. Lenôtre, *Vieilles Maisons, Vieux Papiers*, 2d Ser. (Paris, 1920), 101-25. Lenôtre evidently suspects that Grieve himself was the thief. See also Albert Mathiez, *La Révolution et les Etrangers: Cosmopolitisme et Défense Nationale* (Paris, 1918), 7.

105. *L'Egalité controuvée, ou Petite histoire de la protection, contenant les pièces relatives à l'arrestation de la Du Barry, ancienne maîtresse de Louis XV, pour servir d'exemple aux patriotes trop ardents qui veulent sauver la République, et aux modérés, qui s'entendent à merveille pour la perdre* (Paris, n. d., but signed "Greive, 31 juillet 1793"), copy in Bib. Nat. Another pamphlet by Grieve, also in the Bib. Nat., is entitled *Sur la Belgique, lettre de Georges Greive* ... *au citoyen Denis* ... *Douai, 28 novembre l'an I.*

106. This document, entitled "Mémoire pour Georges Greive Citoyen des Etats Unis d'Amérique Aux Représentants du Peuple composant le Comité de Sureté générale de la Convention nationale," is in the alphabetically arranged series of "Petitions et Réclamations de Divers Colons détenus dans les prisons à différentes époques," D XXV, 77, Arch. Nat., Paris. With it is an earlier document, dated Aug. 12, 1793, which is a denunciation of "Graive Américain" by Citizen Jean Rat, who suspects the former of having been in secret correspondence with Dumouriez at the time of the General's defection in Belgium.

107. This is confirmed by the obituary notice of David Richard Grieve published in the *Gentleman's Magazine*, 63 (Supplement for 1793), 1216, portions of which are quoted by J. H. Trumbull, Mass. Hist. Soc., *Proceedings*, 11 (1871), 8.

108. Printed by Lenôtre, *Vieilles Maisons, Vieux Papiers*, 125, n. 1.

109. See below, Pt. II, chap. 3, Grieve's n. 42.

110. See below, Pt. I, chap. 4, n. 12.

111. See below, Pt. I, chap. 2, n. 33.

112. William Short to William Nelson, Paris, Feb. 7, 1787, Gilpin Papers, Hist. Soc. of Pa.

113. *Ibid.*

114. La Harpe, *Correspondance littéraire*, V, 80-81 (1786); Tourneux, ed., *Correspondance littéraire par Grimm*, XIV, 380-81 (May 1786).

115. Buffon to Chastellux, Montbard, June 10, 1786, in Lanessan, ed., *Oeuvres de Buffon*, XIV, 326-28.

116. Brissot's comments are mentioned in the Editor's notes to the present edition at appropriate places; see, especially, Pt. I, chap. 3, n. 89.

117. *Journal de Paris*, Nov. 16, 1786.

118. La Harpe, *Correspondance littéraire*, V, 215-17.

119. *Mémoires de l'Abbé Morellet*, I, 312. Morellet says that his reply was already half printed, when he yielded to Chastellux's wishes. He kept only

two sets of these printed pages, to which he added transcripts of the rest of his manuscript; one of these he gave to Chastellux, and kept the other for himself. Listed among Morellet's manuscripts, *ibid.*, II, 445, is a "Défense du marquis de Chastellux contre Brissot."

120. 57 (Jan. 1787), 36-39.

121. Although this pamphlet has been attributed to Jonathan Boucher, the Loyalist clergyman, and even to Benedict Arnold, the authorship is established beyond any doubt by Simcoe correspondence now in the D. W. Smith Papers at the Toronto Public Library. In a letter to D. W. Smith, undated but endorsed in Smith's hand as received Jan. 6, 1800, Simcoe writes: "The Pamphlet...mentioned is to be had at Wilkies, St. Paul Church Yard. It was printed about 1787. It is entitled 'Observations on the Travels of the Marquis de Chastellux'—buy two of them. I do not wish to be known as the Author, therefore do not discover that you know me; but ask cursorily." The pamphlet is again referred to in another letter from Simcoe to Smith, Feb. 7, 1800. I am indebted to Mr. Lawrence C. Wroth for calling my attention to this information, contained in a communication from Miss Marie Tremaine of the Toronto Public Library to the John Carter Brown Lib., Aug. 3, 1935.

122. Franklin to Chastellux, Philadelphia, Apr. 17, 1787, Albert Henry Smyth, ed., *The Writings of Benjamin Franklin*, 10 vols. (N. Y. and London, 1905-7), IX, 567-68.

123. Washington to Chastellux, Mount Vernon, Aug. 18, 1786, Fitzpatrick, ed., *Writings of Washington*, XXVIII, 522-24. See below, Pt. I, chap. 2, n. 33.

124. Ezra Stiles to Jefferson, Dec. 8, 1786, Boyd *et al.*, eds., *Jefferson Papers*, X, 584-86.

125. Short to William Nelson, Paris, Feb. 7, 1787, Gilpin Papers, Hist. Soc. of Pa.

126. Ezra Stiles to Jefferson, Apr. 30, 1788, Boyd *et al.*, eds., *Jefferson Papers*, XIII, 118.

127. Watmough, ed., "Letters of James H. Watmough," *Pa. Mag. of Hist. and Biog.*, 29 (1905), 308-9. The citation is from a letter written in Mar. 1787, during Watmough's return voyage to America.

128. Letter of "a French gentleman, settled in one of the United States, to his friend in one of the French West India Islands," *Daily Advertiser* (New York), May 5, 1790.

129. The New York publisher, for example, omitted entirely the concluding part of Chastellux's Letter to Madison (see below, Pt. IV), in which he exhorts the Americans to make Sunday a happy day for the people. Also omitted was Grieve's footnote (Pt. III, chap. 2, n. 53) mentioning the Roman Catholic funeral service for Monsieur de l'Epine at Boston in 1782.

130. For discussions of Chastellux's book in this context see, for example: Bernard Faÿ, *L'Esprit Révolutionnaire en France et aux Etats-Unis à la fin du XVIIIe siècle* (Paris, 1925) (translated by Ramon Guthrie as *The Revolutionary Spirit in France and America, A Study of Moral and Intellectual Relations between France and the United States at the End of the Eighteenth Century* [New York, 1927]); Werner Stark, *America: Ideal and Reality; the United States of 1776 in Contemporary European Philosophy* (London,

1947); Antonello Gerbi, *La Disputa del Nuovo Mondo, Storia di una Polemica, 1750-1900* (Milan and Naples, 1955); Durand Echeverria, *Mirage in the West: A History of the French Image of American Society to 1815* (Princeton, 1957).

131. Lawrence C. Wroth, in John Carter Brown Lib., *Annual Report for 1953-1954* (Providence, 1954), 16-24.

PART I

Chapter 1

From Newport, across Connecticut, to West Point

1. Rochambeau's army was brought to America on a fleet commanded by the Chevalier de Ternay, which left Brest May 2, 1780, and arrived off Rhode Island on July 11. Chastellux came, with Rochambeau, on the flagship *Duc de Bourgogne*. He was one of three *maréchaux de camp* (major generals) ranking directly beneath the Comte de Rochambeau (lieutenant general), the others being Baron (Antoine-Charles du Houx) de Vioménil and the latter's younger brother, Comte (Charles-Joseph Hyacinthe du Houx) de Vioménil. Since Baron de Vioménil outranked him in seniority of service, Chastellux may therefore be considered to have held the third place in the hierarchy of Rochambeau's army. Given his rank (as well as his knowledge of English) it is safe to assume that he was among the first officers to come ashore at Newport. During his sojourn of nearly a year in Newport—or at least for the greater part of it—Chastellux was quartered in the house of Captain John Mawdsley (who had left Newport with the Tories when the English evacuated the city in 1779) on Spring St. The Mawdsley House, at 228 Spring St. (corner of John St.), now owned by the Society for the Preservation of New England Antiquities, is one of the notable examples of colonial architecture extant in Newport; see Maud L. Stevens, "Mawdsley House," Newport Historical Society, *Bulletin*, 97 (July 1936), 14-22; "The Maudsley-Gardner-Watson-Pitman House, Newport, R. I.," *Old-time New England*, 28 (1938), 79-84. The authority for locating the quarters occupied by Chastellux and his brother officers is a document entitled *Etat des logemens occupés dans la ville de Newport par l'armée aux ordres de M. le Cte. de Rochambeau pendant le quartier d'hiver de 1780 à 1781.* A contemporary manuscript copy of this billeting list, once belonging to Dr. Solomon Drowne (1753-1834) of Providence (who was in close touch with the French army during its sojourn in Rhode Island), is now among the manuscripts in the Henry Russell Drowne Collection, owned by the Sons of the Revolution in the State of New York, Fraunces Tavern, New York City. The list has been printed in Edwin M. Stone, *Our French Allies ... in the Great War of the American Revolution, from 1778 to 1782 ...* (Providence, 1884), 221-24, and elsewhere (with varying degrees of accuracy). It should be noted that the numbers used in this *Etat* are not street numbers, but numerals used upon this occasion by the French army to designate the billets.

2. This was not merely a false alarm; the English did in fact have plans, which miscarried, for dislodging the French from Rhode Island before they

had an opportunity to establish their defenses there. For a discussion of this point see William B. Willcox, "Rhode Island in British Strategy, 1780-1781," *Journal of Modern History*, 17 (1945), 304-31, with two British maps from the Sir Henry Clinton Papers, William L. Clements Lib., Ann Arbor, Mich.

3. Considerable information concerning the daily activities which commanded Chastellux's attention during this period will be found in the diaries and memoirs of other French officers, for example, Evelyn M. Acomb, ed., *The Revolutionary Journal of Baron Ludwig von Closen, 1780-1783* (Chapel Hill, 1958), 28-44. Several French maps of Newport and vicinity are extant. Among those in American collections are one signed by Von Closen, in the John Carter Brown Lib.; one in the Library of Congress; and another by Colbert de Maulevrier in the William L. Clements Lib., "*Plan de la Ville, Rade, et Environs de Newport, avec le Campement de l'Armée Françoise près de cette place en 1780, la disposition des ouvrages qu'elle a Executé et le mouillage de l'Escadre*," reproduced in the souvenir program of the *Washington-Rochambeau Celebration, 1780-1955*, 20-21, and in Christian Brun, *Guide to the Manuscript Maps in the William L. Clements Library* (Ann Arbor, 1959), no. 281, facing p. 68.

4. The Chevalier de Ternay, commander of the fleet that had brought the French army to America, died at Newport, Dec. 15, 1780, and was buried in Trinity churchyard there; he was succeeded, as the ranking naval officer with the expeditionary forces, by Destouches, who was in turn succeeded, in May 1781, by Barras.

5. The conference at Hartford marked the first meeting of Rochambeau with his commander in chief, George Washington. Plans for a combined Franco-American operation against British-held New York City were discussed. It should be borne in mind that New York was generally considered the probable objective of the allied armies during the whole period covered by Chastellux's first journal; it was not until the Wethersfield Conference the following May 1781—which Chastellux attended—that the alternative of an operation against Virginia, depending upon the arrival and whereabouts of French naval reinforcements, was seriously discussed. The British occupation of New York also explains Chastellux's circuitous itinerary southward to Philadelphia in 1780; indeed, he was unable to visit New York City during his entire sojourn in the United States.

6. A French squadron under Guichen had been cruising in the West Indies since the early spring of 1780. During the summer Guichen received letters from La Luzerne, the French Minister at Philadelphia, and from Lafayette, urging him to come northward to the United States, but he considered this request contrary to his instructions, and, leaving Santo Domingo on Aug. 16, he proceeded with a convoy of merchant ships to Cadiz, Spain, which he reached on Oct. 24. Edouard Chevalier, *Histoire de la Marine française pendant la Guerre de l'Indépendance Américaine* (Paris, 1877), 194. Louis Gottschalk, *Lafayette and the Close of the American Revolution* (Chicago, 1942), 106, 124, 129, 130-31, 141.

7. Among the new works thrown up by the French was a battery on Hallidon Hill, the height commanding at short range the batteries at Brenton's Point and Goat Island; it was called "Fort Chastellux," but presumably at some subsequent date, for it is not so designated on the contemporary maps just cited. Still later it was known as Fort Harrison and

Fort Denham, while the older name was in turn transferred to present "Chastellux Avenue," a Newport street running back up the hill from the waterfront where the French army disembarked (now King Park). George W. Cullum, *Historical Sketch of the Fortification Defenses of Narraganset Bay* ... (Washington, 1884), 16 and Plate I, Fig. 3; Edward Field, *Revolutionary Defences in Rhode Island* ... (Providence, 1896), 142. A document issued under Chastellux's signature, entitled "Instruction pour le service de l'armée pendant le quartier d'hyver," is preserved in the Miscellaneous Autographs, MSS. Division, Harvard Univ. Lib. The system of guards and patrols, precautions against fire, sanitary arrangements, and other routine matters relating to the French army's winter quarters at Newport are discussed.

8. *Ch.* Both of these gentlemen were made *colonels en second* on their return to Europe: Lynch, of the Walsh Regiment, and Montesquieu of the Bourbonnais Regiment.

Ed. These were Chastellux's aides-de-camp. Isidore Lynch (1755-1838), born in London of an Irish family, was educated at the Collège Louis-le-Grand in Paris, began his military career in the French service as a second lieutenant in the Clare Regiment of which his uncle was colonel. Following his return from America he rose to the rank of lieutenant general (1792) and commanded a division under the orders of Kellermann at the Battle of Valmy. Lynch was imprisoned in 1793, but later resumed his military career, serving as *inspecteur des revues* during the Empire and retiring in 1815. See Ségur, *Mémoires*, I, 508-12; Georges Six, *Dictionnaire Biographique des Généraux et Amiraux Français de la Révolution et de l'Empire*, 2 vols. (Paris, 1934), II, 136.

Charles-Louis de Secondat, Baron de Montesquieu et de La Brède (1749-1824), a grandson of the famous political philosopher, returned to France soon after the victory at Yorktown, but came back to America in Sept. 1782 and was again Chastellux's aide during his New England tour of that year (below, Pt. III). During the French Revolution Montesquieu emigrated to England and as an *émigré* participated in the unsuccessful Quiberon raid of 1795. Although named lieutenant general under the Bourbon Restoration, he spent most of his later life in England, where he had an estate called Bridge Hill near Canterbury. An attractive portrait of Montesquieu (privately owned) is reproduced in Contenson, *Société des Cincinnati*, fig. 127. Concerning Montesquieu's letters from America see the Editor's "Bibliographical Note." Recalling the 1780 journey with Chastellux and Lynch, Montesquieu wrote from Newport, April 3, 1781: "I am still as happy as anyone can be. I traveled five or six hundred leagues this winter, I went through seven of the thirteen United States, I've seen Philadelphia, etc.; in a word, I have *peregrinated* as Montaigne says, with a pleasure which you alone can imagine. My General, the most amiable of men, made the journey I speak of with his two aides-de-camp. The three of us, who were mutually congenial, traveled together on horseback, talking, looking, stopping—in a word, traveling in the full sense of the term. Judge of the pleasure I experienced! We wrote down every evening what we had seen during the day, we supped, and we slept until next morning, but not without having first had a long conversation with the innkeeper. I couldn't understand much of the conversation, but it nevertheless gave me more ease in expressing myself in bad English." Raymond Céleste, "Charles-Louis de Montesquieu à l'Armée (1772 à 1782)," *Revue Philomathique de Bordeaux et du Sud-Ouest*, 6 (1903), 518-19.

9. *Ch.* "Ferries" are places where one crosses over rivers or arms of the sea on boats propelled by oars or sails.

Ed. Chastellux uses the English word throughout his journals. The Bristol Ferry has been replaced in the twentieth century by the Mount Hope Bridge.

10. The Butt's Hill fortifications were erected on the northern end of the island by the British in 1777. They were occupied by the Americans in 1778 and served as a base of operations for the troops under General John Sullivan in the unsuccessful attempt to dislodge the British from Newport known as the Battle of Rhode Island. Butt's Hill was still a key position, manned in part by the French, when Chastellux visited it. Remains of the earthworks may be seen there today (Sprague St., in Portsmouth, between routes 114 and 138), and commemorative markers recall their former significance. The Rhode Island campaign of 1778 included an unsuccessful attempt at joint action between the Americans and French naval forces under D'Estaing—the first such attempt subsequent to the Alliance of 1778. D'Estaing's visit to New England at this time (as well as his failure at Savannah in 1779) had left serious doubts in some American minds about the efficacy of French aid and the possibility of effective Franco-American cooperation. Rochambeau's army had therefore, in 1780, to live down this unfortunate heritage—a fact which must have been often in Chastellux's mind and made him particularly eager, as a responsible French officer, to cultivate American good will and to appreciate intelligently their problems.

11. Warren is, and was, when Chastellux stopped there, in the state of Rhode Island, although it had been a part of the adjoining Massachusetts town of Swansea prior to 1747.

12. Shubael Burr's tavern, no longer standing, was at the southwest corner of present Main and Washington (formerly King) Sts. in the center of Warren; Washington St. leads straight down to the waterfront. Washington stopped here Mar. 13, 1781, on his way to visit the French army at Newport. The building was torn down shortly before 1900. Virginia Baker, *The History of Warren, Rhode Island, in the War of The Revolution, 1776-1783* (Warren, 1901), 31-32, and frontispiece (photograph of Burr's Tavern before demolition); Henry J. Peck, *200th Anniversary of Warren, Rhode Island, Historical Sketch* (Warren, 1947), 22, 69-71.

13. "Mr. Porter" was perhaps Simeon Potter (1720-1806), a well-known Bristol County shipowner, who had attained the rank of major general in the colonial militia; see Joseph J. Smith, comp., *Civil and Military List of Rhode Island, 1647-1800* ... (Providence, 1900), I, index; W. H. Munro, *The History of Bristol, R. I.; The Story of the Mount Hope Lands* ... (Providence, 1880), chap. 24. Colonel Christopher Greene (1737-81) of Warwick, R. I., whom Chastellux had known at Newport, was to meet his death several months later on the Croton River outside of New York; Stone, *French Allies*, 382-85.

14. *Ch.* (note added to 2d ed., 1788). This college is a magnificent building which the state of Rhode Island has had built in a very fine situation on one of the heights which surround the city of Providence. It can accom-

modate more than 200 scholars, but it was barely finished when the war began, and had not yet been inhabited at the time of our debarkation at Newport. Our crossing having been very long (it lasted 70 days, and the troops had previously remained three weeks on board the ships while waiting for a favorable wind in the harbor at Brest) we recognized upon our arrival that out of the nearly 11,000 men comprising the land troops and the ships' crews, we had more than 1200 cases of scurvy. 400 of these were placed in the college at Providence; an equal number were distributed among several churches in Newport, without there being any evidence of dissatisfaction from the inhabitants, regardless of the sect; the rest were sent into barracks that the American troops, who had for three years been obliged to keep watch of the English on Rhode Island, had had built on a neck of land called Popishsquash [Poppasquash Neck, at Bristol]. It will perhaps be useful, for the good of mankind, to note here that it was in this last-named hospital that the sick were cured in the greatest number and the least time. As it was situated on a peninsula which could easily be closed off from the mainland by a mere guard, no disorder was to be feared from the soldiers and sailors and they were permitted to walk about freely. They could thus amble along the hedges and bushes and eat the wild fruit that they were able to find there at this season. Unfortunately vegetables were very scarce on Rhode Island, as the English had destroyed all the gardens. No pains were spared however to gather them, and care was taken to have a special kettle for the scorbutics, in which less meat and more vegetables were put. This precaution which was taken without delay had the best effects. But it will not be inappropriate to add that special orders were required to put this measure in practice, since the then existing rules for the hospital service permitted the administration to make no other expenditure than one pound of meat per patient and at the same time required the use of this entire quantity. The new rules that have been devised under the present Ministry [i.e., *ca.* 1788] allow the doctor freedom to prescribe the type of broth that he judges most appropriate; but it was nearly the end of the eighteenth century before this change was thought of, and how many victims had by then been sacrificed to the exact observation of these rules, which had nevertheless all been devised for the greater good of mankind!

Ed. The college was Rhode Island College, subsequently Brown University. The "college edifice," now known as University Hall, had been built in 1770; the hospital for the French army established there was maintained until the spring of 1782. Concerning the wartime use of the college by both Americans and French, see Walter C. Bronson, *The History of Brown University, 1764-1914* (Providence, 1914), 70-75; Howard W. Preston, "Rochambeau and the French Troops in Providence in 1780-81-82," Rhode Island Historical Society, *Collections,* 17 (1924), 1-23; Allan Forbes and Paul F. Cadman, *France and New England . . . ,* 3 vols. (Boston, 1925-29), II, 135-51; Maurice Bouvet, *Le Service de Santé français pendant la Guerre d'Indépendance des Etats-Unis (1777-1782)* (Paris, 1933, reprinted 1934), 52 ff.; Blanchard, *Journal, passim.*

15. Claude Blanchard (1742-1802) was the chief commissary of Rochambeau's army, and his responsibilities included the establishment of hospitals. Blanchard's journal of his three years' sojourn in America, like those of several of the other French officers, provides an interesting supplement and parallel to Chastellux's account. Under date of Nov. 12, 1780, Blanchard

notes: "The Chevalier de Chastellux arrived in the morning; he was on his way to General Washington's camp and thence to Philadelphia. I gave him dinner and we paid some calls together. In conversing with him respecting the intendant [M. de Tarlé, "*commissaire ordonnateur, faisant fonctions d'intendant*"], whom he did not like and of whom he spoke unfavorably, I remarked how disagreeable it was to our cloth and especially to me to have so mediocre an administrator for chief. He replied that when one is more than thirty, it is better to be the second of a fool than of a man of sense. He departed the next day. The ground was covered with snow." Blanchard, *Journal*, 75-76.

16. Col. Ephraim Bowen (1753-1841) was deputy quartermaster general of the American army in Rhode Island, and as such was in close touch with the French officers concerning problems of provisioning, quartering, etc.; see Stone, *French Allies*, 150-53. Col. Bowen was married to Sally Angell, so that the "Miss Angel" whom Chastellux saw was presumably one of Mrs. Bowen's relatives, perhaps the Miss Nabby or the Miss Polly Angell who received invitations to the "very splendid ball" given by Rochambeau two years later when the French army returned to Providence; Preston, "Rochambeau and the French Troops in Providence," R.I. Hist. Soc., *Collections*, 17 (1924), 20.

17. Mrs Varnum was presumably the wife of Brigadier General James Mitchell Varnum. Deputy Governor Jabez Bowen (1739-1815) was at this time living in a house on North Main St. facing Market Square (subsequently demolished); Stone, *French Allies*, 246-49. When Chastellux returned to Providence with the army in June 1781 he was quartered in the Joseph Russell house (still standing, with modifications, on west side of North Main St.), while Rochambeau, as the ranking officer, was the guest of Deputy Governor Bowen; Preston, "Rochambeau and the French Troops in Providence," R. I. Hist. Soc., *Collections*, 17 (1924), 12-13. Preston's article has photographs of the Bowen and Russell houses.

18. Col. Peck was presumably George Peck (born 1749, Cumberland, R. I.) a lieutenant colonel in the R. I. Militia and commandant of the 2nd Regiment, Providence Co., who later served at Yorktown; Smith, comp., *Civil and Military List of R. I.*, I, 394, 401, 413, 420; Stone, *French Allies*, 508n. General William Heath had been in command of the American forces at Newport when Rochambeau's army arrived. Chastellux had thus come to know him well, and records his favorable impression later on in this journal (see below, Nov. 21, 1780). Heath's dealings with the French can be traced in his own letters to Washington and others, printed in *Heath Papers* (Mass. Hist. Soc., *Collections*, 7th Ser., 5 [1905]), III, hereafter cited as *Heath Papers;* see also his *Memoirs* ... (Boston, 1798).

19. *Gr.* Here are several places of public worship, an university, and other public buildings; and a very brisk trade was carried on even at the worst period of the war for American commerce, viz. in 1782. Mr. Welcome Arnold, a great plumber, and Delegate to Congress from this state, has changed his name by Act of Assembly, since the defection of Benedict Arnold.

20. Chastellux refers to the locality known today as Sterling Hill, Windham Co., Conn., and not to the present village of Voluntown in the town of that name, New London Co., which is some nine miles to the south. At

the time he was writing the town of Voluntown included territory which was later, in 1794, incorporated separately as the town of Sterling.

21. The tavern kept at this time by Jeremiah Angell (1707-86), built by his father Thomas Angell *ca.* 1710, was close to the geographical center of the town of Scituate, on the banks of the Ponagansett River, at a locality later known as Richmond Mills. The building survived until *ca.* 1840; the site was inundated when the Scituate Reservoir was built in the 1920's. Charles C. Beauman, *An Historical Sketch of the Town of Scituate, R. I.* (Phenix, 1877), 32 ff.; *Map of the State of Rhode Island* (N. Y., 1862), from surveys by Henry F. Walling; U. S. Geological Survey, North Scituate and Clayville, R. I., quadrangles, 1955. When the French army moved westward to the Hudson in June 1781 it took a slightly different route from the one followed by Chastellux on his present excursion, making its first encampment at Waterman's Tavern (still standing, near Pottersville, town of Coventry, R. I.). The road from Providence via Angell's Tavern (the Plainfield Pike, State Route 14, but partly relocated because of the reservoir) and the one more to the south via Waterman's Tavern (Scituate Ave.–Matteson Road) join before reaching "Voluntown" (Sterling Hill) and Plainfield, Conn. Chastellux's unfavorable impression of Angell's Tavern, recorded here, perhaps contributed to the decision to march the army via the other route the following June. The staff *projet* or instructions for the march mention: "The camp site is in a rather pretty position.... a brook in front, and behind it the Tavern [Waterman's] and the highway from Providence to Voluntown, which is better than the road which goes by Angell's Tavern. Lodgings for the Divisional headquarters are not very plentiful but there are more than at Angell's Tavern or at the Whipple house." Berthier Papers, No. 8, Princeton Univ. Lib.

22. In the privately printed edition of his *Voyage* (Newport, 1781, p. 4), Chastellux gave the name "Dorrance" in full; but in the Paris 1786 edition he substituted "D***." The English translator, in the London 1787 edition, restored the full name; but the American editor of the New York 1827 edition reverted to "D———." As Chastellux's own lengthy footnote hereinafter indicates, this was one of the controversial passages of the *Travels.*

Dorrance's Tavern still stands in the village of Sterling Hill, Conn. It is on the northern side of State Road 49, just before reaching the crossroads church when approaching from Oneco. The French army, when marching to Plainfield in June 1781, passed through "Voluntown" along the same route taken by Chastellux; in Nov. 1782 the army encamped here, in the fields adjoining Dorrance's Tavern, on its northward march to Boston. A roadmap of the 1781 march and a map of the 1782 encampment are in the Berthier Papers, Princeton Univ. Lib. Berthier's roadmap of the 1781 march indicates "dalens taverne" at "Walen Town." See also Marian D. Terry, ed., *Old Inns of Connecticut* (Hartford, 1937), 236-37, with photograph. The proprietor of the inn was Samuel Dorrance (*ca.* 1708-88), who came to America as a boy from Ulster in northern Ireland; he was a carpenter by trade and lived in Scituate, R. I., until 1771, when he moved to Sterling Hill, Conn. (then a part of Voluntown). From his marriage to Margaret Trumbull in 1748 there were four sons and two daughters. Concerning the eldest son, John, see n. 24, below; one of the daughters, Susanna (b. 1760)—presumably the unfortunate girl whom Chastellux describes—married (1st) William Green of Warwick, R. I., on Jan. 14, 1782, at Voluntown, and (2nd) Benjamin Brewster on Sept.

8, 1786, at Windham, Conn. See Mrs. I. H. Wynne and J. D. Morrell, comps., A Genealogy of the Descendants of George and Margery Dorrance... (1948), typescript in Conn. State Lib., Hartford; Emma Finney Welch, *Dorrance Inscriptions, Old Sterling Township Burying Ground, Oneco, Connecticut* (1909), pamphlet in Conn. State Lib., 5 (inscriptions 9, 10).

23. *Ch.* When a small number of copies of this journal [the Newport, 1781, printing] were received in Europe—seven or eight at most and the only ones sent by the author—the curiosity then excited by everything relative to the affairs of America procured them many readers. Although the author had sent these only to his most intimate friends and had taken the precaution of informing them that it was his intention they should not be given any publicity, they were passed around rapidly from hand to hand; and as people had them only for a short time, they were read with as much haste as avidity. This eagerness could only proceed from a desire to form some idea of the manners of the Americans, concerning which this journal gave several details to which distance and novelty lent some interest. Nevertheless, from an inconsistency, less uncommon in France than in any other country, some people did not hesitate to judge the author on points of propriety, of which he alone was capable of giving *them* an idea: he was taxed with irresponsibility (*légéreté*) and indiscretion for having concealed neither names nor places in relating the adventure of a maiden deceived by her lover. A very simple reflection, and one costing little mental effort, might have convinced them that it was hardly likely that a general officer—a man of forty-five years of age, who was on particularly friendly terms with the Americans, and who has everywhere expressed sentiments of gratitude and attachment to all those from whom he experienced kindness—would allow himself to offend or even to distress honest people who had shown him every attention and for whom he has only words of praise. Furthermore, the simple and even serious manner in which this article is written affords not the least appearance of irresponsibility, and this alone should have been sufficient to forestall the irresponsible criticisms of certain readers. Another reflection might have occurred naturally enough, although it required a bit more thought: The author has attempted, it might have been said, to give us an idea of American manners, which he is certainly very far from satirizing: might it not be possible that among these people so remote from us in every respect, a girl who has given herself too soon to the man she is engaged to, a girl quite without suspicion (as her parents themselves admit), in a country where one is not taught to be suspicious, where morality is so much in its infancy that intercourse between two free persons is deemed less censurable than the infidelities, caprices, and even the coquetries which disturb the peace of so many European families—might it not be possible that such a young woman, as interesting as she is unhappy, should be pitied rather than blamed, that she should still retain all her rights in society and become a legitimate spouse and mother, though her adventure be neither unknown nor even dissimulated? Indeed, how could the author have learned this story? Was it through scandalous gossip in a hamlet where he was a stranger to all but his hosts? "I have since learned" (he has said in speaking of this girl) "that she was with child and near her confinement." How did he learn this? From her own parents, who had made neither mystery nor secret of it. But had these stern judges, when they reached the end of the book, happened to remember what they had read at the beginning, they might have noted that

the author being at Voluntown a second time, two months later [see below, Pt. I, chap. 6, Jan. 7, 1781, and nn. 17, 19], saw Miss D*** suckling an infant, which was continually passing from her lap to her mother's; that she was then cherished and cared for by her whole family. This affecting sight was described with sensibility, and not with malignity. But it is now time to set at rest, not the critics, but men of feeling, whose approbation alone is precious. On still another journey to Voluntown [see below, Pt. III, chap. 3, Nov. 30, 1782, and n. 2], the author had the satisfaction of seeing Miss D*** perfectly happy: her lover had returned, and had married her; he had expiated all his wrongs, nor had they been such as they at first appeared; he had unfortunate circumstances to plead as his excuse, if indeed there can be any excuse for a man who for a single day leaves in such distress the interesting and helpless victim who was unable to resist him.

Gr. The Translator, who has been at Voluntown, and enjoyed the society and witnessed the happiness of this amiable family, is likewise acquainted with the whole of this story. He is so well satisfied with the justness of the liberal minded author's reasoning on American manners in this particular, that he has not scrupled to give the name of this worthy family at length, not apprehending that their characters would suffer the smallest injury, where alone the imputation is of any consequence; nor does he fear opposing the virtue of this family, and of these manners, to European chastity, prudery, and refinement. The circumstances of this story were related to the Translator by Mr. and Mrs. Dorrance, with the same sensibility, and the same innocence, with which they appear to have told them to the Marquis de Chastellux. They are a kind, hospitable, and amiable couple, and the husband is far from being ill informed; he entertained the Translator with many anecdotes of the war, and with some laughable ones respecting General [Richard] Prescott of the British Army, who was brought to his house, after being carried off without his breeches from Rhode Island [July 9, 1777]; but never without expressing a becoming degree of sensibility for his situation, which was peculiarly mortifying, from his gout, his naturally peevish disposition, the humiliating mode of his capture, and the circumstance of its being the second time of his falling into the hands of an enemy, whom he was weak enough to despise and to insult.

Ch. (note added to 2d ed., 1788). Although my note in the first edition is already very lengthy, I cannot refuse myself the satisfaction of inserting here the note which the English Translator, Mr. G***, has kindly added to it. I take this opportunity of rendering him all the justice due him with the more pleasure as his modesty cannot be offended by my praise when it is my own interest that incites me to publish it. It is indeed a full justification of the author of the *Travels* to say that Mr. G***, who in this instance bestows his complete approval on the author, is no less distinguished for the loftiness of his sentiments, his love of mankind, and his zeal for all that is good and honest, than he is for his wide knowledge in literature and the facility and elegance of his style. Here is what he says ... [Chastellux's French translation of Grieve's note, in which, however, he still refrained from spelling out the name of Dorrance].

24. *Gr.* The Translator had a great deal of conversation with this young man, and found him such as the Marquis represents him; but he must likewise add, that he met with a great number of excellent classical scholars, in different parts of the continent, educated at Williamsburgh, Philadelphia,

Yale College, New-Haven, Cambridge, and Providence, and very few deficient, especially to the northward. The war did infinite mischief to the rising generation of America, by interrupting education.

Ed. John Dorrance (1749-1813), who graduated from the College of Rhode Island in 1774, served as tutor there in 1774-75, and as college librarian, 1773-75. He later became a lawyer and judge in Providence and served as a trustee of the college from 1798 until his death. Brown University, *The Historical Catalogue . . . 1764-1934* (Providence, 1936).

25. *Gr.* The Translator, when he travelled in America during the war, always carried wine with him when practicable, for at Baltimore and Philadelphia, those great sea ports, very indifferent wine, *called* claret, was sold at *two dollars,* upwards of 9 shillings a bottle, hard money. Nor was it an uncommon thing to transport wine from Boston to Philadelphia by land, when the arrivals were more fortunate in that quarter.

26. *Gr.* The Translator confirms this assertion, except with regard to the pacific religious sects, in the whole extent of his observations from Virginia to New Hampshire.

27. *Gr.* There is an academy or college here [Plainfield Academy], with four Latin and English masters, and when the Translator was there, he was present at some, not contemptible, public exhibitions of oratory in those two languages.

28. *Ch.* In summer these marshes are dry, as I have since learned—a fact worth noting in order not to give a false idea of this position.

Ed. In the 1781 edition (p. 8) Chastellux had used the word *étangs* (ponds) to describe the marshes; in the 1786 edition he changed this to *flaques d'eau* (literally, puddles or shallow pools) and added the explanatory footnote. As a military man Chastellux, throughout his journey, kept a professional eye peeled for good "positions." The following summer, when the French army marched from Newport to join the American forces on the Hudson, it made its third encampment at Plainfield (June 19-22, 1781)—not on the heights, however, but in the valley to the west of the village.

29. *Gr.* The Translator reached Canterbury on a *Sunday,* a day on which travelling is forbid in the New England states. The family at Buckhouse's [Backus's] Tavern were all at meeting, and it cost him innumerable entreaties, besides the most unequivocal proofs of *Whiggism,* to procure a morsel of the most wretched fare, and to obtain which he was obliged to wait till the meeting was at an end. Both this town and Windham are most beautifully situated, particularly the latter, which is extremely picturesque.

30. Rochambeau's army of four regiments (Bourbonnais, Soissonnais, Saintonge, and Deux-Ponts) also included a separate élite "legion," of foreign volunteers, under the command of the Duc de Lauzun (Armand-Louis Gontaut, later Duc de Biron, 1747-93). His "rough riders" were stationed during the winter of 1780-81 at Lebanon to serve as an advanced post for the main army at Newport, and because forage for the horses was more readily obtainable there. It has also been said that Rochambeau considered Lebanon—which De Lauzun himself compared to Siberia—an appropriate place for the impetuous and, at times, insubordinate duke, De Lauzun's *Mémoires* (Paris, 1822) do not mention the transitory quarters at Windham nor do they speak of Chastellux's subsequent visit to Lebanon (see below, Pt. I, chap. 6, Jan. 5-6, 1781). The Duc de Lauzun does, however, in another

connection, speak of Chastellux's "fickle head which can't concentrate for long on the same ideas." For the story of his life, see R. de Gontaut Biron, *Le Duc de Lauzun* (Paris, 1937).

31. *Gr.* This tavern is called Lebanon Crank, and the Translator has made similar remarks in his journal on the external appearance of, and the kindness that reigns within this little hut; where, a very uncommon circumstance at that time, he found excellent green tea, and fine loaf sugar. He also saw Mrs. Hill feed, and relieve a travelling soldier.

Ed. Lebanon Crank Tavern was in the part of Lebanon known as Lebanon North Parish or Lebanon Crank; "The Crank" was in 1804 incorporated as the town of Columbia. The house which served as Hill's tavern—with subsequent additions—is still standing, privately owned, at the intersection of the two main roads (U.S. 6A and State 87) in the village of Columbia, Tolland Co. Terry, *Old Inns of Conn.*, 233-35, with photographs.

32. East Hartford, on the eastern bank of the Connecticut across the river from Hartford proper ("Hartford Courthouse," as Chastellux calls it), at this time still formed part of the town of Hartford; it was incorporated as a separate town only in 1783; still later, in 1823, the eastern part of East Hartford was in turn separately incorporated as the town of Manchester. Thus, Chastellux's stopping place was probably within the present boundaries of the town of Manchester. "Mr. Mash" was perhaps Daniel Marsh (1732-1818), whose name, along with that of James Marsh, is among those "nominated" by the civil authority of the town of Hartford "to keep houses of public entertainment in said town" for the year 1780 (also for 1781, 1782); "Travel: Highways and Taverns," Conn. State Archives, Hartford County Court Files. Daniel Marsh's third wife was the widow of Caleb Pitkin; his Pitkin stepsons settled in Marshfield, Washington Co., Vermont. Dwight Whitney Marsh, ed., *Marsh Genealogy. . . . giving several thousand descendants of John Marsh of Hartford, Conn., 1636-1895* (Amherst, Mass., 1895), 96. When Chastellux wrote, Connecticut was sending a considerable number of settlers (including Marshes innumerable) to the region that became the state of Vermont, settlement of which had begun in the 1760's at the close of the Seven Years' War. In its "Declaration of Independence" of Jan. 1777 the state was called "New Connecticut," but the name Vermont was adopted the following June. The name of a Daniel Marsh appears among the grantees of the town of Caldesburgh (subsequently the town of Morgan, Orleans Co.) in a charter issued under the authority of the state of Vermont, Nov. 6, 1780. The presence of other recognizable Connecticut and Hartford names on the list of grantees (Wadsworth, Huntington, Pitkin, Cheney, *et al.*) makes it appear likely that this is "our" Daniel Marsh and that the Vermont lands he mentioned to Chastellux were in the wilderness near the Canadian border not far from Lake Memphremagog. Settlement of the town did not actually take place, however, until *ca.* 1800, by which time the rights of most of the original grantees had passed to others; Rev. Jacob S. Clark, "Morgan," in Abby M. Hemenway, ed., *Vermont Historical Gazetteer*, 3 (1877), 282-93.

33. *Gr.* —or something more than eight pounds English.

34. Vermont is situated *west* of New Hampshire and *north* of Massachusetts.

35. *Ed.* This entire sentence was rewritten by Chastellux for the 1786 edition of his work. In the Newport, 1781, edition (p. 10) he had said: "I have

since been assured, at Albany, that this Allen was a very ordinary and very ignorant man, and that he was beginning to lose the credit he had gained in this new country which calls itself the *State of Vermont;* but which, from all appearances, will sooner or later be joined to the state of New York or to the state of Massachusetts." Chastellux's Yorker informant, who had first-hand knowledge of Ethan Allen and his maneuverings—but who proved a poor prophet in respect to the future status of Vermont—was probably General Philip Schuyler, whom he visited at Albany later on during his journey (see below, Pt. I, chap. 5). Indeed, at this very time, Ethan Allen was in secret contact with British agents from Canada—a fact which caused no little concern to Schuyler and others. This flirtation (subsequently referred to as "the Haldimand correspondence") was used by Allen and his coadjutors as a veiled threat to obtain Congressional recognition of Vermont's territorial claims and independent status. See Charles Miner Thompson, *Independent Vermont* (Boston, 1942).

Gr. In the years 1780, 1781, and 1782, the inhabitants of Vermont who were *not* guided by Ethan Allen, annually sent deputies [i.e., "agents"] to Congress, and were once within *one vote* of carrying their point, but had not the peace taken place, it is probable from circumstances, that in case of refusal, they would *at least* have threatened to put themselves under British protection, an event to which the Marquis seems to allude.

36. *Gr.* At the Moravian settlement of Bethlehem is a ferry passed by ropes, like that opposite the invalid hospital [L'Hôtel des Invalides] at Paris, and many others in France, and other parts of Europe.

Ed. See below, Pt. III, chap. 4, n. 47.

37. The "Proceedings of the Hartford Convention of November 1780" will be found in Boyd *et al.*, eds., *Jefferson Papers*, IV, 138-41; they were sent with an accompanying letter, Nov. 22, 1780, by William Bradford, Commissioner from Rhode Island and President of the Convention, to Thomas Jefferson who was then Governor of Virginia. The gathering was known officially as "a Convention of the Commissioners from the States of New Hampshire, Massachusetts, Rhode Island and Providence Plantations, Connecticut, and New York, holden at Hartford in the State of Connecticut." Among the resolutions adopted—which concerned chiefly the states' contributions of "men, money and other supplies" to the Continental Army—was a recommendation that the states represented "appoint a Commissioner or Commissioners to meet for the purpose of entering into Contracts for supplying the Fleet and Army of his most Christian Majesty with Provisions."

38. The house of Colonel Jeremiah Wadsworth (1743-1804) stood in the center of Hartford, on the eastern side of Main St., on the site now occupied by the Wadsworth Atheneum. A commemorative tablet at the entrance of the pseudo-mediaeval building designed by Ithiel Town (1842) recalls the house that Chastellux knew. Forbes and Cadman, *France and New England,* II, 109-11.

39. *Gr.* The Translator had the pleasure of meeting with this accomplished officer, at Baltimore, at Boston, and in Europe. Nature has been very favourable to his exterior, and he unites to the most perfect good manners, and a thorough knowledge of the world, and books, the most unexampled activity in his profession.

Ed. Mathieu Dumas (1753-1837) wrote up his recollections of the American war in his *Souvenirs du lieutenant-général Mathieu Dumas, de 1770 à*

1836 (Paris, 1839), translated as *Memoirs of His Own Time ...*, 2 vols. (Phila., 1839). These are retrospective memoirs, written in the 1820's and not a day-to-day diary or journal. Dumas, like several of the other younger French officers, apparently looked up to Chastellux as a sort of "philosophical" mentor. When inserting in his memoirs some general observations on the United States (pp. 64 ff.), he noted that he had "addressed them to the Chevalier de Chastellux, who, when he took leave to return to France, had asked me to correspond with him. I have transcribed an extract from this correspondence, which contains a faithful picture of the moral and political state of those countries."

40. *Gr.* The Translator cannot forbear adding his testimony to this brilliant but not exaggerated eulogium.

41. Dominique-Louis Ethis de Corny (1736-90) had preceded Rochambeau's army to America, arriving in the spring of 1780 aboard the *Hermione* in the company of Lafayette. As *Commissaire des guerres* he was entrusted with the responsibility of assembling supplies for the expected army. De Corny returned to France ("for reasons of health") in Feb. 1781; during his brief sojourn in America he acquired the rank of lieutenant colonel in the Continental Army. Opinions as to his competence seem to have varied: Claude Blanchard (above, n. 15) entertained a poor opinion of him, and Chastellux apparently shared this view; André Lasseray, *Les Français sous les Treize Étoiles (1775-1783)*, 2 vols. (Macon, 1935), I, 206-11, 603, 627. Not long after his return to France M. de Corny, a widower, married Marguerite Victoire de Palerne, widow of Bagneux de Foacio. The De Cornys became acquainted with Thomas Jefferson during the latter's sojourn in Paris as American minister, and the second Madame de Corny corresponded with Jefferson for many years afterwards. Gilbert Chinard, *Trois Amitiés françaises de Jefferson* (Paris, 1927); Boyd *et al.*, eds., *Jefferson Papers*, X-XVI, *passim*.

42. Chastellux's brief account of Jeremiah Wadsworth's services as purchasing agent for the French army is corroborated and amplified by Wadsworth's own letterbooks and correspondence for this period, now preserved at the Conn. Hist. Soc., Hartford. Wadsworth undertook the task of assembling supplies for Rochambeau's army only a month or so before its arrival in July 1780. In spite of his vigorous efforts, complications developed, especially with M. de Corny. Wadsworth soon withdrew, but after a few months was, during the autumn of 1780, again entrusted with the business in association with John Carter [Church] and continued as agent until the end of the war. Thus he was in charge of preparations for the march of the army from Rhode Island in the summer of 1781, and again when it returned northward in 1782. Many of the initial misunderstandings arose, as Wadsworth pointed out, from lack of adequate interpreters; he himself, for example, knew no French. Such problems in turn make it evident that the English-speaking French officers such as Chastellux must have played a considerable role in maintaining inter-allied harmony. Wadsworth, in a note written from Hartford, Mar. 19, 1781, prior to leaving for conferences in Newport, assured Chastellux that "my friendship for you wou'd alone be a sufficient inducement to come to New Port.... I shall be happy to embrace every opportunity that presents to shew you how much I value your friendship"; Wadsworth Papers, Box 151, Letterbook L, 102, Conn. Hist. Soc.; Wadsworth to Chastellux, May 3, 1781, *ibid.*, Box 153, Letterbook D, 12.

Further evidence of the cordial relations between the two men is to be found in two letters (in English) written by Chastellux to Wadsworth not long after his return to France in 1783; May 31 and July 10, 1783, *ibid.*, Box 135. Speaking of his efforts to expedite a settlement of Wadsworth's account with the French government and of a memorial on the subject that he had transmitted to the Count de Vergennes, the Minister of Foreign Affairs, Chastellux writes: "I wrote half a dozen pages where I mentioned the services of all kinds you did, both to the armies and to the fleet, and I went to Versailles the day before yesterday; I dined with the Count and gave him the memorial to which I added my warmest recommendation. . . . Depend upon it, that I'll make my best endeavour to see that business terminated to your satisfaction. I am sorry indeed to think that you are uneasy, but I rejoice to see the day where I can give you, my dear Colonel, some pledge of the everlasting friendship you inspired to my heart. Neither time nor distance can eradicate from them my American friends, but peculiarly my dear Wadsworth and his worthy friend Carter. I am happy indeed to live in my own countrie with my old friends, but I regrett, and shall always regrett the precious connections of friends beyond the seas." Further documents concerning supplies for Rochambeau's army will be found in Correspondance politique, États-Unis, Supplément, XVII, Archives du Ministère des Affaires Etrangères, Paris (photocopies in Lib. Cong.); see Waldo G. Leland, John J. Meng, and Abel Doysié, *Guide to the Materials for American History in the Libraries and Archives of Paris*, 2 vols. (Washington, 1932 and 1943), II, 850. On Wadsworth's partner, John Carter [Church], see below, Pt. I, chap. 2, Grieve's n. 48.

43. Chastellux met Governor Trumbull again at Lebanon, during his return journey, and upon that occasion added a few more strokes to his portrait of him; see below, Pt. I, chap. 6, Jan. 6, 1781.

44. As Chastellux indicates, Governor Trumbull's projected history was no more than an outline, and was in fact never completed. Trumbull for a long time had in his possession part of the manuscript of a *History of New England* written by John Winthrop, first governor of Massachusetts (published in part in 1790, and completely only in 1825). See the preface to the *Trumbull Papers* (Mass. Hist. Soc., *Collections*, 7th Ser., 3 [1902], IV, xiii-xvi, where a letter from La Luzerne to Trumbull concerning the latter's proposed history is printed. The passage in Winthrop's journal that Trumbull had noted, and which in turn attracted Chastellux's attention, is the following, dated Dec. 25, 1640: "Upon the great liberty which the king had left the parliament to in England, some of our friends there wrote to us advice to send over some to solicit for us in the parliament, giving us hope that we might obtain much, etc. But consulting about it, we declined the motion for this consideration, that if we should put ourselves under the protection of the parliament, we must then be subject to all such laws as they should make, or at least such as they might impose upon us; in which course though they should intend our good, yet it might prove very prejudicial to us"; John Winthrop, *The History of New England from 1630 to 1649*, ed. James Savage, new ed., 2 vols. (Boston, 1853), II, 29-30. In a letter (Lebanon, June 27, 1777) addressed to Baron van der Capellen, Trumbull had also used this same passage to buttress his argument that the colonies had never acknowledged Parliament's right to legislate for them. The letter did duty as pro-American propaganda by being published in both Dutch

and French: *Brieven van hunne Excellenties de Heeren Jonathan Trumbull, en William Livingston . . . aan Johann Derk Baron van der Capellen* (Amsterdam, etc., n.d.; Sabin Nos. 97252, 97254). The Dutch translation was made by Francis Adriaan van der Kemp, probably under the aegis of John Adams. The English text of Trumbull's letter was later printed in Mass. Hist. Soc., *Collections,* 6 (1799).

45. *Ch.* (note added to 2d ed., 1788). At least in winter: in summer it is customary to set forth at sunrise, and to stop at about eight o'clock in the morning to breakfast and to feed your horses. A second stop is made for dinner, and often a third to bait your horses again; but it is not unusual for a traveler who has taken these precautions to post twenty or even twenty-five *lieues* [leagues] with the same horse, and to do so several days in succession.

46. Chastellux softened his comments on General Parsons a bit in the 1786 edition of his *Voyages.* In the earlier Newport edition (1781, p. 14) he had written: "He appeared to me a sensible man, and he is so regarded in his country; *but he does not pass for a great officer:* he is also, what one must never be, in war or in anything else, unlucky. His début was on Long Island, where he was captured, and he has since been in all the bad affairs; *so that he passes for a shrewd and clever man rather than for a good general.*"

47. The Farmington meetinghouse (Congregational Church), built in 1771-72 by Judah Woodruff (*ca.* 1720-1799), still stands, relatively unchanged, and still deserves Chastellux's description: "*un beau Meeting.*" A complete description, with drawings and photographs, will be found in J. Frederick Kelly, *Early Connecticut Meetinghouses, Being an Account of the Church Edifices Built before 1830 Based Chiefly upon Town and Parish Records,* 2 vols. (N. Y., 1948), I, 157-69.

48. *Gr.*—or about two and twenty pence, English money.

49. The house of Phinehas Lewis (1722-1800) was at the northern end of Farmington village. It was subsequently known as the Elm Tree Inn and survives today, considerably modified, as the "Elm Tree Apartment," on Farmington Avenue. Julius Gay, *Farmington Papers* (Hartford, 1929), 87-88, 112; "Farmington Houses and Farmington Owners, 1662-1950," file in Village Library. Chastellux saw Mrs. Lewis (née Norton) again on another visit to Farmington two years later (see below, Pt. III, chap. 3, Dec. 2, 1782, and n. 7).

50. *Gr.* Here the author is a little inaccurate respecting the English language, as the same word *wall-nut,* is applied to the same tree in England, and with no reference whatever to any such use.
Ed. Grieve wins! The word "walnut" has nothing to do with "walls." According to Webster, it derives from the Anglo-Saxon *wealh-hnutu—wealh* meaning foreign or strange.

51. George-Louis Leclerc, Comte de Buffon (1707-88), was personally known to Chastellux, who cherished a lifelong admiration for the great naturalist; it was Buffon who had pronounced the speech welcoming Chastellux to membership in the French Academy (1775). Buffon's *Histoire naturelle, générale et particulière* (1749-88) provided Chastellux, as it did so many of his contemporaries, with a frame of reference for observing natural phenomena. In this instance Chastellux is thinking specifically of Buffon's theory of geological chronology, first outlined in the *Théorie de la Terre* (1749) and perfected in *Des Epoques de la Nature* (1778). Accord-

ing to Buffon, the earth in the first Epoch was a gradually cooling incandescent mass; in the second Epoch the earth cooled into a vitreous globe with surface irregularities of quartz and other glass-like substances; only in the third Epoch did condensing vapors form the waters that by their action on the vitreous materials produced clay, slate, and calcareous rocks. Then came the Epoch of volcanoes, the appearance of the first animals, the separation of the continents, and finally, the seventh or last Epoch, when Man appeared and began his modification of Nature.

In his remark that Buffon "not only expresses himself well, but is always right" (non seulement il parle bien, mais ... il a toujours raison), Chastellux is instinctively refuting the disparagements of certain of Buffon's contemporaries who claimed that the naturalist cultivated an eloquent style at the expense of scientific sobriety (popularization vs. "pure research"). Chastellux had earlier framed a somewhat similar compliment: "M. de Buffon," he had written in his De la Félicité Publique (Bouillon, 1776), II, 124, "has achieved the glory of having created in our day the science of natural history: this science has come from his hands in all its beauty, as Minerva sprang forth from Jupiter's head. He has succeeded both in making it known and making it loved. Never has eloquence been put to finer use: it is as if Demosthenes were writing down the observations of Aristotle." For a useful introduction to Buffon's voluminous writings and his place in the history of science, see the recently published volume: Jean Piveteau, ed., Oeuvres philosophiques de Buffon (Paris, 1954), which includes, pp. 513-75, a valuable "Bibliographie de Buffon," compiled by Mme E. Genet-Varcin and Jacques Roger.

52. Gr.—or about twenty-five pounds sterling.

53. Gr.—or four shillings and sixpence an acre.

54. The Litchfield meetinghouse that Chastellux saw was located in the very center of the village green (on the spot now indicated by the Beecher Monument); the present Congregational Church, a restored early 19th-century structure, is on the north side of the green, a short distance from the site of the two earlier meetinghouses, the second of which was erected in 1762. See the sketch-map of Litchfield drawn by Ezra Stiles in 1762, reproduced in Franklin B. Dexter, ed., Extracts from the Itineraries and other Miscellanies of Ezra Stiles ... 1775-1794 ... (New Haven, 1916), 185; and also Litchfield Historical Society, Some Historic Sites of Litchfield, Connecticut (Litchfield, 1933; reprinted 1954), with map.

55. Two Seymours are recorded among the residents of Litchfield at this time: Moses Seymour, Jr. (1742-1826) and his brother, Samuel Seymour (1754-1837), who were originally from Hartford; George C. Woodruff, A Genealogical Register of the Inhabitants of the Town of Litchfield, Conn. ....from 1720 ... to 1800 ... (Hartford, 1900), 193. The nominations for tavernkeepers presented by the civil authority of the town of Litchfield to the Litchfield County Court, Jan. 24, 1780, include the name of Thomas Phillips among those "recognized" by the court. His name does not appear on the similar lists for 1781 and subsequent years, from which it may be surmised that the persiflate Mr. Phillips resided but briefly in Litchfield and soon moved on to fresher fields; "Travel: Highways and Taverns," Litchfield County Court Files, Conn. State Archives. When Chastellux again passed through Litchfield two years later he stopped at Samuel Sheldon's tavern; see below, Pt. III, chap. 3, Dec. 3, 1782, and n. 9.

56. *Ch.* This is a name given derisively, or merely jestingly, to the inhabitants of the four eastern states. It is thought to come from a tribe of Indians whose lands were occupied by the first settlers and who lived between Connecticut and the state of Massachusetts. In the same way the name of "Buckskin" is given to the inhabitants of Virginia, because their ancestors were hunters and sold buck, or rather deer skins, for it will be seen in the journal of my second *Voyage* that there are no roebucks (*chevreuils*) in Virginia.

Gr. The English army serving in America, and England herself, will long have reason to remember the contemptuous use they made of this term in the late unhappy war, and the severe retort they met with on the occasion. The *English army*, at Bunker's Hill, marched to the insulting tune of "Yankee doodle," but from that period it became the air of triumph, the Io Paean of *America*. It was *cuckoo* to the British ear.

Ed. There appears to be no supporting evidence for the Indian origin of the term "Yankee." In spite of the many theories proposed, ever since Chastellux's time, the *Dictionary of American English on Historical Principles,* ed. Sir William Craigie *et al.,* 4 vols. (Chicago, 1936-44), IV, 2514 ff., concludes that the word is "of unknown origin."

57. For all his laudable efforts to clarify the New England use of such terms as "town," "county," etc. (see above, this chap., Nov. 15, 18, 1780), Chastellux was here entrapped. There was no Washington County in Connecticut, but only a *town* of Washington, so-named and incorporated by the General Assembly in Jan. 1779, from parts of the towns of Litchfield, Woodbury, Kent, and New Milford. To complicate matters further, it should be pointed out that the meetinghouse and cluster of houses that Chastellux passed by were those on New Preston Hill, a mile or so west of the present, and later, valley "village" of New Preston, in the northern part of the "town" of Washington, Litchfield Co. The somewhat dilapidated church now to be seen on New Preston Hill, surrounded by reclaimed "summer places," is an early 19th-century structure (1824) situated not far from the site of the earlier meetinghouse noted by Chastellux. New Preston Hill—Chastellux's "Washington"—is along the old "upper route" from Hartford to Fishkill via Litchfield. Florence S. M. Crofut, *Guide to the History and the Historic Sites of Connecticut,* 2 vols. (New Haven, 1937), I, 441-46, and "Map of Journeys of Washington in Connecticut, 1756-1789," facing p. 68. Chastellux was correct, however, in speaking of a "county of Washington" in Virginia; "belonging," but in the figurative sense only, to the protector of America: Washington County, in the southwestern part of Virginia, was formed and so named in 1776 from a part of Fincastle Co.

58. *Ch.* Two years later [Dec. 4, 1782] the author again went through this place, where he had seen but a few houses and a single inn. The number of houses was almost doubled and there were three very good and very neatly arranged inns. He has remarked the same progress along nearly all the inland roads from Chesapeake Bay to the Piscataqua, that is, over an extent of two hundred leagues. This progress is due in great measure to the misfortunes of the war itself. For the English, being masters of the sea, made, or had it in their power to make, what they called "depredatory expeditions." But this term, too shameful to be admitted into the vocabulary of war, denoted only a small part of the ravages committed; murder and conflagrations were the usual melancholy results of such raids. Hence it

happened that the most prosperous citizens, that is to say, those who combined agriculture with trade and had their plantations near the coasts or mouths of rivers, abandoned them, to seek more tranquil inland habitations. The small capital that they took with them was used for clearing new land and these settlements soon began to prosper. On the other hand, communications by sea becoming impossible, inland routes had to be used: roads were improved and were more frequented; inns multiplied, as did those establishments useful to travelers such as wheelwrights' and blacksmiths' shops. Thus, in addition to liberty and independence, the United States will gain from the war this further advantage: trade and population will have spread throughout the states, and lands which would otherwise have long remained unsettled will have been cultivated so successfully that they cannot henceforth be abandoned.

Gr. Marks of these horrid expeditions [the English raids] were everywhere to be met with in travelling within fifty miles of the coasts or rivers. In one of them it was agitated by the Generals Garth, Tryon, and their officers, to burn the beautiful and popular town of New Haven in Connecticut, with its handsome college, etc. *The latter General was for it,* but happily, more humane and wiser spirits prevailed in the council. The Translator had the opportunity of making the same remarks [i.e., similar to those of Chastellux], not only in a journey from Virginia to New Hampshire, but in many of the interior parts of the continent.

59. Again, Chastellux had his terminology slightly mixed: there was no Milford *County* in Connecticut, only the *towns* of Milford (Fairfield Co.) and New Milford (Litchfield Co.), the latter of which is referred to here. The hamlet on his route was perhaps the locality known today as "Upper Merryall," which is in the very northeastern corner of the fairly extensive town of New Milford, and through which the old route to Fishkill passed.

60. The locality is known today as Bull's Bridge, in the southeastern corner of the town of Kent, Litchfield Co. One of Connecticut's few remaining covered bridges crosses the Housatonic here, below the falls, which are now harnessed by the Connecticut Light and Power Co. When Washington journeyed along this same route on his way to visit the French army at Newport in Mar. 1781—a few months after Chastellux's tour—he paid $215 (Continental currency, no doubt) for "getting a horse out of Bull's Falls," according to the expense account kept by his aide, Col. Tilghman. Acomb, ed., *Von Closen Journal,* 62n.

61. The "Oblong" was theoretically ceded by Connecticut to New York by an intercolonial agreement of 1683, but the new boundary line was not run until 1731, and was not definitively determined until 1880-81. This "equivalent oblong," a strip of land about 1¾ miles (580 rods) wide running along Connecticut's western border from the town of Greenwich north to the Massachusetts line, was to compensate for Connecticut's westward thrust towards the Hudson represented by the town of Greenwich. Concerning the long drawn-out New York-Connecticut boundary disputes see Dixon Ryan Fox, *Yankees and Yorkers* (N. Y., 1940), 128-40; Charles O. Paullin, *Atlas of the Historical Geography of the United States,* ed. John K. Wright (Washington and N. Y., 1932), 75-76, plate 97-E. "The Oblong" is clearly delineated on Claude Joseph Sauthier's "A Chorographical Map of the Province of New York in North America" (London, 1779), which is reproduced in E. B. O'Callaghan, ed., *The Documentary History of the State of New York,*

4 vols. (Albany, 1849-51), I, between pp. 774-75—a map with which Chastellux was probably familiar.

62. The tavern of Col. Andrew Morehouse, or Morhouse (Dutchess County Militia, 3rd Regiment) was in the town of Dover, Dutchess Co., N. Y., on high ground between Tenmile River and its tributary, Swamp River; see Erskine-Dewitt maps Nos. 35 and 102, N.-Y. Hist. Soc. The site of the tavern, demolished in 1877, was in 1962 marked only by a horse chestnut tree and pile of stones in a field at the northwest corner of the junction of State Route 55 (from Webatuck) and the unnumbered connecting road leading westward from it, across State Route 22, into Wingdale village. There is a wood engraving of the Morehouse Tavern in Philip H. Smith, *History of Duchess County* (Pawling, 1877), 160; and a photograph taken before its demolition, in Frank Hasbrouck, ed., *The History of Dutchess County, New York* (Poughkeepsie, 1909), facing p. 182. Across the road from the site of Morehouse's place the still extant Moosehead Tavern, a red brick structure built in the early 19th century, further testifies to the former importance of this crossroads on the east-west route from Hartford to Fishkill and the north-south "Harlem Valley route" (roughly present State Route 22), long used by drovers bringing livestock from Vermont and New Hampshire southward to city markets. Both the Moosehead Tavern and the site of the Morehouse Tavern are on land belonging to the state of New York, adjacent to the Harlem Valley State Hospital. P. H. Smith, *Duchess County*, 161, points out that Morehouse's did not actually stand "in the Oblong" as Chastellux states; although this may be correct, strictly speaking, the tavern appears to have been but a short distance outside the western line of the Oblong and it is likely that the term was rather loosely used to designate the general locality.

63. *Gr.* At Leesburgh in Virginia [Loudun Co.], on my way to visit General Gates [at "Traveller's Rest," near what is now Kearneysville, Jefferson Co., West Virginia], I staid three days at the house of an Englishman, a native of Bristol, a man of five foot high, who united, in his own person, the offices of *Colonel, Justice of the Peace, Parish Clerk*, and *Innkeeper*, nor was he deficient in any of these functions.

64. *Gr.*—Three-pence to five-pence English.

65. *Gr.* The Translator, who as a disinterested, and determined friend to the rights of mankind, and to the principles of the English Constitution, could not but wish success to America in her glorious struggle; as a native of England had many similar occasions for interesting reflections on the vicissitudes of human affairs, and of the wickedness of those who too frequently direct them. But in no instance was this more striking than in Virginia, where he saw the French army encamped [in July 1782] on the very spot [at Alexandria], from whence Braddock set out on his unfortunate expedition against the French, five and twenty years before [in 1755]. The traces of his encampment were still evident. In this expedition Braddock was not only well seconded by the Provincials, but had their advice been followed, his success would have been very different. It is worth observing too, that no less than *four* of the most distinguished of the American Generals, were with him on the expedition. General Washington was his aide-de-camp, and after dissuading him as much as possible from forming his army in the European manner (the mistake which proved fatal to him), received him when mortally wounded in his arms; General [Charles] Lee

was in a detached party from the main body of the army; General [Horatio] Gates served in the army, and General [Adam] Stephen was shot through the body in the engagement: Lee and Gates were Englishmen, and Stephen a Scotchman; all the four were now become inhabitants of Virginia. On the anniversary [1782] of that unfortunate day [July 9, 1755], the Translator dined in the back part of the country at General Gates' ["Traveller's Rest"] with General Stephen, from whom he had many curious particulars; nor was the wonderful revolution in the affairs and minds of men, the subject of less anxious discussion with them, than with the Translator. At the time he is speaking of, indeed, during their whole stay, nothing could be more cordial and sincere than the kind reception given to the French by the Virginians.

66. Numerous gravestones of early Dutch settlers, which the modern tourist can see in the cemetery adjoining the Protestant Reformed Dutch Church of Hopewell (founded 1764, rebuilt 1833), confirm Chastellux's remarks. The church is in "Old Hopewell" on Beekman Road, a mile or so east of Hopewell Junction (town of East Fishkill, Dutchess Co.), the modern "center."

67. Col. Jacob Griffin's house still stands, about two and a half miles beyond Hopewell Junction, when proceeding westward towards Fishkill, on the north side of State Route 82, a short distance east of Sprout Creek; Federal Writers' Project, *Dutchess County* (Phila., 1937), 133. A roadside tablet (erected 1928 by Melzingah Chapter D.A.R. and state of New York), which serves to identify the house, recalls that it was known during the Revolution as "Griffin's Tavern" or "the Rendez-vous," that the Committee of Observation for Rombout Precinct held a famous meeting here Aug. 15, 1775, and that it was "frequented by Washington, La Fayette, Putnam, Steuben, Continental and French soldiers." The 18th-century structure has undergone various modifications and is now in a dilapidated state.

68. The inn—not further identified but presumably along the main street of Fishkill Village—had changed for the better when Chastellux stopped there two years later; it was then kept by Mr. "Boerom." See below, Pt. III, chap. 3, Dec. 5, 1782.

69. Trinity Church (built *ca.* 1769), which served as a hospital during the Revolution, still stands on the south side of the road from Hopewell (State Route 52) as it enters Fishkill Village, and just before it crosses the present Albany Post Road (U.S. Route 9). The "Doctor" (not further identified) was thus well situated to observe Chastellux and his suite ride by. Concerning the organization of the medical services in the French army at this time, and the sharp distinction made between *médecins* and *chirurgiens,* see Bouvet, *Service de Santé,* where the "Code d'Administration" of Jan. 1, 1780, is given.

70. *Gr.* My old friend [Dr. William] Rumney, whom I had the happiness to meet with after an absence of twenty years, during which time he has been settled at Alexandria in Virginia (whose respectable father had been forty years master of the Latin school at Alnwick in Northumberland, and his uncle [the Rev. Joseph Rumney] clergyman of Berwick), had served more than one campaign as colonel, doctor, and surgeon in the army; he is held in the highest esteem, and is on terms of the greatest friendship with General Washington, at whose house I spent some days with him. But it

is impossible to conceive the estimation in which all the medical men, attached to the army, were held during the war, by the people in general, as well as the military. I travelled from Philadelphia to the American camp on the North River, with Mr. Craigie [Andrew Craigie, apothecary-general?] of that department, a most respectable young man, and was witness to the grateful acknowledgements his countrymen seemed everywhere to bestow on him, for the service he was rendering their suffering fellow-citizens, nor indeed could anything exceed the zeal, perseverance, and attention of this department under the most discouraging circumstances.

Ed. Concerning Dr. William Rumney, who served as physician to Washington and his family, see Douglas Southall Freeman, *George Washington, A Biography*, 7 vols. (N. Y., 1948-57), III, 196, 204, 210, 227.

71. Chastellux's escort must have been John Keese, assistant to Col. Hugh Hughes, the deputy quartermaster general who had his headquarters at Fishkill; a letter written by Keese to Maj. Gen. McDougall, Nov. 20, 1780 (Hugh Hughes Letterbook 18, 26-27, N.-Y. Hist. Soc.) states that Col. Hughes was then in Albany, while other correspondence indicates that Keese was customarily in charge of the Fishkill post during his superior's absences. The military depot and barracks were located a mile or so south of Fishkill village on either side of the Post Road (present U. S. Route 9) and extended to the foot of the mountains. The new Interstate Highway 84 crosses the area from west to east, intersecting the Post Road just north of the Cornelius R. Van Wyck House (also called the "Wharton House" from its traditional association with Cooper's novel, *The Spy*), which served as officers' quarters during the Revolution. Archaeological investigations prompted by the construction of the new highway, undertaken in the spring of 1962, have revealed traces of the encampment. A bit farther south along the Post Road, at the corner of Van Wyck Lake Road is a stone marker (erected 1899 by Melzingah Chapter D.A.R.) commemorating the American soldiers who died at the barracks; across the road from the marker is an old milestone indicating "66 miles to New York." Still farther south, some three miles from Fishkill, are markers (N. Y. State, and D.A.R. tablet) recalling the American batteries that guarded Fishkill Clove, or Wiccopee Pass. The camp of the "invalids," visited by Chastellux after leaving the main encampment, was probably located near the summit of the pass. The Editor is especially indebted to Mrs. Charlotte C. Finkel for verification of the above details.

72. Jean-Louis-Ambroise de Genton, Chevalier de Villefranche (1747-84), was one of the French engineers who had served in the American army since 1777. A captain, then major (1778), he was given the rank of lieutenant colonel in 1783. Lasseray, *Français Treize Etoiles*, I, 229-31; Elizabeth S. Kite, *Brigadier-General Louis Lebègue Duportail*...(Baltimore, 1933), 241-45. Several maps drawn by Villefranche have survived, notably his "Plan of West Point," 1780, reproduced in facsimile in Edward C. Boynton, *History of West Point*...(N. Y., 1863), between pp. 86-87; and Justin Winsor, ed., *Narrative and Critical History of America*, 8 vols. (Boston, 1884-89), VI, 462. This map was probably made during the summer of 1780, since the principal fort is called "Fort Arnold"—a designation that was changed to "Fort Clinton" after the discovery of Arnold's treason in Sept. Villefranche's map thus shows the West Point fortifications substantially as they were when Chastellux saw them—with Villefranche himself as one

of his guides—in Nov. 1780. Other maps of slightly later date, which also confirm and illustrate Chastellux's description, are: a map of West Point accompanying Cromot du Bourg's Diary (Hist. Soc. of Pa., reproduced in *Magazine of American History*, 4 [1880], opp. 304, probably drawn by Von Closen, who visited West Point in Mar. 1781, as pointed out by Évelyn Acomb in her edition of the *Von Closen Journal*, 60-61); and the map of West Point included by Louis-Alexandre Berthier in his map of the French army's march from Newcastle to King's Ferry, Aug. 1781, Berthier Papers, No. 15-1, Princeton Univ. Lib. See reproduction of Berthier's map in this volume.

73. Chastellux must have turned west from his southbound route and approached the river from the heights above the present village of Garrison. The route is clearly shown on Villefranche's map (see previous note), and still affords the traveler a suddenly revealed view of West Point.

74. This foraging party under General Stark was part of a larger operation against New York, concerning which Chastellux learned further details from General Heath that evening at West Point (below, n. 79), and when he was at Washington's Preakness headquarters in New Jersey a few days later (below, Pt. I, chap. 2, Nov. 25, 1780, and n. 25).

75. On Nov. 13, Washington had written from his headquarters in New Jersey to General Heath: "The inclosed from the Marquis de la Fayette announces the expected arrival of several French Officers of distinction upon a visit to the Army. Should they pass the posts under your command I am convinced you will pay them every attention and honor due to their Rank. I should wish to have notice of their approach to this Camp, you will oblige me by dispatching an Express as soon as they arrive with you, with an account of the Route which they mean to take." Fitzpatrick, ed., *Writings of Washington*, XX, 343. Lafayette's letter to Heath, dated "Light Camp, November the 13th, 1780," is printed in the *Heath Papers*, III, 128-29: "You know their ranks in the French Army; you know that each nation pays honors agreable to its own regulations; you know my sentiments about appearing to advantage; you know every French officer as well, and the greatest part of them better than I do." Lafayette had been with Heath in Rhode Island when the French arrived the previous July, and had already coached him in such matters; for example, in a long confidential communication of June 11, 1780 (*ibid.*, 66-70), explaining ranks and usages in the French army, he had mentioned that "in the French service they give to the Maréchal de Camp *thirteen guns*." See also Heath's *Memoirs*, where he mentions under date of Nov. 21, 1780: "The troops destined for the grand forage paraded between Nelson's Point and the Church. Just before they marched, Chevalier Chastellux, Major General in the French army, at Newport, and some other French officers, arrived; the detachment defiled before them, and proceeded for the lines. The French officers were much pleased with the appearance of the troops. General Chastellux then accompanied our General over to the Point, and on landing was saluted by the discharge of 13 cannon; after dinner, he took a view of Forts Clinton, Putnam, Willis, etc."

76. It was only two months prior to Chastellux's visit to West Point that Benedict Arnold's treachery had been discovered—on Sept. 25, 1780, when Washington was returning from his conference with Rochambeau at Hart-

ford. Major André had been hanged on Oct. 2; the courts of inquiry related to the event had taken place during October.

77. *Gr.* Mr. Franks is the son of a Canadian Jew.

Ed. David Salisbury Franks (1740-93) was later in France, for varying periods of time between 1781 and 1787, serving as diplomatic courier for Franklin, as vice-consul in Marseilles, and as emissary to Morocco. At one time Franks, who was then finding his business and consular affairs unlucrative and who was expecting war to break out in Europe, considered serving in the French army: "The Marquis de Chatelux, we hear is appointed one of the Generals," he wrote to Jefferson from Bordeaux, Jan. 1, 1785. "He knows me—would perhaps interest himself in my favor; if his military family is not compleat I should be happy to serve under him." Boyd *et al.*, eds., *Jefferson Papers*, VII, 587. For further discussion of Franks see Hersch L. Zitt, "David Salisbury Franks, Revolutionary Patriot," *Pennsylvania History*, 16 (1949), 77-95.

78. The principal West Point fort at the Point had at first been known as Fort Arnold, but was re-named Fort Clinton after Arnold's attempted betrayal of it. See maps cited above, n. 72. (The Fort Clinton located five miles or so farther south, opposite Anthony's Nose, at the entrance to The Highlands, was no longer maintained in 1780, as Chastellux mentions hereinafter, Nov. 22, 1780, and n. 93.) Louis Le Bègue de Presle Duportail (1743-1802) had come to the United States in 1777 with three other French engineers (La Radière, Laumoy, Gouvion), and had soon been given command of the Engineer Corps of the Continental Army with the rank of brigadier general; after the victory at Yorktown he was promoted to major general. In the early years of the French Revolution Duportail was to be Minister of War (1790-91); in 1794 he emigrated to the United States, acquired a farm in Pennsylvania at Swede's Ford near the old Valley Forge encampment, died on his return voyage to France in 1802. Lasseray, *Français Treize Etoiles*, I, 272-77; Kite, *Duportail, passim*. At the time Chastellux visited West Point, Duportail, who had been taken prisoner at the capitulation of Charleston, S. C., in May 1780, had only just been exchanged. Although Chastellux did not therefore meet Duportail during the present journey, he was to see him frequently during the ensuing months—at the Franco-American staff conference at Wethersfield in May 1781 and during the Yorktown campaign.

79. Washington's instructions to Heath, Nov. 16, 1780, are printed in Fitzpatrick, ed., *Writings of Washington*, XX, 350-52. See also below, Pt. I, chap. 2, Nov. 25, 1780, and n. 25.

80. Concerning Guibert see below, Pt. I, chap. 3, n. 35.

81. John Manners, Marquis of Granby (1721-70), colonel of the Royal Horse Guards ("the blues") and later lieutenant general, as well as Member of Parliament from Cambridgeshire, attained fame and wide popularity for his successful campaigning against the French in Germany during the Seven Years' War. His portrait was painted by Sir Joshua Reynolds, appeared on snuffboxes, Worcestershire mugs, and medals, and long survived as a favorite signpost for inns (see the *Pickwick Papers*); Walter Evelyn Manners, *Some Account of the Military, Political, and Social Life of the Right Hon. John Manners, Marquis of Granby* (London, 1899), with reproductions of several of the portraits. General Heath was apparently flattered by his resemblance

to Lord Granby, for in his *Memoirs* (written in the third person) he thus alludes to Chastellux's description of him: "He [Heath] is of middling stature, light complexion, very corpulent, and bald-headed, which led the French officers who served in America, very frequently to compare him to the Marquis of Granby."

82. *Gr.* It may now be mentioned, without any invidious imputation, that the conduct of too many of the British officers, when prisoners in America, was as injurious to the honour and interest of their country, as destitute of good sense and common policy; of this the Translator saw many examples which made him blush for England. At Lancaster in Pennsylvania, in particular, he was present at a court of inquiry, instituted into the conduct of some British officers who had broken their parole more than once, and insulted and beat the inhabitants of the country; nothing could be clearer or more decisive than the evidence, nor more polite and indulgent than the behaviour of the American officers who constituted the court, yet they were openly insulted and contemptuously treated by these magnanimous gentlemen officers. Their names are withheld by the Translator, on account of their families; they were a part of the army taken at Yorktown, with Cornwallis. Captain Grenville [Greville?] of the Guards, and others who conducted themselves really like gentlemen, can say how well they were treated.

Ed. The incidents at Lancaster mentioned by Grieve took place in the spring or summer of 1782, at which time General Moses Hazen's Continental Regiment was stationed there to guard the British prisoners of war. See Franklin Ellis and Samuel Evans, *History of Lancaster County, Pennsylvania* (Phila., 1883), I, chap. 8, 59 ff.

83. See above, this chap., nn. 2, 18.

84. Heath wrote to Rochambeau, Dec. 2, 1780, *Heath Papers*, III, 136-37, "I ... have had the pleasure of hearing from you by Count Chatsleaux and other officers of your army, who made us very happy in visiting this post." Again, on Jan. 29, 1781 (*ibid.*, 168), he wrote: "We have been several times cheered in this dreary world by the friendly visits of some of the gentlemen of your army."

85. *Ch.* A drink made with rum, sugar and water; it is properly speaking punch without lemon.

86. Fort Putnam was named for Col. Rufus Putnam (1738-1824), whose Massachusetts regiment built it in 1778—not for General Israel Putnam ("Old Put"), as Chastellux implies. This fort was restored in the 20th century, and like the other sites mentioned, is now on the premises of the United States Military Academy. Fort Wyllis was named for Col. Samuel Wyllis, commanding the 3rd Connecticut Regiment responsible for its construction. The "battery still lower down and nearer the river," mentioned by Chastellux, was probably Fort Meigs, named for Col. Return Jonathan Meigs, commander of the 6th Connecticut Regiment. Chastellux omits mention of Fort Webb, named for Col. Samuel B. Webb, also of Connecticut, whose regiment built it, although the Colonel himself was a prisoner of war at the time. See maps cited above, n. 72; Boynton, *History of West Point*, 48-68, 153-55; Horace M. Reeve, "West Point in the Revolution, 1778-1783," *The Centennial of the United States Military Academy at West Point, New York, 1800-1902*, 2 vols. (Washington, 1904), I, 137-200.

87. *Gr.*—half a million sterling.

88. *Gr.* The zeal, perseverance, and, I may say, *honour,* which shone forth in the American army, in the most arduous and extraordinary circumstances, almost surpass credibility. They were in general most wretchedly clothed, seldom received any pay, were frequently in want of everything, from the public scarcity of money, and the consequent indifference of the contractors, and had daily temptations thrown out to them of the most alluring nature. This army was composed of all nations, yet they seemed to be pervaded but by one spirit, and fought, and acted with as much enthusiastic ardour as the most enlightened and determined of their leaders. We all remember, when their intolerable distresses drove part of them to revolt in 1781,* when Clinton sent emissaries among them, with the most advantageous offers, and made a movement of his army to favor their desertion, that they disdainfully refused his offers, appealing to their *honour,* and delivered up with indignation, the British emissaries [John Mason and James Ogden], who were executed at Trenton [Jan. 11, 1781]. Mr. Hugh Shield [Shiell], and Mr. John Maxwell Nesbitt [his brother, Alexander Nesbitt, according to other sources], two Irish gentlemen, settled at Philadelphia, who were entrusted with the care of them, informed the Translator, that one of them was an officer of some note [?] in the British army. On the morning of their execution, this gentleman desired Mr. Shiell to accompany him to the necessary, wherein he staid some time, apparently with the hope of effecting his escape, but this failing he addressed that gentleman as follows. "I see, sir, that you are faithful to the trust reposed in you, and that my die is cast; but as you are a gentleman, I hope you will not fail to let General Clinton know, that my fidelity is unshaken, that I die a loyal subject to George the Third, and that I hope he will not forget my family." He then made a hearty breakfast of cold beef, and was executed with his companion on a tree near the river Delaware, full of courage, and making the same declarations. To account for the subordinate situation in which Messrs. Nesbitt and Shiell appear to have acted on this occasion, it is necessary to observe, that on all emergencies the merchants of Philadelphia flew to arms and acted as common soldiers.

Ed. Grieve here refers to the mutiny of the Pennsylvania Line, at Morristown, in Jan. 1781; see below, Pt. I, chap. 4, n. 4.

89. Jean-Baptiste de Gouvion (1747-92), who had come to America in 1777 with Duportail, likewise served brilliantly as engineer (lieutenant colonel, and colonel) in the American army during the remainder of the war. Chastellux did not see Gouvion during the present journey, but was subsequently associated with him in the Yorktown campaign. Lasseray, *Français Treize Etoiles,* I, 234-37.

90. Vicomte Louis de Noailles (1756-1804), a brother-in-law of Lafayette, had arrived in Newport with Rochambeau's army as Lieutenant Colonel of the Soissonnais Regiment; Comte Charles de Damas (1758-1829) was one of Rochambeau's aides-de-camp, with rank of captain. The Chevalier Thomas-Antoine de Mauduit du Plessis (1753-91), who had arrived in Newport as *premier aide-major de l'équipage d'artillerie,* was, however, already a veteran of the American war. He had previously seen service in the Continental Army, 1777-79, and had distinguished himself at Brandywine, Germantown (below, Pt. I, chap. 3, Dec. 2, 1780, and n. 34), Redbank (Dec. 8, 1780, and n. 80), and Monmouth. Lasseray, *Français Treize Etoiles,* I, 304-15.

Chastellux also met these fellow travelers later during his journey, at Philadelphia and at Albany. Still other French officers from Newport were on the road at this time, including the Comte de Custine, Colonel of the Saintonge Regiment, and the Marquis de Laval, Colonel of the Bourbonnais Regiment (below, Pt. I, chap. 3, Dec. 12, 1780). Winter quarters and the consequent lull in hostilities evidently made of this an auspicious time to reconnoiter the country and visit the Americans, and likewise contributed to the morale of the idle and impatient officers.

91. *Ch.* A much used expression in America, and which need not be translated [into French].

92. See above, this chap., n. 5, concerning plans for attack on New York.

93. Fort Clinton on the southern side and Fort Montgomery (not mentioned by Chastellux) on the northern side of Popolopen Creek were on the west bank of the Hudson, opposite Anthony's Nose, at the entrance to The Highlands. The site of Fort Clinton is now included in the Bear Mountain Section of Palisades Interstate Park; remains of the fort's western redoubt may be seen there, not far from the western end of present Bear Mountain Bridge; the Fort Clinton Historical Museum and "Historical Trail," also in the Park, provide a commentary on the capture of the position by the British on Oct. 6, 1777. Later on, when the defenses were concentrated farther north at West Point, the name of Fort Clinton was given to the principal fort there (see above, n. 78). William H. Carr and Richard J. Koke, "Twin Forts of the Popolopen, Forts Clinton and Montgomery, New York, 1775-1777," *Scenic and Historic America,* 5 (July 1937), 1-60, illus. and maps.

Gr. A poor fellow who was sent with a letter from Burgoyne to Clinton inclosed in a silver bullet, miscarried in his message, and lost his life by the sameness of names of the American and British commanders. Falling in, in the woods, with a party of Americans clothed in British uniforms, which they had taken, he inquired eagerly for *General Clinton,* to whom he was instantly conducted, but on discovering that it was not *the Clinton* he was in search of, in the face of a number of spectators, he swallowed the bullet. Emetics and purgatives were instantly administered, which made him disgorge, and the unfortunate fellow was hanged on the next tree.

Ed. Grieve's version of the silver bullet incident indicates that it had already, five years after the event, become crystallized into a pat but slightly garbled anecdote. The facts of the case were reported by Gov. George Clinton in a letter to the N. Y. Council of Safety, Oct. 11, 1777, in Hugh Hastings and J. A. Holden, eds., *The Public Papers of George Clinton,* 10 vols. (N. Y. and Albany, 1899-1914), II, 412-14. The message enclosed in the so-called bullet ("a small silver ball of oval form, about the size of a fusee bullet, and shut with a screw in the middle") was actually addressed *by* Sir Henry Clinton *to* Gen. Burgoyne, from Fort Montgomery, Oct. 8, 1777: "Nous y voici, and nothing now between us and Gates." The messenger, Lt. Daniel Taylor (British 9th Regiment), was apprehended near the American camp at New Windsor on Oct. 10, and was executed as a spy at Hurley, near Kingston, on Oct. 18. The ill-fated silver bullet, long preserved by descendants of Gov. Clinton, has now come to rest in the Fort Ticonderoga Museum, where it is on display with the incriminating message still inside. See the Museum's *Bulletin,* 4 (July 1936), 94-97, which reprints Benson J. Lossing's article on the bullet and drawing of it from the *American*

Historical Record, 3 (Jan. 1874), 8-10; recorded in 1936 as being on loan from Mr. Henry O. Tallmadge, the bullet has since become the property of the Fort Ticonderoga Museum.

94. The several chains strung across the Hudson (at Fort Montgomery, and later, at West Point) are fully described in E. M. Ruttenber, *Obstructions to the Navigation of Hudson's River* ... (Albany, 1860), and in Charles Rufus Harte, *The River Obstructions of the Revolutionary War* (New Haven, 1946, reprinted from the Connecticut Society of Civil Engineers, *62nd Annual Report* [1946]). Links from the chains may be seen in various historical museums, for example, at West Point, Newburgh, Morristown National Historical Park, and Ringwood Manor.

95. "The Clove" here refers to the upper Ramapo Valley stretching northward from Suffern at the New Jersey-New York line; it provided a natural and well-protected passageway between northern New Jersey and New Windsor, situated on the Hudson above The Highlands. Present State Route 17 and the New York Thruway pass through this "Clove." The word, deriving via Dutch from the verb "to cleave" (cf. cloven hoof), is also applied to other localities in southern New York state, and is roughly equivalent to the terms "gulf," "notch," and "gap" used in other parts of the northeastern United States. Chastellux went through The Clove on his return journey northward a few weeks later; see below, Pt. I, chap. 4, Dec. 19, 1780, and n. 10.

96. *Ch*. This officer had already distinguished himself on several occasions, particularly at the retreat of General Sullivan from Rhode Island [Aug. 1778], and at the defense of Mud Island [see below, Pt. I, chap. 3, Dec. 8, 1780, and nn. 75, 76]. He had come to America in 1777. He has since been Major of the Saintonge Regiment, and has served as *Major de Brigade* in the army of Comte de Rochambeau. On his return to France he was made Colonel of the Pondichéry Regiment, and is now in India.

Ed. Further details on the career of François-Louis Teissèdre de Fleury (born 1749) will be found in Lasseray, *Français Treize Etoiles*, II, 425-33, 639-40, and in Le Roy Elwood Kimball, *Fleury in the American Revolution* (N. Y., 1935). For his brilliant conduct at Stony Point the Continental Congress awarded Fleury a special medal, designed and struck in Paris under Franklin's supervision by Benjamin Duvivier. The reverse of the medal depicts the fortified peninsula of Stony Point. Copies of this medal—one of the most attractive of those designed in France for the American government—may still be obtained from the U.S. Mint in Philadelphia. Fleury had gone back to France on furlough in 1779, but returned to America with Rochambeau's army in 1780. At the time Chastellux penned his journal, Fleury was thus at Newport, serving again in the French army, with rank of major, while retaining his higher rank of lieutenant colonel in the American army, from which he was technically on leave. The Stony Point Battlefield Reservation has since 1946 been under the control and jurisdiction of the Palisades Interstate Park Commission; exhibits on display in the museum there are maintained by the American Scenic and Historic Preservation Society. The Stony Point Reservation was in July 1961 designated a "Registered National Historic Landmark" by the Secretary of the Interior.

97. *Gr*. I cannot here resist a pang of sorrow for the dreadful consequences of the late desperate and fatal war. Captain [Francis] Tew of the

17th Regiment [of Foot], as brave an officer, and as amiable a man as ever lived, whom I had long known and esteemed, when serving with our common friend Montgomery in that regiment, here [at Stony Point] lost his life, refusing to take quarter. This gallant man was already perforated with wounds received in Canada and the West Indies, fighting under his Colonel, General Monckton, in the preceding war [the Seven Years' War], and was such a spectacle of a wounded body still in life, as to be particularly pointed out to the King his master's notice at a review of the regiment near London in 1770 or 1771; the King asked him many questions, seemed much affected with his situation, expressed his pity, and—he was left to pine a subaltern, and to follow his regiment once more to scenes of war and a distant climate. He deeply felt this ever after, and chagrin no doubt, added to his despair, had made him wish for death. The fate of my most intimate and lamented friend, [Richard] Montgomery, who fell [at Quebec, in 1775], as he thought in a better cause, and on the very spot where he had attended Wolfe to victory and glory, affords ample food for melancholy reflection, not easy to be effaced from susceptible minds, and who have felt a double loss of friends, in the horrors of this detestable war.

98. The "promontory" pointed out to Chastellux was Teller's Point, or Croton Point, on the opposite (east) bank of the Hudson, some four miles below Stony Point.

99. *Gr.* There is every reason to believe that Arnold's treachery took its date from his connexion with Lieutenant [Christopher] Hele, killed afterwards on board the Formidable in the West-Indies, and who was undoubtedly a very active and industrious spy at Philadelphia in the winter of 1778, whither he was sent for that purpose in a pretended flag of truce, which being wrecked in the Delaware, he was made prisoner by Congress, a subject of much discussion between them, and the commander at New York. That the intended plot was known in England, and great hopes built upon it, long before it was to take place, is certain. General Matthews and other officers who returned in the autumn of 1780, being often heard to declare, "that it was all over with the rebels; that they were about to receive an irreparable blow, the news of which would soon arrive, etc. etc." Their silence from the moment in which they received an account of the failure of the plot, and the discovery of the traitor, evidently pointed out the object of their allusions.

Ed. Grieve's assertion that Arnold's treachery stemmed from conversations with Lt. Christopher Hele, which evidently reflected a belief current at the time, has not been confirmed by recent investigators. Carl Van Doren, for example, in his *Secret History of the American Revolution* ... (N.Y., 1941), 193, states: "There is nothing to support the traditional conjectures that Arnold was won over by the persuasions of some British agent, either Beverly Robinson or Christopher Hele. ... Lieutenant Hele, in command of the British tender *Hotham*, sailed in October 1778 into the Delaware with the Manifesto and Proclamation of the British commissioners. Arrested and jailed by order of Congress, he was in December released on parole not to leave Philadelphia. He may have talked with Arnold that winter, but it is only a guess that he had any influence."

100. *Gr.* Smith's is a very handsome house and beautifully situated, but it was in the same desolate state when the Translator was there in 1780 [*sic*, but evidently a typographical error for 1782].

Ed. The house of Joshua Hett Smith, known to later generations as "Treason House," was situated on a height of land to the west of the main road leading to Haverstraw. The house is no longer standing; the site on "Treason Hill," indicated by a roadside marker, is now occupied by the New York State Rehabilitation Hospital (in West Haverstraw, U.S. Routes 202, 9W). For views of the house before its demolition, and maps, see: Benson J. Lossing, *The Pictorial Field-Book of the Revolution* ... , 2 vols. (N. Y., 1859), I, 720; William Abbatt, *The Crisis of the Revolution, being the Story of Arnold and André* ... (N. Y., 1899), 10 ff.

101. Chastellux is not strictly accurate in stating that André remained on the right (west) bank of the Hudson after his interview with Arnold at Smith's house; actually he did recross to the east bank, where he was arrested. However, it was at Tappan, a few miles below Haverstraw, on the west bank, that he was hanged at noon on Oct. 2, 1780. André's itinerary and timetable are given in Abbatt, *Crisis of the Revolution*, 87-88.

102. Joshua Hett Smith had been acquitted by a court-martial on Oct. 26, 1780, and then turned over to the civil authorities of the state of New York, who held him in the Orange Co. jail at Goshen, where he was detained at the time Chastellux passed by his deserted house. The following spring, in May 1781, he escaped to New York and went to England, returning only in 1801 to America, where he died in 1818. In 1808 was published Smith's *An Authentic Narrative of the Causes which led to the Death of Major André* ... (London, 1808, and N.Y., 1809; Sabin Nos. 83421, 83422), in which Smith, among other things, attempted to "vindicate his own reputation against the illiberal attack of the Marquis de Chastellux in his work stiled 'Travels through North America' "; see pp. vi, 80-81, 97-98.

103. From a later allusion in Chastellux's journal of his 1782 tour (see below, Pt. III, chap. 3, Dec. 7, 1782), it appears that Mr. Smith's inn was at the locality known as "Kakiat" (from the name of an early land purchase from the Indians, called the "Kakiat Patent"). Chastellux is correct in placing Smith's inn at Kakiat, "in Haverstraw," for in his time the designation "Haverstraw" applied to a much larger region than the present town of Haverstraw. Kakiat was a pivotal point on the 18th-century routes leading from the Hudson into northern New Jersey: a "lower road" running south from Kakiat led along the Saddle River to Paramus, while an upper route, to the southwest, went via Suffern through the Ramapo Valley to Pompton. See Erskine-Dewitt maps Nos. 1-A, 36-pt. 2, 113, N.-Y. Hist. Soc.; map of French army's march from Haverstraw to Suffern, Aug. 25, 1781, Berthier Papers, No. 15-2, Princeton Univ. Lib.; U. S. Geological Survey, Thiells, N. Y., quadrangle, 1955. The Presbyterian meetinghouse of Kakiat is still standing at New Hempstead near the junction of State Route 45 and New Hempstead Road. Two or three miles to the southwest, at West New Hempstead near the junction of State Route 306 and Brick Church Road, is "The Brick Church," a mid-19th-century structure on the site of the Dutch Reformed meetinghouse of "Kakeath" (organized 1774, erected 1778; see tablet placed on outside wall of the present building in 1930 by Shatemuc Chapter D.A.R.). The Erskine maps cited above show about halfway between the two meetinghouses, a "Smith's Store," which was presumably Chastellux's stopping place. The localities mentioned are now within the

town of Ramapo (formed from a part of Haverstraw in 1791), Rockland Co., N. Y. I am indebted to Mr. and Mrs. A. C. Leiby for confirmation of this information.

Chapter 2

South through New Jersey

1. From Oct. 9 to Nov. 27, 1780, Washington's army encamped for the second time that year in the vicinity of Totowa (Passaic) Falls (present Paterson, N. J.). The main body of the army was stretched along the base of the hills on the west bank of the Passaic River for a distance of six or seven miles. Washington's headquarters was in Colonel Theunis Dey's house, at Preakness, in a protected valley some distance back from the river. Lafayette was in command of the light infantry corps, stationed in an advanced position on the extreme left of the main army, at the bend of the Passaic (now Hawthorne, a suburb of Paterson, N. J.). See William Nelson, "Washington's Headquarters at Preakness," *Mag. of Amer. Hist.*, 3 (1879), 490-95, which includes a "Map showing the Location of the American Army at Totowa and Preakness, N. J., and Vicinity, October and November, 1780."

2. *Gr.* The guide gave the Marquis (Chastellux) very true information, for the Translator who took the Paramus road [in 1782], had several well founded alarms, in passing through that intricate country. At Hopper's Mill, near Paramus, where he slept among myriads of rats in a milk house, the family assured him, that their quarters were constantly beat up, and horses, men, etc. carried off. At this place there was no lock to the stable door, which they said was here a superfluous article, as these banditti were guilty of every act of violence. He received similar information from his friend Doctor Brown of Bridport in Dorsetshire, but who has been long settled in America, and was attached to the continental army, with whom he breakfasted, at his beautiful little residence next morning.

Ed. Further stories concerning the beatings-up, etc., at Hopper's Mill [Hohokus] will be found in the recent book by Adrian C. Leiby, *The Revolutionary War in the Hackensack Valley, The Jersey Dutch and the Neutral Ground, 1775-1783* (New Brunswick, 1962), 249-50.

3. Chastellux probably turned off to the left from the Ramapo Valley Road (U.S. Route 202) at Pond Church Corner (Oakland), and then passed by Franklin Lake. The "stream which falls into Second River [the Passaic]" is Goffle Brook, near which Lafayette's advanced corps was encamped in a locality called Wagaraw, now part of the borough of Hawthorne. William Arndt Lucas, "Lafayette's Encampment at Wagaraw," New Jersey Historical Society, *Proceedings*, 69 (1951), 15-27, has identified Lafayette's own quarters as the John Francis Ryerson (later Degray) house, a portion of which survives at No. 40 Wagaraw Road, Hawthorne, on the east bank of Goffle Brook. Lucas's excellent map and photographs permit identification of the spot, now nearly engulfed by factories, filling stations, and other urban excrescences.

4. *Gr.* It is impossible to paint the esteem and affection with which this French nobleman is regarded in America. It is to be surpassed only by the love of their illustrious chief [Washington]. He [Lafayette] has found the

secret of winning all their hearts; nor to those who know him is it matter of any wonder. In the gentlest, and most courteous manner, he unites a frankness, which is supposed to be not the general characteristic of his countrymen; his deportment is dignified without pride; and his zeal, activity, and enthusiasm in the cause of America, distinct from all the political views of co-operation with the wishes of his court, added to a sincere and uniform admiration of the greatest and best character of the age, completely endeared this excellent young man to grateful America. The "Marquis" was never spoken of in the hearing of the Translator, without manifest tokens of attachment and affection.

5. Lafayette, who first came to America in 1777, had returned to France in 1779 and remained there for over a year. He arrived in America again in Apr. 1780, bringing to Washington the news of the impending arrival of Rochambeau's army. Lafayette took command of the light infantry corps in Aug. 1780.

6. Chastellux apparently meant that the Americans could not stack or pile their arms in the approved European manner because their "fusils" were not equipped with bayonets or the devices necessary for interlocking them. He also refers obliquely to the fact that the Americans were at this time hoping to receive better equipment from France, and, as an advocate of inter-allied co-operation, expresses (for the benefit of such of his compatriots as might read his journal) his regret that the expected shipments have not been more prompt.

7. *Gr.* Major [William? de] Galvan, with whom I was well acquainted in Philadelphia, was a French West-Indian, who came, as the Marquis de Chastellux mentions, to America on commercial affairs. He was allowed to be an active good officer. During his residence at Philadelphia in 1782, he became enamoured of a beautiful and accomplished widow of the first distinction in the country. Having conceived the most flattering hopes of success to his passion, he was so shocked at finding himself deceived, that he formed the most desperate resolution. After writing a pathetic, but reproachful letter to the object of his love, and another to her female friend [Sally Shippen], sister to Mrs. Arnold [*née* Peggy Shippen], and arranging all his affairs, he spent the day [July 24, 1782] cheerfully in company with some brother officers at the inn where he lodged, but with some serious intervals. As soon as the tea was over, retiring to his room, he locked the door, placed himself opposite the looking glass, and with two pistols, one in each hand, put an end to his existence. On my arrival at Bordeaux, at the end of the war, I fell in company with a gentleman, who for several days was particularly inquisitive about the Major's conduct, what the general opinion of him was, etc. Fortunately, his conduct was irreproachable; had it been otherwise, this gentleman was imprudently searching for pain to himself and me, as he, to my no small surprise and mortification, declared himself to be his brother [François Louis Galvan de Bernoux].

Ed. Von Closen, one of Rochambeau's aides-de-camp, who was in Philadelphia in late August 1782, noted that the ladies of Philadelphia talked a great deal about the Galvan affair and about "the effects of love on the French character"; Acomb, ed., *Von Closen Journal*, 230. A farewell letter addressed by Galvan to his friends, Lt. Col. Brockholst Livingston, Maj. Matthew Clarkson, and William Bingham, is printed in *Pa. Mag. of Hist.*

and Biog., 26 (1902), 407-8. The Editor's attempts to identify the "beautiful and accomplished widow" have been unsuccessful. Galvan's impetuous character appears to have aroused some misgivings at an earlier date; see Washington's private communication to Baron von Steuben, New Windsor, Apr. 30, 1781, Fitzpatrick, ed., *Writings of Washington*, XXII, 8-9.

8. *Gr.* On the universal stoppage of paper money, from its enormous depreciation, the worst of specie, notwithstanding the abilities and activity of Mr. [Robert] Morris, the financier, occasioned great wants in the army, and a total indifference on the part of the contractors; insomuch, that in the end of 1782, the army was in danger of disbanding from absolute necessity. It was on this critical occasion that Colonel [Jeremiah] Wadsworth, whose merit has been so well appreciated by the Author [see above, Pt. I, chap. 1, Nov. 16, 1780, and n. 42], stept in, took the contract on himself, and by his *name* and *influence* restored affairs, and kept the army together. America cannot be too grateful to this gentleman.

9. "Totowa Bridge" was situated in what is now the heart of the city of Paterson, a bit downstream from the modern West St.-West Broadway Bridge; it spanned the Passaic from a spot corresponding to the foot of present Bank St. across to Water St. The Dutch Reformed meetinghouse (built 1755, burned 1827) was on the hillside not far from the northwestern end of the bridge. William Nelson, *History of the Old Dutch Church at Totowa, Paterson, New Jersey, 1755-1827* (Paterson, 1892) 28, corrects Chastellux in several particulars: "The word 'hexagonal' was probably due to a slip in his memory, for in this case, at all events, it was as incorrect as the statement of the distance of the church from the bridge .... The distance was less than five hundred feet .... The exact location of the old church was about thirty feet east of the Totowa road (now Ryle Avenue), about one hundred feet south of Marlock Street." Nelson's account includes a conjectural drawing of the church (frontispiece). See also William Nelson and Charles A. Shriner, *History of Paterson and Its Environs...*, 3 vols. (N. Y., 1920), II, 447-53.

10. Totowa Falls (Great Falls or Passaic Falls), still in the "wilderness" when Chastellux wrote, subsequently became the site around which grew the industrial city of Paterson. One of the sponsors of the "Society for Useful Manufactures," formed in 1791 to exploit the power of the falls, was Alexander Hamilton, who, as is evident from Chastellux's narrative, had been in this vicinity with Washington's army in 1780. The "great cataract," long considered one of the natural wonders of America, and frequently portrayed in paintings and engravings, is still an impressive sight, especially in spring. See Leo A. Bressler, "Passaic Falls: Eighteenth-Century Natural Wonder," N. J. Hist. Soc., *Proceedings*, 74 (1956), 99-106; Harold J. Dahl and George Connor, "The Falls of the Passaic," *Antiques*, 74 (1958), 326-28 (with illustrations from old prints); N. J. Hist. Soc., *Falls of the Passaic*, intro. by Robert M. Lunny (Newark, 1958).

11. The French text reads: "toute sa surface est guillochée, c'est-à-dire creusée par petits carreaux comme les anciennes boîtes de Maubois." Maubois was a well-known 18th-century French turner, who perfected the lathe and related mechanical tools; see Maurice Daumas, *Les Instruments scientifiques aux XVIIe et XVIIIe siècles* (Paris, 1953), 151. It seems probable that *"boîtes de Maubois"* were metal boxes ornamented with a checkered pattern by

means of a *tour à guillocher* or rose-lathe; see Diderot and D'Alembert, eds., *L'Encyclopédie*, VII, article on the word "Guillocher," and *Planches*, Vol. X, plates showing "Tour à guillocher." I am indebted to M. Paul Ahnne, Librarian and Curator of Prints, Musées de la Ville de Strasbourg, for this explanation.

12. Again, Chastellux is recalling the teachings of Buffon in his *Epoques de la Nature* (see above, Pt. I, chap. 1, n. 51).

13. Washington's headquarters was on the farm of Colonel Theunis Dey (1726-87), in a substantial eight-room brick house which had been built in the 1740's. The "Dey Mansion," still standing, was restored in the 1930's and is now maintained as a public museum by the Passaic County Park Commission. It is located on Totowa Road adjoining the Passaic County Golf Course in Preakness Valley Park in the lower Preakness section of Wayne Township, not far from Mountain View, N. J. Washington's letters and orders for the period of his second sojourn here (Oct. 8–Nov. 27, 1780)—printed in Fitzpatrick, ed., *Writings of Washington*, XX—use several different designations in referring to the place: "Head Quarters near Passaic Falls"—"Totowa"—"Prakness," "Prackness," "Preckness," "Pracaness," "Precaness," "Prekaness," or "Preckaness" (reflecting the orthographical whims of different secretaries and aides)—and occasionally, "Col. Dey's."

Chastellux's visit here was not unexpected. On Nov. 4, Lafayette had written from the camp near the Passaic to his brother-in-law the Vicomte de Noailles (then at Newport, R. I.): "Let me know when you're coming. Charlus, I imagine, and Damas, and perhaps the Chevalier de Chastellux, will accompany you. I am very anxious to be informed in advance because I'd like to be at home the day you come and am often roving about." Jean Patou, ed., *Lettres inédites du Général de La Fayette au Vicomte de Noailles, écrites des Camps de l'Armée américaine durant la Guerre de l'Indépendance des Etats-Unis, 1780-1781* (Paris, 1924), 34. As mentioned above (Pt. I, chap. 1, n. 75), Washington had on Nov. 13, written to General Heath at West Point concerning the expected arrival of the French officers. Three days later, Nov. 16, he wrote to Rochambeau: "I shall be extremely happy in seeing the Chevalier de Chattelus, Count de Custine, Marquis de Laval, and Count de Deux Ponts at my Quarters. I will endeavour to render the time, which they spend with the Army, agreeable to them, and when they incline to visit Philadelphia, they may be assured of that permission, which you so politely make to depend upon me." Fitzpatrick, ed., *Writings of Washington*, XX, 357.

14. *Gr.* About five feet ten and a half inches, English.

Ed. See Freeman, *Washington*, III, 6, where Washington is described by George Mercer as "measuring 6 feet 2 inches in his stockings."

15. *Gr.* La Rochefoucauld has said, "That no man is a hero to his Valet de Chambre." Without combatting the general justice of the remark, this excellent man is most certainly an exception. Those who are the nearest to his person love him the most, but this is never separated from a marked degree of respect and admiration. This is not only the universal testimony, but I had myself the high gratification of observing it. Before the war, there was not a gentleman within the circle of his neighborhood, who, having important concerns, or a family to leave behind him, did not close his eyes in peace, could he be so fortunate as to get Mr. Washington for an executor:

an unequivocal proof of his integrity. I have likewise the strongest testimony to refute those injurious insinuations which have been propagated by envy, ignorance, or party malevolence, with the view of depreciating his talents. I had particular business to transact with him in 1782, respecting the estates of an old friend to whom he was executor, but which from peculiar circumstances had been totally neglected by the noble heirs in England, from the year 1771, indeed I may say, from the year 1767. I found his Excellency in winter quarters at Philadelphia; on entering into conversation on the subject, which was of *a most complicated nature,* the General modestly apprized me, that from the active and turbulent situation in which he had long been placed, never having been at his own house in Virginia since the year 1775, but one night on his return from Yorktown, he was ignorant of his own affairs, and was consequently afraid he could afford me but little information respecting those in question: but what was my astonishment, when, after this prelude, he entered into an accurate detail of every thing respecting them, scarcely omitting, as I afterwards found upon the spot, the most minute particular! On my arrival in Virginia, I had an opportunity of perusing, among the papers, many of his letters written whilst in the active management of the affairs, which furnished me with unquestionable proofs of the clearness of his head, the honor and disinterestedness of his heart, and the uncommon perspicuity and elegance of his style; so as to convince me of the identity of the pen that produced those admirable epistolary performances, which did him so much honor during the war, and will ever mark the energy of his mind, and the excellence of his understanding. I have dwelt with the more satisfaction on this particular, as Envy, unable to detract from their merit, has made frequent attempts to rob his fame of the honor of having ever produced them; and what relates to the public opinion concerning himself he always leaves to the determination of others. This heartfelt, but faithful tribute to transcendent virtue and abilities, is the effusion of a mind unaccustomed to flattery, and in any instance where flattery neither has, *nor can have any object.* I had long revered his character before I saw him, and we all know that too much prepossession is generally unfavorable on a nearer view; but to know *him,* establishes and heightens the most favorable ideas; and I saw, and knew this truly great man, only to root in my mind the most sincere attachment, affection, and veneration for his person and character.

16. *Ch.* Lord Stirling died before the end of the war.

Ed. At Albany, Jan. 15, 1783. Although Chastellux was perhaps not aware of it, he passed near Lord Stirling's "extensive estates" a few days later, when journeying from Morristown to the Raritan Valley in Col. Moylan's company. Stirling's mansion was a short distance southeast of the center of Basking Ridge, on what is now called Lord Stirling Road; only brick outbuildings, which once served as slave quarters, survive today.

17. *Le Huron,* a light opera, with music by André E. M. Grétry and libretto by J. F. Marmontel, was first performed in Paris at the Théâtre des Italiens, Aug. 20, 1768. It was based upon Voltaire's "philosophical" tale *L'Ingénu* (1767). The words and music of the operetta, including the lively march which concludes Act II, will be found in the *Collection complète des Oeuvres de Grétry* (Leipzig and Brussels, n.d.), XIV. Perhaps Chastellux, upon hearing the familiar march here in remote New Jersey, recalled its

context in the opera, where it accompanies a parade of soldiers in Lower Brittany who have rallied to the cry "Vaillants Français, courez aux armes; Les Anglais menacent vos ports!"

18. *Ch*. M. de Gimat served in the next campaign at the head of a battalion of light infantry, still under the command of M. de La Fayette. At the siege of Yorktown he attacked and carried jointly with Col. [Alexander] Hamilton the enemy's left redoubt. This attack was made at the same time that Baron de Vioménil attacked the right redoubt, and was equally successful. M. de Gimat was at this time wounded in the foot. Upon his return to Europe he was made Colonel of the Regiment of Martinique.

Ed. Jean-Joseph Sourbader de Gimat had begun his military career *ca*. 1761 in the Guyenne Regiment, of which Chastellux was then colonel. He had come to America with Lafayette aboard the *Victoire* in 1777, and served in the American army (rank of major) as aide-de-camp to "the Marquis"; Gimat accompanied Lafayette on his journey to France in 1779 and returned to America the following year. Lasseray, *Français Treize Etoiles*, II, 418-20.

19. *Gr*. The *heroic* Tarleton has experienced that there is some difference between these dragoons and a surprised party of ill-armed infantry and peasants. This gentleman's forte was in the latter species of war; a forced march, a surprise, and a bloody gazette, are the records of his glory.

20. The French term was currently used in the American army at this time. Washington's General Orders of Oct. 9, 1780, for example, refer to the duties of the "Marechausie." Fitzpatrick, ed., *Writings of Washington*, XX, 142.

21. "Pyes & Powding," in the French text!

22. Grieve here adds in parentheses: "hickory nuts."

23. *Gr*. On my return from the southward in 1782, I spent a day or two at the American camp at Verplank's Point on the North River [Hudson], and had the honor of dining with General Washington. I had suffered severely from an ague, which I could not get quit of, though I had taken the exercise of a hard trotting horse, and got thus far to the northward in the month of October. The General observing it, told me he was sure I had not met with a good glass of wine for some time, an article then very rare, but that my disorder must be frightened away; he made me drink three or four of his silver camp cups of excellent Madeira at noon, and recommended to me to take a generous glass of claret after dinner, a prescription by no means repugnant to my feelings, and which I most religiously followed. I mounted my horse next morning, and continued my journey to Massachu-

setts, without ever experiencing the slightest return of my disorder. The American camp here, presented the most beautiful and picturesque appearance: it extended along the plain, on the neck of land formed by the winding of the Hudson, and had a view of this river to the south; behind it, the lofty mountains, covered with wood, formed the most sublime background that painting can express. In the front of the tents was a regular continued portico, formed by the boughs of trees in verdure, decorated with much taste and fancy; and each officer's tent was distinguished by superior ornaments. Opposite the camp, and on distinct eminences, stood the tents of some of the general officers, over which towered, predominant, that of General Washington. I had seen all the camps in England, from many of which, drawings and engravings have been taken; but this was truly a subject worthy of the pencil of the first artist. The French camp during their stay at Baltimore [late July-Aug. 1782], was decorated in the same style. At the camp at Verplank's, we distinctly heard the morning and evening gun of the British at Kingsbridge.

Ed. The American army was in camp at Verplanck's Point from late Aug. until the end of Oct. 1782 (when it moved to winter quarters near Newburgh). Grieve refers again to his visit to the camp at Verplanck's Point: see below, Pt. I, chap. 4, n. 1; Pt. II, chap. 3, n. 9; Pt. III, chap. 1, n. 1.

24. *Gr.* The English reader will see that the Author makes a small mistake here; it being the custom in America, as in England, to give a lady, *or* a sentiment, or both.

25. The proposed attack against Staten Island, designed as a feint to divert the enemy's attention, was actually part of a larger plan for a surprise attack upon New York itself. Various related movements were under way previous to and during Chastellux's visit at the Preakness Headquarters. At the review on the previous day, for example, he noted that no salute was fired in his honor because "all the troops on the other side of the [Hudson] river" were in motion. On Nov. 21, when approaching West Point, he had passed in review on the east bank of the Hudson the infantry corps under General Stark which was setting out on a foraging expedition towards King's Bridge (see above, Pt. I, chap. 1, Nov. 21, 1780, and nn. 74, 79). Details of the plan, which had been carefully worked out by Washington and Lafayette, may be gleaned from Washington's orders in Fitzpatrick, ed., *Writings of Washington*, XX. See also Gottschalk, *Lafayette and Close of Amer. Rev.*, chap. 7, which skillfully situates Chastellux's visit in the larger frame of events.

26. Chastellux recorded a less complimentary opinion of General Robert Howe in the 1781 edition of his *Voyage* (p. 54), where he wrote: "General Howe, who is one of the oldest major generals, and who enjoys some consideration in his country, although he has never been lucky in war, and is thought not to have much skill. He is a tall man with a rather disagreeable face, which is not embellished by a scar on his nose. I remained a considerable time with him."

27. According to Nelson and Shriner, *History of Paterson*, I, 238, 292-94, the "big-headed boy of Totowa" was Pieter Van Winkle, who was born in 1754 and died at the age of thirty-one, i.e., three years or so after Chastellux visited him. The unfortunate Van Winkle is also described by Samuel Dewees (*A History of the Life and Services of Captain Samuel Dewees...*, John Smith Hanna, ed. [Baltimore, 1844], 174), who recalls that when he was stationed during the Revolution near Passaic Falls "all the soldiers went

frequently to see the falls, and then a great curiosity which was not far from the falls"; and by Dr. James Thacher (*Military Journal* [Boston, 1823], 243, 527), who relates that when Washington inquired of Van Winkle whether he was a Whig or a Tory, the latter replied that "he had never taken an *active* part on either side." This reply apparently became proverbial among the officers who were at Totowa and was recalled by them on numerous appropriate occasions. Many years later, it is related, when Lafayette revisited Paterson during his triumphal tour of the United States in 1824 he recognized Godwin's "Passaic Hotel" as the place where he had once seen the "big-headed man," and made inquiries concerning his fate. Chastellux's own remarks about the deformed creature and the "necessity of an equilibrium between the solids and fluids" betray the 18th-century "philosopher" familiar with such mechanistic theories of human life as those expressed in La Mettrie's *L'Homme machine* (1748) or D'Holbach's *Le Système de la Nature* (1770).

28. In the privately-printed Newport edition of his *Voyage* (p. 55) Chastellux had included the following supplementary details about Mrs. Knox's costume, which were omitted in the 1786 edition: "for she never leaves her husband. Her attire was ridiculous without being neglected; she had made of her black hair a pyramid which rose a foot above her head; this was all decked out with scarves and gauzes in a way that I am unable to describe. A child of six months, and a little girl of three...." The children were Lucy Flucker Knox (1776-1854) and Henry Jackson Knox (1780-1832). From Chastellux's description of his route it may be deduced that the "little farm" where the Knoxes were living was located between the river and the Dey Mansion, probably on the high land to the east of the latter.

29. *Ch.* General [Henry] Knox, who retained this same position in the American army until the peace, commanded their artillery at the siege of Yorktown. One cannot too much admire the intelligence and activity with which he collected from all quarters, transported, disembarked, and conveyed to the batteries the artillery train intended for the siege, and which consisted of more than thirty pieces of cannon or mortars of a large bore. This artillery was always extremely well served, General Knox never failing to direct it, and frequently taking the trouble of aiming the mortars himself. He scarcely ever left the batteries; and when the town surrendered, he had need of the same activity and resources to evacuate and transport the enemy's artillery, which consisted of more than two hundred pieces, with all the ammunition. The rank of major general was the reward for these services.

It may be observed that if the English on this occasion were astonished at the accuracy and the deadly effectiveness of the French artillery, we French were no less impressed by the extraordinary progress of the American artillery, as well as by the capacities and knowledge of a great number of the officers employed in it.

As for General Knox, it would be depriving him of half the praise he deserves to mention only his military talents. An *homme d'esprit*, well informed, good humored, sincere, and loyal, to know him is to esteem him, to see him is to love him. We have mentioned above that he was a bookseller in Boston before the war: which is not strictly accurate; he traded in various articles, and according to the American custom, sold them wholesale and retail. Books, and French books in particular, were part of his trade, but he spent more time reading than selling them. Before the Revolution he was one of the leading citizens of Boston; now he belongs to the whole world through his reputation and his success. Thus have the English unwittingly adorned mankind by awakening talents and virtues where they thought to find but ignorance and weakness.

30. See below, Pt. I, chap. 3, Dec. 6, 1780, and n. 63.

31. *Gr.* This might in some respect be true at the time the Marquis speaks of, but let the southern campaigns [1781] be attended to, and justice will be done to the active zeal, the wonderful exertions, the unabating courage of that great officer General [Nathanael] Greene; other exceptions might be made, but this stands conspicuous.

32. *Gr.* It is impossible for any man who has had the happiness to approach the General, not to admire the accuracy of this description, and the justness and happiness with which it is developed, or to read it without the strongest emotion. It is here above all, the Translator must apologize to his author; it is not possible to do justice to the original, to feel all its elegance it must be read in the language in which it was written. Posterity, future historians, will be grateful to the Marquis de Chastellux for this exquisite portrait; every feature, and every tint of which will stand the test of the severest scrutiny, and be handed down to distant ages in never fading colors.

33. It should be noted here in connection with Chastellux's memorable portrait of Washington that the American leader, for his part, appears to have gained a most favorable impression of his visitor. Washington wrote to Rochambeau from his headquarters at Preakness on Nov. 27, 1780: "I have been very happy for these three days past in the company of the Chevalier De Chatlies and family, the Viscount De Noailles, the Count D'Amat [Damas] and our old acquaintance Du Plessis. I find in these Gentlemen every thing that can command my esteem." Fitzpatrick, ed., *Writings of Washington*, XX, 415. He repeated the same complimentary remarks in another letter to Rochambeau written Dec. 10 (*ibid.*, XX, 456), and a few days later, from his winter headquarters at New Windsor, on Dec. 20, wrote to Benjamin Franklin (then in Paris): "A few days since, by the Chevr. De Chatteleaux, I had the honor to receive your favor of the 19th. of March introductory of him, and thank you for bringing me acquainted with a gentn. of his merit, knowledge, and agreeable manners. I spent several days very happily with him, at our camp near the great Falls of Passaic in New Jerseys before the Army seperated for its cantonments." *Ibid.*, XX, 507. While Chastellux was still at Preakness Washington wrote several letters of introduction for him. To the President of the Congress at Philadelphia, Samuel Huntington, for example, he wrote, Nov. 27: "I have the honor to introduce to Your excellency The Chevalier De Chatellux Major General in the French Army. I was happy in the opportunity which his journey this way afforded me of making the acquaintance of a Gentleman as eminent in the literary world as distinguished for military merit and for the social qualities. The personal knowledge I have acquired of him confirms me in the sentiments with which his reputation had impressed me, and induces me to recommend him particularly to Your Excellency's esteem." *Ibid.*, XX, 403. Further evidence of the cordial relationship established at Preakness is to be found in the later co-operation between the two men (notably at the

Wethersfield Conference and at Yorktown) as well as in their subsequent correspondence, which continued until Chastellux's death in 1788. Chastellux's letters to Washington (unpublished) are preserved among the Washington Papers, Lib. Cong. Washington's letters to Chastellux are printed in Fitzpatrick, ed., *Writings of Washington.*

Chastellux sent Washington a copy of his book soon after its publication in 1786. After reading—or rather, after David Humphreys had translated for him—the "portrait" of himself at Preakness, Washington wrote to the author: "[Humphreys] has also put into my hands the translation of that part in which you say such, and so many handsome things of me, that (although no skeptic on ordinary occasions) I may perhaps be allowed to doubt whether your friendship and partiality have not, in this one instance, acquired an ascendancy over your cooler judgment. Having been thus unwarily, and I may be permitted to add, almost unavoidably betrayed into a kind of necessity to speak of myself, and not wishing to resume that subject, I choose to close it forever, by observing, that as, on the one hand, I consider it an indubitable mark of mean-spiritedness and pitiful vanity to court applause from the pen or tongue of man; so on the other, I believe it to be a proof of false modesty or an unworthy affectation of humility to appear altogether insensible to the *commendations* of the virtuous and enlightened part of our species. Perhaps nothing can excite more perfect harmony in the soul than to have this spring vibrate in unison with the internal consciousness of rectitude in our intentions and an humble hope of approbation from the supreme disposer of all things." Mount Vernon, Aug. 18, 1786, Fitzpatrick, ed., *Writings of Washington,* XXVIII, 522-24.

34. *Gr.* I was acquainted with four brothers of this family; they were all amiable, sensible, and lively men, and remarkably active and useful in the revolution. The colonel [Stephen], in the military line; another brother [John] whom I *suppose* to have been the merchant at Cadiz, was afterwards in America, and clothier general to the army; another [Jasper] is a lawyer at Philadelphia; and Mr. [James] Moylan, who is lately dead at Lorient, was singularly useful in the year 1777, by managing a treaty between the American Commissioners and the Farmers General of France, for an annual supply of tobacco from America, which he concluded *during Lord Stormont's residence at the Court of France,* and many months previous to the open rupture with that Court. I speak of this with personal knowledge of the fact, nor was it so secret as to have escaped the English Ambassador, or the *vigilant Mr. Forth.* There could not be a more direct attack on England and English claims, than this transaction, which *must* have had the sanction of the French Government, yet England was lulled to sleep by her Ministers, or rather was so infatuated as to shut her ears against the most interesting truths. I could say much more on this subject, but why enter into discussions which have long ceased to be either seasonable or useful? England was, literally, in the case of *Quos Deus vult perdere.*

Ed. The several Moylans mentioned by Chastellux and by Grieve were sons, by two marriages, of John Moylan of Cork in Ireland. The names of four of them—Stephen, John, James, and Jasper—occur at various times in the early minutes of the Friendly Sons of St. Patrick, a society of well-to-do Irishmen, chiefly merchants, founded at Philadelphia in 1771. John H. Campbell, *History of the Friendly Sons of St. Patrick . . .* (Philadelphia, 1892); see also below, Pt. II, chap. 2, n. 2. Stephen Moylan (1737-1811), Chastellux's guide, was the first president of the Society; his name is today commemorated by Moylan Park at 25th and Diamond Sts. in Philadelphia. John Moylan was appointed clothier general of the Continental Army on Apr. 17, 1781 (Worthington C. Ford *et al.*, eds., *Journals of the Continental Congress, 1774-1789*, 34 vols. [Washington, 1904-37], XIX, 401-2; XX, 505). James Moylan, who was in Philadelphia prior to the Revolution, was in France during and after the war. He formed a business partnership, known as Barclay, Moylan & Co. of Lorient, with Thomas Barclay (1728-93), another Friendly Son and also U. S. Consul in France. James Moylan's death at Lorient involved his partner in indebtedness and various complications arising therefrom; for the story of Barclay's involvement and its ramifications see Boyd *et al.*, eds., *Jefferson Papers*, XI, 493-500*n* and Index to VII-XII. Jasper Moylan was a lawyer in Philadelphia.

35. The site of "the winter quarters of 1779" is today incorporated into the Morristown National Historical Park, administered by the National Park Service of the Department of the Interior. For a description of the area and map of the points of interest, see Melvin J. Weig and Vera B. Craig, *Morristown National Historical Park, A Military Capital of the American Revolution* (National Park Service, *Historical Handbook*, 7 [Washington, 1950, reprinted 1957]).

36. Arnold's Tavern, the principal inn of Morristown, figures frequently in the annals of the period 1777-81, during which the Continental Army was at several different times stationed in the vicinity. Washington is said to have used it as his headquarters in 1777. It faced the northwest side of Morristown Green (Park Place), but is no longer standing today. P. H. Hoffman's pamphlet, *History of "the Arnold Tavern," Morristown, N. J.* (Morristown, 1903), cites Chastellux's remarks, p. 5, and includes a drawing (evidently an imaginary reconstruction) of the inn.

37. *Gr.* The terms of his acquittal are—*with the highest honour.*

38. *Gr.* General St. Clair's defence on this trial, which was lent to me by Mr. Arthur Middleton, one of the delegates in Congress for South Carolina, is an admirable piece of reasoning and eloquence.
Ed. The *Proceedings of a General Court Martial,...For the Trial of Major General St. Clair August 25, 1778* (Phila., 1778), were held at White Plains, N. Y., under the presidency of Major General Benjamin Lincoln. Evans, No. 16141, reprinted in N.-Y. Hist. Soc., *Collections*, 13 (1881), 1-171.

39. Washington's army moved forward from Morristown (where it had retired into winter quarters after the Battle of Princeton) to the camp on the heights of Middle Brook at the end of May 1777, and remained in the vicinity until July 3, when it again withdrew to Morristown. The camp extended along the upper reaches of Middle Brook, just behind the rim of the natural fortress formed by First Watchung Mountain, which overlooks the Raritan Valley. Erskine-Dewitt map no. 55, N.-Y. Hist. Soc., gives a contemporary plan of the encampment, including the two redoubts on the right mentioned by Chastellux. The modern traveler proceeding southward from Martinsville along Chimney Rock Road (State Route 525) will find (corner of Gilbride Road), before beginning the descent along Middle Brook into the Raritan plain, a Somerset County Historical Society marker recalling this "Position in Readiness." Two miles or so eastward, part way

up the mountainside (above Bound Brook, Middlebrook Ave.), there is a flagpole erected by the Washington Camp Ground Association to commemorate the presumed first flying of the stars and stripes at the Middle Brook Camp in June 1777. Still farther to the eastward is the Washington Rock State Park, traditional site of one of the lookout points used by Washington. The American army again repaired to Middle Brook Heights for winter quarters, Dec. 1778-June 1779 (during which time Washington occupied as headquarters the John Wallace house in what is now the city of Somerville).

40. The "deep vale" is formed by Middle Brook, a tributary of the Raritan, which here flows through First Watchung Mountain down into the plain; it is known today as Chimney Rock Road (New Jersey State Route No. 525). In spite of the devastation inflicted by extensive quarrying operations, the route still presents through part of its course "a Romantick prospect." The French text reads: "ces débris de la nature & ces ravages de la guerre, composoient le tableau le plus poëtique, ou suivant l'expression angloise, le plus romanesque; car c'est précisément ce qu'on appelle en Angleterre a Romantick prospect." Chastellux's use of the English term is interesting evidence of the way in which French writers, at this time, were absorbing from English sources the concept of Romantic scenery, and with it the word romantique, which was gradually adopted in French and came to have a meaning distinct from the older term romanesque. For other examples see Fernand Baldensperger's study, "Romantique," Ses Analogues et Ses Equivalents, Tableau synoptique de 1650 à 1810 (Harvard Studies and Notes in Philology and Literature, 15 [Cambridge, Mass., 1937]).

41. Chastellux refers to three Italian singers, all famous at the time, and familiar to his French friends for whom the Travels were originally written. Giuseppe Millico (b. 1739), composer and male soprano, was an admirer of Gluck and friend of Chastellux's friend, Mlle de Lespinasse. Giusto Ferdinando Tenducci (1736-ca. 1800) was another male soprano, very popular in England, Ireland, and Scotland, where he spent most of his life; his elopement with a pupil at Edinburgh in 1768 further contributed to his celebrity and produced a romantic story by the lady entitled A True and Genuine Narrative of Mr. and Mrs. Tenducci (London, 1768). Gioacchino Caribaldi (b. 1743), the "bouffon," had made appearances at Madame d'Epinay's salon, where Chastellux had probably heard him. Grove's Dictionary of Music and Musicians.

42. Gr. The Translator, as well as most travellers in America, particularly in the middle states, can testify the accuracy of this account.
Ed. Later on, Chastellux did hear the mockingbird—when he was in Virginia in the spring of 1782. See below, Pt. II, chap. 1, Apr. 9, 1782.

43. The huts pointed out to Chastellux on the brow of the mountains were presumably to the northeastward, and not "to the south," as he says. After the Battle of Monmouth Courthouse (now Freehold), June 28, 1778, when Washington's army had sallied forth from the heights in an attempt to disrupt the British withdrawal from Philadelphia across the Jersey lowlands to Sandy Hook, it retired to New Brunswick, and thence northward to Paramus.

44. Philip Van Horne's "manor" was located on the western bank of Middle Brook not far from its junction with the Raritan. The house is

still standing, but in a somewhat less beautiful situation, on property of the American Cyanamid Company, on a knoll to the north of the old turnpike leading from Bound Brook to Somerville, opposite the Company's extensive plant at Calco Circle. A roadside marker (Somerset Hist. Soc.) identifies it as the Van Horne House, built in 1750.

45. A somewhat less indulgent comment on Philip Van Horne's conduct will be found in the journal of the Baroness von Riedesel, wife of the German general, who accompanied her husband during General Burgoyne's disastrous campaign and who was interned with him as one of the Saratoga Convention prisoners. Three times during the autumn of 1779, while negotiations for the exchange of her husband were in progress, the Baroness had occasion to stop at the Van Hornes' house. The first time this family "who gave themselves out for royalists ... showed us much kindness, and begged us to recommend them to General Cornwallis." Three days later—the exchange of prisoners having been countermanded—the Riedesels were forced to retrace their steps and to stop again at the Van Horne house. "This time we found there a nephew of General Washington, with quite a number of other American officers, who within three days had wrought such a wonderful change in the sentiments of these people—they were among those who hang their cloaks to the wind [*die von denen waren, die den Mantel nach dem Winde hängen*]—that we not only saw the daughters of these pretended royalists on the most familiar footing with the anti-royalists, and allowing them all kinds of liberties; but, as they thought we would not now dare to remonstrate, we heard them singing during the whole night, 'God save Great Washington! God damn the King!' Upon our departure the next morning, I could scarcely conceal my indignation." Six weeks later, in Nov. 1779, the exchange having at last been arranged, the Baroness again found herself on the road through Bound Brook: "I did not wish to call again on the Van Hornes, for I despise double dealing people; but we had the fatality of having our wagon break down before their very door, so that I was forced to tarry with them until the damage could be repaired. I did not, however, remain over night at their house; and when they again asked that we should recommend them, and assured us of their devotion to the King, in whose army the head of the family had served as a colonel, I answered coldly that I believed he did not need our recommendations; which reply he was welcome to take as he pleased." William L. Stone, trans., *Letters and Journals relating to the War of the American Revolution ... By Mrs. General Riedesel* (Albany, 1867), 164-65, 167. The Baroness von Riedesel's journal (edited by her son-in-law, Count Henry Reuss) was first printed privately for her family, in 1800, and then published in Berlin, 1801, as *Die Berufs Reise nach America, Briefe der Generalin von Riedesel auf dieser Reise und während ihres sechsjährigen Aufenthalts in America zur Zeit des dortigen Krieges in den Jahren 1776 bis 1783 nach Deutschland geschrieben.*

46. The Cornwallis incident related by Chastellux had presumably taken place on Apr. 13, 1777, during the British raid on Bound Brook up the Raritan from their base at New Brunswick. In his *Remarks on the Travels of the Marquis de Chastellux in North America* (London, 1787), p. 4, Lt. Col. John Graves Simcoe cites this anecdote as an example of the gasconnades of Chastellux and his informants: "When the Marquis de Chastellux relates that he was at the house where Lord Cornwallis came to take Mr.

Lincoln, he forgets to recount that, although his Lordship missed the General, he took what was better, his cannon."

47. *Gr.* Though this freedom prevails among all ranks, it is particularly striking among the middling classes and common people. Not to speak of the New England *bundling,* a practice which has been so often mentioned, the Translator has seen a grave Quaker and his wife sitting on their bench at their door, as is the custom at Philadelphia in the summer evenings and along side of them the apprentice boy of sixteen, and the servant girl, or perhaps one of the daughters of the family, not only kissing and embracing each other, but proceeding to such familiarities as would shock modesty, and draw down the vengeance of the virtuous citizen of London; and all this, not only without reprehension, but even with marks of complacency on the part of the good old folks. Even the *last slip,* is no essential blemish in the character of the frail fair one. Both sexes arrive early at puberty, their constitutions are warm, there are few restraints, and they lose no time in completing the great object, the population of the country.

48. *Gr.* Mrs. Carter is the daughter of General Schuyler, and is now called Mrs. Church; her husband, Mr. John Barker Church, having re-assumed his real name on his return to England since the peace. He is an English gentleman of a very respectable family and connexions; but having been unfortunate in business in London in the outset of life, retired to America, where, from his known principles he was received as a good whig. He took the name of Carter, that his friends might hear nothing of him, until by his industry he had retrieved his affairs. His activity in the revolution, brought him acquainted with General Schuyler, whose daughter [Angelica] he soon after married; and on the arrival of the French troops, got a principal share of the contract for supplying them, in conjunction with Col. [Jeremiah] Wadsworth. Since the war he has returned to Europe, with a very considerable fortune, settled all his affairs, and is happily and honourably restored to his friends and family.

Ch. (note added to 2d ed., 1788). The real name of Mr. Carter, and the one he now bears in England, is *Church.* He comes from a very good family in that country, and was keeping books for one of his uncles, a substantial merchant, when certain reverses that he had suffered in his own fortune, and a desire to travel, led him to cross over to America. He landed at Charleston, and went thence to Philadelphia. This was at the time of the forming of Congress and the general determination to wage war. Mr. Church, a good Whig, that is to say a good Englishman, took the side of the oppressed party. Congress, which was already assembling troops, lacked gunpowder, and two of the very necessary means for obtaining it. They did not know how to get an agent to Europe to buy it, and they had no money. Mr. Church, who as an Englishman did not run the risk of being captured, and who possessed four thousand guineas, offered his person and his purse. He embarked, and at a short distance from the coast was captured by an English cruiser and taken in to Boston. General Gage, who had some suspicion of his secret mission, treated him rather roughly, and among the other threats proffered, announced that he would not set him at liberty: but Mr. Church told the General that he had no claim over an English citizen who had happened to be a passenger on an American vessel; he threatened, in his turn, to take action against Gage in England, and to prosecute him in court, at any time whatsoever, if he dared, in this instance, keep him prisoner. Mr. Gage was frightened and gave in, and Mr. Church proceeded to rejoin Congress, which subsequently employed him as a commissioner for the liquidation of the accounts of the northern army. It was in pursuit of this mission that he went to Albany, where he made the acquaintance of Miss Schuyler, whom he married. The latter, who combines with the intelligence and estimable qualities inherited from her father all the graces of her sex and her age, was at Boston with her husband when we landed at Rhode Island. Mr. Church came thither to transact business with the Administration of our army. His knowledge of our language, and especially his talents, his experience, and his probity made him very useful. In 1781 he became the friend and associate of Colonel [Jeremiah] Wadsworth, and it is to these two foreigners that we of the French army are particularly indebted for having supplied all our needs in foodstuffs, forage, carriages, horses, etc.

49. During the "last war," i.e. the Seven Years' War, Chastellux, then a young officer in his twenties, campaigned in Germany. "Sauerland" is the rugged region of southern Westphalia, east of Cologne, which long maintained the reputation for remoteness and inaccessibility that it had in the 18th century. The Sourland (Chastellux writes "Saourland") Mountains of New Jersey form a range of hills along the borders of Hunterdon, Somerset, and Mercer Cos., to the west of Hopewell. The region was settled in the early 18th century by German immigrants who presumably, as Chastellux surmises, named it for the locality in the old country.

50. Nassau Hall, which at this time housed the entire College of New Jersey, was completed in 1756; it was generally considered the largest building in the British North American colonies. Although it was twice gutted by fire (in 1802 and again in 1855), the exterior walls still preserve the original dimensions of the "immense building" that attracted Chastellux's attention. Paul Norton, "Robert Smith's Nassau Hall and President's House," in Henry L. Savage, ed., *Nassau Hall, 1756-1956* (Princeton, 1956), 3-26. The College of New Jersey (now Princeton University) obtained its charter (1746) from the royal governor of New Jersey (who was an ex officio member of the Board of Trustees), but it was a privately endowed institution and not, as Chastellux thought, built by the colony or state.

51. *Ed.* In the 1786 French text the name appears as "Wederpurn," corrected to "Withersporn" in the second edition. Chastellux's aide-de-camp, Montesquieu, in his summary of the journey (letter to Latapie, Jan. 29, 1781, Raymond Céleste, "Un Petit-fils de Montesquieu en Amérique (1780-1783)," *Revue Philomatique de Bordeaux et du Sud-Ouest*, 5 [1902], 544-50), noted that "the head of this college is a member of Congress, he is a man of sixty, who speaks French well and seems to be master of the ancient Greek and Latin authors." Several less flattering anecdotes concerning John Witherspoon's French accent have survived, but despite the Scotch character of Witherspoon's spoken French, he undoubtedly possessed a good reading knowledge of the language, as the numerous French works surviving from his personal library testify. Concerning the earlier career of Witherspoon (1723-94)—he came to America from Scotland in 1768 to assume the presidency of the College of New Jersey—Grieve adds this footnote:

Gr. This gentleman is so well known in Europe as to render it unnecessary to enter into any particulars respecting him. He certainly played a much more important part on the theatre of this grand revolution, than by heading the low church party, as it is called in Scotland, and displaying his eloquence, as I have seen him, at presbyteries and synods.

52. In the French text Chastellux says "*physique*," which Grieve appropriately renders by "natural philosophy," the common 18th-century English designation which included branches of study corresponding to physics and astronomy, but not biology (natural history).

53. The few books from the college library which survived the Revolution are today on display in a reconstituted 18th-century room in the Princeton University Library—together with books from Witherspoon's personal library acquired by the College after his death. (Among the latter is a copy of the London, 1787, edition of Chastellux's *Travels*; no marginalia!) A partial record of the pre-war library survives in the printed catalogue compiled by President Samuel Davies, *A Catalogue of Books in the Library of the College of New-Jersey, January 29, 1760* (Woodbridge, N. J., 1760; facsimile reprint, with foreword by Julian P. Boyd, Princeton, 1949).

54. According to another version of the story, a cannon ball from one of Capt. Alexander Hamilton's batteries decapitated the portrait of George II when the Americans were dislodging a British garrison from Nassau Hall on the morning of Jan. 3, 1777. Three years after Chastellux's visit to Princeton—in Sept., 1783, when the Continental Congress was meeting in Nassau Hall and when Washington was residing at nearby Rocky Hill—the College trustees commissioned Charles Willson Peale to paint Washington's portrait which, when finished, was to be "placed in the Hall of the college in the room of the picture of the late King of Great-Britain, which was torn away by a ball from the American artillery in the battle of Princeton." The following year Peale's famous painting of "General Washington at the Battle of Princeton" was hung in Nassau Hall, where it has survived down to the present day. See Charles Coleman Sellers, *Portraits and Miniatures by Charles Willson Peale* (Amer. Phil. Soc., *Transactions*, New Ser., 42 [1952], Pt. 1), No. 933, pp. 235, 359; hereafter cited as Sellers, *Peale Portraits;* and Donald Drew Egbert, *Princeton Portraits* (Princeton, 1947). The portrait of George II now hanging in Nassau Hall was acquired only in 1936, at a time when Anglophilia had become more prevalent among the sons of Old Nassau.

55. *Gr.* This is the celebrated *Orrery of Rittenhouse*, the supposed destruction of which made so much noise at the beginning of the civil war, and sullied the English name in the eyes of all enlightened Europe. Justice, however, requires from the Translator to declare, that from his inquiries, and examination on the spot, the report had no other foundation than, that they intended to remove, and send it as a present to the King. It may possibly be said, and would to God that such a conjecture were not too well warranted by the whole conduct of the war, that to this motive only may be attributed its preservation; however that may be, their sudden dislodgement from Princeton preserved the Orrery, and, as far as that goes, the national character.

Ed. For a history of the orrery, acquired in 1771 for the College of New Jersey through John Witherspoon's efforts, see H. C. Rice, Jr., *The Rittenhouse Orrery, Princeton's Eighteenth-Century Planetarium, 1767-1954...* (Princeton, 1954), and "The Rittenhouse Orrery, A Check-list of Items shown in the Exhibition held in the Princeton University Library, May-

June 1954," *Princeton University Library Chronicle*, 15 (1954), 194-206. Chastellux describes, below, Pt. I, chap. 3, Dec. 5, 1780, the similar orrery built by David Rittenhouse for the College of Philadelphia.

56. *Gr.* Lord Cornwallis made one or two attempts to force the small stone bridge over the creek at Trenton, but was so galled by a small battery which commanded it, and a body of chosen men, placed by General Washington in the Mill-house, that he gave up the attempt, from a contempt of his enemy; looking upon them as his certain prey, their retreat over the Delaware, then full of ice, being impracticable; for the same reason, probably he made no attempt to cross the creek in any other part.

57. The engraved map (with which Chastellux was doubtless familiar), published by William Faden (London, 1777), *Plan of the Operations of General Washington against the King's Troops in New Jersey, from the 26th of December 1776 to the 3d January 1777*, provides a good guide to the events and localities in Princeton and Trenton mentioned here. The basic account is William S. Stryker, *The Battles of Trenton and Princeton* (Boston and N. Y., 1898); Alfred Hoyt Bill, *The Campaign of Princeton, 1776-1777* (Princeton, 1948), is a readable re-telling of the story (note, in particular, his reproduction of the so-called "spy's map" of Princeton, original in Lib. Cong.); landmarks and monuments are described in V. Lansing Collins, *Princeton Past and Present*, rev. ed. (Princeton, 1945). The major portion of the Princeton battlefield, on either side of Mercer Road (State Route 583), southwest of the center of Princeton, is now preserved by the state of New Jersey as the "Princeton Battlefield State Park." Mercer Road did not exist in the 18th century; the main route from Princeton to Maidenhead (Lawrenceville), and over which Chastellux traveled, is present U.S. Route 206, a continuation of Princeton's Stockton St.

58. Rensselaer Williams had since 1766 kept an inn in Trenton, known as the "Royal Oak," at several different locations. At the time of Chastellux's visit Williams's tavern was located at the northeast corner of Queen and Third Sts. (present Broad and East Hanover Sts.) on premises formerly belonging to Abraham Cottnam, which Williams had first rented, and then purchased, from Cottnam's executors in Apr. 1779. A newspaper advertisement of this period describing the "tenement," mentions: "a large commodious brick dwelling house two stories and a half high, four rooms on a floor, with convenient upper lodging rooms, a convenient kitchen adjoining, an elegant brick outhouse fronting the street at a small distance, a large convenient barn, stables, carriage house and other outbuildings; a garden containing about three quarters of an acre. It has been a tavern for upwards of two years past, and is a very convenient and an excellent stand for that business or any other, being situate on the street leading directly through the town." Trenton Historical Society, *A History of Trenton, 1679-1929* ... (Princeton, 1929), I, 317-18, and also, 105, "Map of Trenton about 1776."

59. The emblem that ornamented the inn sign appears to have been borrowed from the Continental six-dollar bill, on which the beaver gnawing down a tree also appears, with the same motto. According to "An Explanation of the Devices on the Continental Bills of Credit with Conjectures of their Meaning," which appeared at the time the first bills were issued in the autumn of 1775, the large tree represents the enormous power of Great Britain, which the persevering, steady-working beaver (America) is

reducing within proper bounds. The devices and mottoes on the Continental bills were apparently designed by Francis Hopkinson. See Henry Phillips, Jr., *Historical Sketches of Paper Currency of the American Colonies*, 2 vols. (Roxbury, Mass., 1865-66), II; Benson J. Lossing, "Continental Money," *Harper's New Monthly Magazine*, 26 (1863), 433-47, with redrawings of the emblems; George Everett Hastings, *The Life and Works of Francis Hopkinson* (Chicago, 1926), 240-44.

60. *Gr.* This gentleman was so active and useful in the revolution, that he was long the marked object of tory vengeance. He was obliged, for many months, to shift his quarters every day, and under the necessity of sleeping every night in a different place; but nothing would abate his zeal, he never quitted his government, and was indefatigable in his exertions to animate the people.

61. Chastellux presumably crossed the Delaware by the so-called "Continental Ferry" (earlier known as "Bond's Ferry"), about two miles or so from the center of town, just below the present site of Riverview Cemetery (Lamberton St.). This is not to be confused with the ferry nearer town, the "Trenton Ferry," which was at the foot of present Ferry St. at about the place where the Pennsylvania Railroad bridge spans the river. Trenton Hist. Soc., *History of Trenton*, I, 263-72.

62. *Gr.* This landlord, like his brethren at Richmond and Shooter's-hill, makes his guests pay for the prospect, and he has the same temptations; the ride from Philadelphia here on parties of pleasure being very common in summer, and the situation of his house on the great road to the Jerseys, and the northward, always ensuring him a number of travellers.

Ed. A footnote at page 20 of the English translation of Jacques Pierre Brissot de Warville's *A Critical Examination of the Marquis de Chastellux's Travels . . .* (Phila., 1788), referring to this passage in Chastellux's book, asserts: "In one place amongst many others, when speaking of one Bessonet (whom you mistake for a brother of Benezet's) you say, that he retained none of his Quaker principles, but that of selling at an extravagant price." This rectification of the name of the innkeeper in turn permits identification of the inn. It was rebuilt by Charles Bessonet (also spelled Bessonett) in 1765 on the site of an earlier ferry house, and until the Revolution had a likeness of George III (or George II, according to some sources) emblazoned on its sign. The name was then changed to "The Fountain." W.W.H. Davis, *History of Bucks County . . .*, 2d rev. ed., 2 vols. (N. Y. and Chicago, 1905), I, 321; II, 340. Bessonet's inn still stands (somewhat enlarged and remodeled) on the bank of the Delaware at the northeast corner of Radcliffe and Mill Sts. in Bristol, and is still maintained as a hotel under the name of "Ye Olde Delaware House." Radcliffe St., Bristol's main street, was formerly the post road from Trenton to Philadelphia.

Chapter 3
Philadelphia and Vicinity

1. The English lines ran from the mouth of Conoquonoque Creek on the Delaware (a bit to the north of the present Benjamin Franklin Bridge) westward to the height of land above the Schuylkill now occupied by the Philadelphia Museum of Art; although subsequent urban development has

largely obliterated recognizable topographical features, the lines might be roughly described as running between present Callowhill and Spring Garden Sts. See *A Plan of the City and Environs of Philadelphia, with the Works and Encampments of His Majesty's Forces, under the command of Lieutenant General Sir William Howe, K. B.* (London, W. Faden, 1779), reproduced in J. Thomas Scharf and Thompson Westcott, *History of Philadelphia, 1609-1884,* 3 vols. (Phila., 1884), I, between pp. 360-61; and map of "Redouts near Philadelphia," Henry Cabot Lodge, ed., *André's Journal; from June 1777 to November 1778,* 2 vols. (Boston, 1903), I, between pp. 134-35. Lossing, *Field-Book,* II, 102-3, gives a detailed description of the English lines on a reconnaissance made in 1848; see also the description by Townsend Ward, based on plan of English lines drawn by Col. Lewis Nicola immediately after the evacuation, in *Pa. Mag. of Hist. and Biog.,* 4 (1880), 181-82. For Chastellux's visit to the western part of the lines, see below, Dec. 12, 1780.

2. The "large hospital" was presumably the Pennsylvania Hospital, the cornerstone of which was laid in 1755. The original building is still standing, Pine St. between 8th and 9th; in Chastellux's time this was on the outskirts of the built-up part of the city, the building thus looming large among open fields. The hospital was built "by the bounty of Government and many private persons," and was not an exclusively Quaker enterprise, as Chastellux implies. Edward B. Krumbhaar, "The Pennsylvania Hospital," *Historic Philadelphia* (Amer. Phil. Soc., *Transactions,* New Ser., 43 [1953], Pt. 1), 237-46, illus.; hereafter cited as *Historic Philadelphia.*

3. *Ed.* The house occupied at this time by the French Minister was at the northeast corner of Chestnut and Seventh Sts., not far from the State House (Independence Hall). No longer standing today, it is referred to by Philadelphia antiquarians as "Carpenter's Mansion," the "Old Graeme Place," or "John Dickinson's House," from the names of earlier occupants.

Gr. The French Ambassador's was a very handsome house, hired of Mr. John Dickinson, and very near the seat of Congress. In one of those dreadful storms of thunder with which America is so frequently visited in the summer months, this house, though lower than the State-house, and that of his neighbour, Mrs. Allen, was struck by lightning, and a French officer, sitting alone in one of the rooms, burnt to death; the lightning had set fire to his clothes, and thrown him into a fainting fit, during which, part of his body was miserably scorched, and his private parts reduced to ashes, so that he survived but a few hours; but the principal ravage was in a chamber containing an *iron bedstead,* in which the Ambassador himself slept, by way of security from the bugs; in that room, large blocks of marble were rent in pieces, and torn from the chimney-piece; its effects, in short, were so singular in many respects, and in some so contrary to received opinions, that Mr. Arthur Lee, and Dr. [Benjamin] Rush, thought proper to publish a very long and curious account of it; and indeed, as far as I am able to judge, this stroke presented many new phenomena of electricity. It may be proper to add, that this was the only house in the neighbourhood *unprovided with an electrical apparatus.*

Ed. It was on Mar. 27, 1782, that lightning struck the French Legation, while the Minister himself was absent on a visit to French army headquarters in Williamsburg, Va. The victim was an artillery officer, Monsieur de Meaux. A detailed account of the disaster (which, incidentally, provides numerous details about the house) appeared in the *Pennsylvania Packet* (Phila.), Apr. 2, 1782; although unsigned, this is presumably the "very long and curious account" by Arthur Lee and Benjamin Rush, referred to by Grieve. Further details concerning the injuries suffered by Monsieur de Meaux, who died Apr. 3., are given in *ibid.*, Apr. 6, 1782. Von Closen, no doubt repeating current gossip, explains the absence of a lightning rod on the Minister's residence by the fact that the owner, John Dickinson, was "an enemy and rival of Dr. Franklin's" and thus skeptical of the value of such devices; Acomb, ed., *Von Closen Journal*, 191. For an official report on the damage, see Corr. pol., Etats-Unis, XX, fols. 483-87, Arch. Aff. Etr., Paris.

4. *Gr.* This gentleman lost his leg by a fall from a phaeton. He is a man of exquisite wit, and an excellent understanding. An admirable companion at the table, and the toilet, he was in universal request; he was in all the secrets of his namesake the financier [Robert Morris], and refined in the dark history of political intrigue. Notwithstanding his misfortune, nature did not form him for inactivity.

Ed. After his return to France Chastellux maintained a correspondence with Gouverneur Morris, for whom he entertained a high regard; see above, Introduction, nn. 72, 77.

5. For Samuel Powel, see below this chap., Dec. 1, 1780, and n. 29.

Chastellux describes Henry Pendleton as "grand Juge de la Caroline"; Grieve rendered this "Chief Justice of South Carolina." There was no chief justice of South Carolina after William Henry Drayton's death in 1779 until John Rutledge received his commission on February 18, 1791. Pendleton's commission on Apr. 17, 1776, as "one of the Assistant Judges of this Colony" is found in the records of the Secretary of the Colony, MS Misc. Records, Book A, 1776-1801, p. 4, South Carolina Archives Department. The balance of the salary due him for the period Apr. 1, 1777-82, "as one of the Judges of the State" was compensated by indents 409-11C, *Stub Entries to Indents, C-F*, ed. Wylma Wates (Columbia, 1957), 71. Pendleton's title was Associate Justice after the Revolution; see Renunciation of Dower Book, 1775-87, Pt. 2, 301, as well as Judgments, Bundle B-W 1778, Charleston Court of Common Pleas, S. C. Arch. Dept. The Editor is indebted to W. L. McDowell, Jr., of the S. C. Arch. Dept., for this information.

6. *Ed.* Not long after Chastellux saw him in Philadelphia, Col. John Laurens (1754-82) sailed for France, in Feb. 1781, as a special emissary from the Continental Congress; he returned in late Aug. 1781 just in time to participate in the siege of Yorktown; the following year he lost his life in a skirmish in South Carolina. Among the letters of recommendation that Laurens took to France was one to Franklin from Chastellux, dated Newport, Feb. 1, 1781; Franklin Papers, XXI, 42, Amer. Phil. Soc. Chastellux's aide-de-camp, Baron de Montesquieu, wrote to his friend Saint-Chamans from Newport, Feb. 2, 1781: "You will perhaps see at Versailles a man of ability who is leaving as an emissary of the United States. This is Colonel Laurens, a man of wit and one of the bravest of America's defenders. I made his acquaintance at Philadelphia and had the pleasure of seeing him here a few days before his departure. Talk to him about me, if you see him; he speaks French very well." Beuve, "Un petit-fils de Montesquieu," *Revue Historique de la Révolution Française et de l'Empire*, 5 (1914); see above, Pt. I, chap. 1, n. 8.

Gr. Among the numerous traits that might be cited to do honour to this illustrious young man, so prematurely, and unfortunately lost to his family and his country, the Translator has selected the following, extracted from the journals of Congress... [Resolution of Nov. 5, 1778, recommending Laurens for promotion; and Laurens's reply, Nov. 6, 1778, declining promotion on grounds that it would be an "evident injustice to his colleagues in the family of the commander-in-chief"; Ford *et al.*, eds., *Journals of Cont. Cong.*, XII, 1105-7].

7. *Gr.* Mr. White is the clergyman of St. Peter's church, and brother to Mrs. [Robert] Morris, the financier's lady.

Ed. William White (1747-1836), ordained in 1772, was from 1779 Rector of Christ Church (the parish also included St. Peter's); Bishop of Pennsylvania in 1786; and in 1789 the first Presiding Bishop of the Protestant Episcopal Church in the United States. White was a chaplain of the Continental Congress, and later served as chaplain to the U.S. Senate while it was in Philadelphia. See below, this chap., Dec. 9, 1780, and n. 93.

8. *Gr.* I had the happiness of enjoying the particular acquaintance of General Mifflin. He is a smart, sensible, active, and agreeable little man. I never saw him without thinking of Garrick; he is about the same size and figure, and his countenance sparkles with significance and expression. To him and his brother [George Mifflin] I am indebted for the most hospitable reception, and continued civilities and attention; and the General, besides showing me on the spot, the whole manoeuvres of Germantown, and the proceedings on the Marquis de la Fayette's expedition over the Schuylkill [to Barren Hill], furnished me with many interesting particulars respecting the conduct of the war. I knew there was a disgust, and the cause of it, but all his narratives seemed to be those of a man of honour, unmixed with personal considerations. On signifying my intention of making a tour into the interior parts of Pennsylvania, he was so good as to give me the following letter of introduction, to his friend Colonel [John] Patton, in case I passed by his neighbourhood. I have preserved it as characteristic at once of his own frankness, and American hospitality.

'Dear Patton Mr. ——, my particular friend, will favour you with a visit at the Spring. I have assured him that he will meet with a hearty welcome.
                    Yours,   THO. MIFFLIN.
Philadelphia, 3d May, 1782.'

9. *Ch.* He is at present [i.e., 1786] a colonel in the service of Holland, in the legion of Maillebois.

Ed. Still later, from 1791 to 1793, Ternant served as French Minister to the United States; he was the last representative of the French monarchy, preceding Citizen Genet, the first envoy from the Republic. Lasseray, *Français Treize Etoiles*, II, 433-36. Ternant's portrait, painted *ca.* 1781 by Charles Willson Peale, is in the Independence Hall Collection; Sellers, *Peale Portraits*, No. 859, p. 208, and fig. 113, p. 301.

10. *Ed.* In the 1781 edition of his work (p. 75) Chastellux had identified the object of Colonel Armand's passion as Mademoiselle Beaumesnil (an opera singer), and had written, instead of the sentence as it appears here: "His family having compelled him to renounce the happiness of marrying Mademoiselle Beaumesnil, he thereupon cast himself into the monastery of La Trappe; but he soon left it to go to America, where he has subjected

himself to a more glorious abstinence and to more meritorious mortifications." He also added to the 1786 edition the following footnote:

Ch. M. le Marquis de La Rouërie was then very young: his subsequent conduct has proved that nature, in giving him a susceptible and impassioned mind, has not made him a present likely to be always fatal to him: glory and honor have employed all its activity; and it is worth consigning to history, as well as to this journal, that carrying with him, as he did to America, the heroic and chivalrous courage of the old French nobility, he could so well conform to republican manners, that far from availing himself of his birth, he would only make himself known by his Christian name: hence he was always called "Colonel Armand." He commanded a legion which was destroyed in Carolina, at the battle of Camden and in the rest of that unfortunate campaign. In 1781 he went back to France, purchased there everything necessary for arming and equipping a new legion, and, on his return to America, he advanced the cost to Congress. By the time peace was concluded, he had been promoted to the rank of brigadier-general.

Ed. For a summary of Col. Armand's services in America see Lasseray, *Français Treize Etoiles,* II, 454-62; John H. Stutesman, Jr., "Colonel Armand and Washington's Cavalry," N.-Y. Hist. Soc., *Quarterly,* 45 (1961), 5-42; concerning his subsequent career, G. Lenôtre, *Le Marquis de La Rouërie et la Conjuration bretonne* (Paris, 1899). The young French traveler François René, Vicomte de Chateaubriand, when he called upon President Washington in Philadelphia in 1791, bore a letter of introduction from "Colonel Armand," whom he knew as the lord of a neighboring estate not far from his own Château de Combourg in Brittany. Chateaubriand, *Mémoires d'Outre-Tombe,* Book V, chap. 15, Book VI, chap. 7. A portrait of Colonel Armand, painted by Charles Willson Peale (or possibly James Peale), *ca.* 1783-84, is in the Hist. Soc. of Pa. collections; Sellers, *Peale Portraits,* No. 755, p. 186, and fig. 149, p. 304.

11. Chastellux's French text: "et n'admet pas même l'excuse du grand cousin, *on ne boit pas sans connaître.*" This is an allusion to a scene in *Le Déserteur* (libretto by M. J. Sedaine, music by P. A. Monsigny), a popular comic opera first performed in 1769 and familiar to all of Chastellux's French readers. Cautious and simple-minded Bernard, "the big cousin," when asked to drink a glass with the free and easy dragoon, Montauciel, makes the above reply and thereby provokes an explosion of wrath from the bibulous soldier (Act II, Scene 17). In Charles Dibdin's English adaptation of *The Deserter* Bernard goes by the name of "Simkin," while Montauciel is "Skirmish." For another allusion to *Le Déserteur,* see below, this chap., Dec. 10, 1780, and n. 94.

12. *Gr.* The conduct of the Chevalier de La Luzerne in America justified every idea that has been formed of the superior skill and address of the French nation on embassies, and in the cabinet. He not only conformed to the manners, and customs of the country, but he studied the character of every individual of the least importance. He rose early in the morning, and watched the hour that best suited their convenience, to wait on the members of Congress, and the leading men of state; at dinner he received company of all political complexions, except *offensive* tories; his afternoons were chiefly employed in visiting the ladies, and in passing from one house to another; in these visits he made no political exceptions, but on the contrary, paid his court particularly to the ladies in the suspected families, an evi-

dently wise policy; in this class, he was supposed to have a very agreeable, as well as useful acquaintance, in the two Miss C——'s [Chew ?], who put no restraint upon their tongues, but were well informed of all the transactions of their party. Wherever he could not himself be present, Mr. Marbois, and Mr. Ottaw [Otto], the Secretaries were distributed, so that you could not make an afternoon's visit to a *whig* or *tory* family in the city, without being sure to meet with this political General or one of his aides-de-camp. When he made a public entertainment, and the presence of the tory ladies gave offence to those of the patriotic party, he always pleaded ignorance, contrived to shift the blame from himself, and throw it on the Secretaries, who were left to fight the battle in the best way they could over the tea table; but all this was carried on with undescribable address, and so managed as to keep all parties in good humour with him. He indulged every man's peculiarities, and bestowed the *petites attentions* on all. It is thus the French maintain their ascendency in the cabinet, which is worth a thousand victories, and their superiority in the Courts of Europe, under every varied form of government, from Holland to Constantinople....

13. Concerning Joseph Reed's conduct at the time of the "Carlisle Commission" of 1778, and the controversy involving him, see John F. Roche, *Joseph Reed, A Moderate in the American Revolution* (N. Y., 1957); and the same author's "Was Joseph Reed Disloyal?" *William and Mary Quarterly*, 3rd Ser., 8 (1951), 406-17.

14. *Gr.* I make no doubt that the M. de Chastellux is correct in this assertion, but thus much I can say from personal knowledge, that Mr. Reed is one of the warmest and most strenuous supporters of the present democratic constitution of Pennsylvania, the work of Dr. Franklin, and to subvert which almost all the personal enemies of Mr. Reed have been labouring for some years past. In Philadelphia, in 1782, the parties of constitutionalists, and anti-constitutionalists ran so high, as to occasion frequent personal quarrels. Another fact is well known to many persons in Europe, and to every body in America, that the attack on Dr. Franklin came from a much more powerful and intriguing quarter than that of Mr. Reed, who never was of any weight in *Congress*. Mr. Reed too was much attached to General Washington, whom the opposers of Dr. Franklin's constitution of Pennsylvania, *affected* to hold in no very high respect. I never exchanged a word with Mr. Reed, my only wish is to ascertain the truth.

Ed. This seems the appropriate place to note that Franklin had written to Joseph Reed a warm letter of introduction for Chastellux, whom he characterized as "a soldier, a gentleman, and a man of letters," as well as a "friend to mankind." Franklin to Reed, Passy, Mar. 19, 1780, printed in Smyth, ed., *Writings of Franklin*, VIII, 42. In a letter to Franklin written from Newport, Feb. 1, 1781, Chastellux mentions that at Philadelphia *"vos lettres m'ont valu le meilleur accueil de Mr. Reed et de la Société académique"* (your letters have gained for me a warm welcome from Mr. Reed and from the Philosophical Society). Franklin Papers, XXI, 42, Amer. Phil. Soc.

15. The last part of this sentence has been somewhat changed from the 1781 edition (p. 78), where it originally read: "and they were satisfied with giving him a sort of assistant, who was well disposed towards him and who served only to help him in his difficult mission. The choice fell upon Colonel Laurens, whom I have mentioned above."

16. *Gr.* Colonel [John] Laurens obtained six millions of livres from the French court, the greatest part of which was expended in clothing and necessaries for the American army, on his arrival in Europe in the spring of 1781. Mr. [Alexander] Gillon, who had the commission of commodore from the state of Carolina, and had been sent over to purchase three frigates for that state, came immediately from Holland to Paris, and prevailed on Colonel Laurens, who was of the same state, to purchase a large quantity of the clothing at Amsterdam, a measure highly offensive to the French court, to be shipped on board his frigate the *South Carolina,* which was to sail *immediately,* and besides her great force, carrying twenty-eight forty-two pounders, and twelve eighteens, had the legion of Luxembourg on board. The purchase was made accordingly at Amsterdam, the goods shipped on board the frigate, by which many private purposes were answered to Mr. Gillon, who, on some pretext however, and after many months' delay, and the Colonel's return, removed the goods from the frigate, and shipped them on board two Dutch vessels *to be taken under his convoy;* but to these he soon gave the slip, leaving them in September in the Texel, without saying a word of his intention; finding he did not return, they were conveyed back in October to Amsterdam, and relanded at an enormous expence to America, and to the great loss of the army, for whom they were intended as a supply that winter; yet, on his return, he had address enough to elude every inquiry into this very extraordinary transaction, to which escape, the universal esteem in which Mrs. Gillon, his wife, was held by every person in Carolina, contributed not a little. It may here be proper to correct an error which has slipped into all the English public prints of the day, and particularly into *Dodsley's Annual Register,* on the subject of the frigate, the *South Carolina.* This frigate is mentioned in the list of Admiral Zoutman's fleet in the engagement off the Dogger's Bank in August, 1781. The translator was then at the Texel, saw the Dutch fleet sail, and return after the engagement; during that interval had the frigate lying at anchor before his eyes, and was close to her, on board another vessel off the end of the Haaks, a great shoal at the mouth of the Texel, when the Dutch fleet entered in the most shattered condition. Mr. Gillon is himself a native of Rotterdam, but was on very bad terms with all the officers of the Dutch fleet, and indeed with almost all his countrymen. *Ed.* See Christina H. Baker in *DAB* s.v. "Gillon, Alexander."

17. Reed was at this time living in the official residence provided by the Assembly of Pennsylvania for him as the President of the Executive Council; this was the confiscated house of the Loyalist, Joseph Galloway, situated at the southeast corner of Market and Sixth Sts. The house is no longer standing; see Harold D. Eberlein and Cortlandt Van Dyke Hubbard, *Portrait of a Colonial City, Philadelphia, 1670-1838* (Phila. and N. Y., 1939), 74-75.

18. *Ed.* In the 1781 edition of his *Voyage* (p. 78) Chastellux referred to Mrs. Washington as "*une grosse femme de quarante à quarante-cinq ans,*" which is a bit less respectful than the phrase used in the 1786 edition, "*une femme de quarante à quarante-cinq ans, un peu grasse....*" He also, in the later version, omitted entirely the sentence: "*Je trouve qu'elle ressemble à une princesse allemande*" (I find that she looks like a German princess).

Gr. I had the pleasure of passing a day or two with Mrs. Washington, at the general's house in Virginia, where she appeared to me to be one of the best women in the world, and beloved by all about her. She has no family by the general, but was surrounded by her grandchildren, and Mrs.

Custis, her son's widow. The family were then in mourning for Mr. [John Parke] Custis, her son by a former marriage, whose premature death [Nov. 1781] was subject of public and private regret. He was brought up by the general as his own son, and formed himself successfully on his model. He succeeded him as representative for Fairfax County, and promised to be a very distinguished member of society, but having gone down to Yorktown, after the capture of Cornwallis, to view the works, he caught a malignant fever at one of the hospitals, and was rapidly carried off. The general was uncommonly affected at his death, insomuch that many of his friends imagined they perceived some change in his equanimity of temper, subsequent to that event. It is certain that they were upon terms of the most affectionate and manly friendship.

19. The resemblance to Fabricius and Philopoemen was apparently an afterthought on Chastellux's part. In the earlier version of his book he had written (p. 78): "We found him in his cabinet, lighted by a single candle. It is said that he is hardly more enlightened, figuratively speaking, than he is in the literal sense of the word, but he is an upright man, who espouses no party, and may be relied on." Huntington, as President of the Continental Congress, occupied a residence provided at public expense, the Pemberton house, also known as "Clarke Hall," at the southwest corner of Third and Chestnut Sts. A Congressional resolution of Mar. 30, 1780, had specified "that the house of Joseph Pemberton, hired by the Board of Treasury, be appropriated for the use of the President of Congress"; Ford et al., eds., Journals of Cont. Cong., XVI, 235, 317, 381. See also Edmund C. Burnett, "Perquisites of the President of the Continental Congress," American Historical Review, 35 (1929), 69-76. The Pemberton house was demolished ca. 1800; the "First Bank of the United States" (later Girard's Bank, now National Park Service) was built on the grounds of the estate. John F. Watson and Willis P. Hazard, Annals of Philadelphia, and Pennsylvania..., rev. ed., 3 vols. (Phila., 1891), I, 374-75; Scharf and Westcott, History of Philadelphia, I, 181, illus.; II, 855.

20. Don Juan Miralles, the first Spanish Minister to the United States, had in 1779 rented the Benjamin Chew residence at 110 (now 242) South Third St., next door to the Samuel Powel house (see below, this chap., n. 29). Ex-Chief Justice Chew was at the time "in retirement" from Philadelphia as a former Crown official. The house had originally been built by Charles Willing for his son-in-law, Colonel William Byrd of Westover; it was subsequently acquired by Governor John Penn, from whom Chew purchased it in 1771. After its temporary use by the Spanish representatives—and, for a brief period in the winter of 1781-82, by General Washington—Chew again resumed possession of it. The house is no longer standing. Burton Alva Konkle, Benjamin Chew, 1722-1810... (Phila., 1932), 108-9, 125-26, 191-92. Rendón, the Spanish chargé d'affaires, was evidently a somewhat disgruntled host; see his letter to Diego Joseph Navarro (Captain General of Cuba), Dec. 10, 1780, in which he complains of the expense of lodging Chastellux and retinue; Cunningham Transcripts, Lib. Cong., cited in Carson, The Chevalier de Chastellux, 77.

21. Mrs. Richard (Sarah Franklin) Bache lived in the house built for her father in 1764-65 in a court on the south side of Market St., between Third and Fourth. This house, in which Franklin himself lived after his return from France in 1785 and where he died in 1790, was demolished in 1812. The site, known as "Franklin Court," on Orianna St., is now part of Inde-

pendence National Historical Park. See Edward M. Riley, "Franklin's Home," *Historic Philadelphia,* 148-60.

22. "Mrs. P***" is identified in the 1781 edition of Chastellux's work (p. 79) as "Mrs. Platter"—presumably Elizabeth Rousby Plater, the wife of George Plater (1735-92), delegate to Congress from Maryland and later governor of Maryland.

23. *Gr.* Between 3 and 400,000 pounds sterling.

24. *Gr.* Mr. Morris has certainly enriched himself greatly by the war, but the house of Willing & Morris did a great deal of business, and was well known in all the considerable trading towns of Europe, previous to that period. Mr. Morris had various other means of acquiring wealth besides privateering; among others, by his own interest, and his connexions with Mr. Holker, then Consul-General of France, at Philadelphia, he frequently obtained exclusive permissions to ship cargoes of flour, etc., in the time of general embargoes, by which he gained immense profits. His situation gave him many similar opportunities of which his capital, his credit, and abilities always enabled him to take advantage.

On the strength of his office, as Financier-General, he circulated *his own notes of Robert Morris,* as cash, throughout the continent, and even had the address to get some assemblies, that of Virginia in particular, to pass acts to make them current in payment of taxes. What purchases of tobacco, what profits of every kind might not a man of Mr. Morris' abilities make with such powerful advantages? The house the Marquis speaks of, in which Mr. Morris lives, belonged formerly to Mr. Richard Penn [see below, this chap., n. 27]; the Financier has made great additions to it, and is the first who has introduced the luxury of hot-houses, and ice-houses on the continent. He has likewise purchased the elegant country house formerly occupied by the traitor, Arnold, nor is his luxury to be outdone by any commercial voluptuary of London. This gentleman is a native of Manchester in England, is at the head of the aristocratical party in Pennsylvania, and has eventually been instrumental in the revolution; in private life he is much esteemed, by a very numerous acquaintance.

Ed. A recent study of Robert Morris is Clarence L. Ver Steeg, *Robert Morris, Revolutionary Financier* (Phila., 1954).

25. *Gr.* Very large fortunes were made from nothing during this period, but this state of prosperity was not of long duration; in 1781 and 1782, so numerous were the King's cruisers, and privateers, that frequently not one vessel out of seven that left the Delaware escaped their vigilance. The profits on successful voyages were enormous, but it was no uncommon thing to see a man one day worth forty or fifty thousand pounds, and the next reduced to nothing; indeed these rapid transitions were so frequent, that they almost ceased to affect either the comfort or the credit of the individuals.

Flour shipped on board at Philadelphia, cost *five* dollars, and produced from twenty-eight to thirty-four dollars a barrel in *specie* at the Havana, which is generally but a short run, and the arrival of one European cargo, out of three, amply repaid the merchant, so that notwithstanding the numerous captures, the stocks were continually full of new vessels to supply such as were lost or taken. In short, without having been upon the spot at that period, it is impossible to conceive the activity and perseverance of the Americans. There was scarcely a captain, or even common sailor, who had not been taken six or seven times during the war, nor a merchant who had not been, more than once, rich and ruined.

26. Chastellux's portrait of Robert Morris, as printed in the 1781 edition of the *Voyage* (p. 80), differs in several details from the longer 1786 version given here. The earlier text reads: "Mr. Morris is a large man, very simple in his manners, but well intentioned, and as well versed in public business as in his own. He is the friend of Mr. Franklin, and the decided enemy of Mr. Reed. His house is handsome, closely resembling the houses in London. He lives there modestly, being neither prodigal nor miserly, but incapable of consuming more than thirty thousand pounds a year even though he might have five hundred thousand. I have already mentioned Mr. Powel."

27. In note 24, Grieve states that the house referred to by Chastellux "belonged formerly to Mr. Richard Penn; the Financier has made great additions to it." This was the Masters House, where Penn and his wife Mary Masters Penn lived from 1772-75, on the south side of Market St. below Sixth, next door to the Galloway House; the house was used by Sir William Howe during the British occupation of the city, then by Arnold, and then by John Holker, French Consul, until a fire in Jan. 1780 partially destroyed it. Robert Morris then rebuilt it for his residence, although he obtained formal title to it from the Penns only in 1785. This was the house that Morris later relinquished for the use of the President of the United States from 1790 to 1800, and it thus became known as "The President's House." It was demolished in 1832. See Harold D. Eberlein, "190, High Street (Market below Sixth)—The Home of Washington and Adams, 1790-1800," *Historic Philadelphia*, 161-78.

However, it should be borne in mind that Grieve's information was based on his own visit to Philadelphia in *1782;* it is not certain that Morris was already installed in his new Market Street residence by *Dec. 1780* when Chastellux visited him. More probably he was still in his earlier residence on Front St. below Dock St. Ellis P. Oberholtzer, *Robert Morris, Patriot and Financier* (N. Y. and London, 1903), chap. 9.

28. *Ch.* Mr. Morris has since filled for three years the post of "Financier" or Comptroller General [Superintendent of Finances], which was created for him [in Feb. 1781]. He had for his assistant Mr. Gouverneur Morris, whom I have already mentioned, and who has amply justified the opinion entertained of his talents. It may safely be asserted that Europe affords few examples of perspicuity and facility of understanding equal to his, which adapts itself with the same success to business, to letters, and to sciences.

Ed. For Robert Morris's career as "financier," see E. James Ferguson, *The Power of the Purse, A History of American Public Finance, 1776-1790* (Chapel Hill, 1961).

29. Samuel Powel (1739-93) had been mayor of Philadelphia at the beginning of the Revolution and had continued in this capacity during the British occupation of the city in 1777-78; at the time of Chastellux's visit he "took no part in the government," as mentioned above (Nov. 30, 1780); later, however, when the animosities of the post-occupation period had abated, he again became mayor of the city in 1789. Mrs. Powel (1742-1830), *née* Elizabeth Willing, was the sister of Thomas Willing, business associate of Robert Morris, and of Mary Willing Byrd (whom Chastellux saw in Virginia; below, Pt. II, chap. 4, Apr. 27, 1782). The Powel house, at No. 244 South Third St., is one of the few private Philadelphia homes visited by

Chastellux that is still standing. It has been restored and furnished with appropriate 18th-century pieces (only a few of Powel provenance) by the Philadelphia Society for the Preservation of Landmarks, and is open to the public. Eberlein and Hubbard, *Colonial City*, 365-73, illus. The original panelling from two of the rooms in the Powel House, replaced by copies in the house itself, may be seen in "period rooms" at the Philadelphia Museum of Art and at the Metropolitan Museum of Art (American Wing). An attractive oil portrait of Mrs. Powel, painted *ca.* 1793 by Matthew Pratt, is preserved at the Pennsylvania Academy of Fine Arts; Mrs. Powel is shown leaning on a pedestal with an urn inscribed "Dear Pledge of Chaste and . . . . Farewe[ll]"—presumably an allusion to the recent death of her husband and to that "happiest union" alluded to by Chastellux. W. Sawitzky, *Matthew Pratt, 1734-1805* . . . (N. Y., 1942), plates 30-31, pp. 60-62.

30. Chastellux's remarks about Mrs. Powel, as they were originally printed in the Newport edition of his *Voyage* (1781), apparently caused some comment among those Philadelphians who had seen, or heard about the privately-printed edition of the book. In a letter written to Chastellux (Paris, Dec. 24, 1784) Thomas Jefferson mentioned that when he was in Philadelphia during the winter of 1782-83 an acquaintance repeated to him a few passages from the book containing "strictures on some of the ladies whom you had seen"; but when he later saw the book itself (Marbois's copy) he found that the "malice and curiosity of the world" had "fished out" these passages, and, ignorant of the book as a whole, had concluded that it must be "a collection of personal strictures and satyre," instead of "the most flattering account of America that had ever been written." Jefferson then suggested that such passages, which had given offense, might be omitted in the public edition of the book to which he urged Chastellux to consent. Boyd *et al.*, eds., *Jefferson Papers*, VII, 580-83. In his reply Chastellux assured Jefferson that he had already consented to publication of his book, and added, "De tout ce que j'ai pu hazarder legerement, je ne regrette qu'une plaisanterie, assez innocente cependant sur le gout qu'a Madame Powell pour la conversation. J'ai conçu depuis beaucoup d'estime et d'amitié pour elle" (Of all that I may have ventured lightly, I regret but one of my little jokes, a rather innocent one, indeed, about Mrs. Powell's taste for conversation. I have since conceived great esteem and friendship for her). *Ibid.*, 584-86. In the first trade edition of his book (1786), Chastellux slightly modified the remarks about Mrs. Powel, as a comparison with the following text of the original version will show: "I have already mentioned Mr. Powel, now I must speak of his wife; for contrary to American custom, she plays the leading role in the family—*la prima figura*, as the Italians say. She received me in a handsome house furnished in the English manner and, what pleased me most, adorned with fine prints and some very good copies of the best Italian paintings, for Mr. Powel has traveled in Europe and has been in Rome and Naples, where he acquired a taste for the fine arts. As for Mrs. Powel, she has not traveled, but she has wit and a good memory, speaks well and talks a great deal; she honored me with her friendship and found me very meritorious because I meritoriously listened to her."

In a letter written from Paris, June 21, 1786, to Franklin, who had by then returned home to Philadelphia, Chastellux asked him to present his respects to Mr. and Mrs. Bache, and added: "Je ne doute pas que les dames de Philadelphie ne soient aussi empressées auprès de vous que celles de Paris, et je crois les flatter encore en vous priant de me rappeler à leur souvenir; particulièrement à celui de Mde. Morris, Madame Powel, Madame Meredith, Mesdemoiselles Cadwallader, Madame Craig" (I daresay that the ladies of Philadelphia are as attentive to you as those of Paris were, and I hope to please them in requesting you to remember me to them; especially to Mrs. Morris, Mrs. Powel, Mrs. Meredith, the Misses Cadwallader, Mrs. Craig). Franklin Papers, XXXIV, 95 3/4, Amer. Phil. Soc.

31. *Gr.* There are many striking differences between this account, and that given by General Howe in his public despatches, in his own narrative to the House of Commons, and in the examination of his witnesses. The English General reports, that Washington's camp near Skippack Creek, from whence he moved, was *sixteen* miles from Germantown—the Marquis (Chastellux) says, only *ten*. The English General strongly asserts, that this affair was no surprise (see his *narrative* and his examination of Sir George Osborne); Chastellux seems to be well authorized to call it a *complete surprise*. The General affirms he was prepared for it. Chastellux *proves*, nay, the English General's letters and narrative demonstrate how narrowly, and by what means his army, and the British affairs escaped total ruin. The General says, "The enemy retired near twenty miles to Perkyoming [Perkiomen] Creek, and are now encamped near Skippack Creek, about *eighteen* miles distance from hence." Chastellux asserts that "The retreat was executed in good order, that General Washington took an excellent position within *four* miles of Germantown, so that on the evening of the battle, he was six miles nearer the enemy than before." How shall we reconcile these essential contradictions, which ought unquestionably to be discussed, for the interest of truth, and the benefit of history?

Ed. Grieve's references to General Howe's version of events, here and subsequently, refer to the considerable body of evidence that had been published as a result of the Parliamentary inquiry into the conduct of the war in America. In the course of this investigation, which took place in 1779 soon after Howe's recall, Howe's dispatches to Lord George Germain were laid before the House of Commons and were the subject of debate. Howe himself, on Apr. 29, 1779, delivered a condensed "narrative" in defense of his conduct in America, and subsequently participated in the examination of witnesses, chiefly his own subordinate officers (Cornwallis, Grey, *et al.*). All of this material was printed in John Almon, ed., *The Parliamentary Register; or History of the Proceedings and Debates of the House of Commons*, 17 vols. (1774-80), XI, XII, XIII, and (1802 reprint), X, XI, XII, and found its way into the many controversial pamphlets that followed. Among the latter was *The Narrative of Lieut. Gen. Sir William Howe, in a Committee of the House of Commons, April 29, 1779, relative to his conduct during his late command of the King's troops in North America: to which are added, Some Observations upon a pamphlet* [by J. Galloway], *entitled: Letters to a Nobleman* (London, 1780). Thus the English version of the Pennsylvania campaign of 1777 (including Brandywine, Germantown, Red Bank, and the other Delaware River forts, Whitemarsh, etc.) was not only available to Grieve, but was also known to Chastellux himself when, pursuing his own inquiry into the conduct of the war, he made his reconnaissances of the battlefields in Dec. 1780. In considering his description of the Battle of Germantown this background of controversy should be borne in mind, as well as the fact that he discussed the affair with participants in the action (notably the Chevalier Duplessis-Mauduit); his concluding critique is a professional staff officer's exercise in military theory.

32. Contemporary English maps include: J. Hills, *Sketch of the Surprise of German Town, by the American Forces commanded by General Washington, October 4th, 1777* (London, Wm. Faden, 1784); "Battle of German Town the 4th October 1777," in Lodge, ed., *André's Journal*, I, 102-3. See also Lossing, *Field-Book*, II, 110; Scharf and Westcott, *History of Philadelphia*, I, 354-55.

33. *Ed.* This large stone house, one of the several notable 18th-century Germantown residences still standing, is located at 6401 Germantown Ave. Known as "Cliveden," or the Chew House, it was built in 1763-64 by Benjamin Chew, who sold it in 1779 to Blair McClenachan. Chew bought it back in 1797, and it has remained in the family ever since. Harry M. Tinckom, Margaret B. Tinckom, Grant Miles Simon, *Historic Germantown* (Amer. Phil. Soc., *Memoirs*, 39 [1955]), 102-3, hereafter cited as *Historic Germantown*; Konkle, *Benjamin Chew*.

Gr. In 1782 I visited and passed a very agreeable day at this celebrated stone-house, so bravely, and judiciously defended by Colonel Musgrove, and saw many marks of cannon and musket shot in the walls, doors, and window shutters, besides two or three mutilated statues which stood in front of it. It is a plain gentleman's country-house, with four windows in front, and two stories high, calculated for a small family, and stands single, and detached from every other building, so that defended as it was by six companies, commanded by so gallant an officer, it was calculated to make a long resistance against every thing but heavy cannon.... This house formerly belonged to Mr. Chew, a loyalist, and was purchased by Mr. Blair MacClenachan; who, from a very small beginning, has, by his industry, fairly and honourably acquired a very considerable fortune.

34. *Ch.* Mr. Laurens has since fallen a victim to his too reckless valor; he was killed in Carolina, in a skirmish of little importance, a short time before the signing of the peace.

Ed. Duplessis-Mauduit lost his life in a riot at Port-au-Prince, Santo Domingo, in 1791; see above, Pt. I, chap. 1, n. 90. A touching tribute to him by a brother officer, Anne-Louis de Tousard (who also served in the American army), is found in a rare pamphlet entitled *Aux Mânes du Colonel Mauduit* (To the Shades of Colonel Mauduit), in which "the ramparts of Redbank, the fields of Brandywine, Germantown and Monmouth" are evoked; a copy preserved by Thomas Jefferson is now in the Library of Congress; E. Millicent Sowerby, comp., *Catalogue of the Library of Thomas Jefferson*, 5 vols. (Wash., 1952-59), No. 2594.

35. The last part of this sentence, in Chastellux's text, reads: "car l'expérience, qui est toujours brouillée avec M. de Me[s]nil-Durand, nous apprend que l'ordre profond est celui qui est le plus sujet au désordre et à la confusion, et qui demande par conséquent le plus de flegme et de discipline." Chastellux is being ironic at the expense of Baron de Mesnil-Durand (1729-99), whose writings on tactics were widely debated among French military theorists of the time. Mesnil-Durand's *Projet d'un ordre françois de tactique* (1755) had been followed by other writings, among them his pamphlet attacking Tronson du Coudray's *L'ordre profond et l'ordre mince considérés par rapport aux effets de l'artillerie* (1776). In Aug. and Sept., 1778, at the Camp of Vaussieux in Normandy an elaborate test of Mesnil-

Durand's theories had taken place under the command of Marshal de Broglie. Both Rochambeau and Chastellux had participated in these maneuvers which generally discredited Mesnil-Durand's theories. The latter were based on the use in battle of an extreme form of the *ordre profond* (formation in depth), which he and his supporters called *l'ordre français*, as opposed to the *ordre mince* (thin formation), which they dubbed *l'ordre prussien*. The Comte de Ségur, in his *Mémoires*, I, 139-41, has some lively comments about this controversy, which he likens to the contemporary quarrel of the Gluckists and Piccinnists over musical theory. For a discussion and summary of the military theories which were a part of Chastellux's intellectual equipment, and in the light of which he observed the battlefields of America, see Robert S. Quimby, *The Background of Napoleonic Warfare, The Theory of Military Tactics in Eighteenth-Century France* (N. Y., 1957); and also, R. R. Palmer, "Frederick the Great, Guibert, Bülow: From Dynastic to National War," in Edward Mead Earle, ed., *Makers of Modern Strategy* (Princeton, 1943), 47-73. At other points in his narrative Chastellux indicates his own respect for the writings of one of Mesnil-Durand's critics, Comte Jacques A. H. de Guibert (1743-90), who is generally considered the most brilliant and influential French military theorist of the century, and who was, like Chastellux, a "philosopher" as well as a soldier. Both of them were admirers of Frederick the Great and of Voltaire (who versified Guibert's *Essai général de tactique* [1772] in a poem entitled "La Tactique"), and both were familiar figures in the Paris *salons*. The famous love letters of Mlle de Lespinasse, published posthumously, are addressed to Guibert.

36. *Gr.* Possibly the Marquis [Chastellux] does not know that there were *six companies* of the 40th regiment in this house; no despicable enemy to leave in the rear of such an army as General Washington's was composed of.

37. Gimat was Lafayette's aide-de-camp; see Chastellux's earlier comment, above, Pt. I, chap. 2, n. 18.

38. The members of Congress customarily assembled at the "City Tavern" (no longer standing) on the west side of Second St. between Walnut and Chestnut; see Robert Earle Graham, "The Taverns of Colonial Philadelphia," *Historic Philadelphia*, 322-24, illus.

39. *Ed.* In the earlier edition of his book (p. 87), Chastellux had written, "the line of demarcation being from north to south."

Gr. There is a great probability of seeing this line of demarkation more distinctly marked, by a separation of the federal union into *two parts*, at no very distant day; but not on hostile, or unfriendly terms. This was matter of frequent discussion during my stay at Philadelphia, and seemed to be an opinion which was daily gaining ground. Indeed it seems to be a measure which sooner or later must take place, from the obvious difficulties attending the management, and operations of a confederacy extending from Florida to Nova Scotia, a country, every day increasing in population, and branching out into *new states*. Such a division must, in my opinion, give new force and energy to each part of it, and produce more union and activity in their councils: nor do I see any bad consequences arising from such an amicable separation, except in the case of a war exactly similar to the last, a case which I believe every man will agree is scarcely within the line of possibility. *Local* obstacles to a long continuance of the present state of things, must alone infallibly produce it. They who are acquainted with America will add many reasons, which it is unnecessary for me to enumerate.

40. "I will only add that the Visit of the French noblemen has given pleasure. The Chevalier Chastellux particularly recommends himself by his agreeable manners and literary Accomplishments." James Duane to George Washington, Philadelphia, Dec. 9, 1780, Edmund C. Burnett, ed., *Letters of Members of the Continental Congress*, 8 vols. (Wash., 1921-36), V, 477-80.

41. *Gr.* Mr. Thompson [Charles Thomson (1729-1824)] is an Irishman; his nephew, Mr. Sinclair, is a barrister at York in England.

42. Samuel Adams, as one of the delegates from Massachusetts, was in attendance at the Continental Congress in Philadelphia from June 1780 through Feb. 1781. In a letter to his wife, Nov. 24, 1780, Adams wrote: "I have forgot in my late Letters to tell you, that six Weeks ago, General Ward [Artemas Ward, also delegate from Massachusetts at this time] and myself changed our Lodgings, and are at the House of Mrs. Miller. She is a well bred Woman, and my Situation is agreeable." Harry Alonzo Church, ed., *The Writings of Samuel Adams* (N. Y., 1908), IV, 227. Mrs. Miller was perhaps the "Mrs. Miller, gentlewoman," whose residence is listed in Francis White's *Philadelphia Directory* for 1785 (p. 49) as being on Front St. between Arch and Race.

43. The following sentence concerning Mrs. Theodorick Bland (*née* Martha Dangerfield), included at this point in the Newport 1781 edition (p. 88), was entirely omitted by Chastellux in his 1786 version: "His wife was with him; I believe she might be regarded as one of the pieces of furniture in the house, convenient rather than handsome." In deference to Mrs. Bland's memory it may be added that she apparently charmed some of the other Frenchmen, though she left Chastellux cold. Arthur Lee wrote to Col. Theodorick Bland, from Chatham near Fredericksburg in Virginia, Sept. 27, 1781: "Col. Dangerfield and his family are well; and he has touched some hard money from the French, for his hay, which being unusual is very delightful. Are the French and Spanish ministers still at Mrs. Bland's feet, and have the banks of the Schuylkill still the happiness of seeing her?" Charles Campbell, ed., *The Bland Papers*, 2 vols. (Petersburg, 1840-43), II, 77.

44. The Continental Congress met in the Pennsylvania State House, known today as Independence Hall. Chastellux is not strictly accurate in calling it the *hôtel de ville*, or town hall. It should be borne in mind that the two detached buildings which now flank Independence Hall—the City Hall, built in 1790-91, on the east corner of the square (where the U. S. Supreme Court sat from 1791 to 1800), and the County Courthouse, built in 1787-89, on the west corner of the square (where the U. S. Congress met from 1790 to 1800) —did not exist in 1780 when Chastellux was in Philadelphia. See Edward M. Riley, *Independence National Historical Park, Philadelphia, Pa.* (National Park Service, *Hist. Handbook*, 17 [rev. ed., Wash., 1956]); and, for a more detailed study of the buildings, the same author's "The Independence Hall Group," *Historic Philadelphia*, 7-42. A view of the State House, as it was when Chastellux saw it, is included in the background of Charles Willson Peale's full-length portrait of the French Minister Conrad-Alexandre Gérard (La Luzerne's predecessor), painted in Sept. 1779 at the behest of Congress, and now in the Independence Hall Collection; Sellers, *Peale Portraits*, No. 292, p. 86 and fig. 101, p. 297 (where the name of the subject is confused with that of his brother). Peale's view of the State House and seat of Congress (to which the French Minister was accredited) appropriately

shows it as it appeared when looking from the French Legation (northeast corner of Chestnut and Seventh Sts.), the very view that Chastellux had from the window of his residence during his stay in Philadelphia. See above, this chap., n. 3.

45. The painting, for which Washington sat in 1779, was by Charles Willson Peale; it had been commissioned for the State House by the Executive Council of Pennsylvania to honor the hero of the Philadelphia campaigns. After many vicissitudes it came, in 1943, into the possession of the Pennsylvania Academy of Fine Arts, the present owner. A copy of this portrait, executed in 1959 by C. Gregory Stapko, was in 1960 hung in the "Assembly Room" of Independence Hall in the place where Chastellux saw the original in 1780; the historical evidence for placing it there was in fact supplied by Chastellux's account. A detailed history of the portrait—one of the best known of Peale's several life portraits of Washington, and of which many replicas and copies were made—will be found in Sellers, *Peale Portraits*, No. 904, pp. 226-27, and fig. 357, p. 355. According to Sellers, the flags in the foreground of the painting, representing the Hessian flags captured at Trenton, were painted from the originals—which suggests that it was these same flags that Chastellux saw on the walls of the secretaries' room in the State House.

46. Chastellux's text describes the marble tablets as *below* the casements— "*plusieurs tables de marbre placées au-dessous des croisées.*" This may be interpreted as meaning below the upper range of windows, i.e., between the lower and upper ranges of windows; see Peale's picture of 1779, mentioned above, n. 44, reproduced in this volume.

47. *Gr.* Mr. Wilson is a Scotchman, and is making a fortune rapidly in the profession of the law at Philadelphia. He is about four and forty, a man of real abilities, and Mr. Morris's intimate friend and coadjutor in his aristocratic plans.

Ed. See below, this chap., Dec. 14, 1780, and n. 111.

48. Chastellux noted the works of Montesquieu and D'Aguesseau with obvious satisfaction inasmuch as his aide-de-camp, Baron de Montesquieu, was the grandson of the author of *De l'Esprit des Lois,* and he himself was the grandson of Chancellor Henri-François d'Aguesseau (1668-1751).

49. *Ed.* William Bingham (1751-1804) and Anne Willing Bingham (1764-1801) had been married on Oct. 26, 1780, only a few weeks before Chastellux met them. The newlyweds were probably living at this time in the home of her parents, the Thomas Willings, who had a house (no longer standing) at Third St. and Willing's Alley. See Burton Alva Konkle, *Thomas Willing and the First American Financial System* (Phila., 1937), 22-23 (photograph of Willing House before demolition), 40, 42-43, 118. The Binghams were thus close by the Chew house where Chastellux spent his first night in Philadelphia, and the Samuel Powel house. Mrs. Bingham was a niece of Mrs. Samuel Powel. At the close of the war the Binghams spent some time in Europe, where Chastellux saw them again; it was only after their return that they built the elegant mansion at Third and Spruce Sts. (no longer standing) which figures so prominently in Philadelphia social annals during the last decade of the century. Concerning the Binghams see the series of articles by Margaret L. Brown: "William Bingham, Agent of the Continental Congress in Martinique," "Mr. and Mrs. William Bingham of Philadelphia,"

"William Bingham, Eighteenth Century Magnate," *Pa. Mag. of Hist. and Biog.,* 61 (1937), 54-87, 286-324, 387-434.

Gr. Mr. Bingham, even at this age, returned from Martinico with a very handsome fortune. In the year 1782, he gained a very considerable sum by opening policies on the capture of the Count de Grasse in the *Ville de Paris* [Battle of the Saints, Apr. 12, 1782]; an event, of which there is little doubt he had secret and sure intelligence from his connection with the islands. They first opened at 10, and afterwards were done at 25 and 30 per cent. Very large sums were underwritten, chiefly by the *Whigs,* who were unwilling, and could not be brought to credit this piece of news. Circumstances were peculiarly favourable to this speculation, for, notwithstanding the great intercourse between the West-Indies and the Continent, only *two* accounts of this affair arrived for six weeks after the engagement; the event of which was sooner known, with certainty, in England. The one was in Rivington's New York paper, copied from the Antigua Gazette, and lamely given; besides, that his paper was deservedly in universal discredit: the other was brought to Philadelphia by the *Holker* privateer, Captain Keane, who saw part of the engagement, but whose account contradicted the principal facts in Rivington's. The two fleets having gone to leeward after the battle, no fresh intelligence was received from the *leeward,* or more properly speaking here, in the *windward* islands, so that this gambling was carried to so high a pitch, as to induce the French Ambassador to go in person to the coffee-house to communicate a letter he had received from Martinique, subsequent to the battle; from which fair conclusions might be drawn *against* the capture; but this, instead of putting a stop to the gambling, by encouraging the Whigs, increased it:—Mr. Bingham and his friends in the secret, indulged them to the utmost extent of their enthusiasm; and if the policies were all paid, a matter which began to be a subject of discussion when I left Philadelphia, must have gained *prodigious sums,* for no less than from £80,000 to £100,000 sterling were calculated to have been written. It is a singular circumstance, that the first *authentic* account of this great battle, which appeared in America, was copied from the *London Gazette.* Whereas we had at Boston the account of the loss of the *Royal George,* at Spithead, the *16th day* after the accident, by way of Newfoundland.

50. In the privately-printed edition of Chastellux's *Voyage* (Newport, 1781, p. 89) this sentence reads: "I spent the rest of the evening at Mrs. Powel's, where, as can be imagined, conversation did not lag; it was agreeable and animated and I lingered there longer than I realized." See above, this chap., n. 30.

51. Since the Pennsylvania Assembly had relinquished to the Continental Congress its own meeting hall on the ground floor of the State House, it was itself meeting at this time in a room on the second floor of the building. See above, this chap., n. 44.

52. By "Gallo-Americans" Chastellux means the French officers, like Lafayette and Gimat, who were serving with the American army; while the "French" were those like Noailles, Damas and himself, who were with the French army under Rochambeau, or diplomatic personnel of the French Legation.

53. See *Minutes of the First Sitting of the Fifth General Assembly of the Commonwealth of Pennsylvania, which met at Philadelphia on Monday the Twenty-third day of October, in the year of our Lord One Thousand Seven*

Hundred and Eighty (Phila., 1780; Evans, No. 16934), 329-30, "Tuesday, December 5, 1780, A. M." The discussion that Chastellux heard concerned the setting of a day for the hearing of charges against Francis Hopkinson, Judge of the Court of Admiralty, for maladministration in his office. Hopkinson was charged, among other things, with having used his office to hasten the sale of prize cargoes brought in by privateers in such a way as to benefit certain individuals. He was to be impeached, but was eventually acquitted on Dec. 26, 1780. See also Edmund Hogan's *Pennsylvania State Trials* ... (Phila., 1794), I, 1-62.

54. The "cabinet" or museum of Pierre-Eugène Du Simitière (1736-84) was on the north side of Arch St., below Fifth. He was a voracious collector, not only of natural "curiosities," but also of books and pamphlets; many of the latter, which were sold with the rest of his collections in 1785, are now in the Library Company of Philadelphia. Some of his papers are also in the Library Company, others in the Library of Congress. A number of Du Simitière's portraits of eminent Americans, drawn in Philadelphia *ca.* 1779, were engraved in Paris by Bénoit-Louis Prévost and published there in 1781 through the instrumentality of Gérard, the Minister of France in Philadelphia preceding La Luzerne. The set was pirated in England, where it first appeared under the title *Thirteen Portraits of American Legislators, Patriots, Soldiers* (London, 1783); there were many subsequent reissues and copies. These engravings did much to establish the iconography of the "famous men" therein represented. William John Potts, "Du Simitière, Artist, Antiquary, and Naturalist, Projector of the First American Museum, with some extracts from his notebook," *Pa. Mag. of Hist. and Biog.*, 13 (1889), 341-75; Hans Huth, "Pierre Eugène Du Simitière and the Beginnings of the American Historical Museum," *ibid.*, 69 (1945), 315-25; Edna Donnell, "Portraits of Eminent Americans after Drawings by Du Simitière," *Antiques*, 24 (1933), 17-21, illus.

55. "Fixed air"—*air fixe*—was the term applied at this time to what has subsequently become known as carbon dioxide. The subject was being much studied and discussed in the 1770's, notably by Priestley and Lavoisier, as well as by Chastellux's friends in the Académie des Sciences. "Petrifactions" were also of concern to Buffon and others in the same Parisian scientific circles.

56. The university was at this time located on the west side of Fourth St., near the corner of Arch; the buildings are no longer extant; the site, corresponding to present numbers 58-66 North Fourth St., is marked by a bronze tablet. Chastellux is correct in referring to the "university," for the colonial College of Philadelphia, founded in the 1750's as "the College, Academy, and Charitable School of Philadelphia," had in 1779 been rechartered as the "University of the State of Pennsylvania," which continued to use the old buildings. Through the efforts of the ousted provost, the Reverend William Smith (whose conduct during the British occupation of the city had been, to use Chastellux's phrase, "somewhat equivocal"), the old charter of the college was restored in 1789; but in 1791 the Pennsylvania Assembly merged the college and the state university, which had existed concurrently for two years, into a single institution known as the University of Pennsylvania. See William L. Turner, "The Charity School, the Academy, and the College, Fourth and Arch Streets," *Historic Philadelphia*, 179-86.

During Chastellux's later sojourn in Philadelphia, at the conclusion of his third journey (below, Pt. III) and just prior to his return to France, the University of Pennsylvania gave him the honorary degree of Doctor of Laws. The mandamus of the trustees, dated Dec. 23, 1782, authorizing the provost, vice-provost and professors to grant honorary degrees to several of the visiting Frenchmen, reads in part: "Whereas We have thought proper, that the Degree of Doctor of Laws be conferred on Francis Joannes, Chevalier de Chatelleux, a Gentleman of distinguished literary abilities, and a General officer of high rank in the French Army now in America; and on Francis Barbé de Marbois, Consul of France for certain of these United States: And that the Degree of Doctor of Medicine be conferred on Johannes Franciscus Costé, Physician General, and on Maria Bernardus Borgella, a Physician of Rank, and the Degree of Master of Arts on M. Robilliard, Surgeon General, of the Army of his Most Christian Majesty, now in America, being Gentlemen in their respective professions and of high literary reputations: Now Know Ye that ye are hereby authorized and required to confer on each of them. . . ." Archives, Univ. of Pa. The degrees were thus "conferred" on, or shortly after, Dec. 23, 1782; records of a ceremony, if indeed there was any, are lacking. It will be noted that the university, quite properly, chose to honor only such French army visitors as could be ranked among the "literati." On Coste, see below, this chap., n. 86, and Pt. II, chap. 5, n. 16; on Robillard, Pt. II, App. C, n. 20. Marie-Bernard Borgella seems to have been generally overlooked in writings about French participation in the American Revolution; he is mentioned by Bouvet, *Service de Santé*, 34, 105, as one of the physicians under Coste, but no further details are given, nor has the Editor been able to discover more. The Pennsylvania degrees (a doctorate to Coste and Borgella, but only a master's degree to Robillard) reflect the relative status of physicians and surgeons then existing in the French medical profession.

After his return to France Chastellux was instrumental in obtaining for the university a gift of books presented in the name of the King. Their arrival was duly heralded in the newspapers: "A well chosen collection of books is arrived at New-York in the French Packet le Courier de l'Amérique; they are sent by order of the King of France to his Consul General [Marbois], to be presented to the Universities of Philadelphia and Williamsburg. They have been given at the joint request of the Count de Vergennes, and of the Chevalier (and since his brother's death) Marquis de Chatellaux." *Pennsylvania Journal* (Phila.), July 17, 1784. In acknowledging the gift, Thomas McKean, speaking for the trustees, not only expressed their regard for His Most Christian Majesty, but also their satisfaction "in seeing the name of Chastellux placed in their annals, a name equally distinguished for literary merit and for military fame." The gift consisted of 36 titles in 100 volumes, 92 of which still survive in the University of Pennsylvania Library. Many of the books—predominately history, science, and exploration—were products of the Imprimerie Royale. The presence of several of Chastellux's favorite authors (Buffon, Tacitus, Metastasio, for example), as well as his own book, *De la Félicité Publique* (rev. ed., Bouillon, 1776), suggest that he had a finger in the selection. A detailed account of the gift (including the unexpected controversy provoked by it) and the complete list of books is in C. Seymour Thompson, "The Gift of Louis XVI," *University of Pennsylvania Library Chronicle*, 2 (1934), 37-48, 60-67.

Concerning the similar gift of books to the College of William and Mary, Chastellux's other American *alma mater,* see below, Pt. II, chap. 5, n. 17.

57. *Gr.* The President [Provost] is Dr. [John] Ewing. I had the gratification of being present [Mar. 21, 1782] at a public exhibition at the college, at which the Congress, the President and executive council of the state, General Washington, the French Minister, and all the strangers of distinction, etc. assisted. Some excellent declamations were made in Latin, and in English, by the young men who were about to leave college, and obtain degrees; by no means inferior to those I have heard at Oxford and Cambridge. Their compositions in general were elegant, and their elocution easy, dignified and manly; but, whatever was the subject, the great cause of liberty and their country never was lost sight of, nor their abhorrence of the tyranny of Britain. This language in the mouths of some of these young men, who were the sons of *tories,* illustrated the remark of the shrewd and sensible author of *Common Sense,* that whilst the war was depending, the old prejudiced friends of Britain were dropping off, and the rising generation, in the course of seven years knew nothing of that country but as an enemy, nor saw or heard of any thing but her cruelties and devastation. To them the independence of America appeared as much the natural and established government of the country, as that of England does to an Englishman. "Time and death," says he, "hard enemies to contend with, fight constantly against the interests of Britain; and the bills of mortality, in every part of America, are the thermometers of her decline. The children in the streets are from their cradle bred to consider her as their only foe. They hear of her cruelties; of their fathers, uncles, and kindred killed; they see the remains of burnt and destroyed houses, and the common tradition of the school they go to, tells them *those things were done by the British.*" [Thomas Paine, *Letter to the Abbé Raynal on the Affairs of North America* (Phila., 1782).]

58. Chastellux rewrote this sentence for the 1786 edition of his book. In the 1781 edition (p. 91) it reads: "He is a man of great simplicity and modesty; he is not deeply enough versed in mathematics to understand the books of M. d'Alembert, but he has enough to be acquainted with the movements of the heavenly bodies." Chastellux's aide-de-camp, Montesquieu, noted in a letter to Latapie, Jan. 29, 1781 (Céleste, "Un Petit-fils de Montesquieu en Amérique," *Revue Philomathique de Bordeaux et du Sud-Ouest,* 5 [1902], 544-50), that he saw here at Philadelphia "a machine of the system of the world according to Newton, it was made by an American and seemed to me very beautiful, but guess how this good man is now employed! Verifying the printing of paper money!"—an allusion to Rittenhouse's employ as treasurer of the state of Pennsylvania. The machine seen by Chastellux and Montesquieu in the library of the university was the second of the two orreries built by David Rittenhouse; it can still be seen in the present library of the University of Pennsylvania. See Rice, *The Rittenhouse Orrery,* 39-41, 45-46, 51-52, 60-61, plate XII.

59. Chastellux's text gives the name of "Showell," as does the 18th-century English translation of the work. According to an advertisement in the *Pennsylvania Gazette* (Phila.), Dec. 7, 1774, announcing a course of lectures by Dr. Chovet, his "Anatomical Museum" was then situated in "Vidal's-alley, Second-street." Vidal's Alley was west of Second St., between Chestnut and Walnut. Further details about the anatomical models

are given by Von Closen, who visited the museum on Aug. 31, 1781, while on his way to Yorktown; Acomb, ed., *Von Closen Journal*, 118. After the death of Abraham Chovet (1704-90) his collection of wax models was purchased, in 1793, for the Pennsylvania Hospital, which in turn presented it, in 1824, to the University of Pennsylvania; here the collection remained until its destruction by fire in 1888. See Francis R. Packard in *DAB* s.v. "Chovet, Abraham."

60. The "cabinet" of anatomical models fashioned by Mlle Marie-Catherine Biheron (1719-86), in the Rue Saint-Jacques in Paris, enabled the curious to see corpses in colored wax which opened up to show the internal organs. Although many doctors were hostile, she was encouraged by Jussieu and Villoison in France and by Hunter and Hewson in England. Her collection was purchased for Catherine II of Russia. Didot, *Nouvelle Biographie Générale*, VI, 65. There are in the Franklin Papers, Amer. Phil. Soc., several letters from Mlle Biheron to Franklin, whom she met through their mutual friend, Jacques Barbeu-Dubourg, the French translator of Franklin's works. Barbeu-Dubourg named a mushroom for Mlle Biheron in his *Le Botaniste François* (Paris, 1767), II, 486-87.

61. *Gr.* Mrs. Arnold is said to be very handsome; but this I know, that her two sisters are charming women, and must have been very dangerous companions for a wavering mind, in the least susceptible of the most powerful of all passions. But an apology for Arnold, on this supposition, is too generous for a mind so thoroughly base and unprincipled as his. With what delicacy could be beloved a woman by that miscreant, who made the mysteries of the nuptial bed the subject of his coarse ribaldry to his companions, the day after his marriage!

62. In a letter to Washington, written from Philadelphia, Dec. 5, 1780, Lafayette mentions that "To morrow, my dear General, I will go to Brandiwine with C^{her} de Chattelux, and also to Red Bank, Fort Mifflin, etc. On my return, I hope to find news from France, and I will write you my determination about my going to the south ward." Louis Gottschalk, ed., *The Letters of Lafayette to Washington, 1777-1799* (N. Y., 1944), 135.

63. There were at this time three ferries over the Schuylkill: the Upper Ferry (approximately at present Museum of Art); the Middle Ferry (at Chestnut St.); and the Lower, or Grey's Ferry (Gray's Ferry Ave.), by which Chastellux crossed the river on his way to Chester.

Philippe-Charles-Jean-Baptiste Tronson du Coudray (1739-77) had been commissioned a major general by Silas Deane in Paris, and reached America —preceding Lafayette by several months—in the spring of 1777. He was a brilliant albeit vain and quarrelsome officer, who had published numerous pamphlets on artillery, gunpowder, and military theory. It was on Sept. 16, 1777, while on his way to join Washington's army (then in upper Chester Co. during the withdrawal from Brandywine), that Du Coudray, without dismounting, rode his too-spirited horse on to the ferry, and across it, into the Schuylkill. His death was apparently little regretted among either the Americans or the French, most of whom would have subscribed to Lafayette's remark that "the loss of this muddle-headed man was perhaps a happy accident"; *Mémoires, Correspondance et Manuscrits du Général Lafayette,* 6 vols. (Paris, 1837-38), I, 19. See also Chastellux's own somewhat similar comment, above, Pt. I, chap. 2, Nov. 26, 1780. Du Coudray was certainly one of those whom Richard Peters had in mind when he spoke, in a confidential conversation with Chastellux (below, this chap., Dec. 12, 1780), of certain French officers "who had offered their services early in the war," but "who had not given such an advantageous idea of their country" as the later arrivals. Lasseray, *Français Treize Etoiles*, II, 444-54. Chastellux was aware of Du Coudray's troublesome "conduct" even before his departure for America; see Silas Deane to Chastellux, Paris, Jan. 1777, *Deane Papers*, I, 468-69.

64. *Gr.* Not far from this town, is found an astonishing quantity of asbestos.

65. Assuming that Chastellux recorded correctly what Lafayette told him, there appears to be a discrepancy—already noted by Lossing, *Field-Book*, II, 171-72—between this statement that Lafayette had spent the night before the battle with Washington in Benjamin Ring's house and a tenacious local tradition that it was in Gideon Gilpin's house that he lodged that night. Lafayette himself consecrated the Gilpin house as his "headquarters" when, as "the Nation's Guest," forty-eight years after the battle and forty-five after his pilgrimage with Chastellux, he again visited the Brandywine battle-field on July 26, 1825. According to Lafayette's secretary and traveling companion on that occasion: "At Chadd's Ford the General learned that one of his companions in arms, Gideon Gilpin, under whose roof he had passed the night before the battle, was now confined to bed by age and infirmity, and despaired of being able to join his fellow citizens in their testimony of respect to the General: he went to visit the aged soldier, whom he found surrounded by his family. Gideon Gilpin, notwithstanding his extreme weakness, recognized him on his entrance, and proved by tears of grateful and tender recollection how much this visit tended to the comfort and soothing of his last moments." Auguste Levasseur, *Lafayette in America in 1824 and 1825 . . .*, trans. John D. Goodman, 2 vols. (Philadelphia, 1829), II, 237.

Both "Washington's Headquarters," i.e., the Benjamin Ring house (re-stored 1949), and "Lafayette's Headquarters," i.e., the Gideon Gilpin house (restored 1952), still stand, a half mile apart, on the north side of U.S. Route 1 a mile or so east of Chadd's Ford; they are on the grounds of the State Park, maintained by the Brandywine Battlefield Park Commission, Commonwealth of Pennsylvania, and are open to the public. Markers in front of the two houses were placed there in 1910 by the Delaware County Historical Society; see "Marking of Headquarters of Washington and Lafayette . . . . September 10, 1910," Del. Co. Hist. Soc., *Proceedings*, 2 (1922), 193-229.

66. The map that Chastellux had with him was entitled *Battle of Brandy-wine in which The Rebels were defeated, September the 11th 1777, by the Army under the Command of General Sr. Willm. Howe*, engraved by William Faden (London, 1778). For other maps and accounts of the battle see: "Plan of the Battle of Brandywine, September 11th 1777, compiled from an actual Survey made during the Summer of 1846," accompanying John S. Bowen's and J. Smith Futhey's "A Sketch of the Battle of Brandywine" and Joseph Townsend's "Some Account . . . of the Battle of Brandywine," Hist. Soc. of Pa., *Proceedings*, 1 (1846); Charlemagne Tower, Jr., *The Marquis de La Fayette in the American Revolution . . .*, 2 vols. (Phila., 1895), I, 223-32.

Several landmarks connected with the battle are still extant, notably the

Birmingham Friends Meeting House (erected 1763), adjoining which are various markers and memorial monuments. Along the road from Birmingham Meeting House to Dilworthtown there is a shaft (erected under the auspices of the Chester County Historical Society, 1895) recalling the spot where Lafayette, in Chastellux's phrase, "shed the first drop of blood he offered to Glory."

67. *Gr.* General Howe calls them 10,000 men.

Ed. See Howe's letter to Lord George Germain, Headquarters at Germantown, Oct. 10, 1777, which includes his account of the Battle of Brandywine, *Parliamentary Register* (1802 reprint), X, 426.

68. *Gr.* General Howe's account says, "General Washington detached General Sullivan to his right with [near] 10,000 men, who *took a strong position* on the commanding ground above Birmingham church," and then relates the maneuvres to *dislodge* them. There is a material difference in these accounts.

Ed. See Howe's letter to Lord George Germain, *ibid.*

69. *Ch.* Several persons, among others some English officers who were prisoners, whom I questioned, assure me that Knyphausen's corps crossed the river only in one column at Chadd's Ford; but that it then separated into two parts, one of which turned the battery and the other attacked it in front.

70. Chastellux's text reads "General Wayne"; Grieve changed this to read "General Washington."

71. *Gr.* Howe's account says, there were two divisions, one under Grant, the other under Knyphausen; the fourth and fifth regiments turned the battery.

Ed. See Howe's letter to Germain, Oct. 10, 1777, *ibid.*, 427. John Graves Simcoe in his *Remarks on the Travels of the Marquis de Chastellux* (pp. 5-6 *n.*) makes the following comment: "The Marquis is in doubt whether the British troops who passed Chad's Ford, were in one or two columns. Though I have failed in my enquiries relative to this point, I have met with an anecdote that may illustrate his account, and deserves to be made more generally known. The Marquis was informed that the redoubt which Mr. Washington had thrown up to cover Chad's Ford 'could not be taken unless turned.' Lieutenant Colonel Moncrief (then captain) was in the front of a column which advanced to a redoubt. There was a howitzer in it, loaded with grapeshot, pointed directly towards the column and a man standing by it, with a lighted match in his hand. Colonel Moncrief, with his usual presence of mind, called out 'I'll put you to death if you fire.' The Man threw down the match and ran off. Had he fired he could equally have escaped, and in all probability Colonel Moncrief had not lived to display his energy and abilities in the defence of Savannah and the conquest of Charles Town."

72. The Marquis de Castries had replaced the Comte de Sartine as French Minister of Marine in October 1780. His son, Armand-Charles-Augustin de la Croix de Castries (1756-1842), then Comte de Charlus, was among the young officers serving with Rochambeau's army in America. In a letter to the Minister written from Newport, Apr. 3, 1781, Chastellux sent Castries news of his son, and of his "new daughter," the French Navy; original in French archives, photostat in Lib. Cong., transcription in Carson, The Chevalier de Chastellux, 145-48.

73. *Gr.* Mrs. Withy's inn at Chester, is one of the best on the continent, and a favourite house for parties of pleasure from Philadelphia.

Ed. Mary Withy (or Withey), widow of James Withy, an English officer, acquired Richard Barry's tavern in 1771 and presided over it until 1796. It was situated at the northeast corner of Market and Fifth Sts. Later known as "The Columbia House," it was demolished late in the 19th century to make way for an office building (now Chester-Cambridge Bank and Trust Co.); photographs of the inn before its demolition are in the collections of the Del. Co. Hist. Soc. at Chester. Mrs. Withy's is not to be confused with another 18th-century inn, where Washington wrote his midnight dispatch to the President of Congress after the defeat at Brandywine, the so-called "Washington House," which was also on Market St., between Fourth and Fifth, opposite the Court House; it was demolished only in 1952. Henry Graham Ashmead, *Historical Sketch of Chester, on Delaware* (Chester, Pa., 1883), 86-87 and map.

74. *Ch.* (note added to 2d ed., 1788). We neglected to point out in the first edition of these Travels that if the author has often spoken of the inns and the fare he found there, this was not unintentional; such details are in fact found in all travel journals and give them that note of simplicity and even of artlessness which has hitherto been supposed to constitute the characteristic of this type of book. The author's object has always been to give a correct idea of the region in which he was traveling: the lack of resources offered by a locality might, for example, depict the misfortunes of war or the simplicity of a new settlement, while, on the other hand, the ease and even the luxury that he sometimes met with might offer a striking contrast to the general distress or to the preconceived notions held in Europe about a people believed to be still in its infancy. Wine, for instance, is an article of luxury in America (and even in England), so that finding it in an inn there is as unusual as for a traveler in France to find lodging in rooms hung with damask and ornamented with mirrors, or for him to meet with people along the road who, though curious and quick to criticize, still do not take it amiss when you try to satisfy their curiosity and give them an opportunity to criticize—for whatever is rare is also worthy of remark.

75. A valuable commentary on Chastellux's visit to the river forts is the contemporary map entitled, "The Course of Delaware River from Philadelphia to Chester with the Several Forts and Stackadoes raised by the Americans, and the Attacks made by His Majesty's Land and Sea Forces" published by William Faden (London, 1778, and later issues, with revisions); insets show "A Plan of Fort Mifflin on Mud Island" as well as profiles and plans of the chevaux-de-frise or stackadoes. The map is reproduced, for example, in Leonard Lundin, *Cockpit of the Revolution, The War for Independence in New Jersey* (Princeton, 1940), facing p. 334; Lundin's chap. 11, pp. 334-71, provides a good summary of the events. Contemporary documents, including Major de Fleury's moving journal of the siege of Fort Mifflin, are collected in Worthington Chauncey Ford, ed., *Defences of Philadelphia in 1777* (Brooklyn, N. Y., 1897, reprinted from *Pa. Mag., of Hist. and Biog.*, 18-21 [1894-97], *passim*); Benson J. Lossing's pilgrimage to the river forts in Nov. 1848, recorded in his *Field-Book*, II, 83-93, is still of considerable interest. Remains of the chevaux-de-frise (timbers, anchors, and iron prongs), salvaged from the Delaware in the 1930's, may be seen today at Red Bank Battlefield Park, N. J.

76. Plans of Fort Mifflin drawn by Major Fleury, the French engineer who served there during the siege in 1777—showing it as it was at that time and before the improvements mentioned by Chastellux—are reproduced (from originals in the Sparks Collection, Cornell University Library) in Winsor, *Narrative and Critical History*, VI, 432-35. Concerning Fleury, who was promoted to the rank of lieutenant colonel soon after the siege, see above, Pt. I, chap. 1, Nov. 22, 1780, and n. 96. Although many of the contemporary maps and documents refer to the island where Fort Mifflin was situated as "Mud Island," there was evidently some variation in the names used to designate the different small islands here at the mouth of the Schuylkill; some maps call it "Port Island," others show a small island upstream from it (probably connected at low tide) called "Little Mud Island." This varying terminology explains Chastellux's own reference to "the island on which this fort [Mifflin] was built, *and* the one called Mud Island." See Freeman, *Washington*, IV, 527, n. 34.

77. *Gr.* The person principally employed in sinking the chevaux de frise, and in securing the passage of the river, was one White, who is supposed to have left this channel open designedly, as he afterwards turned out a decided traitor, went over to the enemy, and distinguished himself by every act of hostile virulence against his country.

Ed. "One White" was Robert Whyte, a sea captain established in Philadelphia prior to the war. Taking the hint thrown out by the Translator as a starting-point, John W. Wallace has meticulously collected the corroborative evidence pointing to Whyte's treason in his *An Old Philadelphian, Colonel William Bradford, The Patriot Printer of 1776* (Phila., 1884), 228-42.

78. *Gr.* This is one of the richest spots of land in America, and being part of the proprietary estate, was parcelled out, and sold in lots by the Assembly of the State.

Ed. Province Island is no longer an island; it now forms part of the lowlands at the mouth of the Schuylkill extending eastward from the Penrose Avenue Bridge to the Delaware, northeast of the Philadelphia International Airport.

79. It was in June 1778 (after the British withdrawal from Philadelphia) that Washington instructed his chief engineer Duportail to prepare new plans for the defense of the Delaware. Maps executed by Major Villefranche, one of Duportail's assistants, survive in the Bureau of Land Records, Commonwealth of Pennsylvania, Harrisburg. These recently rediscovered maps are described by Hubertis M. Cummings in two articles: "Draughts by Two of Washington's French Engineers," *Internal Affairs* (Bulletin of Dept. Internal Affairs, Commonwealth Pa., 28 [1960]), 24-28; "The Villefranche Map for the Defense of the Delaware," *Pa. Mag. of Hist. and Biog.*, 84 (1960), 424-34. (Unfortunately neither article reproduces the maps; photostats in Princeton Univ. Lib.) Although the largest of these maps shows the Mud Island fort as it was prior to Duportail's survey and also (by means of a hinged overlay) as it would be after the proposed improvements, the detailed map of the fort referred to in another of the surviving plans (perhaps the very map shown to Chastellux by Major Armstrong on the spot) has not been found. Von Closen, one of Rochambeau's aides, who saw Mud Island in early September, 1781, noted

that they were trying to finish the fort but that the Americans really worked only on threatened places. Acomb, ed., *Von Closen Journal*, 121.

Fort Mifflin was subsequently rebuilt, during President Adams's administration at the time of the threatened war with France in 1798, by another French engineer, Major Anne-Louis Tousard (1749-1817); Tousard had earlier served in the American Revolution and then returned to America as an *émigré* during the French Revolution. The fort was again repaired during the Civil War and was maintained as a military post until the mid-20th century. The old fort proper, forming an enclave within the U.S. Army Engineer Corps military reservation at Fort Mifflin, has recently been relinquished to the City of Philadelphia which is now considering plans for its restoration and maintenance as an historic site. The fort as it exists today in its "seedy limbo" is essentially Tousard's 1798 construction, which itself incorporated the main features of the Duportail-Villefranche plan that Chastellux saw in 1780. Modern photographs will be found in G. Edwin Brumbaugh, *Fort Mifflin on Historic Mud Island in the Delaware River, Philadelphia: Report to the Greater Philadelphia Movement upon historical aspects and preservation problems* (Phila., 1959).

80. The site of Fort Mercer, the Red Bank fort, is preserved at Red Bank Battlefield Park, on the eastern shore of the Delaware, three miles from Woodbury, Gloucester Co., N. J. The outlines of the earthworks are discernible there; salvaged relics of the river obstructions may be seen at the entrance to the park. The "Quaker's house," mentioned by Chastellux, still stands; this is the Whitall House, maintained by the Ann Whitall Chapter of the Daughters of the American Revolution, and open to the public. The occupants of the house at the time of the battle—and of Chastellux's visit— were James Whitall (1717-1808) and his wife Ann Cooper Whitall (1716-97). An itemized claim for damages "done to James Whiteall by the American forces" in 1777, submitted to the state of New Jersey Apr. 17, 1779, mentions as a part of the total claim for £5760-1-0, "one Barn and Hayhouse totally destroy'd and Damages done to Sundry other buildings—£350," and "an Orchard near 300 trees all Grafted Trees—£100"; Frank H. Stewart, *Notes on Old Gloucester County, New Jersey*, 2 vols. (Camden, N. J., 1917, 1934), II, 167. A diary kept during the period of the battle by James and Ann Whitall's son, Job Whitall (1743-97), reflects the family's imperturbability by ignoring details of the fighting, but speaks of the requisitions and of moving other property to safety; *ibid.*, I, 255-61. Duplessis-Mauduit's account of the affair at Red Bank and of Col. Donop's death, as related by him to Chastellux (three years after the event) and recorded here in the latter's *Travels*, is one of the principal (although often unrecognized) sources for all subsequent accounts, and evidently became at an early date intertwined with "local tradition." See, for example, Alfred M. Heston, *Red Bank; ... Defence of Fort Mercer* (Atlantic City [?], N. J., 1900), and Frank H. Stewart, *History of the Battle of Red Bank* (Woodbury, N. J., 1927). Several such accounts suggest that Chastellux was incorrect in assuming that Col. Donop died in the Whitall House, where he was probably first transported with the other Hessian wounded; Stewart believes that he was "taken across Woodbury Creek Dam to the house of Joseph Low where he died October 28." Duplessis-Mauduit had another opportunity to describe the Red Bank affair when accompanying Rochambeau down the Delaware from Philadelphia to Chester on Sept. 5, 1781; Rochambeau's aide, Von

Closen, records in his *Journal* (pp. 121-22) that Donop before dying had given his sword to Duplessis-Mauduit as a special mark of his esteem, and that Duplessis still had it.

81. Virgil, *Aeneid*, Book VI, 450-476. Aeneas, when journeying through Hades, sees among those who have died of love, Dido, who receives in silence his protestations: "She turned away, her eyes fixed on the ground; / nor, as he pleaded, was her face more moved / Than if she stood there, a hard block of flint, / Or cold Marpesian marble."

82. A "Plan of Fort Mercer, at Red Bank, New Jersey," from surveys made in 1842 by T. S. and E. Saunders of Woodbury, is in John W. Barber and Henry Howe, *Historical Collections of the State of New Jersey* (N. Y., 1844), 210. This plan, which has been copied in later works (Lossing, *et al.*), clearly shows the "reduction of the fortifications" effected by Duplessis-Mauduit. The Congressional resolution of Jan. 19, 1778, promoting Duplessis-Mauduit, upon Washington's recommendation, to the rank of lieutenant colonel in the American army reviews in glowing terms his services at Red Bank and specifically mentions that he "made several judicious alterations in the works" there. The resolution also cites Washington's further remark that "he possesses a degree of modesty not always found in men who have performed brilliant actions." Ford *et al.*, eds., *Journals of Cont. Cong.*, X, 64.

83. *Gr.* General Howe calls them *about* 800 men.

Ed. See Howe's letter to Lord George Germain, reporting on the Red Bank affair, Philadelphia, Oct. 25, 1777, *Parliamentary Register* (1802 reprint), X, 438.

84. *Gr.* As there appears to be some little inaccuracy in this account of the conversation, the reader is referred to the Constitution of the Massachusetts, as republished in England with those of the other states [*The Constitutions of the several Independent States of America*... (Phila., 1781, reprinted London, 1782; Sabin, Nos. 16086, 16087)], where he will see the respective privileges and powers of the *Senate* and *Governor* and *Council* clearly discriminated, which are here confounded. The Translator has endeavoured to free the original from its obscurity, the *Senate* being there wholly overlooked, and its duties blended with those of the Governor and Council; and materially to preserve the drift of Mr. Adams' argument.

Ed. Grieve's revisions have been retained in the present text. For an excellent documentary collection of materials relating to the Massachusetts Constitution of 1780, see Robert J. Taylor, ed., *Massachusetts, Colony to Commonwealth: Documents on the Formation of Its Constitution, 1775-1780* (Chapel Hill, 1961).

85. *Gr.* I have some reason to think that the admirable form of government for Massachusetts Bay, is *not* the work of Mr. Samuel Adams, but of Mr. *John Adams*, the present [1786] Minister Plenipotentiary from the United States, in England.

Ed. In the 2nd edition of his book (1788) Chastellux modified his original statement to read "for he [Samuel Adams] had a very large share in the formation of the new laws," and added this new footnote: "This new constitution is generally looked upon as the work of Mr. John Adams; but these two justly celebrated men are no less united by patriotic bonds than by ties of kinship." Still earlier, a few days after his return to Paris, Chastellux had met John Adams and upon that occasion tactfully gave John to understand that he considered *him* the author. That at least is what John thought, for he recorded in his diary, March 8, 1783: "Dined at Passy, the Spanish Ambassador, the Comte de Rochambeau, the Chevalier de Chatelux, Mr. Jay etc. present. Chatelux said to the Abbé Morlaix [Morellet] that I was the Author of the Massachusetts Constitution, and that it was the best of em all, and that the People were very contented with it." L. H. Butterfield *et al.*, eds., *Diary and Autobiography of John Adams*, 4 vols. (Cambridge, Mass., 1961), III, 110.

Although Chastellux's original statement was undoubtedly too strong, he was nevertheless right in continuing to credit Samuel Adams with some share in the Massachusetts constitution, in spite of Grieve's flat contradiction. Both Samuel and John were delegates to the Massachusetts constitutional convention of 1779, and, with James Bowdoin, comprised the three-man sub-committee entrusted with the drafting of a constitution. This sub-committee in turn delegated to John Adams the task of preparing the final draft, which, after a few modifications, was submitted to the people and approved by the necessary majority. The new constitution went into effect in June 1780; with the amendments made at subsequent conventions, it is still the fundamental law of Massachusetts. Louis Adams Frothingham, *A Brief History of the Constitution and Government of Massachusetts* (Boston, 1925); John Adams to E. Jenings, June 7, 1780, in Charles Francis Adams, ed., *Works of John Adams*, 10 vols. (Boston, 1850-56), IV, 213 ff.; William V. Wells, *The Life and Public Services of Samuel Adams...*, 3 vols. (Boston, 1865), III, 80-97 (where Chastellux's statement is cited as evidence that contemporaries thought of Samuel Adams as one of the makers of the Massachusetts constitution).

86. Benezet probably asked for this information in behalf of the Humane Society of Philadelphia founded in 1780 for the recovery of drowned persons; Scharf and Westcott, *History of Philadelphia*, II, 1477. Chastellux must have relayed the request to Dr. Coste, chief physician of Rochambeau's army, who was also stationed in Newport. In a memorandum recounting Coste's services in America, sent to Franklin *ca.* 1783 by Lafayette and Chastellux in an effort to enlist support for obtaining Coste's membership in the Society of the Cincinnati (not generally granted to medical corps officials, who were not considered military officers), it is stated: "In 1780 he was consulted by the Humane Society which had just been formed in Philadelphia. He transmitted to this company a detailed memorandum on the different sorts of asphyxia. The Society expressed its satisfaction to him, by letters of thanks and a diploma of correspondent." Franklin Papers, LVII, 123, Amer. Phil. Soc. Michaud's *Biographie des Hommes Vivants* (Paris, 1816-17), II, 244-45, in the article on Jean-François Coste (1741-1819), cites as one of his publications a "Mémoire sur l'Asphyxie, demandé par la Société Humaine de Philadelphie à l'Ambassadeur de France, Philadelphie, 1780, traduit en anglais"; see John E. Lane, *Jean-François Coste, Chief Physician of the French Expeditionary Forces in the American Revolution* (Somerville, N. J., and N. Y., 1928; reprinted from *Americana*, 22 [1928]), 9-10, and Bibliography No. 16. Lane was unable to locate a copy of this publication, and the present Editor has likewise failed to do so. It seems probable that the "Mémoire" was never actually published, although some of the information supplied by it may have been utilized in the pamphlet on the subject issued by the Humane Society: *Directions for Recovering Persons who are supposed to be Dead, from Drowning...*

(Phila., n.d., Evans, No. 21159); see also broadsides, with extracts from same text, Evans, Nos. 22121.1, 23746.1; copies in Lib. Co. of Phila. Coste's membership in the Humane Society of Philadelphia (*ex humana Societati Philadelphiensi*) is included in the list of his academic honors recapitulated in the diploma of his College of William and Mary honorary degree; see below, Pt. II, chap. 5, n. 17.

87. For a comprehensive and readable account of the life of Benezet see: George S. Brookes, *Friend Anthony Benezet* (Phila., 1937).

88. The pamphlets given to Chastellux by Benezet must have included his *A Short Account of the People called Quakers; Their Rise, Religious Principles and Settlement in America, Mostly collected from different Authors, for the Information of all serious Inquirers, particularly Foreigners*, of which there was also a French version, *Observations sur l'Origine, les Principes, et l'Etablissement en Amérique de la Société connue sous la Dénomination de Quakers ou Trembleurs...*; both were printed in Phila., 1780; Evans, Nos. 16711-16713.

89. Chastellux's remarks on the Quakers, here and in his journal entry of the next day, supplied the main pretext for Brissot de Warville's *Examen critique des Voyages...de M. le Marquis de Chatellux*. More than half (pp. 5-82) of the future Girondist's pamphlet was devoted to a "justification of the Quakers" and to a refutation of what he terms Chastellux's "violent" and "slanderous diatribes" against them. Brissot wrote his attack on Chastellux before his own trip to America in 1788—a journey that did not materially change any of his preconceived and somewhat idealized notions of the country. In his account of the trip Brissot devoted two chapters to the Quakers, reminding his readers "with what insulting frivolity M. Chatelux has treated them in the very superficial Journey that he published," and then, after recalling his own *Examen critique*, states: "I have here been able to compare the portrait I had painted of the Quakers with the originals, and I have convinced myself that, save for a few errors, the portrait is not exaggerated." *Nouveau Voyage dans les Etats-Unis*, 3 vols. (Paris, 1791), II, 167-249. When he was in Philadelphia Brissot apparently arranged for the publication of an English translation of his pamphlet; see above, Check-list, No. 18. Again in his *Mémoires* (ed. Claude Perroud [Paris, 1912], II, 46-47), Brissot recalls the circumstances of his *Examen critique*, which he characterizes as the best of his pamphlets and the one he prefers above all his many other writings. For a discussion of Brissot's pamphlet v. Chastellux in the general context of French thinking about Quakers and about America, see Edith Phillips, *The Good Quaker in French Legend* (Phila., 1932); Antonello Gerbi, *La Disputa del Nuovo Mondo, Storia di una polemica, 1750-1900* (Milan and Naples, 1955), 651-74.

90. *Gr.* In confirmation of this remark, I cannot avoid referring to a circumstance which made a considerable noise at the time, and has been grossly perverted to the discredit of American humanity. Every reader attentive to the events of the war in that country, must recollect the execution [Nov. 4, 1778] of [Abraham] Carlisle and [John] Roberts, two considerable quakers, after the evacuation of Philadelphia by General Clinton; the barbarity of putting to death two members of a sect so peaceable and inoffensive, who *had not borne arms*, and whose principles forbid an active opposition to *any* form of government, was much enlarged upon. In justice

to America, and for the benefit of future historians, I shall give the fact, the truth of which will bear inquiry, as I had it from men of every party and description in that city, and leave the decision to every impartial man. The quakers in America, I speak generally, had long belied their principles, and covertly and openly done every thing in their power to thwart the measures adopted by a vast majority of their countrymen, then in possession of the government; their secret intrigues and open defiance were long over-looked and borne with, until danger became so critical as to demand some precautions for the common safety. A few of the most *active* spirits amongst these pacific and *passive* sectaries were arrested, and sent from the immediate scene of action into Virginia, where they suffered only a temporary restraint from mischief. Carlisle and Roberts, though well known for a malignant hatred to the cause of America, unfortunately for them, escaping this tem-porary exile, continued their clandestine practices until General Howe got possession of the city, when they no longer set any bounds to their invet-eracy. They were both employed by the general, or his honest and grateful agent Mr. Galloway, in the administration of the police, or in other words, they undertook, Carlisle in particular, to discriminate between the loyalists and friends to America. Carlisle granted permission to pass the lines, watched at the gates, to point out obnoxious persons coming in from the country, who were frequently committed to prison on his bare suggestion, and exer-cised, in short, the office of sub-inquisitor to Mr. Joseph Galloway. Nor was this the only method by which they manifested the peaceable principles of their sect. General Howe having received information of a party of militia lying in the woods, in the county of Bucks, at sixteen miles distance, under General Lacey, despatched Lieutenant-Colonel Abercrombie with a con-siderable detachment by the Frankford road to attack them; and one or both of these harmless quakers who would not *bear arms* for the wealth of Britain, conscientiously undertook to conduct this man of blood to a success-ful surprise and massacre of their own countrymen. These, and a variety of other facts being proved against them, after the evacuation of the town, where they had the *presumption* to remain, and there being an evident neces-sity for making an example of these most dangerous of all enemies, lenity would have been as ill-timed as unjust to the suffering citizens. Such, I am sorry to say it, was the undoubted conduct of too many of this once respectable body, during the war, a conduct, which must not only be con-demned by every honourable and feeling mind, but I may venture to say, is wholly repugnant to the principles of a Lettson, a Fothergill, a Barclay, or a William Penn; for, it may be pronounced with no intolerant spirit, that in case of critical emergency, no society can endure such members. In opposition, however, to newspaper reports, and their cries of persecution, I can myself bear testimony to the unpublished licence these quietists gave their tongues in the very seat of Congress, and in defiance of the assembly of the state, and to their ostentatious display of the portraits of the king and queen of England, which, however, there is every reason to believe, was more the result of obstinacy, and the spirit of contradiction, than of loyalty or reason, in this selfish set of people.

Ed. Concerning Carlisle and Roberts, see Scharf and Westcott, *History of Philadelphia,* I, 394. For a discussion of their treason trials, see Charles Page Smith, *James Wilson, Founding Father, 1742-1798* (Chapel Hill, 1956), 119-23.

91. The Quaker meetinghouse that Chastellux visited was probably the "Greater Meeting House" at the southwest corner of Second and Market Streets. None of the Quaker meetinghouses used in 1780 is now standing. The Greater Meeting House was succeeded, as the center of Philadelphia Quakerdom, by the newer and larger structure erected in 1804, and still standing, at Fourth and Arch Sts. See Edwin B. Bronner, "Quaker Landmarks in Early Philadelphia," *Historic Philadelphia*, 210-16.

92. *Gr.* Mention has frequently been made in the public prints of the new sect of *shakers* in Massachusetts Bay, who carry their frantic orgies to still more ridiculous and licentious excesses than the pristine quakers, with George Fox at their head; but I have seen no notice taken of another, which sprung up at Rhode Island about the year 1780. A very comely *young woman* [Jemima Wilkinson, "the Universal Friend" (1752-1819)] is, or pretends to be, impressed with the belief that she is in her person *the saviour of the world* revived, and travels from place to place, attended by twelve young men, whom she calls *her apostles;* who, if the general assertion be credited, have literally followed the precept of "making eunuchs of themselves for Christ's sake." General Gates told me he heard her preach at Rhode Island, and I made an attempt to hear her at Philadelphia in October 1782, but the crowd was so great, and, what is very uncommon in America, so turbulent, that it was impossible to get near the place of worship. Two of her apostles came to the house I boarded in, to obtain lodgings for her, and some of the brethren; by which means I had an opportunity of seeing a specimen of them, but they would enter into no conversation; they were tall, handsome young men, the youngest not above nineteen, with large round flapped hats, and long flowing strait locks, with a sort of melancholy wildness in their countenances, and an effeminate, dejected air, which seemed to justify the truth of what I believe literally to be their unfortunate situation.

Ed. For accounts of "the Universal Friend," see Robert P. St. John, "Jemima Wilkinson," N. Y. State Hist. Assn., *Quarterly*, 11 (1930), 158-75, and John Quincy Adams, "Jemima Wilkinson, The Universal Friend," *Journal of American History*, 9 (1915), 249-63.

93. The Anglican church here described is Christ Church, on Second St. between Market and Arch, built 1727-44, one of the most "handsome" surviving examples of colonial architecture, and still one of the sights of Old Philadelphia. See Robert W. Shoemaker, "Christ Church, St. Peter's, and St. Paul's," *Historic Philadelphia*, 187-98. The "handsome pulpit" (1770) was designed by John Folwell, who also, with Parnell Gibbs, built the Chippendale-style case for the Rittenhouse orrery which Chastellux saw in the library of the College of Philadelphia. The "handsome Minister" was the Reverend William White, Rector of Christ Church from 1779 until his death in 1836 (above, this chap., n. 7).

94. A reference to Sedaine and Monsigny's *Le Déserteur*, Act III, Scene 4 (see above, this chap., n. 11). Montauciel, the dragoon, has always been too busy drinking to learn his letters. Attempting to read a paper on which a comrade has written *"Vous êtes un blanc bec"* (You are a simpleton), he makes nonsense by misreading the words as *"trompette blessé"*; then, when he appeals for help and his prison-mate Alexis (the deserter) reads the sentence correctly, Montauciel takes it as an insult and proceeds to knock his unsuspecting helper down. In the operetta Montauciel spells out the

letters in a humorous arietta, the tune of which was presumably very familiar to Chastellux and his Parisian contemporaries. The entire scene is omitted in Dibdin's English adaptation of *The Deserter.*

In his *Examen critique* (1786), pp. 62-63, Brissot de Warville takes Chastellux severely to task for his "strange citation of the *Deserter*" and "this comparison between the Sectarian who is mistaken, and Montauciel who sees in his Letters what is not there."

95. After the Germantown engagement Washington had retired to Perkiomen Creek and then moved progressively eastward to Whitemarsh, where the army was encamped from Nov. 2 until Dec. 11, 1777, when it again moved westward to winter quarters at Valley Forge. Early in Dec. General William Howe marched out from Germantown towards Whitemarsh, but after a few skirmishes, marched back again, Dec. 8, without assaulting the American position. This episode—like all those connected with the Philadelphia campaign—was much discussed in the Parliamentary inquiry (1779) on the conduct of the war in America and in the pamphlet controversies that ensued. In his dispatch to Lord Germain, Dec. 13, 1777, Howe had written of Whitemarsh: "The enemy's camp being as strong on their center and left as upon their right, their seeming determination to hold this position, and unwilling to expose the troops longer in this inclement season, without tents or baggage of any kind, . . . I returned on the 8th." In the course of the examination of witnesses during the inquiry Major General Grey, one of Howe's subordinates, stated: "I think an attack of the enemy, so very strongly situated as they were at White-Marsh, would have been highly imprudent." *Parliamentary Register* (1802 reprint), X, 449; XII, 19. Chastellux, in his bantering argument with Lafayette (who had been present at Whitemarsh during the American army's encampment there in 1777) implicitly credits Howe with sound military judgment in not attacking the Americans.

The Whitemarsh "position" described by Chastellux can still be reconnoitered, although it is now so well enmeshed in highways and turnpikes, new and old, that it takes an eagle's eye to discover it. The hills and streams mentioned are identified in brackets in the text. Remains of a redoubt may be seen on Fort Hill, which is situated in an exclave of Fort Washington Park (Commonwealth of Pa., Dept. of Forests and Waters) lying just north of the Pennsylvania Turnpike. The entrance is from the old Bethlehem Road, a short distance south of the village of Fort Washington (Montgomery Co.); a granite marker along the highway (erected in 1891 by the Pennsylvania Society of Sons of the Revolution) recalls the 1777 encampment.

For contemporary maps, see an American map (Hist. Soc. of Pa.) reproduced in Freeman, *Washington*, IV, 530; and British maps in H. C. Lodge, ed., *André's Journal*, I, 124-25, 128-29.

96. Mrs. Shippen (*née* Alice Lee) was the wife of Dr. William Shippen the younger (1736-1808), whose residence was at the southwest corner of Fourth and Prune (now Locust) Sts. The house, generally referred to as the Shippen-Wistar House, is still standing. "Miss Shippen," the daughter of the house, was Ann ("Nancy") Hume Shippen (1763-1841), the moving story of whose blighted romance with Louis-Guillaume Otto is the subject of *Nancy Shippen, Her Journal Book, The International Romance of a Young Lady of Fashion of Colonial Philadelphia, with letters to her and about her,* comp. and ed. Ethel Armes (Phila., 1935). This book reproduces

in facsimile the manuscript of a "Menuet of Strasbourg," composed by Otto for Miss Shippen—no doubt one of the "several pieces" which Chastellux heard at the tea party. It was only three months later, on Mar. 14, 1781, that Nancy Shippen was forced by her parents into a tragic marriage with Henry Beekman Livingston. Louis-Guillaume Otto (1754-1817), in 1787, married Eliza Livingston, who died within a year thereafter; in 1790 he married Frances-America ("Fanny") de Crèvecoeur; Otto, later Comte de Mosloy, had a distinguished career in the French diplomatic service, being one of the negotiators of the Peace of Amiens in 1802, Napoleon's minister in Bavaria, etc.

97. *Gr.* It is very certain that any person educated in Europe, and accustomed to the luxury of music and the fine arts, and to their enjoyment in the two capitals of France and England, must find a great void in these particulars in America. This the translator experienced during his residence in that country, and felt the contrast with greater force on his return to Europe. After a long absence, in which he heard scarcely any other music than church hymns, the cannon, and the drum; or viewing any paintings but the little sketches of Cimetiere [Du Simitière], or the portraits of Peele [Peale], of Philadelphia: on his arrival at Bordeaux after the peace, the common orchestra at the theatre afforded him more exquisite delight than he had ever felt from one of Haydn's best symphonies at Bach's, or than he should now feel perhaps at the Westminster commemorations of Handel; and the very moderate exhibition at the Louvre, was, to him, a group of Raphaels, Titians, and Vandykes.

98. Lafayette's own account of the affair at Barren Hill—which took place May 18-20, 1778, about a month before the British evacuation of Philadelphia —will be found in his *Mémoires,* I, 46-48, 75-76; a good recapitulation is in Tower, *La Fayette in the American Revolution,* I, 326-39; a critical examination, with discussion of sources, in Louis Gottschalk, *Lafayette Joins the American Army* (Chicago, 1937), 184-93, 203. A "Plan de la Retraite de Barrenhill en Pensilvanie...le 28 [*sic*] May 1778" drawn by Lafayette's aide-de-camp, Major Michel Capitaine du Chesnoy, is in John Carter Brown Lib. (see *Annual Report, 1953-1954,* 27-28); a variant version of the same map is reproduced by both Tower and Gottschalk.

The three roads mentioned are: Ridge Road, which leads eastward from Swede's Ford (near present Norristown) over the height of land between the Schuylkill and the Wissahickon, and thence into Philadelphia; the Germantown Road, further to the northeast; and the more circuitous route passing through Whitemarsh. The present St. Peter's Lutheran Church at Barren Hill (a short distance northeast of Ridge Pike on the road connecting with the Germantown Pike) is on the site of the earlier edifice; a marker in front of the church recalls that "Here Lafayette's Army took defence behind the Old Stone Wall of the Burial Grounds, when surrounded by the British on May 19, 1778, before they masterfully retreated down the Road westward to Matson's Ford at Conshohocken by way of Spring Mill." Another marker, by the side of Ridge Pike, before reaching Barren Hill when approaching from Philadelphia, mentions the campground of the American troops, and the encampment of the Indian scouts. Chastellux's statement that there was only one ford by which Lafayette could retreat across the Schuylkill appears to be a misconception; he crossed at Swede's Ford (below present Norristown) when he advanced to Barren Hill, but retreated by way of Matson's

Ford (Conshohocken), which was downstream from the former and closer to Barren Hill.

Colonel de Gimat, who was with Chastellux and Lafayette on their pilgrimage to Barren Hill, had participated in the 1778 affair as Lafayette's aide-de-camp.

99. *Gr.* The English had brought with them from New York, a company of players, and the officers themselves frequently performed the principal characters. An excellent trait this for the future historians of the civil war, as well as the *Meschianza*, that illustrious act of folly and infatuation; facts truly characteristic of the dissipation, and decline of a great people.

Ed. The *Meschianza*, an elaborate *fête* in honor of General Howe, managed by Major André, took place on May 18, 1778, a month before the evacuation of Philadelphia by the English; ever since Major André himself published an account of it in the *Gentleman's Mag.*, 48 (1778), 353-57, it has continued to supply copy for antiquarians and historical journalists; Scharf and Westcott, *Hist. of Phila.*, I, 377-82.

100. *Ed.* A map of Philadelphia and environs showing the route taken by the French army in early Sept. 1781 (i.e., nine months after Chastellux's present excursion), indicates the "maison à M^r le Ch^{er} de la Luzerne" on the east bank of the Schuylkill below the Falls. Berthier Papers, No. 16-4, Princeton Univ. Lib. This is presumably "Laurel Hill," one of the confiscated Loyalist estates, which had belonged to Mrs. Samuel Shoemaker, whose husband served as assistant to Joseph Galloway in the civil administration of Philadelphia during the British occupation in 1777-78. According to the terms of the Act of Attainder and Confiscation, the state could rent out such properties until they were sold. Laurel Hill was purchased early in 1782 by James Parr and there is record of a lease to the Chevalier de La Luzerne at that time. It seems likely, however, that La Luzerne rented it from the state still earlier; Joseph Reed and family occupied it during the summer of 1780 until Mrs. Reed's death there in September; La Luzerne might therefore have made arrangements to rent it during the autumn of 1780 and it could thus have been the "pretty country house" that Chastellux saw in Dec. 1780 and which is recorded on the Berthier map of Sept. 1781. "Laurel Hill," also known as the Randolph Mansion (not to be confused with the Laurel Hill Cemetery tract a mile or so up river), still stands on the bluff overlooking the Schuylkill, in East Fairmount Park, between "Ormiston" and "Strawberry Mansion." William B. Rawle, "Laurel Hill, and Some Colonial Dames Who Once Lived There," *Pa. Mag. of Hist. and Biog.*, 35 (1911), 385-414, illus.; Francis B. Brandt and Henry V. Gummere, *Byways and Boulevards in and about Historic Philadelphia* (Phila., 1925), 118-20, illus.; Eberlein and Hubbard, *Colonial City*, 299-300, illus.

Gr. The beautiful banks of the Schuylkill are everywhere covered with elegant country houses; amongst others, those of Mr. Penn, the late proprietor, Mr. Hamilton, and Mr. Peters, late Secretary to the Board of War, are on the most delightful situations. The tasty little box of the last gentleman is on the most enchanting spot that nature can embellish, and besides the variegated beauties of the rural banks of the Schuylkill, commands the Delaware, and the shipping mounting and descending it, where it is joined at right angles by the former. From hence is the most romantic ride up the river to the Falls, in which the opposite bank is likewise seen beautifully interspersed with the country houses of the opulent citizens of the capital.

On your arrival at the Falls, every little knoll or eminence is occupied by one of these charming retreats; among which General Mifflin's stands conspicuous, nor is the exterior belied by the neatness, the abundance, and hospitality which reigns within; the easy politeness, the attention, good sense, gaiety, and information of the owner; the order, arrangement, and elegance of Mrs. Mifflin, who still adhering to her sect, which her husband renounced for "the ear-piercing fife and spirit-stirring drum," possesses all its excellencies, and is what a most amiable female Quaker ought to be, render this (and I speak from knowledge and gratitude) a most delicious abode. Below this house, and close to the Falls, is a building erected by Mr. John Dickinson, the celebrated author of the Farmer's Letters [*Letters from a Farmer in Pennsylvania to the Inhabitants of the British Colonies* (Phila., 1768)], for a select society of friends, who held a weekly meeting there, before the war, during the season for eating shad. Good humour, harmony, and good sense, are said to have characterized these meetings, presided by this eminent and amiable man, whose figure, countenance, and manners always reminded me of the urbanity and virtues so characteristically portrayed in the person of the lamented, great, good man, Lord Rockingham.

Ed. The "elegant country houses" mentioned by Grieve can be identified as follows: The house of "the late proprietor," Gov. John Penn, was "Lansdowne," no longer standing; it was on the west bank of the Schuylkill on a site later incorporated into West Fairmount Park; Horticultural Hall, built for the 1876 Centennial Exposition was on this site, and the name survives in "Lansdowne Drive." Watson and Hazard, *Annals,* III, 270-73. Adjoining the Lansdowne estate was Richard Peters's "tasty little box," known as "Belmont." It is still standing in West Fairmount Park, on Belmont Mansion Drive. Eberlein and Hubbard, *Colonial City,* 254-64, illus. William Hamilton's house, "The Woodlands," which was considerably farther to the south than the two just mentioned, is still standing within the bounds of Woodlands Cemetery (the former grounds of the estate), in West Philadelphia. *Ibid.,* 447-54, illus. General Thomas Mifflin's country house, no longer standing, was on the east bank of the river on Ridge Road at Falls of Schuylkill. For a photograph of the house before its demolition, see Kenneth R. Rossman, *Thomas Mifflin and the Politics of the American Revolution* (Chapel Hill, 1952), facing p. 114. The building erected close to the Falls by John Dickinson was probably the one used by the "Society of Fort St. David's," of which Dickinson was a member. After the war this fishing club merged with a similar and more famous organization—still in existence—"The State [earlier, The Colony] in Schuylkill"; Watson and Hazard, *Annals,* III, 292-93. According to Scharf and Westcott, *History of Phila.* I, 233, the "fort" of the Society of the Fort of St. David's "was on a broad, high rock at the Falls of the Schuylkill, on the east bank, a rude timber shanty, but roomy and convenient."

Antiques (Nov. 1962), a special issue devoted to "The Houses in Fairmount Park," provides a convenient summary of the subject.

101. See above, this chap., Nov. 30, 1780, and n. 1, on the English lines.

102. See above, Pt. I, chap. 1, n. 90.

103. Richard Peters' town residence (no longer standing) was presumably on the north side of Walnut St. near the corner of Third—at least it is recorded as being there at a slightly later date; see Grant Miles Simon,

"Houses and Early Life in Philadelphia," *Historic Philadelphia*, fig. 7, 286. Peters' country house was "Belmont"; see above, this chapter, n. 100.

104. *Gr.* The Marquis might have added, *very beautiful.*

105. James Price, who providentially came to the financial aid of the French in 1780, had also rendered similar services to the Americans at the time of Gen. Montgomery's Canadian expedition in 1775. Price, a Montreal merchant (associated for a time with William Haywood), was one of the comparatively few Canadians who supported the Revolution from the beginning of the war. He was an important source of intelligence to the revolting colonists to the southward, and when Montgomery arrived before Montreal in Dec. 1775 helped negotiate the surrender of the town. Price then advanced funds for the ill-fated campaign against Quebec; on Mar. 29, 1776, Congress named him "Deputy commissary general of stores and provisions for the army of the United Colonies in Canada." The record of his services, payments to him, etc., can be traced in Ford *et al.*, eds., *Journals of Cont. Cong.*, IV-IX, *passim.* See also Justin H. Smith, *Our Struggle for the Fourteenth Colony: Canada and the American Revolution*, 2 vols. (N. Y., 1907). Chastellux apparently saw Price again later on, in Virginia, for he is mentioned as having brought letters from Gov. Harrison to the French army when it was moving northward in the summer of 1782; see Chastellux's letter to Gov. Harrison, New Castle, July 6, 1782, in Stone, *French Allies*, 503. Concerning M. de Corny and the supplying of the French army see above, Pt. I, chap. 1, nn. 41, 42.

106. *Ed.* Chastellux's text gives the names as "MM. Sharp, Flowy et Mutterson"; the Translator corrects "Mutterson" to Madison, but appends this note concerning "Flowy": "There must be an error in this name, but as the Translator can find no similitude between it and that of any of the Southern Delegates he has inserted it literally." Grieve's note must have caught Chastellux's eye and apparently shook his confidence in his own memory or handwriting, for in the 2nd edition of his book (1788) he dropped the name of "Flowy" entirely and referred only to "Sharp et Mutterson." But could not the mysterious "Flowy" have been Governor Richard Howly, delegate from Georgia, whom Chastellux had previously seen on Dec. 5, 1780?

Gr. The Marquis de Chastellux seems unfortunately to have known but little of the Southern Delegates, particularly those of *South Carolina*, whom, without any invidious comparison, he would have found men of the greatest liberality and understanding: as firm in their principles, and as ready to hazard their lives in the defence of their liberty, as the most zealous inhabitant of New England; they possessed, in general, all the taste, urbanity, and enlightened knowledge of polished Europe. In Mr. [David] Ramsay, he would have found a cultivated understanding, a persevering mind, and an active enthusiasm, founded on a thorough knowledge of the cause he was engaged in, and the most perfect conviction of its rectitude. In Mr. [Ralph] Izard, the fire and zeal of a gentleman republican, filled with indignation at the violence and excesses he had *witnessed* in the English government. In Mr. [John] Rutledge, a manly, principled determination to risk and suffer every thing, rather than again submit to the yoke of Britain, with elegant ideas of the enjoyment of life, and all the domestic virtues. In Mr. Arthur Middleton, the plainest manners, with the most refined taste; great reading, and knowledge of the world, concealed under the reserve of the mildest, and most modest nature; a complete philanthropist, but the firmest patriot; cool, steady, and unmoved at the general wreck of property and fortune, as far as he was personally concerned, but with a heart melting for the suffering and woes of others. He [Chastellux] would have found him, in short, a model of private worth, and public virtue, a good citizen, a good father, and an exemplary husband, accomplished in the letters, in the sciences, and fine arts, well acquainted with the manners and the courts of Europe, from whence he has transplanted to his country nothing but their embellishments and virtues. I speak of him with enthusiasm, for he really excited my admiration. He had made a handsome collection of paintings when in Italy, and on his travels, which were mutilated and destroyed by the ruffian hands of the European savages, who took possession of his house in Carolina.

Ed. None of the four Carolinians mentioned by Grieve (David Ramsay, Ralph Izard, John Rutledge, Arthur Middleton) was a delegate to Congress at the time of Chastellux's visit to Philadelphia in Dec. 1780; he does, however, make passing reference to Izard, who had just returned there from a European mission (above, this chap., Dec. 5, 1780).

107. Mrs. Samuel (Margaret Cadwalader) Meredith was the sister of General John Cadwalader, not his daughter, as Chastellux thought.

108. In the 1781 edition of his *Voyage* Chastellux gave the name as "Conway"; Grieve expanded the asterisks of the 1786 edition to "Mr. Chace, formerly a Delegate for Maryland." Conway, however, must have been meant, as General Cadwalader did in fact wound Conway in a duel on July 4, 1778. Thomas Conway, an Irish soldier in the French service who had come as a volunteer to America in 1777, was the chief figure in the so-called Conway Cabal which attempted to oust Washington. After his unfortunate experiences in America, he subsequently resumed honorable service elsewhere in the French army—which no doubt explains why Chastellux, out of deference for a brother officer, delicately omitted his name.

109. "I have changed my lodgings, and am now in Front Street opposite the Coffee House, next door to Aitken's bookstore," Paine had written in a letter to Gen. Nathanael Greene, Sept. 9, 1780; Philip S. Foner, ed., *The Complete Writings of Thomas Paine*, 2 vols. (N. Y., 1945), II, 1190. In a letter written upon his arrival at Lorient in France, Paine wrote to James Hutchinson of Philadelphia, Mar. 11, 1781: "P.S. Please to call at my Lodging and let them know I am well." Several letters, written after his return to America, during the autumn of 1781, are headed "Second Street." The "Coffee House" was the London Coffee House at the southwest corner of Market and Front Sts.; Robert Aitken, binder and engraver, as well as publisher and bookseller, had employed Paine, upon his arrival in America in the winter of 1774-75, as editor of the *Pennsylvania Magazine*. Paine's lodgings, at the time Chastellux visited him, were presumably therefore on the east side of Front St., not far from the corner of Market.

110. *Ed.* Chastellux softened his original comment on Thomas Paine (and on James Wilson) in the 1786 version of his text. In the Newport, 1781, edition (p. 126) this passage reads: "he has now no connection with it, and he owes this disgrace to his bad conduct. Another literary man, more respected although less distinguished, expected us for dinner; this was Mr. Wilson whom I have already mentioned . . . etc." What Chastellux terms Paine's "bad conduct" refers to his newspaper writings in 1778-79 about

the "Silas Deane affair," when his indiscretions concerning clandestine French aid to America prior to the alliance caused serious embarrassment to both American and French officials. See Alfred Owen Aldridge, *Man of Reason, The Life of Thomas Paine* (Phila., 1959), 64-77, 78-100, where La Luzerne's subsequent "sponsorship" of Paine is discussed. Only two days after Chastellux's call on Paine, La Luzerne, in a dispatch to Vergennes, Dec. 16, 1780, spoke of his desire to make further use of Paine's talents. Chastellux's revision of his original remarks about Paine thus reflects the change in the official French attitude towards him. In the 1786 edition Chastellux also added this laudatory footnote:

Ch. Mr. Paine has since published a very interesting pamphlet on the finances of America, entitled *The Crisis,* a reply to Abbé Raynal's History of the American Revolution; and several other works, which confirm the great reputation he so justly acquired by his first production.

Gr. The author is inaccurate in this particular, *The Crisis* was a sort of periodical publication, many numbers of which had appeared previous even to the arrival of the French army in America, and was adapted by Mr. Paine to every great hour, or crisis of the government, whether favorable, or unfavorable; either to urge to energy, and as a spur against supineness, or to give a countenance to misfortune, and stimulate to fresh exertions; the subject of finance was only the occasional topic of *one number* of *The Crisis,* and so great was the weight of this writer, whose situation was very different indeed from that of an English pamphleteer, however ingenious the comparison, that on great emergencies, where almost despondency might be looked for, the whole continent waited with suspense for consolation and council from *Common Sense,* his general appellation. His productions were instantly published in every town, of every state (for every town has a newspaper), on grey, brown, yellow, and black, but seldom on white paper, a very rare commodity; the people took fresh courage, and "have you read *The Crisis?*" was the specific against every political apprehension. In short, never was a writer better calculated for the meridian under which he wrote, or who knew how to adapt himself more happily to every circumstance. Considering the wonderful effect of his pamphlet of *Common Sense,* known to every man in America, and the universal ascendency he had justly acquired over the minds of the people, it is impossible, in a general distribution of cases, to appreciate the share Mr. Paine had in producing this momentous revolution. It were the height of injustice, and ingratitude, to rob him of that share of glory, which if not his only, is at least his noblest recompense.

111. James Wilson's house (no longer standing) was on the southwest corner of Walnut and Third Sts.; it was often referred to as "Fort Wilson" because of its role in the civil disturbances of 1779. See Smith, *James Wilson,* 129-39.

112. *Gr.* So varied and universal are the talents of Mr. Peters, and he is so excellent a companion, that it is not saying too much, to add, that he would form the delight of any society in Europe.

Ed. Examples of Richard Peters' famed witticisms are recorded in H. E. Scudder, ed., *Recollections of Samuel Breck* (Phila., 1877), 213-19.

113. Miss Footman is mentioned in Armes, ed., *Nancy Shippen, Her Journal Book,* 173, 182. She was probably Elizabeth Juliana Footman (1767-

1848), daughter of Richard and Eleanor Footman, who married Edward Shippen, Jr. (1758-1809) in 1785; Sellers, *Peale Portraits*, 194.

114. In his original 1781 text (p. 128) Chastellux identified Miss V*** as "Miss Vining." Grieve restored the name as "Miss Viny." This is presumably the Miss Mary Vining (1756-1821), a native of Delaware, romantically described in an article by Mrs. Henry G. Banning, "Miss Vining, a Revolutionary Belle," *American Historical Register*, 2 (1895), 1190-1205. Although this writer does not mention Chastellux's description, she unwittingly supplies a sequel to it: the dazzling and fascinating Miss Vining, she informs us, "had many offers of marriage from British as well as French officers, but for years could not persuade herself to relinquish her independence." Mary Vining, be it added, died a spinster. See Watmough, ed., "Letters of James H. Watmough," *Pa. Mag. of Hist. and Biog.*, 29 (1905), 308-9.

115. Benjamin Franklin, then in France, was president of the American Philosophical Society at this time.

116. "Three days ago," that is, prior to the time when Chastellux was writing up his journal after his return to Newport. He was elected to membership in the American Philosophical Society at the meeting of Jan. 19, 1781, over a month after his visit to the Society with Reed; the Society's minutes describe him as "Le Chevalier de Chatellux, Marshal of the Field in the Army of France, Chevalier of the Royal Military order of St. Louis and one of the forty members of the French Academy." The six others elected at this meeting were: Lafayette, Ebenezer Hazard, Hon. Thomas Bee of South Carolina, Dr. Hugh Shiell of Philadelphia, Isaac Gray of Philadelphia, and Jared Ingersoll of Philadelphia. In the archives of the Society is a letter (in English) from Chastellux written from Newport, Feb. 25, 1781: "Sir, I received your favour of Jany. 27. The agreable intelligence that you are so kind to give me acquires a new value when it comes from your hands, and meets with your approbation. I expect with impatience the Diploma which shall intittle me to a brothership with you, Sir, and all the worthy members of your Society. Though inferior to them in merit, I hope that none of those learned gentlemen will ever excell me in their attachment for their country and zeal for its success. I am, sir, with a gratitude equal to my respect, your most obedient and very humble servant, Le Chevalier de Chastellux." This letter was read at the Society's meeting of Mar. 16, 1781. Among the papers in the Society's archives is an unsigned handwritten certificate of election made out in Chastellux's name, which was presumably retained in the files as a model form. After he returned to America in 1785 Franklin, as president of the Society, apparently signed and sent out new "diplomas" to members previously elected; in a letter to Franklin written from Paris, Dec. 1, 1786, Chastellux mentions that he has received a diploma from the Philadelphia "Academy" sent by Franklin, but since he already has one dated 1781, he does not understand how it happens that he has been elected a second time. Franklin Papers, XXIV, 173 3/4, Amer. Phil. Soc. In the same letter Chastellux informs Franklin that he has sent five months earlier the two volumes of his *Voyages* and that a second edition is being published. Franklin had the two volumes bound by Robert Aitken, according to an entry under date of Mar. 27, 1787, in the latter's "Waste Book," Lib. Co. of Phila.; information from Willman Spawn.

117. *Gr.* Mr. Holker is the son of the Chevalier Holker, who died a few months ago at Rouen. The latter, being condemned to die for acting as an

officer in the Manchester regiment, in the [Jacobite] rebellion of 1745, made his escape from prison, and fled to France, where he was tempted by the government to establish the Manchester manufactory; this he repeatedly refused, until, from the wretched policy of Mr. Pelham and other Ministers to whom he represented the offers held out to him, with a request of his pardon, he was driven to accept of the proposals of the French court. England knows too well, at this hour, the success with which his endeavours have been crowned. On the arrival of the American commissioners in France, Mr. Holker [i.e., John Holker, "Chevalier Holker," 1719-86] was among the first, and most zealous in his offers of every assistance in his power, and entered into the most intimate connexion with them. In 1777 his son [Jean, or John Holker, 1745-1822] was sent to Paris to be near Dr. Franklin, and had many opportunities of rendering essential services. In 1778 he went out to America with Monsieur Gérard, the first French Ambassador, in D'Estaing's squadron, as Consul General of France. He had not been long in the country before he entered into very advantageous commercial speculations, jointly with his father's countryman, Mr. Robert Morris, and by means of his situation as Consul, had many opportunities of shipping flour, etc. under permissions for the French fleet, in the time of a general and strict embargo; he speculated largely too in paper money, with which he purchased, for almost nothing, a very handsome house at Philadelphia, and an elegant country house, and estate a few miles from that city. Mr. Holker displayed, during the whole war, a state and luxury hitherto strangers in America; his house was the resort of all the first people on the Continent, and after the arrival of the French army, of all their officers of distinction. The French court, however, on some representations of the Chevalier de La Luzerne, thought fit to prohibit their Consuls from all private commerce, a wise regulation universally established by them; and Mr. Holker preferring the advantages of trade, to those of his office, resigned the latter, about the beginning of 1781, which for some time occasioned a coolness between the Minister and him; he had likewise a difference with Mr. Morris on settling their accounts to a very large amount, which has detained him in America, since the peace; but, if I am rightly informed, it is at length terminated. In 1777, I supped with Mr. Deane, *then* a strenuous friend to his country, on his return from Havre de Grace; where he told me, that on giving the usual toasts of "the Congress," etc. after dinner, the old gentleman [i.e., Holker *père*] could not forbear reflecting on the mutability of human affairs, and that he who was an exile, and had nearly suffered death for his zealous attachment to the cause of arbitrary monarchy, should now be as ardent in his wishes for the success of the most pure democracy that had ever been proposed to human understanding. And in fact this is more striking, as the most strenuous supporters of the American war were found in Scotland, and his native town of Manchester; in the very seat, and sources of rebellion against liberty; in the persons of the very actors, in the attempt to overthrow the English constitution, and dethrone the Brunswick family.

Ed. Concerning the elder Holker—who was in 1775 granted *lettres de noblesse* by Louis XVI (thus giving him the title of "Chevalier")—see André Rémond, *John Holker, Manufacturer et Grand Fonctionnaire en France au XVIIIe siècle, 1719-1786* (Paris, 1946). Although concerned mainly with the elder John Holker, Rémond's work also includes some information about the son (pp. 95, 103-4, 112, 119-29). In addition to the material in the official archives of France and the United States, there are papers of John Holker the younger in the manuscripts collections of the Library of Congress and the William L. Clements Library, Ann Arbor. Prior to its partial destruction by fire, Jan. 2, 1780, Holker had lived in the Richard Penn house on Market St.; where he had his establishment at the time of Chastellux's visit has not been precisely determined, perhaps in the Samuel Shoemaker house on Arch St. "Selections from Philadelphia Newspapers of 1772, 1779, 1780," *Pa. Mag. of Hist. and Biog.*, 39 (1915), 115.

118. The American Philosophical Society did not at this time have a building of its own; "Philosophical Hall" (still standing in Independence Square) was not completed until 1789. A notice in the *Pennsylvania Journal*, May 17, 1780, announces a meeting of the Society "at the Library Apartments Carpenters' Hall, Chestnut Street, where future meetings of the Society are to be held, till further notice"; the minutes for Jan. 5, 1781, record the meeting at that date as being held "in the Carpenters Hall, in the room adjoining the Library room [the Library Company of Philadelphia at this time occupied quarters on the second floor of Carpenters' Hall]." Although the minutes for the meeting of Dec. 15, 1780—the one attended by Chastellux—do not record the place, it may be assumed that it was also held in Carpenters' Hall. The members present at this meeting were: Joseph Reed, Patron of the Society; Dr. John Ewing and Mr. Owen Biddle, Secretaries; Col. Lewis Nicola, Curator; Arthur Lee, Rev. Mr. Kunze, Timothy Matlack, Ralph Izard, Marbois, Jonathan Smith, Dr. Hutchinson, Charles Thomson. The memoir on "a singular native plant" mentioned by Chastellux is described in the minutes as an account by Isaac Gray "of a proliferous plant, which he supposes to be one of the species, Cepa [i.e., onion]"; Gray's paper was not printed in the published Amer. Phil. Soc. *Transactions*, nor has the manuscript survived in the Society's archives. The minutes further record that at this meeting: "Major General Chastellux presented to the Society a copy of his Works, De la Félicité publique, by the hands of His Excellency the Patron of the Society. Mr. J. B. Smith upon permission, has the use of the above two volumes for a few days." This presentation copy of Chastellux's book is not in the Amer. Phil. Soc. Lib. today.

119. *Ch.* The two branches of the Delaware form two considerable rivers, the sources of which are several miles distant from each other, but they are only distinguished by the names of the *Eastern* and *Western* [Lehigh] *Branches.*

120. *Gr.* The author has by no means given an adequate idea of Philadelphia, which, however, has so often been described as to render it less necessary; but as he names only one street extending along the river, it may be proper to observe, that parallel with Front Street, are Second, Third, Fourth, Fifth, and Sixth Streets; these are intersected at right angles by Arch Street, State Street, and Market Street, etc. etc. the latter, which is of great breadth, and length, and cuts the center of the city, would be one of the finest streets in the world, were it not for the market situated in the middle of it; but the upper part is occupied by the houses of opulent citizens, and will in time become truly noble. It may be added, that so far from the buildings following the river, they are extended rapidly towards the common, where many new streets were marked out and begun in 1782;

and it may safely be predicted that if the trade of Philadelphia continue to flourish, the plan of William Penn will be accomplished, judging from the very rapid progress of the past, at no very distant period, and the ground be covered with, perhaps, the noblest of modern cities, extending from the Delaware to the Schuylkill. This will be accelerated, too, by the sale of the common, which was taken by the Assembly from the proprietor, Mr. John Penn, at the beginning of the revolution, with the rest of the proprietary estate, in consideration of a certain sum, and disposed of in lots to the best bidders.

121. *Gr.* The votes of the House of Commons, and the account of Messieurs Drummond and Harley, will show the immense sums, in Portugal and Spanish gold alone, sent to America; these, as well as English guineas, found their way, towards the middle period of the war, in great abundance into the American part of the continent, where they circulated in a variety of mutilated forms, the moidores, and six-and-thirties, had all of them holes punched in them, or were otherwise diminished at New York, before they were suffered to pass the lines; from whence they obtained the name of *Robertson's,* in the *rebel* country; but the profits, if any, of that commander, on this new edition of the coin, remain a secret. In the country, almost all the specie of every denomination was cut by individuals, and appeared under the forms of half, quarter, and eighth parts, the latter of which received the name of *sharp shins;* by this arbitrary division of the money, which was never weighed, great frauds were inevitable.

122. *Gr.* The wonderful resources derived in the commencement from this paper money, its extraordinary depreciation, and total disappearance without producing any great shock, or convulsion in an infant country, struggling with a complication of difficulties, will certainly form an epocha in the general history of finances, as well as in that of this great revolution. I saw *hundreds of millions* of paper dollars piled up, effaced, in the office of Congress at Philadelphia, which, never possessing any real value, had served all the purposes of a difficult, and uncommonly expensive war, and were now quietly laid aside, with scarce a murmur on the part of the public; the variety of the depreciation, at different periods, and in different parts of the Continent, whilst it gave rise to great temporary abuses, had been so divided, and balanced, by alternate profit and loss among all classes of citizens, that on casting up the account, some very unfortunate cases excepted, it seems to have operated only as a general tax on the public; and the universal joy on its annihilation, with the satisfactory reflection on the necessity under which it was issued in the critical moment of danger, seemed to conciliate all minds, to a total oblivion of its partial mischief. Here and there great fortunes are to be seen, reared upon its now visionary basis, and families reduced from opulence to mediocrity by means of this destructive medium, but these instances are by no means so frequent as they have been represented in Europe, and were often the result of ill judged, but avaricious speculations; but I repeat it, that the continued use, the general circulation, the astonishing depreciation, and total destruction of such an immense imaginary property, will always exhibit a phenomenon infinitely more striking, than that a few, or even a great number of individuals should have suffered, as must always be the case in every civil commotion. The fact is unparalleled, and will probably stand single in the annals of the world.

123. *Gr.* The author might have added in corroboration of his argument, that the constitution of Pennsylvania is, for this reason, only a constitution of experiment, from seven years to seven years, in which it is expressly reserved to a *Council of Censors,* to revise the past operations of government, to judge of the effects produced from it as then constituted, and to call a *general convention of the people,* for the purpose of amending the deficient parts, and of correcting its exuberancies and vices. It is a glorious experiment, worthy the philanthropic heart, and the enlightened understanding of Doctor Franklin,—*Quod felix, faustumque sit!*

124. *Gr.* The city of Philadelphia is not only at present destitute of public walks, but, in summer, the heat renders walking in the streets intolerably inconvenient; the houses and footpaths being generally of brick, are not even cooled until some hours after sunset. This extreme heat, and the abundance of excellent water, with which Philadelphia is supplied, occasion many accidents among the lower class of people, for it is no uncommon thing to see a labourer after quenching his thirst at a pump, drop down dead upon the spot, nor can the numerous examples of this kind every summer, prevent them from frequently occurring; but it is to be observed, that if the heat be intense, the water is uncommonly cold.

Chapter 4

North through New Jersey and up the Hudson to Albany

1. *Gr.* After Sir Guy Carleton's arrival at New York [May 5, 1782] with the vote of Parliament to discontinue offensive war, the Translator, who was travelling to the northward, and meant to call on General Washington, then in camp at Verplank's Point, on the North River, thought he might with safety take the lower road by Brunswick and Elizabethtown, but he had not been an hour in bed, before he and his companion, a surgeon in the American army, were alarmed by a scattering fire of musketry. Before they had time to dress themselves, and take their pistols, the landlord entered their apartment, and informed them, that a party from Staten Island was marching towards the town, and advised them to make their escape; with much difficulty they got their horses out of the stable, hid their baggage in the church-yard, and hearing the English officer order his men to *form* at the end of town, they took different roads, leaving their servants, who were, one a Scotch prisoner to the Americans, the other an English deserter, and whose conduct appeared very suspicious, to take care of themselves, and the horses they rode on. The Translator, who followed the great road to Newark, was mounted on a white horse, which made him a good object, and had several shot fired at him, but the ground rising, and his horse going at full gallop, the balls luckily fell short. After endeavouring to rouse the country, but without being able to collect a sufficient force, he took shelter at an honest carpenter's, about a mile from the town, where he remained till a little before daybreak, when concluding from the general silence, that the party had retired, he returned, and went to search for his baggage in the church-yard, for which, however, he sought in vain, and his anxiety was not a little increased on not finding his other horse in the stable, nor seeing either of the servants. But from which he was soon

relieved by his friend, who had watched the first moment of the enemy's departure, ordered the baggage up into his room, and assured him that the servants had conducted themselves with the greatest fidelity. His alarm was, it seems, much greater than that of the Translator, as General Washington had declared publicly in orders, that any officer of his army, taken near the lines, unless on duty, should be the last exchanged. The Translator imagines the party to have been Refugees [i.e., Tories, or Loyalists] from Staten Island, who, from their separate institution, under the direction of *a Board* [of Associated Loyalists], not unfrequently set at defiance the orders of the Commander-in-Chief; a remarkable instance of which occurred in the case of Captain [Joshua] Huddy, whom they obtained, under false pretences, from the guard-house, where he was a prisoner, and murdered without either scruple or apprehension. All Europe knows the consequence, in the eminent danger of Captain [Charles] Asgill; and all America saw with shame and indignation the English general [Carleton] unable to enforce discipline in his own army, and shrinking under the apprehensions of irritating Governor [William] Franklin, and his envenomed board of Loyalists. [See below, Pt. II, chap. 1, Grieve's n. 7.]

Ed. Although Grieve's comments on the perils of a journey beyond Princeton in the direction of British-occupied New York pertain to a period two years or so subsequent to Chastellux's narrative, they nevertheless serve to emphasize the bitterness of the guerrilla warfare waged in this region ever since 1776, chiefly between the Whigs and the Tory "refugees" (often former neighbors) who had fled to New York City. The hanging near Monmouth of an American prisoner of war, Capt. Joshua Huddy, Apr. 12, 1782, by a band of refugees, represented the exasperated culmination of this envenomed civil war. Huddy's death in turn involved an English prisoner, young Capt. Charles Asgill, who was chosen by lot, at Washington's direction, to be executed in retaliation. Asgill was eventually released, but not until his "eminent danger" had become a matter of international concern. The Huddy-Asgill affair is the subject of Katherine Mayo's *General Washington's Dilemma* (N. Y., 1938); it is also treated in Freeman's *Washington*, V, 412-14, 419-20, 425, and VI, 64 and *n.*; and has recently been retold by Arthur D. Pierce in *Smugglers Woods* ... (New Brunswick, 1960), chap. 10. Although Chastellux does not mention this affair in later installments of his *Travels*, it must have been a matter of close concern to him during the summer of 1782, when the prompt and discreet action of his close associates, Rochambeau and La Luzerne, contributed greatly to the liberation of Asgill in Nov. of that year.

2. Chastellux's French text gives the name of the landlord as "Hoird," which Grieve interpreted as "Howard." This must have been Col. Jacob Hyer, who was at this time proprietor of the Hudibras Tavern, which stood on the south side of the main highway through Princeton (Nassau St.) to the east of Nassau Hall, near the site of the present University Library. "*Capitan*," i.e., a braggart, "*Il Capitano*" being one of the stock characters in Italian comedy.

3. Bullion's Tavern was situated in the village now called Liberty Corner, about five miles southwest of the village of Basking Ridge. Both villages were, and are, in Bernards Township, Somerset Co. Bullion's Tavern is clearly identified on maps drawn (only eight months after Chastellux's

visit) by Lt. Louis-Alexandre Berthier of Rochambeau's staff, when the French and American armies, bound for Yorktown, encamped there in Aug. 1781. Berthier's original maps are in the Princeton Univ. Lib.; one of those showing Bullion's Tavern is reproduced, with a key to the modern place designations, in *Historical Booklet of Bernards Township, N.J.* (Basking Ridge, N.J., 1960). "Bullons" is also shown on an American map of the period: Erskine-Dewitt map No. 106-A, N.-Y. Hist. Soc. "Bullion," as written here by Chastellux, appears to have been an accepted variant spelling of Boylan, no doubt reflecting pronunciation; see A. Van Doren Honeyman, "The Somerset Boylan Family," *Somerset County Historical Quarterly,* 6 (1917), 98-112. Chastellux's "Mr. Bullion" was perhaps John Boylan (1746-93), son of Aaron Boylan who came to New Jersey from Coleraine in Ireland about 1732. John is reported to have been a "merchant and publisher" [publican?] at Liberty Corner.

4. General Anthony Wayne's quarters were at this time in the house of Peter Kemble, situated along what is now U.S. Route 202, just north of "Tempe Wick Road," which leads into the Jockey Hollow area of Morristown National Historical Park. The Kemble House, though still standing, was much modified during the 19th century and was also moved some distance north of its original location. A marker on the west side of the road, erected in 1911 by the New Jersey Society of the Colonial Dames, recalls that Peter Kemble (1704-89), President of the Royal Council of New Jersey, "lived, died and was buried within these grounds." For a readable account of the mutiny of the Pennsylvania line, which Chastellux missed only by a fortnight, see Carl Van Doren, *Mutiny in January* ... (N. Y., 1943). See above, Pt. I, chap. 1, Grieve's n. 88.

5. The Mandevilles were among the earliest settlers at Pompton Plains; for details concerning the family see, for example, David L. Pierson, *History of the Oranges to 1921* ... (N. Y., 1922), 43-45. The owners of the farms mentioned by Chastellux were probably sons of Giles Mandeville (1708-76). The graves of several generations of the family are in the cemetery adjoining the First Reformed Dutch Church (a recent structure on the old site) along the Pompton Pike, which is the main street of Pompton Plains, Pequannock Township, Morris Co.

6. The tavern kept by Joseph Curtis, located near the junction of the road leading northeast through the Ramapo Valley and of the one (taken next morning by Chastellux) leading northwest to Ringwood and the Clove, must have been in what is now the borough of Pompton Lakes, Passaic Co. The Battleship Maine Memorial on a triangle at Passaic Ave. and Hamburg Pike now indicates the important 18th-century road junction. When proceeding from Pompton Plains to Pompton Lakes, via Riverdale, the modern traveler crosses a bridge over the Pequannock, and at a short distance from it, another over the Wanaque (two tributaries of the Pompton River). See roadmap of the French army's march from Suffern to Pompton Plains (Aug. 25-26, 1780), Berthier Papers, No. 15-3, Princeton Univ. Lib. According to Nelson and Shriner, *History of Paterson,* I, 267, Curtis (Chastellux's "Courtheath") leased from Casparus Schuyler in the summer of 1780 a frame building known in later years as "the Yellow House," which was situated "facing southerly on the road to Paterson at the junction of the Hamburgh Road and the Wanaque Road," and which was removed *ca.* 1890. The same

source records a tradition that Curtis had a tavern sign with a picture of a horse, a fish and a bird, and the doggerel:

> This is the Horse that never ran,
> This is the Fish that never swam,
> This is the Bird that never flew,
> Here's good fare for your horse and you.

Nelson also places in this same house the headquarters of Col. Van Cortlandt, who commanded the N. Y. Brigade stationed in this vicinity during the winter of 1781-82; Washington and his wife were guests of Col. Van Cortlandt on their way to Ringwood and Newburgh, Mar. 28, 1782.

7. *Gr.* Travelling in America was wonderfully expensive during the war, even after the abolition of paper money, and when all payments were made in *specie;* you could not remain at an inn, even the most indifferent, one night, with a servant and two horses, living in the most moderate way, under from *five* to *eight* dollars. At Grant's Tavern at Baltimore, where the Translator staid some days [in 1782], with only one horse and no servant, though he either dined or supped out every day, he never escaped for less than *five* dollars.

I cannot here avoid relating the pleasant manner in which one [Robert] Bell, a shrewd Scotch bookseller and auctioneer of Philadelphia, paid his bills in travelling through the country. I had given him an Irish copy of Sheridan's *School for Scandal,* with the prologue and epilogue taken from Dodsley's Annual Register, which he reprinted [Phila., 1782; Evans, No. 17720] and sold for *a dollar.* In travelling through Virginia some months after, I was surprised to see in many of the inns, even in the most remote parts of the country, this celebrated comedy; and, upon inquiry, found that Mr. Bell, who travelled with his family in a covered cart, had passed in his way to the Springs (the Harrowgate, or Matlock of America), and successfully circulated in payment this new species of paper currency; for, as he observed, "Who would not prefer Sheridan's *Sterling,* to the counterfeit creations of Congress, or *even of* Robert Morris?" Nor was any *depreciation* attempted, where the intrinsic value was so unequivocally stamped with the character of wit and freedom.

8. The Ringwood iron mines and forges, the origins of which date back to about 1737, were exploited after 1764 by a London syndicate, the American Iron Company, through their agent, the German-born promoter Baron Peter Hasenclever (1716-93). In 1771, Robert Erskine, a young engineer born in Dunfermline, Scotland, came to America to assume management of the enterprise. With the arrival of the Revolution the Ringwood iron works produced cannon and munitions for the Americans and turned out links for the great iron chains across the Hudson. Erskine himself became geographer and surveyor-general for Washington's army (his maps, a primary cartographic source for the military history of the war, are preserved today at the N.-Y. Hist. Soc. and elsewhere). Erskine died on Oct. 2, 1780, at the age of forty-five. His widow, whom Chastellux met only two months later, was to be remarried in Sept. 1781 to Robert Lettis Hooper, Jr., of Pennsylvania. The Ringwood iron works, subsequently operated by the Ryerson, Peter Cooper, and Abram S. Hewitt families, prospered until well into the 20th century. In 1936 members of the Hewitt

family gave Ringwood Manor to the state of New Jersey which now maintains it as the Ringwood Manor State Park. What is left of the 18th-century house has been incorporated into an extensive and elaborate Victorian mansion. Robert Erskine's tomb, however, may still be seen in the cemetery on the banks of a small pond on the grounds of the estate. A clock from Erskine's time, as well as original letters and documents, are on display in the mansion. A few miles away "Erskine Lake" commemorates his name. See Albert H. Heusser, *The Forgotten General, Robert Erskine; F.R.S. (1735-1780)* (Paterson, N. J., 1928); Alden T. Cottrell, *The Story of Ringwood Manor,* 6th ed. (Trenton, N. J., 1954).

9. "Duck Sider" is Chastellux's phonetic rendering of Tuxedo, and probably reflects the then current pronunciation; it is written "Duck Cedar" on a mid-19th-century map of Orange Co., N. Y.; G. Denniston, *Survey of Orange County* (Albany, 1863). The word is "derived from Delaware dialect of Algonquian, in which the Wolf Subtribe was called P' tuksit, spelled by Morgan Took-seat. This name is a socio-esoteric term for wolf and signifies literally, 'he has a round foot,' from p' tuksiteu (eu = o)"; Frederick Webb Hodge, ed., *Handbook of American Indians North of Mexico,* 2 vols. (Wash., 1907-10), II. Tuxedo Park, the millionaires' residential colony established here in the latter part of the 19th century, has in turn contributed to the American language the common term for dinner jacket, and its derivatives.

10. Smith's Tavern was situated near the junction of three important routes: the road coming north out of "The Clove" (which Chastellux is here following), the road going west to Chester (which he will take two years later; below, Pt. III, chap. 3, Dec. 7, 1782), and the one leading northeasterly to New Windsor on the Hudson. See Erskine-Dewitt Map No. 36, Pt. 3, N.-Y. Hist. Soc. Heusser, *Robert Erskine,* 152, describes the tavern as "near the point on the road from Arden to Central Valley, where this highway [State Route 17] is intersected by the road from Turner's (Harriman), about where the dwelling known as the old Dickerman House now stands." In the language of the 1960's, its approximate location may be described as not far from the Harriman Interchange (No. 16) of the New York Thruway. "Hern's Tavern," where Chastellux eventually stopped for the night, "a little further" along the road to New Windsor, was presumably on present State Route 32.

11. Knox's headquarters was near present Vails Gate, a few miles southwest of New Windsor. Chastellux stopped there, two years later, when General Gates occupied the same house; see below, Pt. III, chap. 3, Dec. 7, 1782, n. 19 and map there cited.

12. *Ch.* He is at present Secretary of the Legation at the Court of France. This brave and excellent soldier is at the same time a poet of great talents: he is the author of a poem addressed to the American army, a work recently known in England, where, in spite of national jealousy, and the affectation of depreciating everything American, it had so much success, as to have been several times publicly read in the manner of the Ancients.

Gr. The Marquis de Chastellux may be assured that it is not by that part of the English nation who are "jealous of America and who affect to depreciate everything American," that the poem of Colonel Humphreys is admired; it is by that numerous and enlightened class of free spirits, who have always supported, and wished prosperity to the glorious struggle of

America, who rejoiced at her success, and who look forward with hope and pleasure to her rising greatness.

Ed. David Humphreys (1752-1818), one of the "Connecticut Wits," served as secretary to the American Commissioners for negotiating trade treaties with the European powers (Franklin, John Adams, Thomas Jefferson) from 1784 to 1786; during his sojourn in Paris he lived with Jefferson. The Marquis de Chastellux himself translated into French verse Humphreys' poem, *A Poem, Addressed to the Armies* (New Haven, 1780). It was beautifully printed with the English text and the French translation on facing pages: *Discours en vers, adressé aux Officiers et aux Soldats des différentes Armées Américaines* (Paris, 1786; Sabin No. 33803). The French edition was published by Prault, who also published Chastellux's *Voyages.* Humphreys, probably with Chastellux's knowledge and approval, undertook to translate the *Voyages* into English: "I have begun to translate the Travels of the Marquis de Chattelus in America, and expect to make some progress during my voyage to that Continent," he wrote to Jefferson, Mar. 17, 1786; Boyd *et al.*, eds., *Jefferson Papers,* IX, 329-30. However, the publication of Grieve's translation in London early in 1787 evidently rendered Humphreys' labors abortive.

13. "I am in very confined Quarters; little better than those of Valley Forge, but such as they are I shall welcome into them your friends on their return to Rhode Island." Washington to Lafayette, New Windsor, Dec. 14, 1780, Fitzpatrick, ed., *Writings of Washington,* XX, 475. The Thomas Ellison house on the west bank of the Hudson, near New Windsor village, occupied by Washington at this time, was demolished in 1833 or 1834. A New York State roadside marker on River Road, New Windsor, recalls the approximate site. An oil painting of the house by John Ludlow Morton (1792-1871), done in 1832, shortly before the demolition, may be seen at the Knox Headquarters historic house at Vails Gate (N. Y. State Education Department). Two somewhat similar paintings, probably copied at a later date by Morton from his 1832 canvas, and with slightly different foregrounds and figures inserted to vary the composition, are preserved respectively in the collections of the Washington Headquarters and Museum, Newburgh, and of the Historical Society of Newburgh Bay and the Highlands, Crawford House, Newburgh (the latter reproduced in *Old Houses and Historic Places in the Vicinity of Newburgh, N.Y.* (Hist. Soc. Newburgh Bay, *Publications,* 15 [1909]). The editor is indebted to Major Kenneth C. Miller, Historic Site Superintendent, Washington's Headquarters and Museum, for information concerning these paintings and for the photograph of Morton's 1832 painting reproduced in this volume. The Ellison house at New Windsor is not to be confused with the Hasbrouck House (still standing), Washington's better known, and later, headquarters a few miles farther north, at Newburgh, where Chastellux was again Washington's guest in Dec. 1782; see below, Pt. III, chap. 3, Dec. 5, 1782, and n. 15.

14. *Ch.* The author having since been very intimate with Colonel Smith, can take it upon himself to assert that this young man is not only a very good soldier, but an excellent scholar. The manner of his entering into the service merits recounting: he was designed for the profession of the law, and was finishing his studies at New York, when the American army assembled there after the unfortunate affair of Long Island. He immediately resolved to take arms in defense of his country, but his parents disapproving

of this step, he enlisted as a common soldier, without making himself known, or pretending to any superior rank. Being one day on duty at the door of a general officer, he was discovered by a friend of his family, who spoke of him to this general officer. He was immediately invited to dinner; but he answered that he could not quit his duty; his corporal was sent for to relieve him, and he returned to his post after dinner. A few days only elapsed before this general officer [John Sullivan], charmed with his zeal and his inclinations, made him his aide-de-camp. In 1780 he commanded a battalion of light infantry, and the year following was made aide-de-camp to General Washington, with whom he remained until the peace.

Gr. He is now Secretary to the Embassy [Legation] to the court of Great Britain, and has lately married the daughter of his Excellency John Adams, Minister Plenipotentiary to that court.

Ed. William Stephens Smith (1755-1816) married Abigail Adams the younger in London on June 12, 1786.

15. Chastellux, when still a very young officer, had himself published an analysis of Frederick the Great's *Instruction Militaire ... pour ses Généraux;* see above, Introduction, n. 6. Guibert's influential work, *Essai Général de Tactique,* was first published anonymously at Bouillon in Belgium, 1772, by the Société Typographique, also publishers of Chastellux's *De la Félicité Publique,* new ed. (1776). For further comment on the theoretical background of Chastellux's military thought, see above, Pt. I, chap. 3, n. 35.

16. "I had the pleasure of the Chevr. de Chatteleaux's Company on his way to Albany, but the Viscount de Noailles and Count Damas passed, on the other side of the River, without calling." Washington to Lafayette, New Windsor, Dec. 26, 1780, Fitzpatrick, ed., *Writings of Washington,* XXI, 19.

17. Chastellux rewrote this sentence for the 1786 edition. The original version (Newport, 1781, p. 141) was: "Mr. Smith had not, in fact, inspired in me the same confidence that Colonel Moylan had; I only regretted not having seen Governor Clinton."

18. The tavern kept at this time by John Pride (1742-1808) appears to have been situated midway between Poughkeepsie and Hyde Park along the present Albany Post Road (U.S. Route 9), two or three miles beyond the Dutchess Co. Courthouse at Poughkeepsie. Mrs. Amy Ver Nooy, secretary of the Dutchess County Hist. Soc., has kindly informed the Editor that although it has been suggested that the tavern site was near the spring just north of the entrance to the Hudson River State Hospital, no documentary proof has been found to confirm or otherwise establish the location with certainty.

19. *Ch.* (note added to 2d ed., 1788). Fertile as are the lands in Dutchess County and in many other parts of America, it would be a mistake to believe that any exist where the seed, sown as it is in Europe, could produce 30 or 40 for one. The explanation of this extraordinary yield is that the American practice, as pointed out carefully in the text, is to sow very thinly. It is rare to sow but a single bushel to an acre, even in Paris; but it is also rare to sow more than two or three. It is easy to understand that the Americans, who generally have more land than they can cultivate, are more concerned with sparing seed than sparing land. Thus one is liable to reach quite different conclusions about the fertility of America according to the different ways in which travelers present the same subject. If the traveler speaks only of

the relationship of seed to the yield he may give a very high idea of the fertility; but if he speaks only of the quantity of grain harvested from an acre he gives a very unfavorable idea. Two bushels may, in truth, yield sixty. But if they comprise all that has been sown on a single acre, then the total harvest per acre will amount to only seven *setiers* (Paris measure), and thus be much less than what is harvested from an acre of our ordinary lands in France.

20. *Gr.* Flax has become a very great and profitable article of cultivation in the Middle and Eastern States, the principal cultivators are settlers from the north of Ireland, who know the value of it in their own country. In Massachusetts [New Hampshire] there is a very considerable and flourishing settlement, called Londonderry, peopled entirely by emigrants from that city, where they apply themselves particularly to the growth of flax.

21. *Gr.* The Translator had the pleasure of being well acquainted with one of the sons of Mr. Le Roy, a most amiable young man, whom he knew at Amsterdam, when residing with his aunt Madame Chabanel, the widow of a rich merchant, who did a great deal of business with America previous to the war. He saw him afterwards at Philadelphia and Boston, and has only to regret, that his affairs rendered it impossible to accept of a kind invitation to pay him a visit at Strattsborough [Staatsburg]. Mrs. Chabanel's house, at Amsterdam, was open to all the Americans in Holland during the war.

Ed. John Adams, then U.S. Minister in Holland, was several times at Mrs. Chabanel's house in Aug. and Sept. 1780; Butterfield *et al.*, eds., *Diary of John Adams*, II, 446-47.

22. Chastellux's stopping place was in what is now the village of Upper Red Hook, east of U.S. Route 9, in the present township of Red Hook, which until 1812 formed part of Rhinebeck. Edward M. Smith, *Documentary History of Rhinebeck* (Rhinebeck, 1881), 85-86, records a tradition that one Jacob Thomas "kept a tavern during the Revolutionary War, and sold a great deal of liquor for a great deal of money"; Christopher Colles, *A Survey of the Roads of the United States of America* (N. Y., 1789, facsimile, ed. Walter W. Ristow, Cambridge, 1961), plate 22, shows "Thomas's" tavern in Red Hook. This is the "Thomas House," or "old brick tavern," still standing in the center of the village of Upper Red Hook.

23. *Gr.* Arnold was brought up to the business of an apothecary, being taken from his mother, out of charity, by Doctor [Daniel] Lathrop of Norwich in Connecticut, who was at once a physician, surgeon, apothecary, merchant, and shopkeeper, as is usual in America; after his apprenticeship expired, his master gave him 500 *l.* and letters of recommendation to his correspondents in London, by which means he obtained credit for some thousands, and returning to Connecticut, settled at New Haven, set up an equipage, with ten horses, a carriage, and a number of servants, failed in two years, and was thrown into jail, where he remained till released by a bankrupt act passed by the Assembly. He then first got with child, and afterwards married the daughter of Mr. [Samuel] Mansfield, High Sheriff of New Haven, much against the will of the latter; who at length became reconciled to him, and employed him as a supercargo to the West Indies, where he usually went in the spring, and returned in the autumn with molasses, rum, and sugar. In winter he went among the Dutch towards the head of Hudson's River, and into Canada, with various sorts of woollen goods, such as stockings, caps, mittens, etc. etc. and also cheese, which sold to great profit in

Canada. These articles he either exchanged for horses, or purchased them
with the money arising from his sales. With these horses, which generally
made a part of a Connecticut cargo, together with poultry, corn, and fish,
he went to the islands, whilst his father-in-law was selling the rum, molasses
and sugars of the last voyage, and collecting woollens for Arnold's next
winter trip to Canada. It was in these voyages that Arnold became an expert
seaman, which qualified him for the command of the fleet on the lakes
[Champlain], where he behaved with his usual gallantry against a much
superior enemy. The Translator had an opportunity, during his residence at
Porto Rico during the war, of seeing several of these Connecticut sloops
make very advantageous sales of their little cargoes. After disembarking
their horses, they ran their vessels up to the quay, and converted them into
retail shops, where they dealt out their onions, potatoes, salt fish, and *apples*
(an article which brought a very high price) in the smallest quantities, for
which they received hard dollars, although *it is a fact,* that specie was
uncommonly scarce in this *Spanish* island, almost all the intercourse being
carried on in *paper dollars,* whilst the *French* part of the neighboring island
of Hispaniola [Santo Domingo] was full of Spanish money, and the French
fleet and army were paid in dollars from the Havana. The Translator hopes
that he shall here be pardoned a digression on the subject of this *charming
island,* which in the hands of any other nation would certainly become one
of the most valuable possessions in the American Archipelago. Its central
situation between the windward and leeward islands, its capacious harbor,
the number of springs and rivers with which it is watered (the latter abound-
ing with fish), the excellence of its soil, the greatest part of which is nearly
in a virgin state, the strong position of the peninsula of St. John, are
advantages, which if in the possession of a great *active* maritime power, such
as France or England, can scarcely be appreciated. In the possession of Spain,
it is at most but a negative advantage; for I am well assured that the King
only receives the inconsiderable revenue of 100,000 piasters from this island,
whilst he expended, in the course of the late war, no less than *eight millions*
on the fortifications, which I had the *very singular favour* to visit, accompanied by the first engineer, and the strength of which is now deemed not
less formidable than those of fort Moro, and the Havana. Nor could England, with her then force in the West Indies, have attacked this island
with any prospect of success, though most persons in Jamaica were sanguine
for such an expedition. Besides an immense train of very fine artillery, three
of the best regiments in the Spanish service were there in garrison, in full
health, viz.: the regiments *de Bruxelles, de la Couronne,* and *de la Victoire,*
and a most numerous militia. Indeed, so secure did they think themselves,
that they embarked, when I was there, the regiment de la Couronne, consisting of 1200 men for Carthagena. The interior of the country, which I was
likewise allowed to visit, is delightful; land may be had for nothing, but
every settler must not only be a Catholic, but a rigid one, the *Inquisition*
having an officer here; he must likewise marry, and wretched is his choice,
within a year, nor is he ever allowed to remove any property from the island,
should he wish to quit it, except what he can carry off clandestinely. Several
Irish are settled here, but all under the predicament of sacrificing to the most
gloomy superstition, the most arbitrary jealousy of despotic power, and to
the most horrid state of nuptial slavery, with the ugliest and filthiest of
women. The officers of the *Dragon* man-of-war of 60 guns, and of the
frigates which were lying there, and the military in garrison were anxious

to peruse the European and American Gazettes I had with me, but even this communication was obliged to be confined to very few, and under the strictest injunctions of secrecy, for our mutual safety. In other respects it is impossible to have met with a more hospitable reception.

24. From Chastellux's description it would appear that his route took him northwesterly from the present main highway (U.S. Route 9) in the direction of Claverack Landing (now the city of Hudson), thence back eastward for a stretch to Claverack "center," where the meetinghouse was situated. The limestone formation that attracted his attention was perhaps the Becraft Hills south of Hudson.

25. *Gr.* The Marquis having, in his account of Totowa Falls [above, Pt. I, chap. 2, Nov. 23, 1780] observed that there is little or no calcareous stone in *this country,* by which I am at a loss to know whether he means the state of New Jersey, where he then was, or the United States in general; I take this opportunity of mentioning, that limestone abounds in a great part of the Continent; the interior parts of Pennsylvania, Maryland, and Virginia in particular are intersected by immense strata of this invaluable stone, which lie everywhere exposed to the day, or very near the surface.

26. *Gr.* With great submission to the Author, he appears to have laid a greater stress on this phenomenon than it has any claim to from its singularity; every mountainous country in Europe abounds with such appearances, which, though curious, may possibly be accounted for on principles more simple, and less *systematical,* than those great convulsions so enthusiastically imagined by the disciples of the *Buffonic* school.

27. This phenomenon, which Chastellux attributes to the Dutch heritage of the settlers, has been interpreted by other historians as a consequence of the manorial system of land tenure characteristic of this part of the Hudson valley. See, for example, Dorothy Canfield Fisher's perceptive discussion of "The Gentry's Last Stand" in *Vermont Tradition* ... (Boston, 1953), 55-100, 419-85.

28. Presumably this refers to Abraham Van Buren, who kept an inn (no longer standing) on what is now Hudson St. His son, Martin, born there in 1782, later became President of the United States. Edward A. Collier, *A History of Old Kinderhook* ... (N.Y. and London, 1914), 386, 414, and facing p. 376, reproduction of an "old print" (probably apocryphal) of "Martin Van Buren's Birth-place."

Chapter 5

Albany and the Saratoga Battlefields

1. "Mrs. Carter" was General Schuyler's daughter, Angelica Schuyler Carter (or, later, Church), whom Chastellux had known at Newport; see above, Pt. I, chap. 2, Nov. 28, 1780, and n. 48.

2. *Ed.* Elizabeth Schuyler's marriage to Alexander Hamilton had taken place at Albany on Dec. 14, 1780.

Ch. Colonel Hamilton is so well known by all those who have had any connection with America, that it would be unnecessary to mention him more particularly here, were not this journal, at length destined for publication, likely to fall into the hands of several readers who have been unacquainted with, or have forgotten, many details relative to this revolution, in which their interest can still be aroused. Colonel Hamilton, a native of Saint Croix, and some time settled in America, was destined to the profession of the law, and had scarcely completed his studies, when General Washington, versed as all great men are in the discovery of talents and in the employment of them, made him both his aide-de-camp and secretary, a post as eminent as it is important in the American army. Henceforth correspondence with the French, whose language he speaks and writes perfectly, the details of every kind, political and military, entrusted to him, developed those talents that the General had known how to discover and put in activity; while the young soldier, by a prudence and secrecy still more beyond his age than his information, justified the confidence with which he was honored. He continued to serve in this capacity until the year 1781, when desirous of distinguishing himself in the command of troops, as he had done in all his other functions, he took command of a battalion of light infantry. It was at the head of this battalion that, jointly with M. de Gimat, he carried by assault one of the enemy's redoubts at the siege of Yorktown. The reader will perhaps be surprised to hear that the next year, before the peace was made, Mr. Hamilton turned lawyer and became a member of Congress. The explanation of this enigma is that the war being considered as at an end, it was necessary for him to think of his fortune which was very inconsiderable. Now the profession of "lawyer," which combines those of [our French] *avocat, procureur* and *notaire*, is not only the most respected in America, but likewise the most lucrative; and there is no doubt that, with such talents and such knowledge, Mr. Hamilton must be in time of peace as in time of war one of the most highly regarded citizens in his new country. He is now living in New York.

    Gr. To this just eulogium, the Translator takes the liberty of adding, that Colonel Hamilton is a most elegant writer, and a perfectly accomplished gentleman, and as such could not fail of distinguishing himself in the first European circles. His account of the behaviour and death of the unfortunate André, to which he was a witness, published at the time in the American and English prints, does equal honour to his understanding and his heart.

    Ed. Hamilton's account—including the oft-quoted phrase, "Never, perhaps, did any man suffer death with more justice, or deserve it less"—is found in his letter to John Laurens, Oct. 1780, printed in successive editions of his writings, for example, in Henry Cabot Lodge, ed., *Works of Alexander Hamilton*, Federal ed., 12 vols. (N. Y. and London, 1904), IX, 209-23; and most recently in H. C. Syrett and J. E. Cooke, eds., *Papers of Alexander Hamilton* (N. Y., 1961), II, 460-70. It was, as Grieve states, published in newspapers soon after the event—in the *Pennsylvania Gazette* (Phila.), among others, as early as Oct. 25, 1780. Hamilton also wrote of André's fate in letters to his fiancée, Elizabeth Schuyler: Sept. 25, Oct. 2, 1780; Lodge, ed., *Works of Hamilton*, IX, 206-8; Syrett and Cooke, eds., *Hamilton Papers*, II, 441-42, 448-50.

    3. The home of General Philip Schuyler (1733-1804), an attractive brick Georgian house erected in the 1760's, is still standing at the corner of Clinton and Catharine Sts., and at the head of Schuyler St., in Albany. "Schuyler Mansion," acquired by the state of New York in 1911, is one of the historic sites administered by the State Department of Education. "The Pastures," as it was originally called, has been restored to its 18th-century appearance, with Schuyler family furniture and other contemporary souvenirs on display.

For a description, including an introductory historical sketch of the house and its owner, see Anna K. Cunningham, *Schuyler Mansion, A Critical Catalogue of the Furnishings and Decorations* (Albany, 1955). Although dated a few years after Chastellux's visit, the following map gives a good idea of the extent of the city and of the location of Schuyler's house, then well outside the town: "A Plan of the City of Albany Surveyed at the request of the Mayor Alderman and Commonalty By Simeon De Witt, 1794," reproduced in Arthur J. Weise, *The History of the City of Albany, New York* ... (Albany, 1884), 412-13, and in Cuyler Reynolds, comp., *Albany Chronicles* (Albany, 1906), 384-85. See also the sketch-map of Albany in 1786 in F. B. Dexter, ed., *Stiles's Itineraries*, 394. A small but graphic delineation of the Schuyler house is included in Plate 26 of Colles, *A Survey of the Roads of the U.S.* (1789).

4. In the 1781 edition of his book (p. 148), Chastellux describes Mrs. Hamilton and Peggy Schuyler in these terms: "Mrs. Hamilton, his second daughter, who lacks none of the attributes of a pretty woman; ... Miss Peggy Schuyler, his third daughter, who lacks only teeth to be as pretty as her sister."

5. Chastellux did not here mention Schuyler's gout in the earlier version of his text (p. 148), which reads: "As for the General he is a man of about fifty, of tall stature, and with a noble and gentle face."

6. In the 1781 text of Chastellux's *Voyage* (p. 149) the last part of this sentence reads: "but he could not serve as our guide, because his health is delicate and he was suffering from gout."

7. One of the letters of introduction to General Clinton had been written by Washington at New Windsor on Dec. 19: "I have the pleasure of introducing to you the Chevr. de Chattelleaux Majr. Genl. in the French Army, and the Viscount de Noailles and the Count Damas who are anxious to see the Northern Frontier of New York, and may perhaps go as far as Lake George. As they are gentlemen of the first rank in France, I would wish every attention paid to them. You will be pleased to offer them an escort if they incline to go beyond Saratoga, and will recommend them to persons on whom they may confide as guides, or for any assistance of which they may stand in need." Fitzpatrick, ed., *Writings of Washington*, XX, 500.

8. Chastellux slightly softened his original remark by qualifying General Clinton's talents, in the 1786 edition, as "*peu distingués,*" whereas in the 1781 edition (p. 150) he had termed them "*très médiocres.*"

9. The island noted by Chastellux was presumably Van Schaick's Island (now in the city of Cohoes, Albany Co.), to which Gen. Schuyler withdrew in Aug. 1777 at the time of Burgoyne's invasion. Gen. Gates, who took over the command from Schuyler here, described the island as "made by the sprouts of the Mohawk River joining with Hudson River, 9 miles north of Albany." Gates to Washington, Aug. 22, 1777, Washington Papers, Lib. Cong. The island a little higher up, which was fortified, was Peobles' (or Peebles') Island (now Haver, or Havre, Island, in Waterford, Saratoga Co.); remains of the earthworks thrown up in 1777 are still visible there.

10. *Gr.*—about 1200 English feet.

11. *Gr.* Madame la Comtesse de Genlis in speaking of this cataract in one of the notes to her *Veillées du Château*, says it is only 50 feet, but from other accounts confirming this of M. de Chastellux, I am inclined to think, that

it is between 70 and 80 feet. This invaluable and correct writer, the pride of her son, and of humanity, has in this instance been unavoidably misled by the American travellers she consulted.

Ed. See Madame de Genlis' once popular children's book, *Les Veillées du Château, ou Cours de morale à l'usage des enfans* (Paris, 1782, and many subsequent editions and translations). Little Pulcheria's question, "Mama, what is the eye trouble called cataracts?" in turn leads her didactic mama to explain in a digressive footnote that the word is also used in geography and to cite several examples, such as the Falls of the Rhine at Schaffhausen, the cataract of the Nile, Niagara, and one "three leagues from Albany in New York which is about fifty feet high."

12. Cohoes Falls, one of the natural wonders of America in Chastellux's time, is still visible in the city of Cohoes, Albany Co., New York. Although derivations of the water for industrial purposes have diminished the cataract to a mere trickle, the empty shell of rocks and cliffs is more or less intact. A pen and wash drawing by John Trumbull, dated Sept. 27, 1791, shows the site in its former splendor, much as it must have appeared to Chastellux and his traveling companions. Trumbull's drawing is now in the Addison Gallery of American Art, Andover, Mass.; see Theodore Sizer, *The Works of Colonel John Trumbull, Artist of the American Revolution* (New Haven, 1950), 88 and fig. 40. John James Audubon also depicted Cohoes Falls, in the landscape background of his "Goosander," *The Birds of America* (London, 1827-38), Plate 331 (1836). The Irish poet Thomas Moore penned some "Lines written at the Cohos, or Falls of the Mohawk River," first printed in his *Epistles, Odes and Other Poems* (1806) and included among the "Poems relating to America" in his collected *Works*. Moore had apparently read his Chastellux (although he entertained a low opinion of French travelers and their rosy views of America), for he is at pains to point out in a footnote to the poem that whereas Isaac Weld in his *Travels through the States of North America* (London, 1799, with engraved plate of Cohoes Falls) gives the height of the cataract as fifty feet, "the Marquis de Chastellux makes it seventy-six."

13. The passage beginning with this sentence was considerably edited by Chastellux for the 1786 edition of his *Travels*. The text of the 1781 edition (pp. 152-53) reads:

My plan, and that of my traveling companions, was to send and ask General Schuyler to have us for dinner; I had observed however that Mrs. Schuyler was a big Dutchwoman, with a rather serious disposition, and that she appeared to be the mistress of the house: I thought it best not to treat her in too cavalier a fashion, and as I knew that she was informed of my return, I thought it more appropriate to temporize, and I did well to do so. Indeed, Colonel Hamilton came to see me during the morning, appeared a bit embarrassed and gave me no invitation. I promised to call on the General during the evening, and I invited all the foreigners to my house for a dinner, which was not as successful as the supper of the previous day. At six o'clock in the evening we were sent for in sleighs and went to General Schuyler's house. We found him in his drawing room alone with Mr. and Mrs. Hamilton; we were told that Mrs. Schuyler was indisposed and we took this at face value. However, conversation began between the General, the Vicomte de Noailles, and myself. We had already talked two days earlier of certain rather important facts concerning the northern campaigns.... [etc.] he suggested letting us read his political and military correspondence with General Washington; we accepted the proposition with great pleasure, and leaving the rest of the company with Mr. and Mrs. Hamilton, we went into another room where we found Mrs. and Miss Schuyler by the fireside, appearing to be in rather good health. The General opened his portfolio.... [etc.]

Although Chastellux decided to delete some of his references to Mrs. Schuyler in the trade edition of his book, he nevertheless confided in a letter to Thomas Jefferson (Paris, Dec. 27, 1784) that these remarks were not undeserved and that they were to a certain extent counterbalanced by his praise of her husband. Boyd *et al.*, eds., *Jefferson Papers*, VII, 584-85.

14. *Papier à la Tellière:* fine quality paper, such as that used for official legal documents in France; the term derives from the name of Chancellor Le Tellier (1603-85), who had it manufactured. It might be understood here to mean "legal size" paper, or "foolscap."

15. Schuyler's letter, which Chastellux summarizes here, was written from Saratoga, Nov. 4, 1777, and was addressed to Congress (John Hancock, President), not to Washington, as Chastellux thought. Schuyler's retained copy of it—perhaps the very manuscript that Chastellux had in his hands—is in Schuyler's Letterbook (Nov. 19, 1776-July 1, 1778), 373-80, no. 1401, Schuyler Papers, MS Div., N. Y. Pub. Lib. The letter was printed in *Proceedings of a General Court Martial...for the Trial of Major General Schuyler, October 1, 1778* (Philadelphia, 1778; Evans, No. 16142, reprinted in N.-Y. Hist. Soc., *Collections*, 12 [1879], 191-97).

16. The abortive Canadian expedition of Feb. 1778, which was related to the Congressional maneuverings against Washington and in favor of Gen. Horatio Gates (the so-called "Conway Cabal"), is discussed at length in Gottschalk, *Lafayette Joins American Army*, chap. 8. Lafayette's own account is in his *Mémoires*, I, 154 ff.

17. Schuyler's "memoir," summarized here by Chastellux, dated Oct. 9, 1778, is in Washington Papers, Lib. Cong.; see John C. Fitzpatrick, ed., *Calendar of the Correspondence of George Washington, Commander in Chief of the Continental Army, with the Officers*, 4 vols. (Wash., 1915), I, 784. Inasmuch as the memoir is dated from Fredericksburg [now Patterson, Putnam Co.], N. Y., Washington's headquarters at the time, it was probably a reply to a verbal request for information, and not to a *letter* from Washington, as Chastellux thought; this supposition is further confirmed by the fact that no such letter from Washington to Schuyler is recorded in either Fitzpatrick's *Calendar* or *Writings of Washington*.

18. *Ch.* This is the name given on English maps to the wilderness situated between Lake Ontario, the St. Lawrence River, and Lakes George, Champlain and the Sorel River.

19. Washington's long letter to Schuyler, dated from his headquarters at Fredericksburg [Patterson], N. Y., Nov. 20-21, 1778, is printed in Fitzpatrick, ed., *Writings of Washington*, XIII, 297-305.

20. Schuyler's letter to Washington, Saratoga, Nov. 30, 1778, is in Washington Papers, Lib. Cong.; see Fitzpatrick, ed., *Calendar*, II, 872. Washington's reply, dated Middle Brook [N. J.], Dec. 18, 1778—not mentioned here by Chastellux—is printed in Fitzpatrick, ed., *Writings of Washington*, XIII, 429-33.

21. *Gr.* From these accounts it appears very evident that General Carleton acted with great prudence in retaining the force he did in Canada, for which he has been blamed by some, when Burgoyne went on his expedition; in the catastrophe of which, 1,500 or 2,000 men more would probably have made little difference, but the want of which would have totally enfeebled the defence of Canada, and thrown that province into the hands of the United States. The American ideas too, on the subject of an expedition into Canada, and which may possibly be carried into execution at some future period, merit the attention of the English government, more particularly as America, since she is put in possession of the Kennebec and the boundary line cuts the Sorel River below Lake Champlain, can now carry on her operations at her ease, and unmolested on the lakes, and by Arnold's route; but, in fact, Canada must, on a rupture, follow the fortune of the United States; that province can only be prevented from falling rapidly before such a force as the Eastern States can put in motion, by *very strong* forts built at the head of the Kennebec, St. Croix, and Connecticut Rivers, by forts on *both* sides of the Sorel, where cut by the boundary line, on *both* sides the St. Lawrence where it joins that river, at *the head* of the carrying place above Niagara, on the English side, where a new carrying place must if possible be formed, and *opposite* the fort of Detroit and Michilimackinac. All must be *strong, regular* works, capable of containing garrisons with stores sufficient to stop the progress of an enemy's army, till relief can arrive from the interior of the country, where 6 or 8,000 regular forces must be kept, besides strong garrisons at Quebec and Montreal, the fortifications of which must be repaired and strengthened. Unless England is determined to adopt, and rigorously to maintain all these necessary defences, perhaps after all inadequate, it is impossible that Canada should long resist an American expedition. On such a tenure, and at such an enormous expence, will that province be worth holding? Mr. [Thomas] Paine, in his admirable *Letter to the Abbé Raynal* [*on the Affairs of North America* (1782), Postscript], makes the following judicious observations on this subject:—"Respecting Canada, one or other of the two following will take place, viz.; if Canada should become populous, it will revolt; and if it does not become so, it will not be worth the expence of holding. But Canada *never will* be populous.... Britain may put herself to great expences in sending settlers to Canada; but the descendants of those settlers will be Americans, as other descendants have been before them. They will look round and see the neighbouring States sovereign and free, respected abroad, and trading at large with the world; and the natural love of liberty, the advantages of commerce, the blessings of independence, and of a *happier climate and a richer soil* will draw them *southward;* and the effect will be, that Britain will sustain the expence, and America reap the advantage.... One would think that the experience Britain has had of America, would entirely sicken her of all thoughts of *continental* colonization; and any part she might retain, will only become to her a field of jealousy and thorns, of debate and contention, for ever struggling for privileges, and meditating revolt. She may form *new settlements,* but they will be for us; *they will become part of the United States of America;* and that against all her contrivances to prevent it, or without any endeavours of ours to promote it. In the first place she cannot draw from them a revenue until they are able to pay one, and when they are so, they will be above subjection. Men soon become attached to the soil they live upon, and incorporated with the

prosperity of the place; and it signifies but little what opinions they come over with, for time, interest and new connections will render them obsolete, and the next generation know nothing of them.... To speak explicitly on the matter, I would not, were I an European power, have Canada, under the conditions that Britain must retain it, could it be given to me. It is one of those kind of dominions that is, and ever will be, a constant charge upon any foreign holder.... There are, I doubt not, thousands of people in England, who suppose that these places [Canada and Nova Scotia] are a profit to the nation, whereas they are directly the contrary, and instead of producing any revenue, a considerable part of the revenue of England is annually drawn off to support the expence of holding them."

What it costs England to maintain Canada alone, may be known from the following accurate *abstract*, verified by the treasury accounts, of the *expences of that Province, from the 1st of June, 1776, to the 24th of October, 1782, being six years and four months:*

	£	s.	d.
Military-Ordinaries,	688,385	18	2½
Extraordinaries,	4,510,790	12	7
Civil Establishment and			
Contingencies	100,343	8	9
Total,	£ 5,299,519	19	6½
Which for 6 years			
4 months, is			
	£ 836,766	6	3 per annum

It is true that the war extraordinaries must not be taken into the estimate of a peace establishment, but will not the independence of the United States render a larger force necessary than during the former peace, besides the garrisons above mentioned, etc.; and is war so very improbable in that quarter? Perhaps the most fortunate event for Britain will be, to receive the news, some spring or other, after the opening of the St. Lawrence, that Canada has been taken in the winter, with little or no bloodshed.

22. Concerning "the Indian Expedition" against the Six Nations, see A. C. Flick, "New Sources on the Sullivan-Clinton Campaign in 1779," N. Y. State Hist. Assoc., *Quarterly Journal*, 10 (1929), 185-224, 265-317. Flick calls attention, pp. 210-11, to "The Forgotten Campaign of 1778"—i.e., the expedition planned for 1778 but not carried out—and Schuyler's share in it. Congress appropriated funds for this campaign in June 1778, but it was subsequently postponed to the following year, when it was placed under the command of Gen. John Sullivan; Washington in a letter to Congress, Oct. 27, 1778 (Fitzpatrick, ed., *Writings of Washington*, XIII, 159), enclosed a report drawn up by Schuyler, Gov. Clinton, and Gen. Hand advising a postponement of the "enterprize against Chemung." Schuyler's "proposed plan," which Chastellux read at Albany (not further identified), was presumably drafted during the late winter or early spring of 1778. Washington continued to seek Schuyler's advice: see, for example, his letter of Apr. 19, 1779 (*ibid.*, XIV, 407-9) in reply to Schuyler's letters of Apr. 3 and 8, 1779. For a further comment by Chastellux on Sullivan's 1779 expedition, see his note, below, Pt. III, chap. 4, n. 25.

23. The Indians that Chastellux saw at Schenectady were displaced persons, chiefly Oneidas and some Tuscaroras (but no Mohawks, as he implies),

who had remained faithful to the Americans and were being supported at
their expense, whereas most of the Six Nations were allied with the British.
They had been driven from their villages and deprived of their normal
livelihood by Tories and other Indians to whom they were an object of
special vengeance. Franklin B. Hough, *The Northern Invasion of October
1780 ... against the Frontiers of New York* (N. Y., 1866), 31-32. Hough cites
a document according to which Jellis Fonda contracted in July 1780 to
supply 390 rations daily to "destitute Oneidas and Tuscaroras at Schenectady"—a figure approximating Chastellux's estimate of 350. Hough also
mentions that "the cinders of their camp fires may still [i.e., 1866] be traced
on the brow of the hills southeast of the city [of Schenectady]." See also
Lossing, *Field-Book*, I, 278, 282; Walter H. Mohr, *Federal Indian Relations,
1774-1788* (Phila. and London, 1933), 184-85.

24. *Gr.* Dr. Franklin, whose amiable and philosophic mind sincerely
laments all the evils attendant on humanity, used frequently to regret the
painful necessity under which he foresaw America would shortly find herself of using violence against the savages, from the bloody scenes into which
they were led by the policy of the English Government. The Translator has
often heard him express himself with the utmost sensibility on the subject,
and suggest many expedients to prevent the probability of matters being
urged to that horrid extremity, but reason, philosophy and eloquence were
in vain opposed by good and wise men to the headlong career of that
mad war.

25. Chastellux is here shaking his finger at the disciples of Rousseau who
extolled man in a state of nature and decried the corrupting effects of civilization. Chastellux's own doctrine, as elaborated in his book *De la Félicité
Publique,* was that men were gradually achieving happiness through the
progress of Reason and Enlightenment.

26. *Gr.* The principal part of Burgoyne's artillery was conveyed to Philadelphia, where I saw a very fine park, formed of them and the pieces taken
from the Hessians, in various engagements.

Ed. Examples of cannon surrendered by Burgoyne under the terms of the
Convention of Oct. 17, 1777, may be seen today at Saratoga National Historical Park, at the Saratoga Battle Monument (Schuylerville), etc.

27. In the 1781 edition (p. 162) this sentence reads: "I inquired the price
of them: I was astonished to learn that they cost from four to five dollars
(*piastres*); this is almost double what our own cost."

28. The hospital visited by Chastellux was presumably the same that
Dr. James Thacher described in his *Military Journal,* 108-9, under date of
Aug. 30, 1777: "The hospital [at Albany] was erected during the last French
war, it is situated on an eminence overlooking the city. It is two stories high,
having a wing at each end and a piazza in front above and below. It contains
forty wards, capable of accommodating five hundred patients, besides the
rooms appropriated to the use of surgeons and other officers, stores, etc."

29. Saratoga, here and in subsequent passages, designates "Old Saratoga,"
now Schuylerville, on the west bank of the Hudson River, and not Saratoga
Springs, ten miles or so west of the river, where the spa and race tracks
later developed.

30. Burgoyne's "accounts" had been published early in 1780 under the
title: *A State of the Expedition from Canada, as laid before the House of*

Commons, By Lieutenant-General Burgoyne, and verified by evidence; with a collection of authentic documents, and an addition of many circumstances which were prevented from appearing before the House by the prorogation of Parliament (London, 1780). The book is illustrated with six maps engraved by William Faden, all with the publisher's date, Feb. 1, 1780. Chastellux may have seen a copy of this book before he left France at the beginning of May 1780; in any case, he had seen it before he made his visit to the Saratoga battlefield, and no doubt had a copy of it beside him when he wrote up his notes at Newport a few weeks later. Burgoyne's book is a revised and augmented version of the evidence he had submitted in 1779 to the Parliamentary committee investigating the conduct of the war; after the surrender of 1777 he had been allowed to return to England as a prisoner on parole and was able to appear in his own defense at the time of the inquiry. Some of the documents concerning Saratoga had thus found their way into print even before the publication of the book. See above, Pt. I, chap. 3, n. 31.

31. It should be borne in mind that Chastellux's winter reconnaissance of the Saratoga battlefield was made about three years and two months after the event, when traces of the battle were relatively fresh. His guide [perhaps Col. Jacob Lansing] was a veteran of the fighting, and he of course had an opportunity to discuss matters with Gen. Schuyler and other participants. Much of the battlefield is today included in the Saratoga National Historical Park. For a convenient recapitulation of events and description of the ground, with diagrams and maps facilitating identification of the features mentioned by Chastellux, see Charles W. Snell and Francis F. Wilshin, *Saratoga National Historical Park, New York* (National Park Service, *Hist. Handbook*, 4 [Wash., 1950, rev. ed., 1959]). See also William L. Stone, ed., *Visits to the Saratoga Battle-Grounds, 1780-1880* (Albany, 1895), 63-87, which reprints Chastellux's description. The most complete recent account of Burgoyne's expedition and its termination at Saratoga is Hoffman Nickerson, *The Turning Point of the Revolution . . .* (Boston, 1928).

32. The "plan of it published by General Burgoyne" refers to the two maps included in *A State of the Expedition from Canada . . . By Lieutenant-General Burgoyne,* both of them drawn by W. C. Wilkinson, Lt. 62nd Regiment, Assistant Engineer, and engraved by W. Faden: "Plan of the Encampment and Position of the Army under His Excellency Lt. General Burgoyne at Swords House on Hudson's River near Stillwater on Septr. 17th with the positions of that part of the Army engaged on the 19th Septr. 1777"; and "Plan of the Encampment and Position of the Army under His Excellency Lt. General Burgoyne at Braemus Heights on Hudson's River near Stillwater, on the 20th Septr. with the Position of the Detachment &c in the action of the 7th of Octr. & the Position of the Army on the 8th Octr. 1777."

33. *Ch.* Lincoln was not wounded until the next day.

34. *Ch.* "Jockey" is a word used in America to describe horse-traders as well as those who train horses.

35. On General Schuyler's house at Saratoga [Schuylerville], see below, this chap., n. 45.

36. According to a careful local historian, the house pointed out to Chastellux was probably that of Jane McCrea's brother John, which stood on the west bank of the Hudson (within the limits of the present town of

Northumberland, Saratoga County), opposite the mouth of Moses Kill, which flows into the river from the east and which is about half way between the villages of Fort Miller and Ford Edward; Jane's father had died several years prior to the Revolution. See William H. Hill, *Old Fort Edward, before 1800*... (Fort Edward, N.Y., 1929), 373, 272-75. Hill's work provides a judicious compendium of the available evidence (much beclouded by tradition and romance) concerning Jane McCrea's family and the story of her death on July 27, 1777, which proved to be an unexpected boon to American morale by contributing greatly to enlistments during the weeks that preceded the final defeat of Burgoyne's expedition. Hill's book also clarifies for the modern tourist the perplexing multiplicity of Jane McCrea markers and monuments in and about Fort Edward. These include: (1) the so-called "Jane McCrea House," along Broadway in the center of the village, which was the house of her friend Mrs. Sara McNeil, and from which she departed to be escorted to her Tory lover, David Jones, serving in Burgoyne's approaching army; (2) a Jane McCrea monument (erected in 1901 by Jane McCrea Chapter, D.A.R.), on upper Broadway (opposite High School), former site of the "Jane McCrea tree" (see Lossing, *Field-Book*, I, 97), claimed by some to be the site of the murder; (3) a marker along the highway (U.S. 4) beside the Hudson, two miles or so south of Fort Edward village, near the site of Jane McCrea's original burial place, from which her remains were removed in 1822 to the "old cemetery" in the village; and (4) her final resting-place and monument, erected in 1852, in the Union Cemetery, along Broadway, between Fort Edward and Hudson Falls.

37. Chastellux was not mistaken in thinking that Jane McCrea's fate offered a most pathetic subject for eloquence and poetry. His compatriot Hilliard d'Auberteuil, for example, published in 1784, "à Philadelphie" [i.e., Paris], *Miss Mac Rea, roman historique*, in which he contrasted "the ferocity of the Savages and the virtues of their chiefs, as well as American innocence and the vices of Europe." In his American epic, *The Columbiad*, Joel Barlow portrayed Jane McCrea under the name of "Lucinda." The de luxe edition of *The Columbiad* published at Philadelphia in 1807 includes (facing p. 240) an engraving by Anker Smith of "The Murder of Lucinda"—for the subject attracted artists as well as poets and novelists. Sketches for a painting of Jane McCrea's murder were made by John Trumbull, *ca.* 1790, but the proposed canvas was never executed; see Sizer, *Works of Trumbull*, 74. John Vanderlyn's painting of the episode, 1803, is now in the Wadsworth Atheneum, Hartford, Conn. Such early examples are but the beginnings of a vast flood of books and pictures. Many of the prints—including the inevitable Currier and Ives lithograph—may be seen in the Old Fort House Museum, Fort Edward, N.Y. An extensive Jane McCrea bibliography compiled by James A. Holden forms an appendix to his article, "Influence of Death of Jane McCrea on Burgoyne Campaign," N.Y. State Hist. Assoc., *Proceedings*, 12 (1913), 249-310. And Jane McCrea's soul still goes marching on, through historical pageants and centennials....

38. The old fortification at the river's edge, built during the Seven Years' War, had been razed in 1775. W. H. Hill, *Old Fort Edward*, 374, concludes that the relocated fort described by Chastellux was the blockhouse on the hill "just north of what is now Case Street" (near present high school), and points out that Chastellux's account is "the only description of its kind" that he has found. This post, which had been but lightly garrisoned after

Burgoyne's defeat in 1777, was reinforced in 1780 as a result of the Indian raids of that year.

39. The destruction observed by Chastellux was of very recent date, having been effected in Oct. 1780 by raiding parties of Indians and Tories, proceeding south from Canada via Lake Champlain, under Major Christopher Carleton. 1780 was long known in the vicinity as "the year of the great burning." At this same time other raids took place as far east as the settlements in the White River Valley in Vermont (Royalton, Bethel); while parties under Sir John Johnson, Butler, and Brandt, proceeding from Niagara, had carried destruction into the Mohawk Valley settlements. Hough, *The Northern Invasion of 1780.* See above, Dec. 27, 1780, for the rumors of further raids that Chastellux heard at Schenectady; and Pt. I, chap. 1, Nov. 21, 1780, for his mention of Tory prisoners at Fishkill. It was currently supposed at the time, not without reason, that these raids against the northern frontier settlements had been timed to coincide with the expected betrayal of West Point by Arnold.

40. The "great cataract" near the northernmost bend of the Hudson, called "Chepontuo" by the Indians, is now known as Glens Falls. It acquired its present name some years after Chastellux's visit, from Colonel John Glen (the same whom Chastellux met at Schenectady; see above, Dec. 27, 1780), who acquired the land after the war and built mills there. It is famed in story as the scene of several chapters of James Fenimore Cooper's *The Last of the Mohicans,* but, like Cohoes and Totowa, is now imprisoned in the unromantic surroundings of an industrial city. Chastellux apparently did not have time to turn aside from his road long enough to visit another notable cataract, still nearer Fort Edward—the falls (Baker's) at what is now the city of Hudson Falls.

41. *Gr.* Two of the most melancholy garrisons in France.

42. *Ch.* This bird can neither be classed in the species of quails, nor in that of partridges; it is larger than the former, and smaller than the latter; the feathers of the wings and body are nearly of the same color as the *perdrix grise* (gray partridge), those of the belly are mixed with gray and black, as with our [European] *bartavelle* (rock partridge). The throat of the cock is white, that of the hen yellow, both ornamented with a handsome black collar. It whistles like the quail, but with more force; and has four notes, whereas the quail has only three. In other respects its habits are more like the *perdrix rouge* (red-legged partridge) than the quail, for it perches and always moves about in a flock: it likes woods and marshes. This bird is very common in America, more so in the south than in the north. I do not exaggerate in asserting that in one winter only, and within a circle of five or six leagues, the [French] officers in winter quarters [1781-82] at Williamsburg and York [in Virginia], killed upwards of six thousand, and that they bought as many again of the Negroes, who caught them in little snares. Nevertheless, the following spring, there was no appreciable diminution of their numbers.

Ed. Chastellux is probably referring to the Bob-white (*Colinus virginianus*), often called (erroneously) "quail" in the northern states and "partridge" in the South.

43. *Ramasse:* a local term used at Mont Cenis and other places in the Alps to describe a sled for descending steep slopes.

44. *Gr.* This is a matter in which General Burgoyne's honour and human-ity seem to be directly called in question. The General in his examination of witnesses on the inquiry into the failure of his expedition before the House of Commons, was particularly anxious to exculpate himself on the subject, and to prove not only that it always was *necessary* in a military point of view to destroy this house, but that General Schuyler himself after-wards admitted that *necessity*—in opposition to which we have here the assertion of a man of rank distinguished in the military and literary world, as well as the General [i.e., Chastellux], who on the testimony of General Schuyler, asserts, '*Que le Général Burgoyne fut à peine de l'autre côté de la creek, qu'il fit mettre le feu à la maison du Général Schuyler, plutôt par humeur, que pour la sûreté de son armée, etc. etc.*' The Translator knows General Burgoyne to be a soldier of honour, who in that capacity never wishes to forget the paramount duties of the citizen, and the man; the Marquis de Chastellux too, deservedly stands high in the public estimation; it is with infinite concern therefore, that the Translator finds himself unable to refute the injurious assertion, or reconcile the contradiction. That the matter may be fairly brought to issue, he subjoins an extract from General Burgoyne's speech in the House of Commons, in answer to "a call upon him by Mr. Wilkes, for explanation respecting the burning of the country during the progress of the army under his command."

"I am ignorant," said the General, "of any such circumstance; I do not recollect more than one accident by fire; I positively assert there was no fire by order or countenance of myself, or any other officer, except at Sara-toga. That district is the property of Major-General Schuyler of the Amer-ican troops; there were large barracks built by him, which took fire the day after the army arrived upon the ground in their retreat; and I believe I need not state any other proof of that matter being merely accident, than that the barracks were then made use of as my hospital, and full of sick and wounded soldiers. General Schuyler had likewise a very good dwelling-house, exceeding large store-houses, great saw-mills, and other out-buildings, to the value altogether perhaps of *ten thousand pounds;* a few days before the negotiation with General Gates, the enemy had formed a plan to attack me; a large column of troops was approaching to pass the small river, preparatory to a general action, and were *entirely covered from the fire of my artillery by those buildings.* Sir, I avow that I gave the order to set them on fire; and in a very short time the whole property I have described was consumed. But, to show that the person most deeply concerned in that calamity did not put the construction upon it which it has pleased the honourable gentleman to do, I must inform the House, that one of the first persons I saw, after the convention was signed, was *General Schuyler.* I expressed to him my regret at the event which had happened, and the reasons which occasioned it. He desired me to think no more of it; said *that the occasion justified it,* according to the principles and rules of war, and *he should have done the same upon the same occasion,* or words to that effect. He did more—he sent an aide-de-camp to conduct me to Albany, in order, as he expressed, to procure me better quarters than a stranger might be able to find. This gentleman conducted me to a very elegant house, and to my great surprise, presented me to Mrs. Schuyler and her family; and in this General's house I remained during my whole stay at Albany, with a *table of more than twenty covers* for me and my friends, and every other possible demonstration of hospitality; a situation, painful it is true in point of sensibility at the time, but which I now contemplate with some satisfaction, as carrying undeniable testimony how little I deserved the charges of the honourable gentleman."

Ed. The passage quoted (italics are Grieve's) is found in *The Substance of General Burgoyne's Speeches, on Mr. Vyner's Motion, On the 26th of May; and upon Mr. Hartley's Motion, On the 28th of May, 1778* ... (London, 1778; Sabin, No. 9257), 8-10. The same pamphlet, of which there were several subsequent editions, includes Burgoyne's remarks on the "necessary evil" of the Indian alliance and on "the case of Miss Mecree ... which was accident, not premeditated cruelty"; see above, this chap., n. 36.

45. The farmhouse in which Chastellux and his friends stayed is still standing, on the right bank of Fish Creek on the southern outskirts of the present village of Schuylerville. This Schuyler farmhouse, comparatively little changed since the 18th century, has recently been acquired by the U.S. Government as an outlying unit of the Saratoga National Historical Park, the main section of which is located ten miles to the south; see above, this chap., n. 31. The meetinghouse and handful of dwellings comprising the settlement at "old Saratoga" were, in Chastellux's day, all located south of Fish Creek; see W. L. Stone, *Visits to the Saratoga Battle-Grounds*, 75-77n.

46. General Burgoyne's position, on a hill on the western outskirts of the present village of Schuylerville, where he made his last half-hearted stand before surrendering, is marked today by the obelisk-like Saratoga Battle Monument, a historic site administered by the N.Y. State Education Department.

47. "Plan of the Position which the Army under Lt. Genl. Burgoine [*sic*] took at Saratoga on the 10th of September [*sic*, for October] 1777, and in which it remained till the Convention was signed," one of the engraved maps included in *A State of the Expedition from Canada ... By Lieutenant-General Burgoyne.*

48. The "Field of Grounded Arms," where the English forces stacked their arms, is on the river flats along the west bank of the Hudson, in present Schuylerville, east on Ferry Street over the Canal Bridge. The surrender, when "they filed off before Gates's army," took place about a fifth of a mile south of the Schuyler House, along the river road.

49. Madame von Riedesel's own account of the incident will be found in her lively journal. "I confess that I feared to come into the enemy's camp," she writes, "as the thing was so entirely new to me. When I approached the tents, a noble looking man came toward me, took the children [Augusta, then aged six; Frederika, three; and Carolina, two] out of the wagon, embraced and kissed them, and then with tears in his eyes helped me also to alight. 'You tremble,' said he to me, 'fear nothing.' 'No,' replied I, 'for you are so kind, and have been so tender to my children, that it has inspired me with courage.' He then led me to the tent of General Gates, with whom I found Generals Burgoyne and Phillips, who were upon an extremely friendly footing with him. Burgoyne said to me, 'You may now dismiss all your apprehensions, for your sufferings are at an end.' ... The man, who had received me so kindly, came up and said to me, 'It may be embarrassing to you to dine with all these gentlemen; come now with your children into my tent, where I will give you, it is true, a frugal meal, but one that will be accompanied by the best of wishes.' 'You are certainly,' answered I, 'a husband and a father, since you show me so much kindness.' I then learned

that he was the American General Schuyler.... As soon as we had finished dinner, he invited me to take up my residence at his house, which was situated in Albany, and told me that General Burgoyne would, also, be there." Stone, trans., *Riedesel Letters and Journals*, 134-35. The Riedesels are the subject of Louise Hall Tharp's *The Baroness and the General* (Boston, 1962).

50. The Baroness von Riedesel (*ibid.*, 136-37) gives this version of the story: "Even General Burgoyne was deeply moved at their magnanimity, and said to General Schuyler, 'Is it to *me*, who have done you so much injury, that you show so much kindness!' 'That is the fate of war,' replied the brave man, 'let us say no more about it.'"

51. See above, this chap., n. 32.

52. For an authoritative discussion of the diffusion and influence of Montesquieu's works, see Paul M. Spurlin, *Montesquieu in America, 1760-1801* (University, La., 1940), where Chastellux's anecdotes are placed in a more general context. See above, Pt. I, chap. 1, n. 8; chap. 3, Dec. 4, 1780, and n. 48.

53. Chastellux took with him a letter from Col. Hugh Hughes, Albany, Jan. 1, 1781, addressed to Capt. Walter Pynchon of Great Barrington, Mass. The latter was informed that "Major General Chevalier De Chaslux and five other gentlemen belonging to the French Army" would be passing through his neighborhood, and was requested to furnish fresh horses and forage from the public stores if necessary. "As your Public Houses are rather inconvenient for these gentlemen," Hughes added, "it will be more suitable to procure private Lodgings for them and put their Servants and Horses at a Tavern. If you can, correct the Directions that I have given them from Barrington to Hartford by the way of Canaan etc." Chastellux presumably did not deliver this letter, as his route took him directly from Nobletown [Hillsdale] to Sheffield without passing through Great Barrington. Hughes's retained copy of the letter to Capt. Pynchon is in his Letterbook No. 11, N.-Y. Hist. Soc.; the Editor is indebted to Mrs. Charlotte C. Finkel for calling his attention to it.

Chapter 6

From Albany back to Newport

1. Nobletown was in the "District of Claverack," in what is now the town of Hillsdale, Columbia Co., N.Y., along the eastern border of the state. It was one of the towns west of the Taconic Range surveyed under Massachusetts authority in the 1750's in defiance of New York claims, and presumably took its name from Robert Noble, a recalcitrant tenant of Rensslaerwyck, who was a leader in the anti-rent warfare that raged in this region for a decade or more in the 1750's and 1760's. Nobletown's pivotal location on the Albany-Hartford route is clearly shown on Sauthier's "Chorographical Map of New York," O'Callaghan, ed., *Doc. Hist. of New York*, I, 774-75. The name of the tavernkeeper (not further identified) should perhaps be spelled "Mackinson."

2. Chastellux's host was probably Capt. Stephen Dewey (1719-96) and the house the one occupied in the 19th century by his grandson, the Rev. Orville Dewey. This house, although modified in appearance, is still stand-

ing, privately owned, on the west side of Sheffield's Main St. (U.S. Route 7). According to local tradition it was at one time used as a tavern. I am indebted to Mr. Howard S. Mott of Sheffield, and to Mr. Willard C. French of the Sheffield Public Library, for help on this point. See also Louis Marinus Dewey, comp., *Dewey Genealogy and Family History* (Westfield, Mass., 1898). Some of the western Massachusetts Deweys migrated northward to western Vermont and eventually produced such notables as Admiral George Dewey and John Dewey, the philosopher.

The Greuze painting that Miss Dewey called to Chastellux's mind was presumably the one now in the National Gallery of Scotland, Edinburgh, and concerning which Diderot embroidered a touching tale in his report on the Salon of 1765; see Diderot, *Salons*, ed. Jean Seznec and Jean Adhémar, 2 vols. (Oxford, 1957-60), II, 145-48, fig. 54. Another of Greuze's variations on the dead bird theme is in the Louvre.

3. Chastellux in his French text calls it *l'Abrégé de la Philosophie de Newton*. This could have been Henry Pemberton's *A View of Sir Isaac Newton's Philosophy* (London, 1728), Colin Maclaurin's *An Account of Sir Isaac Newton's Philosophical Discoveries* (London, 1748), or more probably one of the several textbooks which popularized knowledge of Newtonian science, such as John Rowning's *A Compendious System of Natural Philosophy* (London, 1744), or Benjamin Martin's *Philosophia Britannica: or, a New and Comprehensive System of the Newtonian Philosophy, Astronomy, and Geography* (Reading, Eng., 1747).

4. The village of Canaan is now in the *town* of North Canaan (incorporated in 1858 from Canaan), Litchfield Co., Conn.

5. See above, Pt. I, chap. 1, Nov. 19, 1780.

6. Chastellux's text reads, "et telle est l'excellente police de ce pays, que nul chemin n'est dépourvu de ce qui peut servir à leurs besoins." The word *police* is probably used here only to mean general social organization, or state of civilization; Grieve, apparently misinterpreting it and taking it to mean governmental "police power," appends a long footnote explaining that "the respective governments of America never dreamt of compelling persons to keep public houses, or blacksmith's and wheelwright's shops, nor could such a regulation be enforced without infinite difficulty, even in established and arbitrary governments."

7. "Gilbert's House" was presumably in or near the present village of New Hartford, in the northeast corner of the town of that name, Litchfield Co. See note on the "Old North Country Road" from Albany to Hartford, and map of a portion of it, in Crofut, *Guide*, I, 408, 449-51. The name of John Gilbert is among those licensed to keep public houses in the town of New Hartford for 1780, 1781 and 1782; "Travel: Highways and Taverns," Litchfield Co. Court Files, Conn. State Archives.

8. The name of Dudley Case is among those licensed to keep public houses in the town of New Hartford for 1780, 1781, and 1782; "Travel: Highways and Taverns," Litchfield Co. Court Files, Conn. State Archives. From Chastellux's description it would appear that Case's Tavern was on the east bank of the Farmington River, within the limits of the present town of Canton, Hartford Co. The Farmington River here flows southward to the town of Farmington, where it makes a sharp bend back to the northward; Chastellux thus crossed the river again next day (probably near

present Avon), having journeyed over the hills and cut across the chord of the bow. The old Albany-Hartford road passed through this section along a route corresponding roughly to present U.S. Route 44.

9. *Gr.* It is to be hoped that it will be long, very long ere the *barbarous* prejudices and punishments of polished Europe shall be introduced into this happy country. At present, the natural commerce between the sexes universally takes place, to the exclusion of exotic vices, and without involving the weak and unprotected female in all the horrors of shame, misery and child-murder. Here libertinism is by no means the consequence of an accidental frailty, nor is the mother, who in following the strong impulse of Nature, has given a member to society, thrown an outcast upon the world, lost to herself, and compelled to become vicious. The error of passion, though condemned, is venial, and she is neither driven to despair by cruelty, nor excluded from the sweet prospect of giving birth to future offspring, under the sanction of every legitimate and sacred title. Nothing is more common in this country, than such slips in the first violence of an early puberty, nor less frequent than a repetition of the same weakness.

10. Here again Chastellux seems to foreshadow the taste for picturesque scenery generally associated with the Romantic period of the early 19th century. It was on the top of Talcott Mountain that Daniel Wadsworth (1771-1849, the son of Chastellux's friend, Col. Jeremiah W., and founder of the Wadsworth Atheneum) built a country residence called "Monte Video" *ca.* 1810. An account of this estate, which was laid out in the approved romantic manner with a pseudo-Gothic tower on a sightly eminence, is given by Benjamin Silliman in his *Remarks Made on a Short Tour between Hartford and Quebec in the Autumn of 1819* (New Haven, 1820), which also includes (p. 27) a description of the enormous masses of greenstone rock lying in confusion on the western slope of the mountain. Engravings of "Monte Video" after drawings by Daniel Wadsworth appear in Silliman's book; it was later painted by John Trumbull (private collection) and by Thomas Cole (*ca.* 1828, now in Wadsworth Atheneum); these pictures in turn supplied designs for Staffordshire pottery (the so-called "Wadsworth Tower" pattern). See "Monte Video," Conn. Hist. Soc., *Bulletin*, 19 (1954), 22-25, 32, illus.; "Connecticut Views on Staffordshire China," *ibid.*, 20 (1955), 1-12, illus.

11. The famous equestrian statue of Peter the Great, still to be seen in Leningrad, was the work of the French sculptor Etienne-Maurice Falconet (1716-91), who left Russia in 1778 after quarreling with his Imperial patroness Catherine, before the formal inauguration of his masterpiece in 1782. The statue, which has been characterized as an "Encyclopedist on horseback," was mounted on a huge block of granite extracted from the Finnish marshes. Although Chastellux had not himself visited Russia, he was familiar with models and engravings of Falconet's work, and had probably seen the elegant illustrated folio published in Paris, 1777, by the engineer responsible for moving the pedestal to St. Petersburg: Comte Marin Carburi de Ceffalonie, *Monument élevé à la gloire de Pierre-le-Grand, ou Relation des travaux et des moyens mechaniques qui ont été employés pour transporter à Pétersbourg un Rocher de trois millions pesant, destiné à servir de base à la statue équestre de cet Empereur; avec un Examen physique et chymique du même rocher* (Paris, 1777), 48 pp., 12 plates.

12. David Bull's tavern, known as "The Bunch of Grapes," stood on the west side of Main Street, near the corner of present Asylum St. "A Plan of Main Street, Hartford, showing the buildings and occupants at the period of the American Revolution," in John Warner Barber, *Connecticut Historical Collections* (New Haven, 1836), 148; Terry, *Old Inns of Conn.*, 241.

13. Concerning this regiment, which had been recruited by Col. Christopher Greene (above, Pt. I, chap. 1, n. 13), see Lorenzo J. Greene, "Some Observations on the Black Regiment of Rhode Island in the American Revolution," *Journal of Negro History*, 37 (1952), 142-72; for a general survey of the subject, see Benjamin Quarles, *The Negro in the American Revolution* (Chapel Hill, 1961). Several of the other French officers comment in their diaries on the Negro soldiers; for example, Acomb, ed., *Von Closen Journal*, 89, 92. The Comte de Charlus, soon after his arrival at Newport, noticed among the American troops stationed at the northern end of the Island Negro sentinels whose white shirts made them look to him "exactly like the black Harlequins on the stage"; Duc de Castries, ed., "Souvenirs inédits du Comte de Charlus," *Revue de Paris*, 64 (July 1957), 94-110.

14. The Duc de Lauzun had his headquarters in the house of David Trumbull, a son of the Governor; this house, called "Redwood," somewhat changed in appearance by subsequent modifications, still stands on the western side of the green at Lebanon. The residence of Governor Jonathan Trumbull and the building he used as the "War Office" also still face the green or "parade," although both have been moved a short distance from their original sites. The restored Governor Trumbull House is owned and maintained by the Connecticut D.A.R. See above, Pt. I, chap. 1, Nov. 15, 1780, and n. 30; and also Forbes and Cadman, *France and New England*, II, 99-108.

15. *Ch.* There are also a great many "flying squirrels" in Connecticut. They are smaller than the others, which they resemble fairly closely in their shape and their fur. It is well known that what gives them the name of "flying squirrels" is their skill in keeping themselves in the air by means of a long membrane, or skin, attached to the lower part of their feet: this is folded up under their bellies when they are still; but when they want to jump from one tree to another they spread their feet and this skin makes a sort of sail which holds them in the air, and even helps them move. There is to be seen everywhere in North America still another species of squirrels, called "ground squirrels" [chipmunks], because they do not climb trees and live underground as rabbits do. Their hair is shorter, and of a tawny color striped with black; these animals are very pretty and quite tame.

16. See above, Pt. I, chap. 1, Nov. 16, 1780.

17. See above, Pt. I, chap. 1, Nov. 13, 1780, and n. 23. Nearly two years later, when Claude Blanchard, Chief Commissary of the French army, passed through Voluntown, he noted in his *Journal*, 180: "On the 9th [Nov. 1782], the army proceeded to Watertown [Voluntown], where I saw the inn, Dorancy Tavern, of which the Chevalier de Chastellux gives so handsome a description in his printed and rather highly embellished *Voyage*. Moreover, the two young ladies of whom he speaks were no longer there and they both were married." Presumably Blanchard had by this time al-

ready read Chastellux's *Voyage* in the privately printed (Newport, 1781) edition—a book which must have circulated rather extensively among the French officers.

18. The quotation is from Metastasio, *Demofoonte* (1733), Act III, Scene 5. Chastellux had more than a passing familiarity with the works of the Italian poet Pietro Metastasio (1698-1782), whom he had praised highly in his own *Essai sur l'union de la poésie et de la musique* (The Hague and Paris, 1765), and in which, incidentally, he had quoted (p. 32) these same lines from *Demofoonte*. Letters addressed by Metastasio to Chastellux, concerning the topics treated in the latter's *Essai*, will be found in Bruno Brunelli, ed., *Tutte le Opere di Pietro Metastasio*, 5 vols. (Milan, 1943-54), IV, 397, 435; see also V, 695.

19. *Ch*. See what has been said in a note at the beginning of this journal [above, Pt. I, chap. 1, n. 23].

20. Claude Blanchard, Chief Commissary of the French army, then stationed at Providence, noted in his *Journal*, 85-86: "On the 7th [Jan. 1781], melted snow and rain; on the 8th, wind from the north and sudden cold, very sharp. I saw the Chevalier de Chastellux, who was returning from his journey, with which he appeared pleased. He told me that the Academy of Philadelphia [Amer. Phil. Soc.] had chosen him an associate member; that he had collected some notes respecting the American revolution, that he would not content himself with mere observations, and that he would publish a complete work." Blanchard, when re-copying his journal some years later (1794), added this footnote: "I do not perceive that he has kept his promise. He has had the account of his journey printed in two volumes, and some agreeable details are to be found in it, but many trifling matters, mediocre pleasantries and eulogiums, often but little deserved, of persons who had flattered him. Brissot de Warville has sharply criticised this work."

A month or so later, on Feb. 3, 1781, Blanchard entertained at dinner Chastellux, Vioménil, Mrs. Nathanael Greene, and Mrs. Angelica Schuyler Carter.

21. *Ch*. I wish to reward those who have had the patience to read through this journal by laying before them the charming passage of Metastasio, from which these last words are borrowed.

> L'onda dal mar divisa
> Bagna la valle e 'l monte;
> Va passeggiera in fiume,
> Va prigioniera in fonte;
> Mormora sempre e geme,
> Fin che non torna al mar:
>
> Al mar, dov'ella nacque,
> Dove acquistò gli umori,
> Dove da' lunghi errori
> Spera di riposar.

Ed. The passage is from Metastasio's *Artaserse*, Act III, Scene 1. *Artaserse* was first performed at Rome in 1730 with music by Leonardo Vinci, and many time subsequently throughout the century, with music by a long line of other composers, including Gluck, Piccinni, Scarlatti, Cimarosa. An English version, with both words and music by Thomas Augustine Arne, was first performed at Covent Garden in 1762. In place of Chastellux's French translation of the song, the Editor offers his readers the following, from Arne's *Artaxerxes*:

> Water parted from the sea,
>   May increase the river's tide;
> To the bubbling fount may flee,
>   Or thro' fertile vallies glide:
>
> Yet in search of lost repose,
>   Doom'd like me, forlorn to roam,
> Still it murmurs as it flows,
>   Till it reach its native home.